SUBSTANCE USE DISORDERS AND ADDICTIONS

To my parents and Viv, for supporting me throughout my education and career.

*To Melissa, for always knowing when I need to work and when
I need to take a break. She always seems to magically know what I need to
get things done and makes everything about me better.*

*To Margaret, Charlie, and Nicholas, for the well-needed
breaks of Monopoly,* Star Wars, Arthur, Thomas, *Minecraft, Wii, trains,
the park, the pool, hiking, and other distractions while writing this book.*

SUBSTANCE USE DISORDERS AND ADDICTIONS

Keith Morgen

Centenary University
Discovery Psychotherapy & Wellness Centers

Los Angeles | London | New Delhi
Singapore | Washington DC | Melbourne

FOR INFORMATION:

SAGE Publications, Inc.
2455 Teller Road
Thousand Oaks, California 91320
E-mail: order@sagepub.com

SAGE Publications Ltd.
1 Oliver's Yard
55 City Road
London EC1Y 1SP
United Kingdom

SAGE Publications India Pvt. Ltd.
B 1/I 1 Mohan Cooperative Industrial Area
Mathura Road, New Delhi 110 044
India

SAGE Publications Asia-Pacific Pte. Ltd.
3 Church Street
#10-04 Samsung Hub
Singapore 049483

Acquisitions Editor: Nathan Davidson
Development Editor: Abbie Rickard
eLearning Editor: Gabrielle Piccininni
Production Editor: Tracy Buyan
Copy Editor: Diane Wainwright
Typesetter: Hurix Systems Pvt. Ltd.
Proofreader: Pam Suwinsky
Indexer: Beth Nauman-Montana
Cover Designer: Candice Harman
Marketing Manager: Jenna Retana

Printed in the United States of America

Library of Congress Cataloging-in-Publication Data

Names: Morgen, Keith, (Keith J.), author.

Title: Substance use disorders and addictions / Keith Morgen.

Description: Thousand Oaks : SAGE Publications, [2017] | Includes bibliographical references and index.

Identifiers: LCCN 2016013694 | ISBN 9781483370569 (pbk. : alk. paper)

Subjects: | MESH: Substance-Related Disorders—therapy | Behavior, Addictive—therapy

Classification: LCC RC564 | NLM WM 270 | DDC 362.29—dc23 LC record available at https://lccn.loc.gov/2016013694

This book is printed on acid-free paper.

16 17 18 19 20 10 9 8 7 6 5 4 3 2 1

CONTENTS

Editors' Preface

INTRODUCTION TO THE SERIES *COUNSELING AND PROFESSIONAL IDENTITY IN THE 21ST CENTURY*

While time, energy, and money have been poured into programs that target borders and drug trafficking, ignorance and naiveté, and even skill development in learning how to "just say no," the reality is that substance use remains a major concern for all in this 21st century. Advances in our understanding of the psychosocial, biological, and neurological contributors to the development and maintenance of substance disorders and addiction have led to innovation in our approaches to both prevention and intervention. While much of what we have done in the past took on a "one size fits all" mentality, this research has helped us understand the highly unique and individualized nature of substance abuse and addiction. The text that you currently hold in your hands, *Substance Use Disorders and Addictions* by Keith Morgen, reflects the latest in what we know of the etiology, the prevention, and the intervention of substance abuse and addiction.

In an area with many more questions than answers, *Substance Use Disorders and Addictions* provides clear direction in assessment, diagnosis, treatment, and prevention programming of substance use disorders and additions. Dr. Morgen demonstrates his gift in being able to take difficult concepts and constructs tied to things such as the psychoneurology of substance abuse and addiction and present them in easy-to-grasp language, supported by an ample array of rich case illustrations. *Substance Use Disorders and Addictions* is an essential reading for students and clinicians, regardless of their professional specialty or treatment focus.

While we are proud of the content and topics covered within this text, we are more than aware that one text, one learning experience, will not be sufficient for the development of a counselor's professional competency. The formation of both your professional identity and practice will be a lifelong process. It is a process that we hope to facilitate through the presentation of this text and the creation of our series ***Counseling and Professional Identity in the 21st Century***.

Counseling and Professional Identity in the 21st Century is a new, fresh, pedagogically sound series of texts targeting counselors in training. This series is NOT simply a compilation of isolated books matching that which is already in the market. Rather, each book, with its targeted knowledge and skills, will be presented as but one part of a larger whole. The focus and content of each text serve as a single lens through which a counselor can view his or her clients, engage in his or her practice, and articulate his or her own professional identity.

Counseling and Professional Identity in the 21st Century is unique not just in the fact that it "packages" a series of traditional texts but that it provides an *integrated* curriculum targeting the formation of the readers' professional identity and efficient, ethical practice. Each book within the series is structured to facilitate the ongoing professional formation of the reader. The materials found within each text are organized in order to move the reader to higher levels of cognitive, affective, and psychomotor functioning, resulting in his or her assimilation of the materials presented into both his or her professional identity and approach to professional practice. While each text targets a specific set of core competencies (cognates and skills), competencies identified by the professional organizations and accreditation bodies, each book in the series will emphasize each of the following:

1. The assimilation of concepts and constructs provided across the text found within the series, thus fostering the reader's ongoing development as a competent professional;

2. The blending of contemporary theory with current research and empirical support;

3. A focus on the development of procedural knowledge with each text employing case illustrations and guided practice exercises to facilitate the reader's ability to translate the theory and research discussed into professional decision making and application;

4. The emphasis on the need for and means of demonstrating accountability; and

5. The fostering of the reader's professional identity and with it the assimilation of the ethics and standards of practice guiding the counseling profession.

We are proud to have served as co-editors of this series, feeling sure that all the texts included, just like *Substance Use Disorders and Addictions*, will serve as a significant resource to you and your development as a professional counselor.

Richard Parsons, PhD
Naijian Zhang, PhD

AUTHOR'S PREFACE

PERSPECTIVES ON THE CURRENT STATE OF THE COUNSELING PROFESSION: HOW IT PERTAINS TO THIS BOOK

I read a number of excellent books while writing this text. In the course of reading these other works, I began to see a common theme that substance use disorder and addiction counseling is defined as a practice that is based on the following criteria: (1) Substance use disorder and addiction counseling is evidence-based (e.g., motivational interviewing or brief structural family therapy—both of which will be discussed in this text); (2) Substance use disorder and addiction counseling should approach clients from a positive perspective; (3) The practice of substance use disorder and addiction counseling is complicated but relies on a collaborative stance between counselor and client, as well as between counselor and the other areas of influence in the treatment process (e.g., family, courts, or medical services); and (4) Substance use disorder and addiction counseling is built on solid ethical principles and emphasizes social justice and multicultural considerations for the best treatment and welfare of the client. These books all had titles such as *Substance Abuse Counseling* or *Addiction Counseling*. However, the four components listed above can also be used to describe the core components of the counseling profession for all disorders. That is why I chose to open this book with a discussion on what exactly the profession of "substance use disorders and addiction counseling" is, is not, and perhaps can one day be, at least how I see it.

One unique aspect of the addiction field is that those providing treatment for individuals with substance use and addictive disorders can be physicians, psychologists, psychiatrists, licensed professional counselors (LPCs), social workers, or addiction counselors. But concerns remain about how adequately trained these professionals treating addiction are in providing such services (Miller, Scarborough, Clark, Leonard, & Keziah, 2010). In addition, concerns remain regarding the curricular and clinical practice content of the training (Morgen & Miller, 2013). Historically, these concerns arose because addiction counselors could receive certification without formal training in addiction or counseling (Miller et al., 2010). However, recent advances are strengthening the training process. For example, in 2009, the Council for Accreditation of Counseling and Related Programs (CACREP) finalized guidelines for addiction counseling education in relationship to knowledge, skills, and practices. CACREP also contains curricular mandates for the inclusion of addictions material into the core of professional counseling training. Other guidelines for training and competencies in addiction counseling were produced by the Center for Substance Abuse Treatment (CSAT) and the Substance Abuse and Mental Health Services Administration (SAMHSA). In addition, the National Addiction Studies Accreditation Commission (NASAC) was established to standardize addiction training. Finally, there is also an increased emphasis of the master's degree as an entry-level requirement for practice, but in some states only a high school diploma or general equivalency diploma is required for credentialing in the addiction profession (Miller et al., 2010).

Certification

Certification provides a professional standard that is governed by an organization, thus establishing a common minimum competency for professionals. While there are state requirements for substance abuse counseling licensure and certification guidelines, there is a lack of nationwide continuity. This lack of congruence of standards between states produces a confused profession, even more confused trainees and students looking to enter the profession, and clients who do not understand the differences. For example, a client once asked me, "What is the difference if I receive addiction treatment from an addiction counselor or a psychologist or a counselor or a social worker?"

I did not have an answer the client could understand. The real answer is just too confusing and basically is summed up in the remainder of my Preface.

There are different certifications offered by various agencies both domestically and internationally (el-Guebaly & Violato, 2011). For example, the International Association of Addictions and Offender Counselors (IAAOC), which is a division of the American Counseling Association (ACA) working in conjunction with the National Board of Certified Counselors (NBCC), has developed standards and a program for the certification of master's-level addiction counselors. One requirement for the master addiction counselor (MAC) credential is a passing score on the Examination for Master Addiction Counselors (www.nbcc.org). As of the writing of this book, the MAC application requirements are under review.

According to the National Association of Alcoholism and Drug Abuse Counselors (NAADAC), the National Certification Commission for Addiction Professionals recognizes three levels of substance abuse certifications: the national certified addiction counselor level I (NCAC I), the national certified addiction counselor level II (NCAC II), and the MAC. The NAADAC also acknowledges additional specialties, such as the national certified adolescent addiction counselor (see Table 1 for a

Table 1   NAADAC Certifications and Associated Eligibility

Certification Type	Eligibility
National Certified Addiction Counselor – Level I	GED, High School Diploma, or higher.
	Current credential or license as a Substance Use Disorder/Addiction counselor issued by a state or credentialing authority.
	At least three years full-time or 6,000 hours of supervised experience as a Substance Use Disorder/Addiction counselor.
	At least 270 contact hours of education and training in Substance Use Disorders/Addiction or related counseling subjects. Must include six hours of ethics training and six hours of HIV/AIDS-specific training within the last six years. At least 50% of training hours must be face-to-face.
	Passing score on the NCAC I examination within four years of the application.
National Certified Addiction Counselor – Level II	Bachelor's degree or higher in Substance Use Disorder/Addiction and/or related counseling subjects (social work, mental health counseling, psychology) from a regionally accredited institution of higher learning.
	Current credential or license as a Substance Use Disorder/Addiction counselor issued by a state or credentialing authority.
	At least five years full-time or 10,000 hours of supervised experience as a Substance Use Disorder/Addiction counselor.
	At least 450 contact hours of education and training in Substance Use Disorder/Addiction. Must include six hours of ethics training and six hours of HIV/AIDS-specific training within the last six years. At least 50% of training hours must be face-to-face.
	Passing score on the NCAC II examination within four years of the application.
Master Addiction Counselor	Master's degree or higher in Substance Use Disorders/Addiction and/or related counseling subjects (social work, mental health counseling, psychology) from a regionally accredited institution of higher learning.
	Current credential or license as a Substance Use Disorder/Addiction counselor or professional counselor (social worker, mental health, marriage and family, professional counselor, psychologist, psychiatrist, medical doctor) issued by a state or credentialing authority.
	At least three years full-time or 6,000 hours of supervised experience as a Substance Use Disorder/Addiction counselor.
	At least 500 contact hours of education and training in Substance Use Disorder/Addiction. Must include six hours of ethics training and six hours of HIV/AIDS-specific training within the last six years. At least 50% of training hours must be face-to-face.
	Passing score on the MAC examination within four years of the application.

(Continued)

Table 1   (Continued)

Certification Type	Eligibility
National Dependence Specialist	Bachelor's degree or higher in a healing art (i.e., substance use or mental health disorders, nursing, respiratory therapy, or pharmacology etc.) from a regionally accredited institution of higher learning.
	Current credential or license in a healing art (i.e., substance use disorders, nursing, respiratory therapy, or pharmacology, etc.) issued by a state or credentialing authority.
	At least three years full-time or 6,000 hours of employment in a health care profession (i.e., substance use disorders, nursing, respiratory therapy, or pharmacology, etc.).
	At least 270 contact hours of education and training in healing art. Must include at least 40 hours of nicotine-specific education, six hours of ethics training, and six hours of HIV/AIDS-specific training within the last six years. At least 50% of training hours must be face-to-face.
	Passing score on NDS examination within four years of the application.
National Certified Adolescent Addictions Counselor	Bachelor's degree or higher in Substance Use Disorders/Addiction and/or related counseling subjects (social work, mental health counseling, psychology) from a regionally accredited institution of higher learning.
	Current credential or license as a Substance Use Disorder/Addiction counselor issued by a state or credentialing authority.
	At least five years full-time or 10,000 hours of supervised experience working in Substance Use Disorder/Addiction and/or related counseling subjects. Must include two and a half years or 5,000 hours of supervised experience working with adolescents.
	At least 270 contact hours of education and training in Substance Use Disorder/Addiction and/or related counseling subjects. Must include at least 70 contact hours of training related to adolescent treatment, six hours of ethics training, and six hours of HIV/AIDS-specific training within the last six years. At least 50% of training hours must be face-to-face.
	Passing score on the NCAAC examination within four years of the application.
National Certified Peer Recovery Support Specialist	GED, High School Diploma, or higher.
	Minimum of one year full-time of direct practice (volunteer or paid) in a peer recovery support environment.
	At least 125 contact hours of peer recovery focused education and training to include education in documentation, community/family education, case management, crisis management, Recovery-Oriented Systems of Care (ROSC), screening and intake, Identification of Indicators of substance use and/or co-occurring disorders for referral, service coordination, service.

Certification Type	Eligibility
	planning, cultural awareness and/or humility, and basic pharmacology. Must include a minimum of six hours of ethics and six hours of HIV/AIDS-specific training within the last six years. At least 50% of training hours must be face-to-face.
	Minimum one year of recovery from Substance Use/Co-Occurring Mental Health Disorders (self-attestation).
	Passing score on the NCPRSS examination within four years of the application.
National Endorsed Student Assistance Professional	Bachelor's degree or higher in Substance Use Disorder/Addiction and/or related counseling subjects (social work, mental health counseling, psychology) from a regionally accredited institution of higher learning.
	Current credential or license as a Substance Use Disorder/Addiction counselor issued by a state or credentialing authority.
	At least 4,500 hours of supervised experience (volunteer or paid) in Substance Use Disorder/Addiction, to include at least 3,000 hours of direct service delivering student assistance services.
	At least 100 contact hours of education and training in Substance Use Disorder/Addiction and/or related counseling subjects including six hours of ethics training and six hours of HIV/AIDS-specific training within the last six years. At least 70 hours must be related to student assistance services. At least 50% of the 70 hours must be face-to-face training.
	Passing score on the NESAP examination within four years of the application.
National Clinical Supervision Endorsement	Bachelor's degree or higher in Substance Use Disorder/Addiction and/or related counseling subjects (social work, mental health counseling, psychology) from a regionally accredited institution of higher learning.
	Current credential or license in Substance Use Disorder/Addiction and/or related counseling subjects (social work, mental health counseling, psychology) issued by a state or credentialing authority for the past five years.
	At least five years full-time or 10,000 hours overall of employment as a Substance Use Disorder/Addiction counselor. This must include a minimum of two years full-time or 4,000 hours performing direct clinical supervision, and 200 hours of received supervision as a clinical supervisor.
	At least of 30 contact hours of education and training specific to Substance Use Disorder/Addiction clinical supervision. In addition, must include six hours of ethics training and six hours of HIV/AIDS-specific training within the last six years. At least 50% of training hours must be face-to-face.
	A passing score on the NCSE examination within four years of the application.

(Continued)

Table 1 (Continued)

Certification Type	Eligibility
National Endorsed Co-Occurring Disorders Professional	Bachelor's degree or higher in Substance Use Disorder/Addiction and/or related counseling subjects (social work, mental health counseling, psychology) from a regionally accredited institution of higher learning.
	Current credential or license in Substance Use Disorder/Addiction and/or related counseling subjects (social work, mental health counseling, psychology) issued by a state or credentialing authority for the past five years.
	At least five years full-time or 10,000 hours of supervised experience in Substance Use and Mental Health Disorders treatment, to include two and a half years full-time or 5,000 hours of supervised experience working with co-occurring persons.
	At least 70 contact hours of education and training in co-occurring disorders. Must include six hours of ethics training and six hours of HIV/AIDS-specific training within the last six years. At least 50% of training hours must be face-to-face.
	Passing score on the NECODP examination within four years of the application.

Source: www.naadac.org.

review of several of the certification exams and their associated applicant criteria and content). However, counselors' level of certification or licensure will dictate their scope of practice in regard to their state regulations.

The confusion—in part—is that each credentialing body has different requirements for certification. And many of these requirements vary across agency and state. Morgen and Miller (2013) attempted to summarize the overall mission of these varied bodies and concluded that they all share three general goals: (1) Each defines a core set of counselor roles, (2) each addresses a set of expected addiction counseling competencies, and (3) each makes use of assessment measures and exams to evaluate these competencies in those seeking credentialing. But Morgen (2011) noted that many credentialing bodies and states differ in opinion regarding the content and quantity of competencies required for addiction counseling credentialing.

To add another layer of confusion, some credentialing organizations actually have different levels of certification. For example, the International Certification and Reciprocity Consortium (IC&RC), a national organization of certifying boards providing national reciprocity of certification, has three levels of certification: (1) certified addiction counselor, (2) certified drug counselor, and (3) alcohol and drug counselor. Each level has different training, education, and supervision requirements experience (the higher the certification level, the greater degree of requirements exist; http://www.internationalcredentialing.org/).

Licensure

Licensure is the most rigorous form of professional regulation (Morgen & Miller, 2013). Unlike certification, which can be granted nationally (e.g., the NBCC national certified counselor status), state law establishes licensure; thus, each state determines the requirements for licensure. Licensure eligibility typically consists of two criteria: (1) a graduate degree (master's or higher) in the addiction counseling, counseling, or (in some states) psychology professions; and (2) post-graduate supervised hours of clinical work in the counseling or addiction counseling profession. However, different states have different requirements for licensure in regard to the degree type eligibility, graduate course work required, the professional identity and training of the clinical supervisor, and the number of clinical hours performing professional or addiction counseling (and related) services (Morgen, Miller, & Stretch, 2012).

Accreditation

Accreditation applies to the graduate counselor education or counseling psychology training program within a college or university that educates and trains students in the addiction counseling or counseling discipline. Accreditation procedures are designed to verify the quality and standardization of the graduate education. In the accreditation process, standards are clearly specified for the training of addiction or counseling practitioners, for instance, the mandated academic course content or the expected experiential practicum or internship components of the graduate program. Programs that meet or exceed the specified standards are then accredited. In 2009, CACREP recognized addiction counseling as a counseling specialty and thus outlined the accreditation requirements for any addiction counselor graduate program. Table 2 shows these requirements.

In addition, CACREP (2015) also embeds required addictions training within the core professional counseling curriculum. Thus, a graduate master's program (e.g., clinical-counseling) leading to eligibility as a licensed professional counselor must integrate addictions content into the curriculum. For example, CACREP stipulates that theories and etiology of addictions and addictive behaviors be included in the content covered within the course(s) meeting the human growth and development domain of the graduate counseling curriculum. Some studies have shown that CACREP counseling programs currently satisfy these standards, meaning that addictions content is currently being covered (Iarussi, Perjessy, & Reed, 2013). However, though there has been some discussion in the literature regarding

Table 2   CACREP (2015) Addiction Counseling Standards

1. FOUNDATIONS

   a. history and development of addiction counseling

   b. theories and models of addiction related to substance use as well as behavioral and process addictions

   c. principles and philosophies of addiction-related self-help

   d. principles, models, and documentation formats of biopsychosocial case conceptualization and treatment planning

   e. neurological, behavioral, psychological, physical, and social effects of psychoactive substances and addictive disorders on the user and significant others

   f. psychological tests and assessments specific to addiction counseling

2. CONTEXTUAL DIMENSIONS

   a. roles and settings of addiction counselors

   b. potential for addictive and substance use disorders to mimic and/or co-occur with a variety of medical and psychological disorders

   c. factors that increase the likelihood for a person, community, or group to be at risk for or resilient to psychoactive substance use disorders

   d. regulatory processes and substance abuse policy relative to service delivery opportunities in addiction counseling

   e. importance of vocation, family, social networks, and community systems in the addiction treatment and recovery process

   f. role of wellness and spirituality in the addiction recovery process

   g. culturally and developmentally relevant education programs that raise awareness and support addiction and substance abuse prevention and the recovery process

   h. classifications, indications, and contraindications of commonly prescribed psychopharmacological medications for appropriate medical referral and consultation

   i. diagnostic process, including differential diagnosis and the use of current diagnostic classification systems, including the Diagnostic and Statistical Manual of Mental Disorders (DSM) and the International Classification of Diseases (ICD)

   j. cultural factors relevant to addiction and addictive behavior

   k. professional organizations, preparation standards, and credentials relevant to the practice of addiction counseling

   l. legal and ethical considerations specific to addiction counseling

   m. record keeping, third party reimbursement, and other practice and management considerations in addiction counseling

3. PRACTICE

   a. screening, assessment, and testing for addiction, including diagnostic interviews, mental status examination, symptom inventories, and psychoeducational and personality assessments

b. assessment of biopsychosocial and spiritual history relevant to addiction

c. assessment for symptoms of psychoactive substance toxicity, intoxication, and withdrawal

d. techniques and interventions related to substance abuse and other addictions

e. strategies for reducing the persisting negative effects of substance use, abuse, dependence, and addictive disorders

f. strategies for helping clients identify the effects of addiction on life problems and the effects of continued harmful use or abuse, and the benefits of a life without addiction

g. evaluating and identifying individualized strategies and treatment modalities relative to clients' stage of dependence, change, or recovery

h. strategies for interfacing with the legal system and working with court referred clients

Source: CACREP (2015, pp. 18–19).

the nuts and bolts of how to integrate addiction counseling content into the general professional counseling standards (e.g., Lee, Craig, Fetherson, & Simpson, 2013), there are still unanswered questions regarding the degree and quality of the addiction content integration into the counseling curriculum (Morgen, Miller, Chasek, DePue, & Ivers, 2015a, 2015b). For instance, if you consider the topic of addiction etiology and addiction behaviors, that seems to be a very expansive topic to try and integrate into even one or two full class sessions. Or if there is an addiction course, what is the quality of that course, and how do the students integrate this content into their broader counseling training?

CACREP program accreditation is defined as designating the "acceptable" degree of training. So a graduate from a CACREP addiction counseling program could be seen as "more of an addiction counselor" than a graduate from a non-CACREP program. In essence, counselor or addiction counselor identity (as defined by CACREP and accepted by ACA and numerous states) is being shaped by program accreditation status (i.e., CACREP or other). If you consider this paradigm against the broader backdrop of all the different addiction certifications and academic/professional eligibility requirements, you begin to see how the CACREP issue is just one more component of a long national dialogue regarding the issue of counselor identity.

If CACREP is playing a role in establishing the credentialing of an addiction counselor (or professional counselor), then perhaps more discussion regarding what exactly constitutes addiction counseling (or professional counseling) training seems warranted. That is why some other accrediting and professional counseling organizations are developing and growing in response to the CACREP standards. The alternate movement is *not* anti-accreditation or anti-CACREP. Any counselor would agree in a split second about how critical curricular oversight and accreditation are to the practice of training counselors. Training must be rigorous with a core of standard content and skills instilled in all counselors via the classroom and field experiences. The reasons for these new bodies seem more aligned with a desire for a clearer, and more unified, definition of what it means to be a counselor or addiction counselor. Some of these new or growing groups are the Alliance for Professional Counselors and the Master's in Psychology and Counseling Accreditation Council (MPCAC). In the future, some of these (or other) organizations could also take a role in organizing the accreditation process focused on acceptable training and experience for qualification for licensure as an addiction counselor. For example, Table 3 reviews the accreditation for counseling programs within MPCAC. The reader can see where there is room for the inclusion of addiction counseling curricular and training matters within the existing standards (or where standards can expand to include addiction counseling content).

For some counselors/programs, CACREP is problematic due to the following reasons. First, some training programs do not have the faculty resources to meet the CACREP mandate for faculty size. These programs would not be able to achieve CACREP accreditation and would thus be seen as perhaps "less-than" or offering a "poor quality" of training not appropriate for licensure. This seems unfair and not the norm across other mental health disciplines. For instance, some clinical or counseling psychologists graduate from non-American Psychological Association (APA) accredited doctoral programs (the program either is not accredited or currently seeking accreditation). These psychologists, though they may be shut out from some jobs that specify a graduate from an APA program, can get licensed in their state—it just may take extra paperwork and time due to the non-APA status of their doctoral degree-granting program. Second, these same psychologists, though not graduates from an APA program, would still be identified as psychologists. Would a graduate from a non-CACREP program be identified as a professional counselor? This is still a question left unclearly answered.

There is also a subtle undertone indicating that counseling (as defined by CACREP and ACA) is different than counseling psychology. There is a strong emphasis on counselor professional identity within the counseling discipline. This is a good thing! However, some arguments center on CACREP's (2015) stipulation regarding faculty identity and training:

> Core counselor education program faculty have earned doctoral degrees in counselor education, preferably from a CACREP-accredited program, or have related doctoral degrees and have been employed as full-time faculty members in a counselor education program for a minimum of one full academic year before July 1, 2013. (p. 6)

In this case, a counseling psychologist could be a member of the core counseling faculty but only if he or she had been teaching in a program since (at minimum) July 1, 2012. The critical term there is *core* faculty. Core faculty are the heart of the counselor education program. In essence, they are the ones who instill the

Table 3 Master's in Psychology and Counseling Accreditation Standards

Professional counselor identity, ethical behavior, and social justice practices. Including but not limited to: assisting students to acquire knowledge related to the history of the helping profession; professional counseling roles and functions; ethical standards related to professional organizations in the field of counseling; and public policy processes including system advocacy strategies on behalf of the profession, clients, and the communities that counselors serve.

Human development and wellness across the life span. Including but not limited to: the study of life span development; maturational and structural theories of human development; wellness counseling theories; strategies to deal with developmental processes and transitions; human behavior; disabilities; environmental, contextual and multicultural factors that contribute to healthy human development and relevant culturally competent counseling practices; and the promotion of social justice in society.

Neuroscientific, physical, and biological foundations of human development and wellness. Including but not limited to: facilitating students' acquisition of new knowledge related to neuroscience, health and wellness; addictions; and the use of neuroscientific research findings for culturally competent counseling practices and social justice advocacy interventions.

Ecological, contextual, multicultural, social justice foundations of human development. Including but not limited to: the study of culture from ecological, contextual, multicultural, and social justice perspectives; evidence-based strategies for working with diverse groups (related to but not limited to age, race, culture, ethnicity, disability, sexual orientation, gender, class, religion/spirituality); the impact of power, privilege, and oppression and micro/macro aggressions on human development; and culturally competent counseling and social justice advocacy interventions.

Counseling, consultation, and social justice advocacy theories and skills. Including but not limited to: training in preventive counseling; consultation; individual, group, couples, marriage, family and addictions counseling; systems change intervention strategies and skills; and social justice advocacy interventions.

Group theory, practice, and social justice advocacy. Including but not limited to: principles of group dynamics, group process, and group leadership; theories and methods of group counseling; and the application of group work theory and practice to organizational dynamics and social justice advocacy in different environmental settings (e.g., family, school, university, workplace, and community settings).

Career and life development. Including but not limited to: the study of vocational/career development theories and decision-making models; career assessment instruments and techniques; occupational and related educational systems; career development applications; career counseling processes/techniques; and the application of social justice theories to people's vocational/career development.

Assessment of human behavior and organizational/community/institutional systems. Including but not limited to: assessment and diagnosis of individual psychiatric disorders as defined by classification systems such as the *Diagnostic Statistical Manual (DSM)* and the International Classification of Diseases (ICD); understanding of defined diagnostic disorders relative to the helping context; knowledge of cultural biases associated with classification systems; assessment strategies designed to promote healthy human functioning; and assessment strategies that focus on organizational/community/ social justice advocacy dynamics as they impact human development, wellness, and the perpetuation of psychiatric disorders as listed in various classification systems.

Tests and measurements. Including but not limited to promoting an understanding of the theoretical and historical basis for, as well as knowledge of cultural biases associated with: assessment techniques; testing methods; knowledge of various types of tests and evaluation strategies that result in

(Continued)

Table 3   (Continued)

knowledgeable selection, administration, interpretation; and use of assessment/evaluation instruments and techniques that foster social justice among diverse client populations.

Traditional and social justice-oriented research and evaluations. Including but not limited to: quantitative and qualitative research design and methods; statistical analyses, principles, practices, and application of needs assessments; the design and process of program evaluation; organizational, community, and social justice advocacy evaluation strategies; and knowledge of cultural biases associated with research practices.

Practicum/Internship experiences. At least two (2) academic terms of supervised field placement experiences that focus on issues related to the promotion of mental health, human development, wellness, cultural competence, and social justice advocacy (at least three semester hours or five quarter hours per academic term in a counseling and/or related human service setting with 300 hours of supervised field training). The practicum/internship experience (commensurate with program goals and State licensure requirements) shall be completed under the clinical supervision of appropriately credentialed professionals (e.g., licensed professional counselor, social worker, marriage and family therapist, school counselor, psychologist, or physician with a specialty in psychiatry).

Source: MPCAC Accreditation Manual (2016).

professional identity of counseling into the next generation of counselors (i.e., their students). Consequently, counseling psychology professionals who align with ACA/CACREP would be ineligible from serving as a core faculty member if not meeting this July 1, 2013, benchmark.

If the counseling psychologist could qualify for the LPC in their state, why then are they deemed not eligible to serve as core faculty (due to graduating from an APA and not CACREP accredited doctoral program) and instill the counseling identity they obviously endorse as evidenced by their licensure (e.g., LPC) and (perhaps) certification status (e.g., National Certified Counselor)? This seems confusing to me (and many others, thus one of the reasons why you see these alternate CACREP organizations developing). Besides adding more layers to the already multilayered field, it also narrows who can be "defined" as a counselor eligible to train future addiction (and professional) counselors. Thus, more confusion.

So how does this all associate with a book on substance use disorders and process addictions?

Actually, it is imperative. As evidenced by the numerous certifications and other credentials that permeate the addiction counseling profession, *who you are* in a professional identity sense—these days—seems linked with the organization or credentialing body through which you are aligned. That would be easy and fine if there were only one body and all of the profession was in agreement. However, as clearly seen in this Preface, that is not the case. Thus, in the addiction profession and the larger professional counseling body there are competing organizations and professional identity definitions that in the end only serve to confuse the broader purpose of a unified profession. Though there has been some dialogue regarding more collaboration and/or merging of organizations (e.g., NAADAC and IC&RC), this degree of unification has not yet begun on a broad scale. Consider Table 4, which describes the different levels of substance abuse counselor scopes of

Table 4 Model Scopes of Practice and Career Ladder for Substance Use Disorders Counselors

Category 4

Practice of Independent Clinical Substance Use Disorder Counselor/Supervisor – An Independent Clinical Substance Use Disorder Treatment Counselor/Supervisor typically has a master's or other postgraduate degree and is licensed to practice independently. The scope of practice for Independent Clinical Substance Use Disorder Counselor/Supervisor can include:

1. Clinical evaluation, including screening, assessment, and diagnosis of Substance Use Disorders (SUDs) and Co-Occurring Disorders (CODs)

2. Treatment planning for SUDs and CODs, including initial, ongoing, continuity of care, discharge, and planning for relapse prevention

3. Referral

4. Service coordination and case management in the areas of SUDs and CODs

5. Counseling, therapy, trauma informed care, and psycho-education with individuals, families, and groups in the areas of SUDs and CODs

6. Client, family, and community education

7. Documentation

8. Professional and ethical responsibilities

9. Clinical supervisory responsibilities for all categories of SUD Counselors

The Independent Clinical Substance Use Disorder Counselor/Supervisor can practice under the auspice of a licensed facility, within a primary care setting, or as an independent private practitioner. It is the responsibility of the Independent Clinical Substance Use Disorder Counselor/Supervisor to seek out clinical supervision and peer support.

Category 3

Practice of Clinical Substance Use Disorder Counselor – The Clinical Substance Use Disorder Treatment Counselor typically has a master's or other postgraduate degree. Depending on the jurisdiction, persons in this position either have not attained their license, or the license is restricted to practice only under supervision of a Category 4 Independent Clinical Substance Use Disorder Counselor/Supervisor. Category 3 Clinical Substance Use Disorder Counselor scope of practice can include:

1. Clinical evaluation, including screening, assessment, and diagnosis of Substance Use Disorders (SUDs) and Co-Occurring Disorders (CODs)

2. Treatment planning for SUDs and CODs, including initial, ongoing, continuity of care, discharge, and planning for relapse prevention

(Continued)

Table 4   (Continued)

3. Referral

4. Service coordination and case management in the areas of SUDs and CODs

5. Counseling, therapy, trauma informed care, and psycho-education with individuals, families and groups in the areas of SUDs and CODs

6. Client, family, and community education

7. Documentation

8. Professional and ethical responsibilities

9. Clinical supervisory responsibilities for categories Levels 1 and 2 as well as Substance Use Disorder Technicians

The Substance Use Disorder Counselor 3 can only practice under the auspice of a licensed facility, within a primary care setting, and under clinical supervision of a Clinical Substance Use Disorder Counselor 4.

Category 2

Practice of Substance Use Disorder Counselor – The Scope of Practice for the category of those with a bachelor's degree includes the following activities with clinical supervision of a Clinical Substance Use Disorder Counselor or other state approved supervisor:

1. Clinical evaluation, including diagnostic impression or Screening, Brief Intervention, and Referral to Treatment Referral (SBIRT)

2. Treatment planning for SUDs and CODs, including initial, ongoing, continuity of care, discharge, and planning for relapse prevention

3. Referral

4. Service coordination and case management for SUDs and CODs

5. Counseling, therapy, trauma informed care, and psycho-education with individuals, families, and groups

6. Client, family, and community education

7. Documentation

8. Professional and ethical responsibilities

9. Clinical supervisory responsibilities for all categories of SUD Counselors

The Substance Use Disorder Counselor 2 can only practice under the auspice of a licensed facility, within a primary care setting, and under the clinical supervision of Clinical Substance Use Disorder Counselor/Supervisor or Clinical Substance Abuse Counselor.

Category 1

Practice of Associate Substance Use Disorder Counselor – The Scope of Practice for the category of those with an associate's degree include the following activities with clinical supervision from a Clinical Substance Abuse Counselor or state approved supervisor and/or administrative supervision of a Substance Abuse Counselor:

1. Diagnostic impression, and Screening, Brief Intervention, Referral to Treatment (SBIRT)

2. Monitor treatment plan/compliance

3. Referral

4. Service coordination and case management for SUD

5. Psycho-educational counseling of individuals and groups

6. Client, family, and community education

7. Documentation

8. Professional and ethical responsibilities

The Associate Substance Use Disorder Treatment Counselor can only practice under the auspice of a licensed facility or a primary care setting, and under the clinical and/or administrative supervision of an Independent Clinical Substance Use Disorder Counselor/Supervisor and a Clinical Substance Use Disorder Counselor or the administrative oversight of the Substance Use Disorder Counselor.

Technician

Practice of Substance Use Disorder Technician – The Scope of Practice for the category of those with a high school diploma or a GED include the following activities with clinical supervision from a Clinical Substance Abuse Counselor/Supervisor, Clinical Substance Abuse Counselor or state approved supervisor and/or administrative supervision of a Substance Abuse Counselor:

1. Diagnostic impression, and Screening, Brief Intervention, Referral to Treatment (SBIRT)

2. Monitor treatment plan/compliance

3. Referral

4. Service coordination and case management for SUD

5. Psycho-educational counseling of individuals and groups

6. Client, family, and community Education

7. Documentation

8. Professional and ethical responsibilities

The Substance Use Disorder Technician can only practice under the auspice of a licensed facility or a primary care setting, and under the clinical and/or administrative supervision of Clinical Substance Use Disorder Counselor/Supervisor, Clinical Substance Abuse Counselor, or the administrative oversight of the Substance Use Disorder Counselor.

Source: SAMHSA (2011a, pp. 4–6).

practice as defined by SAMHSA (2011a). Different levels have varying degrees of education and training, and thus differing scopes of practice. If you examine Figure 1, you will see how these SAMHSA levels relate with the licensure and certification regulations across all the states.

Look at all that has been discussed so far throughout this Preface. The take-home message here is that the discipline covered by a book titled *Substance Use Disorders and Process Addictions* is varied, layered, at times inconsistent, and most important, fragmented. Now, we take some time to further examine how and why this fragmentation exists.

Figure 1   Types of State Individual Substance Abuse Counseling by Licensing/Certification Categories

State	Category 4: Independent Clinical Substance Use Disorder Counselor/ Supervisor	Category 3: Clinical Substance Use Disorder Counselor
AL	Certified Clinical Supervisor	Master's Level Addiction Professional
AK	Administrator	Chemical Dependency Clinical Supervisor
AZ	Independent Substance Abuse Counselor	Alcohol and Substance Abuse Counselor
AR	Certified Clinical Supervisor	Advanced Alcohol and Drug Counselor
CA		Certified Addiction Specialist; Certified Drug, Alcohol & Addictions Counselor; Certified Alcoholism & Other Drug Addictions Recovery Specialist; Registered Addiction Specialist; Certified Addiction Treatment Counselor; Certified Alcohol & Other Drug Counselor; Certified Alcohol and Drug Counselor II; Certified Chemical Dependency Counselor; Certified Substance Abuse Counselor
CO		Licensed Addiction Counselor
CT	Certified Clinical Supervisor	Certified Addiction Counselor
DE	Certified Clinical Supervisor	Certified Alcohol and Drug Counselor
DC		Addiction Counselor II
FL	Certified Addiction Professional	Certified Addiction Counselor
GA	Certified Clinical Supervisor	Certified Addiction Counselor, Level II
HI	Certified Clinical Supervisor	Certified Substance Abuse Counselor – Master's Degree or Higher
ID	Certified Clinical Supervisor, Advanced Certified Alcohol and Drug Counselor	Certified Alcohol and Drug Counselor
IL	Certified Advanced Alcohol and Other Drug Abuse Counselor, Certified Supervisor Alcohol and Other Drug Abuse Counselor	Certified Reciprocal Alcohol and Other Drug Abuse Counselor
IN	Licensed Clinical Addiction Counselor	Licensed Addiction Counselor

Category 2: Substance Use Disorder Counselor	Category 1: Associate Substance Use Disorder Counselor	Substance Use Disorder Technician
Certified Alcohol and Drug Professional	Associate Certified Addiction Professional	Associate Addictions Professional
Chemical Dependency Counselor II	Chemical Dependency Counselor I	Counselor Technician
Licensed Associate Substance Abuse Counselor		Licensed Substance Abuse Technician
Alcohol and Drug Abuse Counselor		
Certified Addiction Counselor Level III	Certified Addiction Counselor Level II	Certified Addiction Counselor Level I
Certified Addiction Counselor – Provisional	Counselor in Training	
	Certified Associate Addiction Counselor	
Addiction Counselor I		
	Certified Addiction Specialist	Certified Behavioral Health Technician
Certified Addiction Counselor, Level I		Registered Alcohol and Drug Abuse Technician (RADT)
Certified Substance Abuse Counselor – Bachelor's Degree	Certified Substance Abuse Counselor	
		Idaho Student of Addiction Studies
Certified Alcohol and Other Drug Abuse Counselor		Certified Associate Addictions Professional

(Continued)

Figure 1   (Continued)

State	Category 4: Independent Clinical Substance Use Disorder Counselor/ Supervisor	Category 3: Clinical Substance Use Disorder Counselor
IA	International Advanced Alcohol and Drug Counselor	International Alcohol and Drug Counselor
KS		Clinical Addiction Counselor
KY		Alcohol and Drug Addiction Counselor
LA	Certified Clinical Counselor	Licensed Addiction Counselor
ME	Certified Clinical Supervisor	Licensed Alcohol and Drug Counselor
MD	Approved Alcohol and Drug Supervisor	Certified Professional Counselor – Alcohol and Drug
MA		Licensed Alcohol and Drug Counselor 1
MI		Certified Alcohol and Drug Counselor
MN		Licensed Alcohol and Drug Counselor
MS	Licensed Clinical Addiction Counselor	Certified Addiction Counselor
MO	Registered Supervisor	Provisional Licensed Professional Counselor
MT		Licensed Addiction Counselor
NE		Licensed Alcohol/Drug Counselor
NV		Clinical Alcohol and Drug Abuse Counselor
NH	Licensed Clinical Supervisor, Master Licensed Alcohol and Drug Counselor	Licensed Alcohol and Drug Counselor
NJ		Licensed Clinical Alcohol and Drug Counselor
NM		Licensed Alcohol and Drug Abuse Counselor
NY		Credentialed Alcoholism and Substance Abuse Counselor
NC	Certified Clinical Supervisor	Licensed Clinical Addictions Specialist
ND		Licensed Professional Counselor
OH		Independent Chemical Dependency Counselor
OK		Licensed Alcohol and Drug Counselor
OR		Certified Alcohol and Drug Counselor III

Category 2: Substance Use Disorder Counselor	Category 1: Associate Substance Use Disorder Counselor	Substance Use Disorder Technician
Certified Alcohol and Drug Counselor		
Addiction Counselor		
Certified Addiction Counselor	Registered Addiction Counselor	Addiction Treatment Assistant
Certified Alcohol and Drug Counselor	Alcohol and Drug Counseling Aide	
Certified Associate Counselor – Alcohol and Drug	Certified Supervised Associate Counselor – Alcohol and Drug	
Licensed Drug and Alcohol Counselor II	Licensed Drug and Alcohol Counselor Assistant	
	Certified Recovery Support Worker	
Certified Alcohol and Drug Counselor		
	Alcoholism and Substance Abuse Counselor Trainee	
Certified Substance Abuse Counselor		
Licensed Associate Professional Counselor		
Chemical Dependency Counselor III	Chemical Dependency Counselor II	
Certified Alcohol and Drug Counselor		
Alcohol and Drug Evaluation Specialist, Certified Alcohol and Drug Counselor II	Certified Alcohol and Drug Counselor I	

(Continued)

Figure 1   (Continued)

State	Category 4: Independent Clinical Substance Use Disorder Counselor/ Supervisor	Category 3: Clinical Substance Use Disorder Counselor
PA	Certified Clinical Supervisor	Certified Advanced Alcohol and Drug Counselor
RI	Licensed Chemical Dependency Professional/ Licensed Chemical Dependency Clinical Supervisor	Advanced Chemical Dependency Professional II
SC	Certified Clinical Supervisor	Certified Addictions Counselor II
SD	Certified Chemical Dependency Counselor Level III	Certified Chemical Dependency Counselor Level II
TN		Alcohol and Drug Abuse Counselor
TX		Certified Clinical Supervisor
UT		Licensed Substance Abuse Counselor
VT		Alcohol and Drug Abuse Counselor
VA	Licensed Substance Abuse Practitioner	Certified Substance Abuse Counselor
WA		Chemical Dependency Professional
WV	Clinical Supervisor Certification	Advanced Alcohol and Drug Counselor
WI	Intermediate Clinical Supervisor, Clinical Supervisor-in-Training	Clinical Substance Abuse Counselor
WY	Addictions Therapist	Provisional Addictions Therapist (PAT)

Category 2: Substance Use Disorder Counselor	Category 1: Associate Substance Use Disorder Counselor	Substance Use Disorder Technician
Certified Alcohol and Drug Counselor	Certified Associate Addiction Counselor: Associate's Degree Not Required	Certified Allied Addiction Practitioner
Advanced Chemical Dependency Professional	PCDP Provisional Chemical Dependency Professional	
Certified Addictions Counselor I		
Certified Chemical Dependency Counselor Level I		
Licensed Chemical Dependency Counselor	Counselor Intern	
Certified Substance Abuse Counselor		
	Certified Substance Abuse Counselor Assistant	
		Chemical Dependency Professional Trainee
Alcohol and Drug Counselor		
Substance Abuse Counselor		
Certified Addictions Practitioner	Addictions Practitioner Assistant	

Source: The National Association of State Alcohol and Drug Abuse Directors (2013).
Note: Categories based on SAMHSA Consensus Group Career Ladder and Scope of Practice (February 2011).

Professional Identity and Addiction Counseling

The question of professional identity within the counseling profession still exists today (Calley & Hawley, 2008; Cashwell, Kleist, & Schofield, 2009; Chronister, Chou, & Chan, 2016; Mellin, Hunt, & Nichols, 2011; Myers, Sweeney, & White, 2002; Nassar-McMillan & Niles, 2011; Prosek & Hurt, 2014; Remley & Herlihy, 2009). One possible reason for the continual debate around professional identity may lie in the multitude of specialty fields (e.g., addiction, career, and school) within counseling (Gale & Austin, 2003; Myers, 1995). This is a true distinguishing factor from the professions of psychology, psychiatry, and social work in that counseling is the only one of these "mental health" disciplines that licenses/certifies specialty areas. There is, though, a critical issue in need of discussion. Specialty areas such as career counseling and school counseling only denote a practice area (career issues) or population (K–12 students), whereas addiction counseling actually entails the profession of counseling for a *Diagnostic and Statistical Manual of Mental Disorders* (*DSM-5*; APA, 2013) disorder class (Substance-Related and Addictive Disorders). Consequently, all these licenses and certification statuses are focused on the treatment of one *DSM-5* disorder class.

Stop and think about this for a moment. No other *DSM-5* disorder class has a similar model. For instance, there are no licensed anxiety disorder counselors. Nor are there state and national bodies certifying expertise in bipolar disorders in a similar fashion as the addictive disorders (i.e., is there an NBCC credential called the Master Bipolar Disorders Counselor?).

Henriksen, Nelson, and Watts (2010) criticized the counseling specialty system and argued how the counseling specialties do not define counseling but merely denote a practice area, and that counseling specialty licensure/credentialing implies that only a small proportion of the counseling profession is qualified to work with this population. As you have seen thus far in this Preface to the book, the addiction area is one such area of specialization that comes with a separate licensure/credentialing process. As a practicing counselor who works with the addiction population and trains counselors to work with this population, I firmly believe that training is required and must be rigorous and extensive. At the same time, things get a little confusing if you stop and deconstruct the process. Here's why.

Consider the human development counseling domain and the requirement that all counselors receive training in the areas of addiction etiology and addiction behaviors. The graduate student in a CACREP program preparing them for licensure as an LPC receives (as per CACREP, 2015) at least some exposure to these topics in some courses. They move on and become licensed as LPCs.

An addictions counseling license requires extensive course work and training. Obviously, a student in an addiction counseling master's program receives a degree of training and classroom exposure to these topics that are both intensive and pervasive across numerous courses and educational experiences (classroom, practicum, internship, and perhaps "brown-bag" lecture series common in graduate programs). But in many states, the LPC is eligible to counsel and diagnose within the full breadth of the *DSM*, which includes substance use disorders. For example, in New Jersey, where I practice, an LPC has basically the same clinical purview over work with addictions as does a licensed clinical alcohol and drug counselor (LCADC). I perform counseling for substance use and addictive disorders as an LPC. One door down, my colleague does so as an LCADC. Though there are some clear and critical regulatory differences between the LCADC and LPC, for this argument, both legally permit for the counseling of a client struggling with, for example, cocaine use disorder recovery or alcohol use disorder.

Obviously, for the LPC (and the LCADC) in New Jersey (and nationwide), the ACA ethics of adhering to competency apply here. The LPC should only work with the addictions if he or she has the training and experience to work with that population from an empirically supported and theoretically and clinically sound framework. That is one of the pressing questions. Yes, CACREP dictated student exposure to addiction content while in a graduate program leading to licensure as an LPC. But is that all that is needed? That seems far too brief in breadth and scope. So clearly, more training is needed. But how much? What classes? How many hours of supervised postgraduate work? If you recall from above, different certifications specified different requirements. Though the CACREP standards are present for counselors seeking an LPC, do they do enough to adequately train the counselor? Would or could other standards do better? In addition, these questions do not come up in the same manner for any other *DSM-5* disorder. These questions directly pertain to a book such as this because it is the content in this type of book (and other related texts) that would constitute the material for training.

These are hard questions because there really is not any precedent in a discipline beyond addiction counseling. If counselor trainees wish to specialize in major depressive disorder, there are no national certifications, CACREP standards, or state licenses dictating requirements specific to major depressive disorder (or any other *DSM-5* disorder other than the substance-related and addictive disorders). The counselor trainees, in their postgraduate hours for licensure accrual, seek out supervision, training, and other continuing education experiences to make certain that they ethically develop a competency to work with clients struggling with major depressive disorders. But the story changes if the desired area of expertise is substance use and addictive disorders. The new counseling graduate accruing licensure hours or the already-licensed LPC, however, has to sift through the various state and national regulations, as well as the status quo/culture that sometimes seems to ignore the LPC's ability to work with addictions via his or her state scope of practice (typically, this occurs because the addiction license or certification is the clearest way to establish a degree of competency and training in the addiction counseling area). For example, I have had countless graduate students (where I teach and from across the nation in the audience at some of my ACA talks) say that they never were certain if LPCs could work with the addictions because they see the addiction license and/or certification in their state separate from the LPC, counselors holding both the LPC and addictions license/certification, as well as the varied national certifications only focused on addiction (e.g., no NBCC certifications for any other *DSM-5* disorder classes). Again, obviously training and clinical experience are mandatory for any counselor who wishes to work with the addictions. *And again, this statement holds for a counselor wishing to work with any other DSM-5 disorder class. The substance use and addictive disorders require no degree of training and experience to competently work with clients that is any different than the degree of training and experience required to work competently with anxiety, mood, bipolar, personality, psychotic, and all other disorders.* The difference is in the context in which the addiction counseling profession sits (e.g., separate state license/certification, no similar national certification/credentialing system, and a certification/credentialing system with multiple organizations and levels) as opposed to the other *DSM-5* disorder classes.

So coming back full circle, I felt this chapter needed to be written because the reader needs to understand the overall structure of the profession (i.e., this Preface) as well as the research and theory that go into the provision of services (i.e., Chapters 1–11). Take a moment and go back over the Preface. This is the general outline of the profession (at least how I see it, though others feel the same):

- Regulations for addiction counseling licensure and/or certification vary by state.
- Regulations for LPCs pertaining to work with addiction issues vary across some states.
- There are multiple (and competing) national certifications that all demonstrate competence working with the addictive disorders.
- There are varying levels of what can be considered a substance abuse counselor.
- There is a CACREP set of guidelines for the counseling specialty of addiction counseling.
- Those who may be engaged in the act of counseling for an addictive disorder can include a licensed addiction counselor from a CACREP program, an LPC from a CACREP program, an LPC from a non-CACREP program, a psychologist, or a social worker.

- CACREP identifies professional counselor identity, so some counselors (e.g., counseling psychology background) may not be considered a "counselor" and not eligible as a core counseling education faculty member.
- There is no standard and agreed-upon amount of training and education for someone not from an addiction counseling graduate background in regard to course work, supervised hours, and postgraduate experience. Many of these certifications and licenses overlap in areas of competency, class hours, and other matters, but the presence of so many similar credentials indicates a series of nuanced (or major) differences within the discipline pertaining to the expertise needed to practice as an addiction counselor (or other title) as per the specific credential criteria.
- In many cases, professional identity seems dependent upon areas of competence that are externally defined.

In 2011, I gave a talk at the ACA Conference in New Orleans which I titled "Will the Real Addictions Specialist Please Stand?" I want to give you a feel for the profession so you can see why that title made such sense to me (and others). This also sets the stage so you can understand my professional opinions and biases as the author of this book. They are as follows.

My Opinions and Biases

First, I do not conceptualize addiction counseling as a specialty area. I agree with Henriksen et al. (2010), who felt that type of specificity does more harm than good. I see counseling as a unified profession. In my case, I engage in the act of professional counseling for those who struggle with substance use disorders and addictive disorders. That is my perspective in regard to how I chose to write this book. I believe school counseling and career counseling are specialty counseling areas, but because addiction counseling (as named by CACREP) pertains to the counseling to treat a *DSM-5* disorder class, the specialty designation is misused. My evidence to back my claim is the absence of any other counseling license designated for a specific *DSM-5* disorder class. *Any arguments made about the need for training, experience, and competency in the addiction profession are identically relevant for the counselor in the treatment of any other* DSM *disorder class.* Substance use disorders and addictive disorders, in that sense, are not unique from the rest of the *DSM-5.* Training is critical. Supervision is critical. As with any other disorder, the counselor must be competent to practice.

This idea about specialty areas may have some additional support in some of the recent work of Bobby (2013):

CACREP must reexamine its accreditation structure to determine how it can accredit the overall counseling program being offered and not specialty areas within that counseling program. This could be accomplished if CACREP makes a decision to simply accredit counseling programs at the entry level, while offering guidelines for best practice in specialized practice areas or settings. Another option might be for CACREP to accredit programs' postgraduate certificate or educational specialist add-on degrees for students who want to opt for more specialized training. (p. 42)

Though still recognizing "addiction counseling" as a specialty area, it does move CACREP toward perhaps a much more useful model of setting up the necessary postgraduate training structure so all counselors can have a standard level of recognized training to facilitate counseling competence in the addictions. For LPCs, this could greatly benefit those who were misinformed that they *needed* the addiction license in a state where the full *DSM* is covered under the LPC's scope of practice.

Second, I believe that co-occurring disorders are the norm across all substance use disorders counseling. Whether *DSM-5* diagnosable or subsyndromal, any client who presents with a diagnosable substance use disorder (especially at the moderate or severe levels) also presents with *something else*—sometimes multiple other issues. That is why the case that runs throughout this book is of a woman with major depressive disorder, opioid use disorder, and sex addiction. This is the severity and complexity of many of the clients that students will face. I felt it imperative that the reader understand that clients with substance use and a co-occurring disorder are not a special subpopulation; instead, they are *the* population. I felt some books on substance use disorders, whether outwardly or in a more subtle manner, implied to the reader the message that co-occurring disorders are more unique than the norm. I tried to interject this text with as many co-occurring examples as I could to attempt to show the concept as prevalent and expected within the SUD treatment population.

Third (and this goes back to bias #1), I see this as a *counseling text for work with the substance use disorders* and not an *addiction counseling text.* This is more than just a fun play on semantics. I found many addiction counseling texts seemed to "claim" general counseling concepts. For instance, I once obtained a text on ethics in addiction counseling. I thought it was going to give me an applied review of ethical principles and codes through the addiction counseling perspective. Instead, I got a basic review of ethical principles (like you would find in any counseling text) with the "addiction" content being the examples provided about competency or boundaries. I am not trying to reinvent the wheel here. Many of these concepts are included in any good text on the subject matter (e.g., motivational interviewing, relapse prevention, cognitive-behavioral therapy). I do not try to condense these mammoth topic areas into a chapter, as I have found that sometimes leaves students feeling like they "rushed" through a theory and there must be more somewhere. I also do not try to "introduce" the reader to these concepts that are standard across counseling texts (addiction and otherwise). I consider this book a conversation. We step into the subject matter and review some (but not all) of the relevant content, all the while trying to emphasize the application to substance use disorders, addictive disorders, and co-occurring disorders.

I always felt that what was missing from texts I read for myself and used in the classroom as a professor (and one time student) was the stated opinions and biases of the author. That is why I spent these first pages explaining my perceptions of the field this book covers. I am neither right nor wrong. These are just my thoughts as someone who has spent over 20 years in the substance use disorders and addictions profession. In the end, if you agree (even somewhat) with my perspective, then turn the page and we'll start the conversation. If you do not agree, then that is cool as well. I am always at the ACA Conference each year. If you happen to see me in the halls, or attend a talk/poster of mine, please feel free to come up to me, say hi, let me know where we agree, where we disagree, and what you think about how I see the profession. And how *you* see the profession.

In the interim, enjoy the book. . . .

—*Keith*

ACKNOWLEDGMENTS

This book is the summation of my over 20 years in the substance use disorders and addictions profession. I have encountered countless people over the years who have shaped and challenged and disputed my ideas, all which have resulted in how I see this profession today. It's easiest to start at the beginning and go forward.

Dating back to the mid-1990s, David Kerr, Ed Lyons, Dr. Judy Waters, and the hundreds of residents with whom I talked during my initiation into the profession as a researcher/grant writer at Integrity House, a therapeutic community in Newark, New Jersey. Dave Kerr is one of the pioneers of the therapeutic community process (and substance use disorders and addictions treatment), so having access to his perspectives and knowledge on a daily basis laid the foundation for my thinking. Ed Lyons, as a clinical director, took me through the pragmatics of how treatment operates. Finally, Dr. Judy Waters was my first mentor and partner in (what feels like) millions of conversations about academic theory and empirical findings regarding treatment, relapse, and other addictions counseling concepts. She introduced me to Dave—and thus, this field and my career—so thank you, Judy. And thank you, Dave and Ed.

What feels like an eternity ago, I was trained at Lehigh University's Counseling Psychology Doctoral Program. Dr. Arnie Spokane stands out as the psychologist who instilled in me the pressing need to be a fluent expert in a specific area of inquiry but to also be very aware of the broader counseling picture and to look where your area fits into the bigger professional narrative. He said that as professionals we oversee the profession and that if you look hard enough in a critical way, you will see where the problems lie with the field at that time. Then, it is your job to try and address them. Consequently, many of my thoughts on the profession (outlined in the Preface and influencing how I wrote this book in general) are directly due to Arnie (a long time ago) telling me that I was allowed to do that. Thanks, Arnie.

The biggest "break" in my career came when I was fortunate to have been accepted as a predoctoral fellow in the Behavioral Science Training Program in Drug Abuse Research, funded by the National Institute on Drug Abuse and housed at the prestigious National Development and Research Institutes (NDRI) in New York City. Here, I gained my first doses of true professional training. The directors then were Dr. Greg Falkin and (the late) Dr. Bruce Johnson. They were rigorous, challenging, and in their own ways, supportive. Greg would spend hours with me in patience, encouraging me along the way until your dissertation chapter, article, or conference paper was done. Bruce, supportive and mentoring in his own way, would see me at the copier, say hi, and ask if that paper "is ever going to get done or what?" I think that in my own practices as a professor and research mentor, I have adopted both their styles. So Greg, Bruce, thanks.

I remained at NDRI for a postdoctoral fellowship and then for a few years as a senior research associate. Here, I got to work with and learn from some of the giants in the profession like Drs. George De Leon, Gerald Melnick, Alexandre Laudet, and David Kressel. They imparted to me a tremendous wealth of knowledge about the profession, so George, Gerald, Alexandre, and Dave, thanks.

In my "professional" career since NDRI, I have worked with some amazing colleagues on various projects. Dr. Janetta Astone-Twerell, at Samaritan Village, takes me back to my days at Integrity as we work on various TC projects. The fact that she calls me for research advice or statistical problem solving is always flattering in that, for such large and important projects, she trusts my opinion. I still learn little things here and there when we talk about the status of the profession from an administrative end. This informs my work, so Janetta, thank you.

Dr. Tina Maschi (Fordham University) and I have worked together for 10 years on a variety of projects focused on older adult prisoners. It was this work that directly influenced and informed my research and clinical focus on including older adult issues into the substance use disorders discussion. That is why, unlike many other books, there is an older adults section for each chapter in this book. As a social worker, her perspectives widened my views on countless treatment and policy matters in the substance use disorders profession. So Tina, thank you.

I spent several years within the governance of the ACA division called the IAAOC. I started as a committee chair (spirituality), moved on to secretary, and then was so fortunate to have been elected as president 2013–2014. My time with IAAOC was transformative in how it helped sharpen my thinking on some critical areas of relevance to me (training, licensure, credentialing). Some of the IAAOC and ACA members who were pivotal in this process were Drs. E. J. Eissic, Jerry Juhnke, Geri Miller, Todd Lewis, Bryce Hagedorn, Jack Culbreth, Trevor Buser, and Craig Cashwell. To all of you, thank you.

I have worked with a countless number of clients over the years across many settings. Their stories of recovery success, setback, failure, and resilience always informs how I treat, how I research, how I teach, and how I theorize within this profession. The human being never fails to amaze me. Those who I think will succeed wind up struggling, whereas people who seem like they are going to fall away to addiction summon strength and become role models for others in recovery. To all of you, thank you.

Finally, my colleagues at Centenary University. Specifically, the past president (Dr. Barbara-Jayne Lewthwaite) and current provost/VPAA (Dr. Jim Patterson), who have always been supportive of my work and efforts on behalf of the college. In addition, the psychology and counseling department chair (Dr. Harriett Gaddy), who always values, encourages and supports my work within the department with our students. Barbara, Jim, Harriett, and all of my Centenary colleagues, thank you.

And to you. Thank you for bothering to see how I conceptualize this profession we seem to share.

SAGE would like to acknowledge the following reviewers:

Kevin A. Freeman, Mercer University

Bill McHenry, Texas A&M University–Texarkana

Nancy E. Sherman, Bradley University

Richard S. Takacs, Carlow University

ABOUT THE AUTHOR

Keith Morgen is Associate Professor of Counseling and Psychology at Centenary University (Hackettstown, New Jersey), where he teaches in the undergraduate psychology and graduate counseling programs. Dr. Morgen's research on substance use, trauma, and prisoner mental health has been published in major scholarly journals such as *Traumatology, Therapeutic Communities, The Gerontologist, The Professional Counselor, Journal of Correctional Healthcare, Journal of Addictions and Offender Counseling, Alcoholism Treatment Quarterly, Applied Research in Quality of Life, Journal of Drug Issues,* and *Journal of Alcohol and Drug Education.* In addition, Dr. Morgen presents papers at major conferences such as the American Counseling Association, American Public Health Association, American Psychological Association, and the College on Problems of Drug Dependence. Dr. Morgen is a former president (2013–2014) of the International Association of Addictions and Offender Counselors (a division of the American Counseling Association). Dr. Morgen is a Licensed Professional Counselor (New Jersey) and Approved Clinical Supervisor and practices counseling part-time at Discovery Psychotherapy & Wellness Centers in Morristown, New Jersey. He is a past recipient of the Centenary College Distinguished Teaching Award. Dr. Morgen received his PhD in Counseling Psychology (Lehigh University) and was a National Institute on Drug Abuse funded Predoctoral and Postdoctoral Research Fellow at National Development and Research Institutes in New York City.

SAGE was founded in 1965 by Sara Miller McCune to support the dissemination of usable knowledge by publishing innovative and high-quality research and teaching content. Today, we publish over 900 journals, including those of more than 400 learned societies, more than 800 new books per year, and a growing range of library products including archives, data, case studies, reports, and video. SAGE remains majority-owned by our founder, and after Sara's lifetime will become owned by a charitable trust that secures our continued independence.

Los Angeles | London | New Delhi | Singapore | Washington DC | Melbourne

Section 1

Addiction and the Brain, and the Introduction to the Case of Samantha

CHAPTER 1

This chapter covers the psychopharmacology and neuropsychology concepts relevant to any discussion of substance use disorders and addictions. Following this chapter is the case of Samantha. This is a conceptual case (created from my experiences with dozens of clients of similar diagnoses) that you will follow at various key points in the book and review via the content covered in the book at that time.

Chapter 1

SUBSTANCE USE DISORDER AND ADDICTION

Basic and Brief Psychopharmacological and Neuropsychological Review

OPENING THOUGHTS

Any discussion of substance use disorder and addiction must start in the brain. You are treating a psychological, neurological, and medical condition *of the brain.* Understanding *how* the substance(s) can act on the brain and *how* these actions may influence thought, emotion, and behavior is critical to understanding the substance use disorder and addiction condition. However, I want to emphasize that the information in this chapter in no way represents a complete and thorough coverage of the pertinent psychopharmacological and neuropsychological concepts. That is impossible. There are countless texts devoted entirely to the content here in Chapter 1. Consequently, my goal for this chapter is simple: I want you to learn content from the following pages and (perhaps more important) realize that there are other areas you need to learn more about and have an initial direction and leads to go address that inquiry. So this is where we start.

CENTRAL NERVOUS SYSTEM

The human brain is built of two cell types: neurons (numbering in the 100 billion range) and an even larger number of glia. Each is addressed below.

Neurons

Neurons communicate via a series of circuits. These circuits are the foundation for all we are, experience, and feel. Thus, our thoughts, emotions, and behaviors are all rooted in neurons. Figure 1.1 displays the four parts of the neuron anatomy (cell body, axon, dendrites, and synapse). The cell body consists of the nucleus and receives all the input information and is consequently the origin of all neurotransmitter and action potential activation. Action potential is when a neuron membrane is depolarized beyond its threshold. The axon is the "sending" component that transmits a signal down the neuron to the synapse. Here, in the synapse, the neurotransmitters are released. This is how neurons speak to one another as the neurotransmitter signals are received by the dendrites on nearby neurons. In brief, neurons serve three functions: inhibition, excitation, and neuromodulation. Inhibition is the process of one neuron releasing an inhibitory neurotransmitter. Excitation is the neuron releasing an excitatory neurotransmitter. Neuromodulation involves one neuron impacting neurotransmission, typically at somewhat of a distance. Many receptors and neurotransmitter systems are involved with substance use disorder and addiction, including dopamine, serotonin, norepinephrine, glutamate, gamma-aminobutyric acid (GABA), acetylcholine, the endogenous opiate system, and the cannabinoid system (Pinel, 2013).

Figure 1.1   Neuron Anatomy

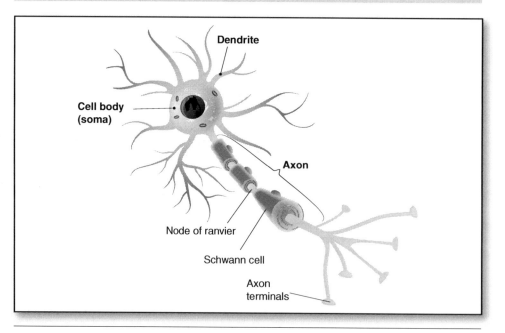

©iStockphoto.com/ttsz

Glia

These are supporting cells of the central nervous system and can outnumber neurons by a margin of 10 to 1. Glia used to be considered the glue of the central nervous system that holds neurons together. However, recent work has uncovered

Figure 1.2 Neurotransmitters Relevant to Substance Use Disorders

Neurotransmitter	Distribution in the Central Nervous System	Functions Affected	Drugs That Affect It
Dopamine	Midbrain, Ventral tegmental area (VTA), Cerebral cortex, Hypothalamus	Pleasure and reward, Movement, Attention, Memory	Cocaine, Methamphetamine, Amphetamine. In addition, virtually all drugs of abuse directly or indirectly augment dopamine in the reward pathway
Serotonin	Midbrain, VTA, Cerebral cortex, Hypothalamus	Mood, Sleep, Sexual desire, Appetite	MDMA (ecstasy), LSD, Cocaine
Norepinephrine	Midbrain, VTA, Cerebral cortex, Hypothalamus	Sensory processing, Movement, Sleep, Mood, Memory, Anxiety	Cocaine, Methamphetamine, Amphetamine
Endogenous opioids (endorphin and enkephalin)	Widely distributed in brain but regions vary in type of receptors, Spinal cord	Analgesia, Sedation, Rate of bodily functions, Mood	Heroin, Morphine, Prescription painkillers (Oxycodone)
Acetylcholine	Hippocampus, Cerebral cortex, Thalamus, Basal ganglia, Cerebellum	Memory, Arousal, Attention, Mood	Nicotine
Endogenous cannabinoids (anandamide)	Cerebral cortex, Hippocampus, Thalamus, Basal ganglia	Movement, Cognition and memory	Marijuana
Glutamate	Widely distributed in brain	Neuron activity (increased rate), Learning, Cognition, Memory	Ketamine, Phencyclidine, Alcohol
Gamma-aminobutyric acid (GABA)	Widely distributed in brain	Neuron activity (slowed), Anxiety, Memory, Anesthesia	Sedatives, Tranquilizers, Alcohol

Source: From "Impacts of Drugs on Neurotransmittion," by National Institute on Drug Abuse, 2007 (https://www.drugabuse .gov/news-events/nida-notes/2007/10/impacts-drugs-neurotransmission).

that glia are now known to have substantial influence over various central nervous system processes. Specifically, some glia cells regulate neurotransmission and are involved in the reuptake process for various excitatory neurotransmitters.

Neurotransmitters

Numerous neurotransmitters form the language via which neurons communicate and we live and breathe. At any given moment, all you feel, think, and do can be linked all the way back to these chemicals—neurotransmitters—which are passed between neurons in the synapse. A comprehensive review of the neurotransmitters is beyond the scope of this chapter and text. However, Figure 1.2 provides a brief review of the neurotransmitters involved with the substance use disorder and addiction conditions.

BRAIN AREAS ASSOCIATED WITH SUBSTANCE USE AND ADDICTION

The brain is made up of a few areas with strong connections to the addiction process. These areas handle dozens of functions, and substance use or the recovery from substance use can impact functioning within these areas as well as the many thousands of connections, or tracts, between these structures (Pinel, 2013). Some key areas are discussed below.

Brain Stem

The hindbrain is made of the cerebellum, pons, and medulla. Typically, the midbrain, pons, and medulla are all tied together and described as being the brain stem (Pinel, 2013). The brain stem is theorized to handle such functions as motor control, language, attention, fear and pleasure regulation, the regulation of cardiac and respiratory function, regulation of the central nervous system, and the maintenance of consciousness. Figure 1.3 shows the location of the brain stem, cerebellum, pons, and medulla.

Anatomically, the brain stem is the most interior and primitive brain area. Several components of the brain stem are theorized to be involved with substance use disorder and addiction, including the ventral tegmental area (VTA), substantia nigra (SN), and dorsal raphe nucleus (DRN). The VTA is involved in the substance and natural reward circuits of the brain and is critical for cognition and emotion (Pinel, 2013). In addition, the VTA's neurons project to several other key brain areas relevant to substance use disorders and addiction, such as the prefrontal cortex (PFC). The SN plays a role in reward seeking and learning. The DRN also

Figure 1.3 Anatomy of the Human Brain, Showing Brain Stem and Other Areas

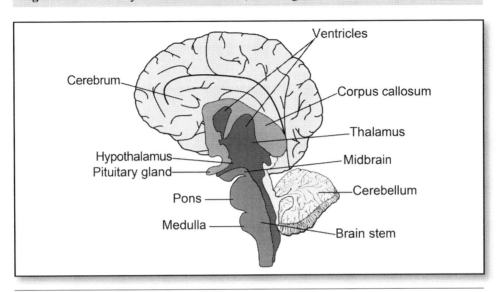

contributes to learning and memory functions, as well as playing a role in affect (Holtz, 2010).

Basal Ganglia

The basal ganglia sits between the brain stem and cortex and consists of areas relevant to substance use disorder and addiction. The nucleus accumbens (NAc) contributes to the cognitive processes of motivation, pleasure, reward, and reinforcement (Pinel, 2013), as well as playing a role regarding responses to novel stimuli (Holtz, 2010). The amygdala is involved with memory and decision-making and emotional processes; specifically, the consolidation of emotional memories (Pinel, 2013). Figure 1.4 shows the location of the basal ganglia and associated areas within the brain linked with addiction, such as the subthalamic nucleus (Pellouox & Baunez, 2013) and the caudate nucleus (Bohbot, Del Balso, Conrad, Konishi, & Leyton, 2013).

Cortex

This is the outermost and most advanced brain area. Pinel (2013) and Holtz (2010) reviewed how the cortex consists of several areas linked with substance use disorders and addiction: the anterior cingulate cortex, dorsolateral prefrontal cortex, orbitofrontal cortex, insular cortex, and the hippocampus. The anterior cingulate

Figure 1.4   Drawing of the Brain Showing the Basal Ganglia and Thalamic Nuclei

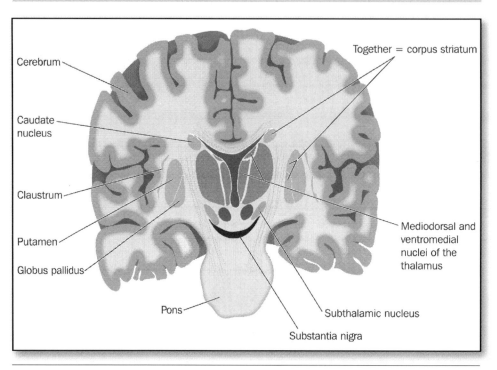

cortex is responsible for such functions as reward anticipation, empathy, emotion, impulse control, and emotion. It helps to modulate emotional responses. The dorso-lateral prefrontal cortex is involved in executive functions, which include working memory as well as cognitive flexibility and planning. This area is frequently discussed as relevant to problems with attention and motivation. In addition, this area is activated in risky or moral decision-making processes involving a cost/benefit analysis of several potential decisions. The orbitofrontal cortex may be involved with linking affect to reinforcement as well as the decision-making processes. The insular cortex is associated with exposure to substance-related triggers, and this brain area is involved with a host of functions, including the processing of negative emotional experience (Critchley, Wiens, Rotshtein, Öhman, & Dolan, 2004) as well as the integration of sensory input from multiple sources (Taylor, Seminowicz, & Davis, 2009). Finally, the hippocampus plays a critical role in the integration of emotion and memory as well as having an influence on long-term memory (Pinel, 2013). Figure 1.5 displays the general human brain anatomy and the functions associated with these areas. Just about all these areas are in some manner influenced by the addiction process, whether during the active use and/or recovery periods.

Figure 1.5 Human Brain Anatomy, Function Area, and Mind System

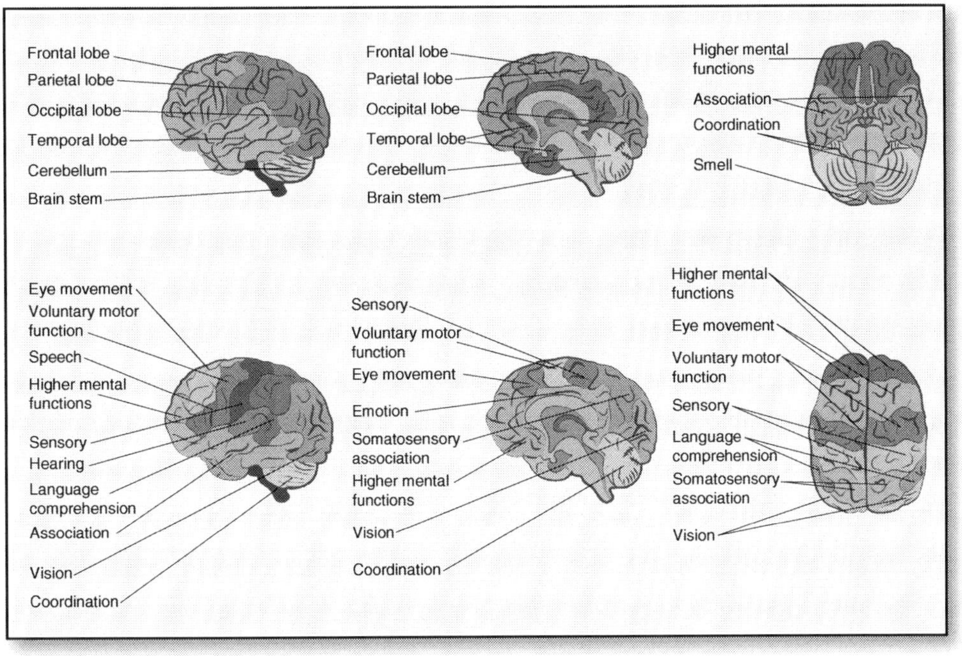

Adapted from © Can Stock Photo Inc./eveleen.

Dopamine Pathways

As discussed in Figure 1.2, dopamine plays a pivotal role across most substances discussed in this text. There are four dopamine pathways in the brain, with the first three being involved in the substance use disorder and addiction process: mesolimbic, mesocortical, nigrostriatal, and tuberorinfundibular. Each is briefly discussed below.

The mesolimbic pathway runs between the ventral tegmental area to the nucleus accumbens. However, the dopamine cells of the mesolimbic pathway also project to other areas relevant to substance use disorders and addictions, including the amygdala, bed nucleus of the stria terminalis (BNST), and lateral hypothalamus. The mesocortical pathway extends to the frontal lobes and includes several structures believed to have an important role in the addictive process, such as the dorsolateral prefrontal cortex (Dagher, Owen, Boecker, & Brooks, 1999), the orbitofrontal cortex, and the anterior cingulate (Bush, Luu, & Posner, 2000). For example, the prefrontal cortex facilitates the control of impulsive behavior. Any alteration in this area, such as via substance use, could lead to increased impulsivity and possible substance use. The third dopamine pathway in the brain is the nigrostriatal pathway, which primarily controls movement and may explain some motor deficits in substance-using individuals (Gardner & Ashby, 2000). The fourth pathway, the tuberoinfundibular pathway, does not play a role in substance use and addiction.

PSYCHOPHARMACOLOGY: BASICS

Route of Administration

The specific format in which a substance is administered will have a major impact on four key concepts: (1) the speed in which the substance begins influencing the body, (2) how this substance is distributed throughout the body, (3) the intensity of the effect, and (4) the speed in which any side effects will be experienced. There are a few ways that substances are administered, with most being divided between the enteral or parenteral routes.

Enteral Substance Administration

Substances administered via the enteral route enter into the bloodstream through the gastrointestinal system (Stahl, 2013). This route is most typically administered orally via a liquid or tablet. Another enteral route is sublingual via the blood-rich tissues found under the tongue.

Parenteral Substance Administration

This route entails the injection of the substance directly into the body (Stahl, 2013) and is typically the preferred route if a rapid onset of substance effects is desired. There are a few types of parenteral administration. Subcutaneous administration is the injection of a substance right below the skin surface, with the advantage being slow absorption into the body. This process (called "skin popping" by illegal substance users) thus provides the substance available for absorption over a period of time. Intramuscular administration injects the substance directly into the muscle. Since muscles are blood rich, the intramuscular process administers the substance into the body quicker than the subcutaneous method. The intravenous method injects the substance directly into the vein; thus, this provides a direct and immediate access to the bloodstream (Stahl, 2013).

Other Routes of Administration

Transdermal administration involves the absorption of a substance through the skin surface. Intranasal administration involves "snorting" the substance through the nose, allowing the substance to enter the system through blood-rich sinus tissues. Inhaling administers the substance into the system via passing through the microscopically thin (1/100,000th of an inch) layer between the air and the circulatory system via the blood-rich tissues in the lungs (Stahl, 2013).

Distribution and Transport

DeVane (2004) underscored the case-by-case nature of substance distribution, with the process influenced by countless variables such as gender, age, muscle tissue ratio, or degree of hydration at the time of substance administration. Substances also need to move to a site of action in the body. However, some types of chemicals move more freely than others. For example, water-soluble compounds can mix easily with blood plasma and can thus be easily moved throughout the body. Alcohol is an example of a water-soluble compound. Other compounds must bind with fat molecules in order to move throughout the body. These compounds are called lipid soluble. While a lipid-soluble compound is bound to the fat molecules the compound cannot be eliminated from the body, but it also cannot produce the intended effect. Thus, the compound must detach from the lipid molecules and enter the bloodstream to reach the site of action desired.

Biotransformation

Biotransformation is usually focused in the liver, although other organs, such as the kidneys, might also be involved. There are essentially two forms of biotransformation: zero-order biotransformation and first-order biotransformation processes. In the zero-order biotransformation process, the biotransformation mechanism(s) can quickly become saturated if a large amount of the substance is taken. Despite the potentially heavy concentration of that substance in the blood, only a set amount can be biotransformed each hour. For example, alcohol works from a zero-order biotransformation process in that if an individual drinks alcohol more rapidly than the body can metabolize it, intoxication occurs. First-order biotransformation process entails a set percentage of the substance biotransformed each hour, independent of the substance concentration in the blood. Many substances are biotransformed through a first-order biotransformation process (Doweiko, 2015; Pinel, 2013).

First-Pass Metabolism

The human digestive tract is designed to filter all content first through the liver. This is called the first-pass metabolism effect (DeVane, 2004). Thus, any toxin ingested can be isolated and the biotransformation process started before any damage occurs. However, one consequence of the first-pass metabolism is that the effectiveness of oral medication is diminished. For instance, much of an orally administered dose of morphine is biotransformed by the first-pass metabolism before it reaches the site of action in the brain, thus greatly limiting the analgesic effectiveness (this is why morphine is administered via intravenous) (Doweiko, 2015).

Elimination

Biotransformation changes the chemical structure of a substance so that it becomes more water soluble and then removed from the circulation by the organs filtering the blood. Kidneys are the most common blood-filtering organ, but the lungs, sweat glands, and biliary tract are sometimes also involved in the process of drug elimination (Doweiko, 2015; Pinel, 2013). Depending on the substance, this process might take hours or even days. Again, the ultimate goal of the biotransformation process is to allow the enzymes to transform the substance molecule(s) into a water-soluble metabolite that can be easily eliminated from the body.

Half-Life

The concept of a half-life provides an estimate of substance effectiveness, duration of the effect, and the length of time that the substance will remain in the body. There are several different types of half-life, with each briefly discussed below.

The distribution half-life is the length of time a substance takes to move into the general circulation postadministration. For example, this is critical in pain management, as the physician would obviously want a medication to quickly get into the circulation to reach the site of action to control pain. Another example is Narcan (naloxone), which is used to treat opiate overdoses. Clearly, the emergency condition of an overdose mandates a substance having rapid action once administered. Cloos (2010a, 2010b) reviewed the two subtypes of distribution half-life. The alpha half-life is the period after the peak blood concentration for the substance. The beta half-life is the amount of time for the concentration to decline as the substance biotransforms and evacuates the body. For instance, beta half-life is the criteria used to classify benzodiazepines as short, intermediate, or long acting.

The therapeutic half-life is the time for the body to inactivate 50% of a substance. It is usually linked to a single dose of a substance, but regular dosing can alter the therapeutic half-life of the substance. The elimination half-life is the time required to eliminate 50% of a single dose of the substance from the body (Doweiko, 2015).

Tolerance/Neuroadaptation

Tolerance is a shortened duration and decreased intensity of substance effects after repeated and chronic administration of the substance (i.e., the neurons have adapted to the presence of the substance in the system). Doweiko (2015) noted that if the substance is prescribed by a physician this process is called *neuroadaptation,* though it is called *tolerance* when focused on illegal substance use. There are a few types of tolerance, which are addressed below.

Metabolic tolerance involves the body becoming more efficient at biotransforming the substance. For instance, many people with substance use disorders (e.g., alcohol, heroin) report the need to administer more of the substance in order to reach the same degree of intoxication. Behavioral tolerance involves the brain and body appearing normal despite the heightened amount of substance in the system. Cross-tolerance occurs when two or more substances focus on a similar receptor site. For example, both alcohol and benzodiazepines share a receptor site for the inhibitory neurotransmitter GABA. Thus, as the drinker grows tolerant of alcohol, that tolerance will cross over to benzodiazepines, thus limiting their effectiveness even if there is no history of prior benzodiazepine use (Pinel, 2013; Stahl, 2013).

The Blood-Brain Barrier

Twenty percent of the blood pumped through the circulatory system makes it to the brain. Consequently, the brain is vulnerable to toxins delivered via the bloodstream. As a protection, the brain has a circulatory system of various cells (endothelial, pericytes) that operate a selective screening process. Of note, lipid-soluble molecules can pass through the endothelial cells. This blood-brain barrier weakness plays an important role in addiction, as numerous substances are lipid-soluble (Holtz, 2010).

INTERFACE BETWEEN SUBSTANCE USE, NEUROPSYCHOLOGY, AND PSYCHOPHARMACOLOGY: BASIC CONSIDERATIONS

Substance use disorder and addiction can be classified as a chronic disorder, primarily located in the brain, that impacts cognition, emotion, and behavior (Goldstein & Volkow, 2002). However, this text is a practical and applied exercise. No counselor needs to know everything (as that is impossible). However, a counselor must know what is needed to be known, including where to seek additional information. As I am not a neuropsychologist or psychopharmacologist, my knowledge and experience with the issues reviewed in Chapter 1 focus on the application of these concepts in the counseling process. If seeking more detailed reviews of these issues, there are numerous quality sources that provide a detailed neuropsychological and psychopharmacological treatise on substance use disorder and addiction (see Koob, 2013; Koob, Arends, & Le Moal, 2015).

In the sections below, neuropsychological issues relevant to specific substance use (and some process addictions) are reviewed from a counseling perspective of influences on client thought, emotion, and/or behavior.

Alcohol

Numerous cognitive deficits are documented in alcohol use-disordered clients (e.g., Fama & Sullivan, 2014). Two of the more severe examples of adverse influences of alcohol on cognition are Wernicke-Korsakoff Syndrome (WKS) and alcohol-induced dementia. WKS is a common alcohol-induced cognitive impairment caused by a lack of vitamin B1 (thiamine) in the brain as a result of malnutrition. WKS primarily presents as a dramatic decline in memory capability while other cognitive properties remain unchanged (Kopelman, Thomson, Guerrini, & Marshall, 2009). Alcohol-induced dementia, caused by overconsumption of alcohol, produces severe cognitive impairments in such areas as executive functioning and emotion regulation (Asada et al., 2010).

Particularly relevant to counseling, chronic alcohol drinkers (especially those who would quality for a *Diagnostic and Statistical Manual of Mental Disorders,* 5th edition [*DSM-5*]; American Psychiatric Association, 2013, alcohol use disorder diagnosis) typically demonstrate significant neuron loss in the frontal cortex area. This area governs working memory, attention, mood regulation, and various skills involved in judgment and risk taking (Sullivan & Pfefferbaum, 2005). Pitel et al. (2010; as reviewed in Fama & Sullivan, 2014) noted a pattern of cognitive deficits as heterogeneous and dependent on factors such as (but not limited to) age, gender, drinking history, and concurrent psychiatric or medical diagnoses. Executive functioning deficits are also linked with relapse, and these executive functioning deficits remain well into extended-term alcohol recovery (Fama & Sullivan, 2014). Other neurological deficits are also relevant. For instance, Fein, Torres, Price, and Sclafani (2006) noted lasting visuospatial deficits, which impact the ability to focus on relevant stimuli for a task. In addition, critical deficits exist in the social-cognition arena where Townshend and Duka (2003) underscored the difficulty in emotional processing for those with an alcohol use disorder history, where individuals responded intensely to facial expressions of fear but showed deficits to anger and disgust expressions. Similarly, Monnot, Lovallo, Nixon, and Ross (2002) found deficits in alcohol use-disordered individuals in recognizing the emotional tone in conversation. Memory, however, seems to produce mixed results. For instance, Noël et al. (2012) noted how recovering alcohol use-disordered individuals struggle with memory coding and retrieval issues, whereas Fama and Sullivan (2014) found that both remote (information from months ago) and implicit memory (learning from prior exposure to the content) for this population remains intact.

Cocaine

Literature suggests that cocaine use leads to changes in several brain areas, including the prefrontal cortex (Franklin et al., 2002) and anterior cingulate cortex

(Kaufman, Ross, Stein, & Garavan, 2003; Li et al., 2008). Sudai et al. (2011) discussed how cocaine use may inhibit new cell development in the hippocampus, thus impairing memory. In addition, cocaine use may cause new extensions on dendrites (Robinson & Berridge, 2001). More dendrite branches in the NAc may collect a greater volume of nerve signals coming from areas such as the hippocampus and amygdala. The additional linkages to the hippocampus and amygdala may explain the intense craving paired with cocaine-associated memories (Nestler, 2005). These brain areas seem relevant to such common cocaine use symptoms as intense craving, vulnerability to drug-related stimuli, various psychiatric symptoms, and impaired judgment (Koob et al., 2015).

Hester, Dixon, and Garavan (2006) found a strong attentional bias for cocaine-related words and visual stimuli, which seems to highlight the role of attention as involved in the neuropsychological pathology linked with cocaine use and how this diminished attention may be a variable to predict cocaine relapse (Verdejo-Garcia, 2014). Other issues include prefrontal and temporal brain region changes (e.g., reduced gray matter) potentially contributing to memory deficits (Hulka, Wagner, Preller, Jenni, & Quednow, 2013), poor facial emotion expression (Fernandez-Serrano, Lozano, Perez-Garcia, & Verdejo-Garcia, 2010), and executive functioning deficits predicting poor treatment engagement and poor treatment outcomes (Verdejo-Garcia, 2014).

Opioids

Soyka et al. (2011) highlighted that opiates (such as heroin) are known to impair cognitive functioning with specific impairments to the frontal cortex and hippocampus. Specific to heroin, Pau, Lee, and Chan (2002) found that heroin addiction has a negative effect on impulse control but not on attention and mental flexibility/abstract reasoning. Other studies document the deterioration of the brain's white matter, which may impact decision-making abilities, behavior regulatory ability, and responses to stress (Li et al., 2012; Liu et al., 2011). Overall, as the abstinence period lengthens, some see a return to better functioning for verbal memory but not inhibitory control or psychomotor function. However, the research on neurological recovery following opiate use disorder is mixed (Rass, Schacht, Marvel, & Mintzer, 2014).

Cannabis

There still exists a debate regarding specific neuropsychological impairment due to cannabis use disorder, though some evidence indicates possible problems with daily life tasks (Cattie & Grant, 2014). However, two meta-analyses examined any lasting effects of cannabis, with deficits noted in learning, memory, verbal language, and various executive functions (Grant, Gonzalez, Carey, Natarajan, & Wolfson, 2003; Schreiner & Dunn, 2012).

Methamphetamine

Numerous neuropsychological deficits in long-term methamphetamine users are noted in the literature, including abstract reasoning, cognitive flexibility (Scott et al., 2007), and behavioral regulation (Kim et al., 2005). Most methamphetamine use-disordered individuals show behaviors common for those with frontal systems dysfunction such as impulsivity, apathy, and sensation seeking (Iudicello, Bolden, Griglak, & Woods, 2014). Furthermore, others have discussed how the risky decision making and poor judgment demonstrated may be linked to the toxic effects of methamphetamine on the dopaminergic system (Paulus, Tapert, & Schuckit, 2005).

Rippeth et al. (2004) found between 33% and 50% of all methamphetamine use-disordered individuals experience learning and memory issues. Iudicello et al. (2011) found prospective memory failures (remembering to perform an action at some point in the future based on a time period or in response to a specific environmental cue relevant to daily life tasks such as adhering to a medication schedule or attending scheduled counseling sessions) in those with a chronic methamphetamine use history. In addition, failure to sustain long-term attention may be linked to damaged areas such as the anterior cingulate cortex (London et al., 2004; McKetin & Mattick, 1998). Other deficient brain areas (e.g., prefrontolimbic) may be responsible for the difficulties with facial affect recognition (Iudicello et al., 2014).

Inhalants

Tagaki, Lubman, Cotton, and Yucel (2014) noted the limited scope of inhalant research, thus impeding a fuller knowledge on the lasting neurological deficits from inhalant use. However, some work has found that chronic inhalant use has serious neurological and neuropsychological effects, likely due to damage of neuronal membranes (Meadows & Verghese, 1996). Inhalants cause brain stem dysfunction and a variety of motor, cognitive, and sensory deficits (Rosenberg, Grigsby, Dreisbach, Busenbark, & Grigsby, 2002). Symptoms could include irritability, tremor, ataxia, slurred speech, or decreased visual acuity, and difficulty with attention and executive functions (Tagaki et al., 2014).

Sample Process Addictions: Gambling and Sex

Process addictions share similar neurological traits as substance-related addictions. One key difference is that substance-related disorders typically cause some degree of damage and/or change to the brain as a result of repeated exposure to the substance. Though dissimilar in that manner, the process addictions do have a neurological foundation of relevance for counselors who encounter these individuals. Two common process addictions (gambling and sexual behavior) are briefly addressed.

Pathological gambling is associated with frontotemporal dysfunction (Brand et al., 2005) and shows impaired attention and concentration abilities, as well as elevated levels of impulsive behavior and novelty seeking coupled with diminished levels of self-directedness and cooperation (Forbush et al., 2008). However, despite pathological gambling being consistently associated with a blunted mesolimbic-prefrontal cortex activity to nonspecific rewards yet increased activity when exposed to gambling-related stimuli, little is actually known about the neuropsychological components of impulsivity and decision making in those with pathological gambling (van Holst, van den Brink, Veltman, & Gourdriaan, 2010).

Drug-cue-reactivity and craving studies of nicotine, cocaine, and alcohol highlight the role of some key brain areas, including the ventral striatum, dorsal anterior cingulate, and amygdala (Kuhn & Gallinat, 2011). In regard to compulsive sexual behavior, Voon et al. (2014) found that these regions were activated during viewing of sexually explicit materials across the groups with and without compulsive sexual behavior, but the activation was stronger for the compulsive sexual behavior group. This finding suggests neurological similarities across the substance use and compulsive sexual disorders.

NEUROPSYCHOLOGY AND COUNSELING ISSUES

Brickman, Rabinowitz, Coates, Cohn, and Kidder (1982) presented a model (see Figure 1.6) that conceptualizes the client's responsibility for developing the maladaptive behavior (i.e., addiction) and the client's responsibility for changing the maladaptive behavior (i.e., recovery). In the model, responsibility for the development and changing of the addictive behavior mostly aligns with the moralistic model of addiction (e.g., criminal acts, lack of willpower, or no desire to be a "better" person). The polar opposite, with no responsibility for development or changing of the addictive behavior, is most aligned with the disease model of addiction (e.g., the disease comes on and dissipates on its own).

So how does the neuropsychology and psychopharmacology discussed in this chapter pertain to this model? One answer lies in recent work done by Steenbergh, Runyan, Daugherty, and Winger (2012), who surveyed the National Association of Alcoholism and Drug Abuse Counselors regarding the relationship between addiction counselor perceptions of client responsibility for their addiction development and recovery and the counselor exposure to addiction-relevant neuroscience theory and research. Most critical, the counselors' level of neuroscience exposure was negatively correlated with their ratings of client responsibility for the development of an addiction but positively correlated to ratings of client responsibility for recovery. Steenbergh and colleagues argued that these relationships reflect that addiction

Figure 1.6   Brickman's Model

| | | Is the person responsible for changing the addictive behavior? | |
		YES	NO
Is the person responsible for the development of the addictive behavior?	YES	**MORAL MODEL** (War on Drugs) Relapse = Crime or Lack of Willpower	**SPIRITUAL MODEL** (AA and 12-Steps) Relapse = Sin or Loss of Contact With Higher Power
	NO	**COMPENSATORY MODEL** (Cognitive-Behavioral) Relapse = Mistake, Error, or Temporary Setback	**DISEASE MODEL** (Heredity and Physiology) Relapse = Reactivation of the Progressive Disease

Source: Adapted by Marlatt (n.d.) from Brickman et al. (1982).

counselors were using neuroscience theory and research in their conceptualizations of how clients both developed an addiction and the client responsibility for personal recovery. In terms of Brickman's model, this would be a compensatory model reflecting no responsibility for addiction development but personal responsibility for recovery. This is the quadrant of the model relevant to the substance use disorder treatment process.

If you consider the concepts reviewed here in Chapter 1, there are numerous instances where one can see how neuropsychological and psychopharmacological factors influence the addiction development. Furthermore, though there are a number of cognitive deficits a newly recovered individual needs to grapple with, the individual client is still responsible for managing his or her recovery. However, this is where a counselor and/or treatment program could make some subtle accommodations to account for these deficits so that the client has the best possible chance for successful early treatment and recovery.

CLOSING THOUGHTS

I am not a neurologist, neuropsychologist, or psychopharmacologist. However, you do not have to be deeply trained in these areas to appreciate the neurological and psychopharmacological aspects of substance use disorders and addictions. When reading this book, think of how different substances (and process addictions) may impact client behavior in the early, mid-, or long-term recovery period when you see them in counseling. For instance, the next few chapters focus on interviewing, assessment, and later on, counseling practices. Consider the deficits noted above regarding executive functioning, attention, memory, emotion regulation and recognition, and impulse control, and ask yourself the following questions:

1. Are treatment programs and counselors asking new-to-recovery clients more than they are cognitively capable of providing? For example, a neuropsychological argument could be made that many of the standard practices, such as a multihour intensive outpatient group (attention deficits) or a biopsychosocial assessment requesting self-report for past mental health or addiction behaviors (memory deficits), fall outside of what the client is able to perform (Bates, Bowden, & Barry, 2002) and thus contribute to client frustration and negative early treatment experiences.

2. Substance use disorder treatment (especially in early recovery) is focused on new coping skill development. This requires a lot of cognitive work both in session and out (e.g., homework). Is there a mismatch between the client's neurocognitive capability and the higher-order cognitive processing required for effective early counseling progress (Bates, Buckman, & Nguyen, 2013)?

3. Does the profession need a new definition of the construct we currently call *denial*? Neurocognitive deficits resulting in poor planning, rational thought, and impulse control may better explain how and why clients seem to downplay or deny the severity of their problem(s). As Goldman (1995) argued over 20 years ago, neuropsychology may better conceptualize what the treatment profession considers denial.

CONCLUSION AND QUESTIONS TO CONSIDER

This is more of an introduction to this section of each chapter. Here, I offer some concluding thoughts and I also pose some questions to consider that build exponentially upon one another across the chapters. For example, in all the remaining chapters, I pose at least one question to consider related to that chapter's content as seen through the perspective of the neurocognitive and psychopharmacology content reviewed in Chapter 1.

QUESTIONS TO CONSIDER AS YOU MOVE ON TO CHAPTER 2

How much of this content in Chapter 1 did you NOT know (or know as well) prior to reading this chapter? Does this content alter your perceptions of addiction in any manner? If so, how, and how will that changed perspective influence your treatment philosophy?

SECTION I REVIEW

CASE OF SAMANTHA

The following is a case pieced together from several different clients (of both genders) with whom I have worked over the years. Overall, the individual in this case (Samantha) is a work of fiction. Her experiences, though, were inspired by the experiences of many of the above-referenced clients and pieced together in such a way to create a realistic teaching example while still being certain that each clinical fact is a conglomeration of a few different clients. Again, in the end, Samantha is entirely 100% a work of fiction.

Below is the case background information. Following the various sections of the text, this case is revisited and conceptualized using that content. For instance, the assessment and diagnostic considerations of the case will be discussed in one area, while the applications of cognitive-behavioral therapy would be reviewed elsewhere. The goal is to have a case you follow through the content in the text in a sequential manner as you would in clinical practice. Instead of trying to cram all that content (and it is a lot) into one case study, there is the opportunity to take a slower pace and review the case through the various lenses you would use as a practicing professional in the addictions field. None of this is a complete examination of Samantha. My goal is to simply expose you to some concepts in application with a case realistic to the substance use disorder's profession. Now, please let me introduce you to Samantha.

Case of Samantha

Samantha is a 31-year-old unmarried woman who came to intensive outpatient co-occurring treatment following a 10-day inpatient hospitalization and a follow-up three-week partial hospitalization for major depressive disorder and opiate (prescription pain medication) use disorder. This was Samantha's first treatment episode for any addiction or mental health issue.

Samantha's Depression History

Samantha was never diagnosed with depression until her recent hospitalization. Until that time, she did a very good job of hiding her symptoms. Samantha always suspected she had depression but did not want to do anything about it out of shame and worry. Growing up, she had seen her family's subtle ridiculing of a cousin who struggled with mental illness. She recalled her father telling her that anyone who gets depressed or anxious is just "weak" and needs to "grow up," whereas her mother would say things such as "They just need to get over it, stop being lazy, and feel better." These sentiments stuck with Samantha. At various times in college, for example, Samantha had considered seeking mental health treatment services at the college counseling center. In fact, twice she had actually made an appointment but cancelled both times. She feared her parents or her professors would find out she had depression and would consider her weak. Samantha carried her resistance to admit her depression and seek help into her professional life. After earning her MBA, she went to work for a major corporation. Some of the executives discussed how they liked her intense work ethic and stated that she would definitely thrive in the corporate world because she does "not let things get to her." This just further instilled her need to keep her depression secret. Her depression would vacillate between periods of relative stability (no depressed mood) and severe depressed mood. When depressed, the episode would run for approximately 3 to 6 weeks before tapering down.

Samantha's Sex Addiction History

About 10 years ago, while still in college, Samantha recalled a period of intense depression. One day, she was walking in the halls of her dorm and a "guy who was always hitting on me but I had no interest in" again began "doing some real heavy flirting with me." Samantha said the following:

> I don't know what really happened or why. I just decided I feel real crappy so why not. I grabbed him and kissed him. We went to his room. It was 100% consensual but I totally used him. I didn't look at him. I didn't kiss him again. I just screwed him and left right when it was done. I actually think I was still readjusting my skirt when I left his room, I left that quick. But it wasn't out of shame. I didn't feel like a slut. I felt some control. I felt a little less depressed. I felt like maybe I could somewhat control how bad I feel with sex. I felt the depression again later on, or maybe it was always there and I just saw it again. Who knows? So, the next day I tried again with another guy because I was feeling depressed still. And yeah, it worked again. For a bit, the self-esteem seems to improve. Mood lifts. It may all just be my misreading things, but it felt better. That's when I began to figure out my depression medication was sex.

Samantha started using sex as her "medication" for depressed mood. If Samantha woke up feeling her major depressive disorder symptoms as too overwhelming, she would make a conscious decision to go find someone to have sex with. She recounted how just thinking that she was going to have sex was enough to even start her feeling more in control and somewhat less depressed. Samantha listed dozens upon dozens of men she had sex with. Some were one time only and a few were "regulars who knew it was only sex." However, she would never skip class or dismiss other responsibilities for sex. Samantha said she remembered her reasoning as being "I'm not a sex maniac as long as I get my work done and show up where I am supposed to be."

Samantha slowly began to feel out of control regarding her sexual behaviors. She became increasingly worried when she saw herself having sex with as many as six different men over the course of a weekend. She was also starting to have sex with men from work, but as she said, "very discreetly." About two months before she started working with me, she started having sex with a few "regulars" in a bathroom at the company. Samantha said she would feel her depressed mood worsen, her worthlessness grew, she felt out of control, and felt as if she "needed the sex to ground myself enough to get through a big presentation to the board that afternoon." She reported that on more than one occasion she went right from having sex to the board room.

Samantha's Opiate Use History

Approximately one year prior to starting work with me, Samantha was in a car accident that left her with back pain and required her to have shoulder surgery. Samantha was prescribed Percocet for the pain. The accident and surgery left Samantha again feeling depressed with another episode of major depressive disorder slowly growing. In addition, Samantha recalled how she knew she was in "no mood or condition" for sex. She slowly started to notice how the Percocet did make her "feel better all around. The injuries and also the mood. Again, for a little while at least."

Samantha recalled one contentious phone call with her supervisor at work regarding a project that did not resolve well. During the call, Samantha remembered she had forgotten a few key data tables. She felt her mood worsen and her self-worth diminish with each angry and "demeaning" word her supervisor said. Samantha then said the following:

I don't know what it was. I hung up the phone and thought, shit, this is the angry boss and bad environment I now have to know awaits me whenever I get back to work after I am done recuperating. I couldn't deal with the depressed mood. I felt like I was worth crap. Like my MBA was a joke and I'd be lucky to get a job putting the salt on the fries at McDonald's. I was due for another Percocet dose. One pill. Don't know why, I took three. I felt calmer. Then I dozed off. When I woke up, I remembered being shocked at how "well" it got my mind off my boss. So, I started taking two or three instead.

Eventually, Samantha recovered and a few weeks later she was back at work. However, she found herself seeking out opiate pain medication more and more. She liked that the pills let her not feel a need to have sex as often. She felt like this helped with her self-pride and gave her more control. Furthermore, she said, "Sex takes time. The pills take a few seconds." She started to doctor shop and also illegally purchase pills from dealers.

Samantha recognized she was out of control. One morning, she was feeling increasingly depressed and also feeling a craving for more opiates. Samantha had a big meeting at 1:30 p.m. It was now 11:45 a.m. Samantha, during her lunch hour, drove to a nearby city (an hour away at a typical rate of speed) "going at least 90 mph there and back so I could get the pills and return in time for my meeting." Samantha saw she needed help when she arrived back to the office at 1:20 p.m. For a moment, she felt a thrilling sense of victory in having accomplished the task on time. She then recognized how fast she drove and how much she risked her life and her employment just for a few pills. Samantha attended the 1:30 p.m. meeting, then called out sick the rest of the day and that afternoon made an appointment for an intake screening that led to her admission to an inpatient, then partial hospitalization program.

SECTION II

COMPONENTS OF CLINICAL TREATMENT PLANNING

CHAPTERS 2-4

These chapters cover the basics of interviewing, assessment, and diagnosis. Following the chapters is a review of the case of Samantha using these concepts as well as a discussion of ethical and curricular/training issues relevant to interviewing, assessment, and diagnosis.

Chapter 2

INTERVIEW, SCREENING, AND ASSESSMENT

PURPOSE OF INTERVIEWING, SCREENING, AND ASSESSMENT

Initial interview, screening, and assessment are integrated tools. First, the initial interview serves as a data-gathering dialogue where the counselor can also begin to craft the narrative regarding the need for treatment and what strengths the client brings to the treatment process. Second, the interview also informs the need for any screening applications. Screening is not just testing, but rather a purposeful and applied clinical measurement to determine the existence of various problems. Third, assessment is a more comprehensive application where the pervasiveness or severity of various problems (including substance use disorder) may be further determined. In brief, the initial interview, screening, and assessment serve such functions as conceptualizing the problem or problems, clarifying the severity of these problems, and informing/motivating the client for the need for treatment. Consequently, the interview, screening, and assessment phases of the initial sessions eventually inform the diagnostic and treatment plan development process (see Figure 2.1). Furthermore, these critical tasks are conducted not only within a substance use disorder (SUD) treatment facility. Beginning with the Institute of Medicine's (1990) call to expand substance use screening efforts beyond the SUD treatment arena, the substance use interview, screening, and assessment processes have expanded to such populations as emergency room (ER) patients (e.g., Lank & Crandall, 2014), primary health care practices (e.g., Stoner, Mikko, & Carpenter, 2014), and college/university counseling centers (e.g., Denering & Spear, 2012) in an attempt to target not only those with diagnosable substance use disorders but also those individuals who present with unhealthy use that does not yet rise to a diagnostic level.

Figure 2.1   The Process From Interview and Assessment to Treatment Planning

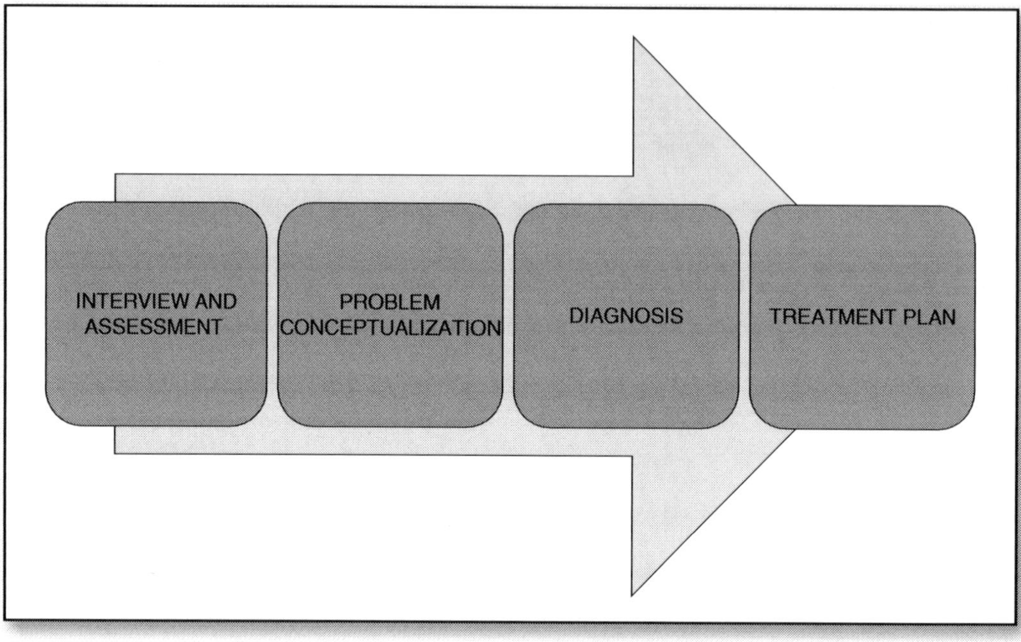

INTERVIEW AND ASSESSMENT → PROBLEM CONCEPTUALIZATION → DIAGNOSIS → TREATMENT PLAN

Need for Strengths-Based Interviewing, Screening, and Assessment Focus

If not careful, the interview, screening, and assessment procedure can become entirely focused on the negative. That is why the strengths section in our discussion comes right at the start (as opposed to at the end of the chapter in other similar texts, whereas other texts virtually ignore this critical issue). Think of all the measures used in the substance use and mental health disciplines. Even if focused on a positive concept by definition (e.g., self-esteem), the measure is typically conceptualized for use to determine the deficit (e.g., lack of client self-esteem). Thus, any clinical interview at the onset of substance use disorder treatment must contain just as much detail on the positive and strengths as we tend to focus on the negative.

For example, Laudet, Morgen, and White (2006) found that social supports, spirituality, religiousness, life meaning, and 12-step affiliation buffer stress effects on enhanced life satisfaction, with the buffer constructs accounting for 22% of the variance in life satisfaction. Though this study was focused on individuals already well into the treatment and recovery process, the buffer constructs are perfect examples of strengths to assess. Each of these key strengths-based concepts is addressed below.

Social Support. Laudet et al. (2006) noted that empirical evidence has linked social support to increased health, happiness, and longevity (Lin, 1986). Among substance users, lower levels of social support has shown to be a reliable predictor of relapse (Havassy, Wasserman, & Hall 1993), while higher levels of social support predict a diminished rate of substance use (Humphreys & Noke, 1997; Noone, Dua, & Markham, 1999; Rumpf, Bischof, Hapke, Meyer, & John, 2002). Moreover, social support is a significant concept in the perceived well-being of those with co-occurring substance use and psychiatric disorders (Laudet, Magura, Vogel, & Knight, 2000). This social support can come from friends, family, support group/community, and nonsecular organizations (e.g., church, synagogue, mosque).

Spirituality and Religion. Laudet et al. (2006) highlighted that religious and spiritual beliefs function as protective factors between life stressors and overall perceived quality of life (e.g., Culliford, 2002; Miller & Thoresen, 2003). Evidence shows an inverse relationship between involvement in religion (e.g., attending services, considering religious beliefs important) and substance use (Johnson, 2001; National Center on Addiction and Substance Abuse at Columbia University, 2001). For instance, religiosity reduced the impact of life stress on both the initial level of substance use and the rate of increasing substance use over time among adolescents (Wills, Yaeger, & Sandy, 2003). Possible benefits of religious involvement may include avoidance of drugs, time-occupying activities incompatible with substance use, and the adoption of prosocial values (Morjaria & Orford, 2002).

In addition, a growing body of empirical research supports the notion that religiousness and spirituality may enhance the likelihood of attaining and maintaining recovery from addictions, and recovering persons often report that religion and/or spirituality are critical factors in the recovery process (e.g., Flynn, Joe, Broome, Simpson, & Brown, 2003; Kaskutas et al., 2014). Moreover, there is evidence that spirituality may assist recovering individuals avoid future substance use and that among recovering individuals, higher levels of religious faith and spirituality are associated with a more optimistic life orientation, higher stress resilience, and more effective coping skills (Brown, Tonigan, Pavlik, Kosten, & Volk, 2013).

12-Step Affiliation. Laudet et al. (2006) emphasized that affiliation with 12-step fellowships, both during and after treatment, is a cost-effective and useful approach to promoting recovery from substance use problems (e.g., Greenfield & Tonigan, 2013; Humphreys & Moos, 2001; Humphreys et al., 2004). Furthermore, evidence suggests that 12-step affiliation benefits extend to psychosocial functioning and enhanced quality of life (e.g., Gossop et al., 2003; Moos, Finney, Ouimette, & Suchinsky, 1999). The principal helpful components likely include the sense of social support and the reduced stigma associated with being in a community with others who share similar struggles (Morgen & Morgan, 2011; Morgen, Morgan, Cashwell, & Miller, 2010).

Coping Skills. Coping skills are a critical component of the treatment and recovery process (Martindale, Sejud, Giardina, McGowan, & Dolan, 2013). Coping strategies include cognitive, behavioral, emotional, communication, and social strategies to deal with the various life stressors faced by those in recovery. Consequently, an inquiry into where an individual feels strong in withstanding daily stressors will help focus on their areas of coping strength. Some questions I ask to accomplish this task include the following:

- Can you think of a recent time you were really stressed but still managed to get a task done? What was the task, what was causing the stress, and how did you manage to accomplish this feat?
- Do you have any specific strategies to relax? What are they, and how well do they work?
- How do you handle any negative thoughts that appear?

CONTENT OF THE INTERVIEW

Substance Use History

Table 2.1 covers all the substances for evaluation in addition to alcohol. It is critical to inquire regarding all substances and not just the primary substance. Furthermore, it is imperative to understand how substances interact with alcohol due to the high prevalence rates of individuals using other substances in conjunction with alcohol (regardless if the alcohol use rises to the level of an alcohol use disorder). The information derived from this inquiry will guide treatment recommendations as well as further screening or assessment.

Best practice dictates that the following areas be addressed:

1. Age at first use. Early first use of substances (before 15 years old) is typically associated with the development of future substance-related disorders (Piehler, Véronneau, & Dishion, 2012). Consequently, age at first use may have diagnostic or prognostic implications. For example, recent admissions data from the Treatment Episode Data Set (Substance Abuse and Mental Health Services Administration [SAMHSA], 2015) revealed that of all the admissions reported in 2013, 55.5% of admitted clients reported an age of first substance use of 17 years old or younger (see Table 2.2).

Table 2.1 Commonly Abused Substances for Assessment in Addition to Alcohol

Substance	Form	Administration	Street Names	Short-Term Effects	Long-Term Effects	Combined With Alcohol	Withdrawal Symptoms
Cocaine	White powder, white crystal	Snorted, smoked, injected	Blow, bump, candy, crack, rock, snow	Narrowed blood vessels; enlarged pupils; increased body temperature, heart rate, and blood pressure; headache; abdominal pain and nausea; euphoria; increased energy, alertness; insomnia, restlessness; anxiety; erratic and violent behavior; panic attacks, paranoia, psychosis; heart rhythm problems, heart attack; stroke, seizure, coma	Loss of sense of smell, nosebleeds, nasal damage and trouble swallowing from snorting; infection and death of bowel tissue from decreased blood flow; poor nutrition and weight loss from decreased appetite	Greater risk of overdose and sudden death than from either drug alone	Depression, tiredness, increased appetite, insomnia, vivid unpleasant dreams, slowed thinking and movement, restlessness
Heroin	White or brown powder	Injected, smoked, snorted	Brown sugar, dope, junk, smack	Euphoria; warm flushing of skin; dry mouth; heavy feeling in the hands and feet; clouded thinking; alternate wakeful and drowsy states; itching; nausea; vomiting; slowed breathing and heart rate	Collapsed veins; abscesses (swollen tissue with pus); infection of the lining and valves in the heart; constipation and stomach cramps; liver or kidney disease; pneumonia	Dangerous slowdown of heart rate and breathing, coma, death	Restlessness, muscle and bone pain, insomnia, diarrhea, vomiting, cold flashes with goose bumps ("cold turkey"), leg movements

(Continued)

Table 2.1 (Continued)

Substance	Form	Administration	Street Names	Short-Term Effects	Long-Term Effects	Combined With Alcohol	Withdrawal Symptoms
Inhalants	Paint thinners or removers, degreasers, dry-cleaning fluids, gasoline, lighter fluids, correction fluids, permanent markers, electronics cleaners and freeze sprays, glue, spray paint, hair or deodorant sprays, fabric protector sprays, aerosol computer cleaning products, vegetable oil sprays, butane lighters, propane tanks, whipped cream aerosol containers	Inhaled	N/A	Confusion; nausea; slurred speech; lack of coordination; euphoria; dizziness; drowsiness; disinhibition, lightheadedness, hallucinations/delusions; headaches; sudden sniffing death due to heart failure (from butane, propane, and other chemicals in aerosols); death from asphyxiation, suffocation, convulsions or seizures, coma, or choking	Liver and kidney damage; bone marrow damage; limb spasms due to nerve damage; brain damage from lack of oxygen that can cause problems with thinking, movement, vision, and hearing	Dangerously low blood pressure potential	Nausea, loss of appetite, sweating, tics, problems sleeping, and mood changes
LSD	Tablet; capsule; clear liquid; small, decorated squares of absorbent paper that liquid has been added to	Swallowed or absorbed through mouth	Acid, Blotter, Blue Heaven	Rapid emotional swings; distortion of a person's ability to recognize reality, think rationally, or communicate with others; raised blood pressure, heart rate, body temperature; dizziness and insomnia; loss of appetite; dry mouth; sweating; numbness; weakness; tremors; enlarged pupils	Frightening flashbacks (called Hallucinogen Persisting Perception Disorder [HPPD]); ongoing visual disturbances, disorganized thinking, paranoia, and mood swings	May decrease the perceived effects of alcohol	Unknown

Marijuana	Greenish-gray mixture of dried, shredded leaves, stems, seeds, and/or flowers; resin (hashish) or sticky, black liquid (hash oil)	Smoked, eaten (mixed in food or brewed as tea)	Blunt, Bud, Dope, Ganja, Grass, Green, Herb, Joint, Mary Jane, Pot, Reefer, Skunk, Smoke, Trees, Weed; Hashish: Boom, Hash, Hemp	Enhanced sensory perception and euphoria followed by drowsiness/relaxation; slowed reaction time; problems with balance and coordination; increased heart rate and appetite; problems with learning and memory; hallucinations; anxiety; panic attacks; psychosis	Mental health problems, chronic cough, frequent respiratory infections	Increased heart rate, blood pressure; further slowing of mental processing and reaction time	Irritability, trouble sleeping, decreased appetite, anxiety
MDMA	Colorful tablets with imprinted logos, capsules, powder, liquid	Swallowed, snorted	Adam, Clarity, Ecstasy, Eve, Lover's Speed, Molly, Peace, Uppers	Lowered inhibition; enhanced sensory perception; confusion; depression; sleep problems; anxiety; increased heart rate and blood pressure; muscle tension; teeth clenching; nausea; blurred vision; faintness; chills or sweating; sharp rise in body temperature leading to liver, kidney, or heart failure and death	Long-lasting confusion, depression, problems with attention, memory, and sleep; increased anxiety, impulsiveness, aggression; loss of appetite; less interest in sex	May increase the risk of cell and organ damage	Fatigue, loss of appetite, depression, trouble concentrating

(Continued)

Table 2.1 (Continued)

Substance	Form	Administration	Street Names	Short-Term Effects	Long-Term Effects	Combined With Alcohol	Withdrawal Symptoms
Metham-phetamine	White powder or pill; crystal meth looks like pieces of glass or shiny blue-white "rocks" of different sizes	Swallowed, snorted, smoked, injected	Crank, Chalk, Crystal, Fire, Glass, Go Fast, Ice, Meth, Speed	Increased wakefulness and physical activity; decreased appetite; increased breathing, heart rate, blood pressure, temperature; irregular heartbeat	Anxiety, confusion, insomnia, mood problems, violent behavior, paranoia, hallucinations, delusions, weight loss, severe dental problems ("meth mouth"), intense itching leading to skin sores from scratching	Masks the depressant effect of alcohol, increasing risk of alcohol overdose; may increase blood pressure and jitters	Depression, anxiety, tiredness
Dex-tromethor-phan	Syrup, capsule	Swallowed	Robo, Triple C, Cough medicine brands typically have name including "DM"	Euphoria; slurred speech; increased heart rate, blood pressure, temperature; numbness; dizziness; nausea; vomiting; confusion; paranoia; altered visual perceptions; problems with movement; buildup of excess acid in body fluids	Unknown	Increased risk of adverse effects	Unknown
PCP	White or colored powder, tablet, or capsule; clear liquid	Injected, snorted, swallowed, smoked	Angel Dust, Boat, Hog, Love Boat, Peace Pill	Delusions, hallucinations, paranoia, problems thinking, a sense of distance from one's environment, anxiety	Memory loss, problems with speech and thinking, depression, weight loss, anxiety	Increased risk of coma	Headaches, sweating

| Prescription Opioids | Tablet, capsule, liquid, suppository | Injected, swallowed, smoked, snorted, rectal | Codeine: Captain Cody, Cody, Lean, Sizzurp, Purple Drank

Hydrocodone or dihydrocodeinone: (Vicodin, Lortab, Lorcet):

Vike, Watson-387

Hydromorphone (Dilaudid):

D, Dillies, Footballs, Juice, Smack

Meperidine (Demerol):

Demmies, Pain Killer

Methadone (Dolophine, Methadose):

Oxycodone (OxyContin, Percodan, Percocet): | Pain relief, drowsiness, nausea, constipation, euphoria, confusion, slowed breathing, death | Miscarriage, low birth weight, neonatal abstinence syndrome. In older adults a higher risk of accidental misuse or abuse as many older adults have multiple prescriptions, increasing the risk of drug-drug interactions | Dangerous slowing of heart rate and breathing leading to coma or death | Restlessness, muscle and bone pain, insomnia, diarrhea, vomiting, cold flashes with goose bumps ("cold turkey"), leg movements |

(Continued)

Table 2.1 (Continued)

Substance	Form	Administration	Street Names	Short-Term Effects	Long-Term Effects	Combined With Alcohol	Withdrawal Symptoms
			O.C., Oxycet, Oxycotton, Oxy, Hillbilly Heroin, Percs Oxymorphone (Opana): Biscuits, Blue Heaven, Blues, Mrs. O, O Bomb, Octagons				
Prescription Sedatives	Pill, capsule, liquid	Swallowed, injected, snorted	Barbiturates: pentobarbital (Nembutal), phenobarbital (Luminal): Barbs, Phennies, Red Birds, Reds, Tooies, Yellow Jackets Benzodiazepines: alprazolam (Xanax), chlordiazepoxide (Limbitrol), diazepam (Valium), lorazepam (Ativan), triazolam (Halcion): Candy, Downers, Sleeping Pills, Tranks	Drowsiness, slurred speech, poor concentration, confusion, dizziness, problems with movement and memory, lowered blood pressure, slowed breathing	Unknown	Further slows heart rate and breathing, which can lead to death	Must be discussed with a health care provider; barbiturate withdrawal can cause a serious abstinence syndrome that may include seizures

	Liquid, tablet, chewable tablet, capsule	Sleep Medications: eszopiclone (Lunesta), zaleplon (Sonata), zolpidem (Ambien): Forget-me Pill, Mexican Valium, R2, Roche, Roofies, Roofinol, Rope, Rophies		Unknown	Further slows heart rate and breathing, which can lead to death	Must be discussed with a health care provider; barbiturate withdrawal can cause a serious abstinence syndrome that may include seizures
Prescription Stimulants	Swallowed, snorted, smoked, injected, chewed	Amphetamine (Adderall, Benzedrine): Bennies, Black Beauties, Crosses, Hearts, LA Turnaround, Speed, Truck Drivers, Uppers Methylphenidate (Concerta, Ritalin): JIF, MPH, R-ball, Skippy, The Smart Drug, Vitamin R	Increased alertness, attention, energy; increased blood pressure and heart rate; narrowed blood vessels; increased blood sugar	Heart problems, psychosis, anger, paranoia	Masks the depressant action of alcohol, increasing risk of alcohol overdose; may increase blood pressure and jitters	Depression, tiredness, sleep problems

(Continued)

Table 2.1 (Continued)

Substance	Form	Administration	Street Names	Short-Term Effects	Long-Term Effects	Combined With Alcohol	Withdrawal Symptoms
Steroids	Tablet, capsule, liquid drops, gel, cream, patch, injectable solution	Injected, swallowed, applied to skin	Nandrolone (Oxandrin), oxandrolone (Anadrol), oxymetholone (Winstrol), stanozolol (Durabolin), testosterone cypionate (Depo-testosterone): Juice, Gym Candy, Pumpers, Roids	Headache, acne, fluid retention (especially in the hands and feet), oily skin, yellowing of the skin and whites of the eyes, infection at the injection site	Kidney damage or failure; liver damage; high blood pressure, enlarged heart, or changes in cholesterol leading to increased risk of stroke or heart attack, even in young people; aggression; extreme mood swings; anger ("roid rage"); paranoid jealousy; extreme irritability; delusions; impaired judgment	Increased risk of violent behavior	Mood swings; tiredness; restlessness; loss of appetite; insomnia; lowered sex drive; depression, sometimes leading to suicide attempts
Bath Salts	White or brown crystalline powder sold in small plastic or foil packages labeled "not for human consumption" and sometimes sold as jewelry cleaner; tablet, capsule, liquid	Swallowed, snorted, injected	Bloom, Cloud Nine, Cosmic Blast, Flakka, Ivory Wave, Lunar Wave, Scarface, Vanilla Sky, White Lightning	Increased heart rate and blood pressure; euphoria; increased sociability and sex drive; paranoia, agitation, and hallucinations; psychotic and violent behavior; nosebleeds; sweating; nausea, vomiting; insomnia; irritability; dizziness; depression; suicidal thoughts; panic attacks; reduced motor control; cloudy thinking	Breakdown of skeletal muscle tissue; kidney failure; death	Unknown	Depression, anxiety, problems sleeping, tremors, paranoia

Source: Table produced from National Institute on Drug Abuse (NIDA, 2016).

Table 2.2 Age of Primary Substance First Use: Treatment Episode Data Set (2013) Results

Age (years)	N	%
11 and younger	105,610	6.4%
12-14	350,768	21.2%
15-17	460,941	27.9%
18-20	297,613	18.0%
21-24	179,978	10.9%
25-29	119,759	7.2%
30-34	62,545	3.8%
35-39	33,989	2.1%
40-44	19,813	1.2%
45-49	11,587	0.7%
50-54	6,004	0.4%
55 and older	3,720	0.2%
TOTAL	1,652,327	100.0%

Source: SAMHSA (2015).

2. The frequency and amount of the substance use, as well as the route(s) of administration for each substance, assist the interviewer in gauging the trajectory of substance use increase over time. For instance, a drinker who went from a six-pack per night to over 20 beers per night reflects key diagnostic information regarding drinking progression. Similarly, the client who reports a one-bag of heroin use (snorted) last year but now reports injecting approximately multiple bags per day also demonstrates a dramatic increase in substance use and reduced client capacity to rein in the addictive behavior (see Tables 2.3, 2.4, and 2.5).

3. Questions regarding consequences of use helps the clinician pinpoint areas of dysfunction caused by the addiction, such as deficits at school (e.g., Hollar & Moore, 2004), work (e.g., Frone, 2009), home (e.g., Dunne, Burrell, Diggins, Whitehead, & Latimer, 2015), and family (e.g., Juhnke & Hagedorn, 2006), as well as financial, legal, or medical problems (e.g., Miller, 2015).

4. An examination of any prolonged (30 days or longer) abstinence period is also critical. Reasons both for the abstinence as well as the return to substance use helps the clinician create a timeline for the waxing and waning of

Table 2.3 Primary Substance Reported at Admission: Treatment Episode Data Set (2013) Results

Substance	N	%
Alcohol	631,578	37.6%
Heroin	316,797	18.9%
Marijuana	281,991	16.8%
Other Opiates	149,863	8.9%
Methamphetamine	130,033	7.7%
Cocaine/Crack	102,387	6.1%
All Others[1]	66,463	4.0%

[1]All others includes the following primary substances: Benzodiazepines, Barbiturates, Amphetamines, PCP, Non-prescription Methadone, Hallucinogens, Over-the-Counter Medications, Inhalants, and Stimulants

Source: SAMHSA (2015).

Table 2.4 Substances Used and Reported at Admission (Minimum 5%): Treatment Episode Data Set (2013) Results

Substance	N	%
Cocaine/Crack	1,365,297	81.1%
Alcohol	911,900	54.2%
Marijuana	630,762	37.5%
Heroin	375,043	22.3%
Methamphetamine	205,691	12.2%
Benzodiazepines	96,687	5.7%

Source: SAMHSA (2015).

Table 2.5 Route of Administration for Primary Substance: Treatment Episode Data Set (2013) Results

Route of Administration	N	%
Oral	756,028	45.7%
Smoked	454,545	27.5%
IV or IM	293,720	17.8%
Inhaled	142,269	8.6%
Other	7,362	0.4%

Source: SAMHSA (2015).

substance use common in an addiction history. Specifically, what were the psychosocial constructs that contributed to the abstinence as well as the return to substance use? The Timeline Followback (TLFB; Robinson, Sobel, Sobel, & Leo, 2014) is a clinical tool that helps the clinician see the schedule of substance use and abstinence over a prolonged period of time. The TLFB can be administered by an interviewer (or client administered) and asks clients to retrospectively estimate their substance use anywhere between 7 days to 2 years prior to the interview date. In clinical settings, the TLFB serves as a motivational tool to contribute to efforts designed to increase client motivation and readiness for treatment.

Psychiatric History

As discussed in Chapter 3, there is a clearly established relationship between substance use and psychiatric disorders (e.g., Atkins, 2014). Recent admissions data in the SAMHSA (2015) Treatment Episode Data Set reflected that 33.1% of admitted clients in 2013 came to SUD treatment with a co-occurring psychiatric disorder. There is also a growing perspective that co-occurring psychiatric symptoms in the SUD treatment population are the norm and not the exception (e.g., Drake, Mueser, Brunette, & McHugo, 2004; SAMHSA, 2005). Consequently, the interview focused on psychiatric history should be mindful that most clients will have a current and/or past experience of an outright diagnosable *Diagnostic and Statistical Manual of Mental Disorders* (5th ed.; *DSM-5*; American Psychiatric Association, 2013) psychiatric disorder or the presence/history of subsyndromal experiences that, though not rising to a diagnosable level, still cause distress.

This interview is complicated. For example, the clinician must address the following matters:

- Is there a history of an independent *DSM-5* diagnosed psychiatric disorder?
- Regardless of history, is the client demonstrating any current symptoms that may reflect a psychiatric disorder?
- What is the history of the client's psychiatric symptom experiences in conjunction with substance intoxication, withdrawal, or prolonged abstinence?
- Are there any instances of distressful emotional experiences that may resemble diagnosable disorders but fail to adhere to any nosology?

However, there are a few challenges inherent within this process. First, as we will review in the next chapters, there is tremendous overlap between substance use and psychiatric symptoms. For example, experiences of anxiety, depressed mood, or paranoia are symptoms of numerous psychiatric disorders but also occur in various instances of substance intoxication or withdrawal. Considering that many clients enter treatment or an ER setting while still actively using or in the early withdrawal phase, it can become very difficult to tease out the temporal and causal relationship (if any) between substance use and psychiatric symptoms. Second, recall that as a clinician you are asking about this complicated and typically unclear relationship with an individual who (due to substance use past and present) is not the best equipped to provide a lucid and organized recollection of all symptoms and experiences. The deficit in memory may be due to limited memory capacity when having been intoxicated or due to the current memory and other cognitive deficits as discussed in Chapter 1.

Due to these issues, the interview may not result in a definitive answer. But the interview (for any clinical area) is not designed to produce a definitive outcome. As emphasized by Ivey, Ivey, Zalaquett, and Quirk (2012), the clinical interview is designed to start the framework of the client narrative. Out of this interview, the narrative may produce additional questions in need of clarification. Thus, the interview provides the basis for deciding what additional screening and assessment measures may be needed to crystallize the client's psychiatric experiences.

Client Perspective on Spirituality

"But I'm not spiritual." I hear that from countless counseling students and SUD clients. One of the big obstacles to working with spirituality is to first recognize that any good assessment of spiritual support extends beyond a simple census-type *yes* or *no* question during the interview process. That is why and how my colleagues and I first posed the concept of considering spirituality as a core component of countless counseling microskills such as empathic listening and patience (Morgen et al., 2010). In this paper, we likened spirituality to a puzzle piece perceived as "missing," thus explaining why and how all of counseling is looking for it. But in the end, spirituality may be right out there in the open as these counseling microskills.

So whether a counselor trainee, a new counselor, or an experienced veteran of the profession, spirituality needs to be considered in a twofold manner. First, how does the counselor define and think about the concept of spirituality? This needs to be far from a dichotomous *I have* or *do not have* answer. If the counselor is that rigid in the spiritual definition, his or her assessment for this critical support ingredient will be limited.

Second, the same intrapersonal work counselors do to come up with a spirituality definition and understanding also needs to be applied to all their clients—in essence, a spiritual development parallel process between clients and their counselors. If clients state that they have no spirituality, the counselors need to investigate if that is truly so. Perhaps clients do not; that is OK. Or perhaps clients do but just do not recognize the existence of spiritual elements in their lives.

Cook (2004) reviewed this concept of multiple definitions for spirituality. Some may not seem "spiritual" as we tend to typically consider it. But if you consider spirituality as a factor that helps improve recovery potential while enhancing individuals' health, these alternate definitions seem to make sense. Some of Cook's broad categories of spirituality are listed below:

Relatedness. This pertains to the quality of interpersonal relationships within individuals' lives.

Transcendence. This is clients' recognition of the transcendent quality of the human existence.

Humanity. This area of spirituality focuses on the distinct quality of humanity within individuals' lives.

Core, force, or soul. This can be conceptualized as individuals' inner strength.

Meaning. Do people have a purpose to their lives?

Authenticity and truth. Do individuals feel as if they are living a life truthful to whom they wish to be?

Values. Similar to authenticity above, do clients feel as if they have a sense of self-worth?

Self-knowledge. Do people have a good grasp of who they are and what they wish to become?

So the question to consider is how to assess spirituality. Instead of asking, "Are you spiritual?" instead the counselor should inquire about some of Cook's (2004) areas listed above. For example, clients who outright deny being "spiritual" very likely are experiencing some cognitive and emotional issues relevant to meaning in their life or the quality of their interpersonal relationships. If clients feel a strength in these areas, for instance, how and why does this positive component contribute to their recovery? Explore those areas. That is a discussion and assessment of spirituality!

Conversely, if clients feel a deficit in these areas, explore this gap. How and why does this "lacking" bother them? In this case, the spiritual discussion is one of how being without this support impedes their recovery and perhaps leaves them vulnerable for a relapse. How do interventions for support, like the 12 steps, then play a role in bolstering of their spiritual support?

The counselor needs to be informed about issues of spirituality across counseling and as applied to the specific treatment of substance use disorder. One good place to start is to review the most recent spirituality competencies as endorsed by the Association for Spiritual, Ethical and Religious Values in Counseling, which is a division of the American Counseling Association. The most recent version can be found in Cashwell and Watts (2010) and reviews the issues of counselor world-view, counselor self-awareness, spiritual development, communication, assessment, and diagnosis and treatment in the context of how a counselor engages with the concept of spirituality.

The best assessment tool is the interview. The unstructured dialogue between client and counselor allows the counselor to investigate countless areas of value to the treatment process. But in regard to spirituality, counselors need to be informed on matters of spirituality so that they can be flexible and see the spirituality inquiry as an open-ended (and not closed) question. It is not a matter of *yes* or *no* but rather a matter of *how* and *why*.

Medical History

A complete medical history (present and past medical problems, surgeries, and medications) is crucial for clients presenting with a substance use disorder. Many substance users neglect their health and thus come to treatment with numerous medical ailments (e.g., Lima et al., 2009; Morgen, Astone-Twerell, Hernitche, Gunneson, & Santangelo, 2007). For each of the medical conditions, the clinician must determine if the symptoms are related to or independent of substance use. This is primarily accomplished by making inquiries regarding the temporal or causal relationships between the medical issues and substance use. Furthermore, there are medical conditions that are associated with a class of substances. Myriad medical ailments are linked with various substances (see Table 2.6).

Family History

The family history provides several meaningful elements. First, a reported family history of substance use disorder may indicate a client's genetic predisposition for the disorder (Agrawal & Lynskey, 2008). Second, the family history also provides a thorough overview of how substance use has entered the family system and the resulting consequences (Lander, Howsare, & Byrne, 2013). The Center for Substance Abuse Treatment (CSAT, 2004a) recommends the following content be included in any family history inquiry as part of the interview:

- Client family of origin history, including substance use by member(s) and any instances of family dysfunction (e.g., abuse, neglect)
- Romantic relationship status and history, including whether substance use ever caused dysfunction or the ending of a relationship (e.g., marital tension due to substance use, past relationships ending due to substance use)
- Any children?

Table 2.6   Medical Ailments Associated With Various Substances of Abuse

HIV, Hepatitis	Gastrointestinal
Heroin	Cocaine
Cocaine	Heroin
Methamphetamine	Prescription Opiates
Cardiovascular	MDMA (Ecstasy)
Cocaine	Musculoskeletal
Heroin	Inhalants
Inhalants	MDMA (Ecstasy)
Marijuana	Steroids
MDMA (Ecstasy)	Kidneys
Methamphetamine	Heroin
PCP	Inhalants
Stimulants	MDMA (Ecstasy)
Respiratory	Liver
Cocaine	Heroin
Heroin	Inhalants
Inhalants	Steroids
Marijuana	
PCP	
Prescription Opiates	
Nicotine	

Source: NIDA (2012).

- Substance use by other member(s) of the family? If yes, the substance(s) used, frequency, and for how long the use has occurred
- Has substance use caused the client or other family member(s) to be alienated from the rest of the family
- Current or past instances of domestic abuse or other abuses (physical, sexual, verbal, emotional)
- Overall quality of current family unit

Social History

A thorough psychosocial history reviews the overall landscape of a client's life and how the client's substance use (and any psychiatric issues) possibly impacts these key areas. First, the interview should examine the client's career history due to addiction issues commonly influencing workplace performance (Frone, 2009).

Specifically, the interview should include current employment status, employment history, satisfaction with current employment, and whether substance use has ever impacted work performance.

Second, educational history is examined. Educational attainment informs the clinician of the client's potential employment options posttreatment as well as whether substance use derailed the client's schooling. For example, when working in a therapeutic community, I typically encountered clients who had failed to obtain a high school diploma (i.e., dropped out of school) due to substance use. Thus, the clinician should inquire about the highest educational level obtained as well as any substance-related reasons for any aborted schooling, for example, if clients reveal that they started community college but never finished the last 20 credits. The clinician should investigate if substance use played any role (direct or indirect) in why clients stopped their education and never returned to finish.

Third, many SUD clients come to treatment with an extensive criminal justice history as well as current legal issues (e.g., CSAT, 2005; Morgen, Maschi, Viola, & Zgoba, 2013). Clients may be referred from drug court, a parole/reentry system, or enter treatment with current charges such as drug possession or driving while intoxicated/driving under the influence. Consequently, the interview will determine such factors as any stresses on the client due to pending legal matters, the potential for the client to have treatment disrupted due to a prison sentencing, as well as any other offices/individuals you will need to engage with (e.g., parole officer, attorney) during the client's treatment.

Fourth, client financial health should also be investigated. In my experiences, client financial health may play one of two roles in the client's case. In some scenarios, the client is experiencing money issues and may turn to selling substances or engaging in prostitution to augment their income. In this scenario, the financials are integrated into the other dysfunctional addictive behavior(s). However, in some other situations, the client experiences stress regarding an uncertain financial standing, and this pressure can serve as a stressor for returning to substance use.

Fifth, though not an area of the interview, all critical information should be corroborated by a collateral informant (typically a spouse, parent, significant other, or other family member). Not only does the clinician obtain verification and clarification of interview information, the corroboration seeking initiates the process of incorporating the key members of the client's life in treatment. As per ethical and legal practices, corroboration with collateral informants can only occur following signed written authorization by the client.

Sixth, especially considering the neuropsychological impact of substance use discussed in the prior chapter, a brief examination of basic mental status functioning is warranted. The mental status examination is a useful component of an SUD intake interview (Anderson & Parker, 1997). If (or when) the client is capable of being examined (i.e., not intoxicated), the mental status examination should cover all the following areas:

- Appearance
  - General appearance
  - Motor status
  - Activity
  - Facial expression
- Characteristics of talk
  - Blocking
  - Preservation
  - Flight of ideas
- Emotional state
  - Mood (e.g., depressed, manic)
  - Affect (e.g., anxious, labile)
- Content of thought
  - Hallucinations
  - Delusions
  - Compulsions
  - Obsessions
  - Ritualistic behaviors
  - Depersonalization
- Orientation
  - Person
  - Place
  - Time
  - General confusion
- Memory
  - Remote past experiences
  - Recall of long-ago and recent past experiences

Recommended Interview Content

The interview provides the baseline information. Typically, much information will be clinically irrelevant, but you do not always know that prior to inquiring. Furthermore, some information may at first seem irrelevant only to become critical later in the counseling relationship. In brief, the recommendation made countless times (e.g., Brooks & McHenry, 2015; Donovan, 2013; Lewis, Dana, & Blevins, 2015; Stevens & Smith, 2013) is to acquire as much history and current functioning information as possible. Consequently, based on the above recommendations, the clinical interview must cover the following areas.

- Referral source
- Primary presenting problem
- History of substance use disorder and any past treatment(s)
- Current substance use (frequency, amount, administration)
- History of psychiatric disorders or symptoms and any past treatment(s)
- Current psychiatric symptoms
- History of/current suicidal ideation, intent, plans, or acts
- History of/current homicidal (harm to others) ideation, intent, plans, or acts
- History of/current nonsuicidal self-injury ideation, intent, plans, or acts
- Living arrangements
- Marital/relationship status
- Any children (if applicable)
- Family of origin history
- School and work history
- Mental status
- Insight and judgment

SCREENING AND ASSESSMENT

The interview is over, but some questions may remain regarding substance use, psychiatric symptoms, or motivation/readiness for treatment. As noted in Figure 2.1, screening and assessment both complement and supplement the interview data for the purposes of diagnosis and treatment planning. We start with the biological screening of recent substance use (i.e., drug testing).

Drug Testing

Verebey and Meenan (2011) noted that drug testing is important for the selection of appropriate treatment planning as well as identifying those currently in treatment as a mechanism to catch some of the earliest signs of a relapse. According to SAMHSA (2012), drug testing in SUD treatment serves one or more of these functions:

- A component of the initial assessment for the SUD evaluation
- A screening tool to prevent any adverse pharmacotherapy effects (for example, opioid screen to verify opiate levels prior to naltrexone treatment)
- A mechanism to evaluate and reevaluate the appropriate level of care
- A way to monitor the client's use of substances and/or adherence to pharmacotherapy regimen

Considering the prevalence of dishonesty about substance use and/or continued substance use despite known and experienced consequences, drug testing is a critical screening tool to manage substance use disorder (DuPont & Selavka, 2015). Federal mandatory guidelines include procedures, regulations, and certification requirements for drug-testing laboratories, determine the drugs tested, and set cutoff concentrations for detecting these substances. The federal mandatory guidelines recommend that the initial screening test identify the presence of the following commonly abused drugs or their metabolites (SAMHSA, 2012): amphetamines (amphetamine, methamphetamine), cocaine metabolites, marijuana metabolites, opiate metabolites (codeine, morphine), and phencyclidine (PCP). Most drug testing retrospectively identifies recent substance use in settings where that information is of diagnostic significance (e.g., ER) or where the information has value in reinforcing an abstinence mandate (e.g., SUD treatment, workplace, schools).

Drug-testing technology includes sweat, oral fluid, and hair in addition to urine. Regardless of testing procedure, each form uses highly reliable science. Sweat, oral fluid, and hair specimen testing are performed at a limited number of specialized laboratories, whereas urine testing is performed at most clinical laboratories (DuPont & Selavka, 2015). The level of a drug or drug metabolite in the urine is influenced by recent fluid consumption and does not correspond with blood levels. Urine test results are either positive or negative at specific cutoff levels. A cutoff strategy is also used for sweat patches and hair tests. Whereas urinalysis is subject to dilution related to fluid consumption, hair biomarker tests can be used to distinguish between light, moderate, and heavy use of drugs and alcohol. However, this procedure is more expensive than the simple positive or negative result from drug urinalyses. Consequently, hair testing may not be a cost-feasible option for many SUD treatment clinics.

Blood has the briefest window of detection because most drugs are cleared at measurable levels from the blood within 12 hours or less. Urine is quite different, with a detection window of about 1 to 3 days (SAMHSA, 2012). Head hair grows at the average rate of about 0.5 inch per month. Newly created hair cells incorporate substances used from the blood on that day, creating a day-by-day registry of substance use. Hair-test reporting cutoffs report positive results only when a person has used a drug at least four to six times (at typical nonmedical doses) per month. Thus, positive hair testing results are considered reliable indicators of chronic substance use. Table 2.7 reviews some basic information for the various types of testing.

NIDA Clinical Trials Network Common Data Elements

There is an almost endless collection of measures to assess all facets of substance use disorder, process addictions, and craving, and countless co-occurring

Table 2.7 U.S. Department of Health and Human Services Federal Mandatory Workplace Guidelines Cutoff Concentrations for Initial and Confirmatory Drug Tests in Urine

Initial Test Analyte	Federal Cutoff Concentrations (ng/mL)
Marijuana metabolites	50
Cocaine metabolites	150
Opiate metabolites (Codeine/morphine[1])	2,000
6-Acetylmorphine (6-AM)	10
Amphetamines[2] (Amphetamine/methamphetamine)	500
Phencyclidine (PCP)	25
Methylenedioxymethamphetamine (MDMA)	500

Confirmatory Test Analyte	Federal Cutoff Concentrations (ng/mL)
Amphetamine	250
Methamphetamine[3]	250
MDMA	250
Methylenedioxyamphetamine (MDA)	250
Methylenedioxyethylamphetamine (MDEA)	250
Cannabinoid metabolite (delta-9-tetrahydrocannabinol-9-carboxylic acid)	15
Cocaine metabolite (benzoylecgonine)	100
Codeine	2,000
Morphine	2000
6-Acetylmorphine (6-AM)	10
PCP	25

[1] Morphine is the target analyte for codeine/morphine testing.

[2] Methamphetamine is the target analyte for amphetamine/methamphetamine testing.

[3] To be reported positive for methamphetamine, a specimen must also contain amphetamine at a concentration equal to, or greater than, 100ng/mL.

Source: SAMHSA (2012, p. 5).

disorders. The question I am asked by students and trainees all the time is "Which ones do I pick and why?" In brief, my response is that the lengthy list of assessments is not an endless à la carte menu from which you select. Rather, there needs to be a reasoned and clinically based selection process. The bulk of the information feeding that selection process comes from the client interview data as well as any prior clinical information available (e.g., client treatment folder).

Consistent with the move toward empirically based practices in treatment (e.g., van Wormer & Davis, 2012) and assessment (e.g., Donovan, 2013), NIDA's Clinical Trials Network produced the common data elements (CDE) collection of assessments for use in electronic health records. NIDA brought together a team of experts to develop a consensus on the best brief screening and initial assessment tools for SUDs in general medical settings. The creation and adoption of a core set of validated common data elements and the inclusion of such consensus-based data elements for general medical settings will enable the integration of SUD treatment within mainstream health care (Ghitza et al., 2013; Ghitza, Gore-Langton, Lindblad, & Tai, 2015). Though these CDEs were developed for a general medical setting, they do present a good basic best practices for screening and assessment in SUD, while selecting other measures that complement or supplement these CDEs. Each CDE is addressed below.

Alcohol Use Disorders Identification Test-Concise (AUDIT-C). The AUDIT-C is a brief alcohol screening instrument that reliably identifies hazardous drinkers or those with an active alcohol use disorder. The AUDIT-C is a modified version of the 10-item AUDIT. The AUDIT-C consists of 3 items scored on a 0 to 12 scale. Each AUDIT-C item has five options valued from 0 points to 4 points. In men, a score of 4 or more identifies hazardous drinking or active alcohol use disorder. In women, a score of 3 or more identifies hazardous drinking or active alcohol use disorder. Generally, the higher the score, the more likely it is that a person's drinking is problematic (Bush, Kivlahan, McDonell, Fihn, & Bradley, 1998).

Drug Abuse Screen Test (DAST-10). The DAST-10 is a 10-item self-report instrument condensed from the 28-item version. The DAST-10 provides a brief self-report instrument for screening. The DAST-10 measures the degree of the consequences related to substance use and is administered via a self-report or interview format (Skinner, 1982). The DAST-10 may be reproduced for noncommercial use (clinical, research, training purposes) as long as credit is given to author Harvey A. Skinner, Department of Public Health Sciences, University of Toronto.

Patient Health Questionnaire (PHQ-2). The PHQ-2 is a self-administered version of the Primary Care Evaluation of Mental Disorders for common mental health disorders administered by health care professionals. The PHQ-2 targets frequency of depressed mood, with scores ranging from 0 to 6. A cutoff score of 3 is used for screening purposes and states that a cut point of 2 would enhance sensitivity.

The PHQ-2 screens for potential depression via inquiries about the degree of experienced depressed mood and anhedonia over the past 2 weeks (Gilbody, Richards, Brealey, & Hweitt, 2007; Kroenke, Spitzer, & Williams, 2003; Spitzer, Kroenke, & Williams, 1999).

Single Question Screening Test. This test identifies the numeric count of instances of maladaptive use of prescription drugs or the use of illegal drugs during the last 365 days. The specific item is, "How many times in the past year have you used an illegal drug or used a prescription medication for nonmedical reasons?" Smith, Schmidt, Allensworth-Davies, and Saitz (2010) reported that of eligible primary care patients ($N = 394$), the single screening question was 100% sensitive and 73.5% specific. This item serves as an excellent quick screening for individuals within a primary care or non-SUD treatment environment (e.g., ER, college/university counseling center, primary medical care office). For those in an SUD treatment facility, this type of data is typically obtained via other more relevant screening measures (such as the Addiction Severity Index) and/or the clinical interview.

Clinical Decision Support (CDS) for Substance Abuse. The CDS is composed of initial screening and assessment questions to provide primary care providers with a clinical decision tool for identifying SUD for treatment referral. It serves as a model for use of some of the NIDA CDEs discussed above. The individual is first administered a 1-item screener (e.g., the single-question screening test) and then completes the DAST-10. Next, a few additional items are added to further clarify the need for SUD referral. These questions focus on the type of substance used, frequency of use, noting any intravenous substance administration, and any current SUD treatment status. Field testing of the CDS is currently ongoing (Tai, Lindblad, Gore-Langton, Ghitza, & Subramaniam, 2012).

Areas of Focus

Donovan (2013) explained the choice of instrument as contingent upon whether the assessment process is in the screening (determination of a problem), problem assessment (further development of clinical clarity regarding the problem), or treatment (factors that may impede or facilitate treatment effectiveness) stage. Table 2.8 lists a small example of the myriad measures available for use.

Table 2.8 Examples of Measures Relevant to the Assessment of Substance Use Disorders, Addiction Disorders, and Associated Disorders

Domain	Instrument	Original Reference
Alcohol	CAGE Questions	Mayfield et al., 1974
	TWEAK	Russell et al., 1991
	Alcohol Use Disorders Identification Test (AUDIT)	Saunders et al., 1993
	Michigan Alcoholism Screening Test (MAST)	Selzer, 1971
	Brief Michigan Alcoholism Screening Test (bMAST)	Pokorny et al., 1972
	Short Michigan Alcoholism Screening Test (sMAST)	Zung, 1984
	Michigan Alcoholism Screening Test – Geriatric (MAST-G)	Blow et al., 1992
	Alcohol Timeline Followback	Sobell & Sobell, 2000
Cocaine	Cocaine Selective Severity Assessment	Kampman et al., 1998
	Cocaine Craving Questionnaire	Tiffany et al., 1993
	Cocaine Craving Questionnaire – Brief	Sussner et al., 2006
	Cocaine Expectancy Questionnaire (CEEQ)	Jaffe & Kilbey, 1994
	Cocaine High Risk Situations Questionnaire (CHRSQ)	Michalec et al., 1992
Opiate	Subjective Opiate Withdrawal Scale (SOWS)	Handelsman et al. 1987
	Objective Opiate Withdrawal Scale (OOWS)	Handelsman et al., 1987
	Short Opiate Withdrawal Scale	Gossop, 1990
	Opiate Addiction Severity Inventory (OASI)	Gu et al., 2008
	Prescribed Opioids Scale (PODS)	Banta-Green et al., 2010
Cannabis	Cannabis Expectancy Questionnaire (CEQ)	Young et al., 1997
	Cannabis Problems Questionnaire	Copeland et al., 2001
	Cannabis Abuse Screening Test	Legleye et al., 2007
General Substance Use	Addiction Severity Index (ASI)	McLellan et al., 1992
	Inventory of Drug Use Consequences	Tonigan & Miller, 2002
	DrugCheck Problem List (PL)	Kavanagh et al., 2011
	Desire for Drug Questionnaire (DDQ)	Franken et al., 2002
	Substance Use Disorders Diagnostic Schedule	Hoffman & Harrison, 1995
	Semi-Structured Assessment for Drug Dependence and Alcoholism	Pierucci & Lagha et al., 2005
	Substance Abuse Relapse Assessment	Schonfeld et al., 1993
	Relapse Situation Appraisal Questionnaire	Meyers et al., 1996

(Continued)

Table 2.8 (Continued)

Domain	Instrument	Original Reference
Process Addictions	South Oaks Gambling Screen (SOGS)	Lesieur & Blume, 1987
	Canadian Problem Gambling Index	Svetieva & Walker, 2008
	Gambling Related Cognitions Scale	Raylu & Oei, 2004
	Compulsive Sexual Behavior Inventory	Coleman, Miner, Ohlerking, & Raymond, 2011
	Sexual Dependency Inventory-Revised	Delmonico, Bubenzer, & West, 1998
	Garos Sexual Behavior Index	Garos & Stock, 1998a, 1998b
	Yale Food Addiction Scale (YFAS)	Gearhardt, Corbin, & Brownell, 2009
	Nonsuicidal Self-Injury Assessment Tool	Whitlock & Purington, 2013
	The Ottawa Self-Injury Inventory	Nixon et al., 2015
	Clinician-Rated Severity of Nonsuicidal Self-Injury	APA, 2013
General Mental Health	California Psychological Inventory	Gough, 1975
	NEO Personality Inventory	Costa & McRae, 1992
	Minnesota Multiphasic Personality Inventory (MMPI-2)	Hathaway et al., 1989
	Millon Clinical Multiaxial Inventory	Millon, 1992
	Symptom Checklist 90 (SCL-90)	Derogatis, 1977
	Beck Anxiety Inventory	Beck et al., 1988
	Beck Depression Inventory	Beck et al., 1961
Physical Health	CDC Health-Related Quality of Life (CDC HRQOL– 4)	CDC, 1993
	Patient Health Questionnaire (PHQ-9)	Kroenke et al., 2002
Treatment Related	Circumstances, Motivation, Readiness, and Suitability Scale	DeLeon et al., 1994
	TCU Treatment Motivation Assessment	Simpson & Joe, 1993
	Client Assessment Inventory	Kressel et al., 2000
	Stages of Change Readiness and Treatment Eagerness Scale	Miller & Tonigan, 1996

Note: Information on most of these measures, including source location, availability (free/payment), and other relevant content, can be located at the University of Washington Alcohol and Drug Abuse Institute's Substance Use Screening and Assessment Instruments Database (http://lib.adai.washington.edu/instruments/).

SPECIAL POPULATIONS

Adolescents

The American Academy of Pediatrics Committee on Substance Abuse (2011) recommends that substance use screening should occur at all routine adolescent clinical visits. Screening may incorporate a variety of screening tools. Following screening and assessment, knowledge of the available resources for adolescent treatment is essential. These resources must be tailored to the individual adolescent. For example, if working with a high-risk or criminal justice-involved adolescent population, screening/assessment for criminal thinking may be warranted. Furthermore, adolescent screening and assessment must also take into account neurological and developmental issues. Prefrontal development (associated with cognitive control) occurs throughout adolescence, and adolescents may be vulnerable to high-risk choices and sensitive to the rewarding properties of substances, thus increasing the potential for SUDs (Beckett & Taylor, 2010). Incorporating this neuropsychological theory into the screening and assessment decision process (Boucher & Sandhu, 2013) leads to a long list of negative outcomes associated with adolescent substance use, such as accidents, suicide, and impairments in the educational, occupational, and/or interpersonal realms. Knight, Becan, Landrum, Joe, and Flynn (2014) emphasized that a modular approach to adolescent screening and assessment is needed so that agencies can customize the screening/assessment process (using some of the measures listed in Table 2.8 and/or others) to produce individual client reports based on reliable assessment instruments. Knight and colleagues emphasized that, unfortunately, little is known regarding the use of a modular screening/assessment package tailored for adolescents.

Older Adults

Morgen (2015) recently reviewed several impediments to effective screening and assessment of SUD (or substance misuse) in the older adult population. First, older people may underreport their substance misuse due to perceived stigma. Second, ageism may distract clinicians from signs of substance misuse, such as low energy and mood changes, which may instead be misattributed to general physical illness or depression. Third, stereotyping may blind detection of symptoms, for instance, ignoring substance use in older women due to the misnomer that substance use is an uncommon occurrence for this population. In addition, when performing an interview, it is crucial to identify the psychosocial factors that may make substance misuse more likely in older adults, for instance, issues such as bereavement, retirement, or physical immobility.

SAMHSA (2011) also highlighted the complexities in assessing older adult SUDs and related psychiatric conditions such as major and mild depression and dysthymia. For example, older adults may demonstrate depression-like symptoms such as hopelessness, worry, and loss of interest in tasks deemed once pleasurable. Furthermore, *DSM* diagnostic criteria are also different than for younger adults, and there are no established older adult *DSM* diagnostic guidelines (e.g., Morgen & Voelkner, 2014). SAMHSA (2011) reviewed other diagnostic issues, such as how in major depression impairment in functioning is less severe as compared to younger adults and how minor depression is often not detected in older adults.

Screening for substance misuse in older adults is primarily limited to alcohol. The most commonly used screen for older adults is the Short Michigan Alcoholism Screening Test-Geriatric Version (SMAST-G) (Blow et al., 1992). The SMAST-G identifies problems common for older adults, such as drinking after a significant loss. Other alcohol measures designed specifically for the older adult population include an adaptation of the AUDIT (SAMHSA, 2001), with sensitivity and specificity shown for a cutoff score of 5 for older men and 3 for older women.

Cognitive impairment associated with alcohol misuse might present as amnestic disorders and/or a more global loss of cognitive function (Liu & Satterfield, 2015). Consequently, cognitive function must be screened. Older adults can be screened via the Mini-Mental State Examination (Folstein, Folstein, & McHugh, 1975) or Addenbrooke's Cognitive Examination (Mioshi, Dawson, Mitchell, Arnold, & Hodges, 2006).

CONCLUSION AND QUESTIONS TO CONSIDER

The interview—consisting of the dialogue between counselor and client—is the most imperative component of the entire process whereby the counselor learns about the client, his or her SUD and addiction struggles, history, and the myriad other co-occurring and associated disorders and psychosocial factors that all collide within the life of an individual in treatment for SUD. Out of the interview, a more formal and standardized assessment process commences to both validate the findings from the interview as well as expand on these matters with data that can drive treatment and diagnostic decisions.

QUESTIONS TO CONSIDER AS YOU MOVE ON TO CHAPTER 3

Question 1: Can you think of any specific problems a client with cognitive deficiencies (due to substance use) would encounter in the interview and assessment process? How could you as a counselor (or program administrator) reorganize some day-to-day interview tasks to better accommodate for this client?

Question 2: This chapter is all about asking clients questions. Whether in the interview or via assessment measures, it is about asking questions. Going back to Chapter 1, which parts of the brain are being activated when being asked various types of questions in the interview and assessment process?

Chapter 3

Diagnostic Issues

DSM-5 *Overview for Substance-Related Disorders*

The *Diagnostic and Statistical Manual of Mental Disorders* (5th ed.; *DSM-5*; American Psychiatric Association [APA], 2013) provides a classification system for the diagnosis of a substance use disorder (SUD) across 10 drug classes including alcohol, cannabis, phencyclidine, other hallucinogens, inhalants, opioids, sedatives, stimulants, tobacco, and other/unknown. Diagnosis is made by specifying the substance of disorder (e.g., alcohol use disorder [AUD]). If the substance is part of a larger class, such as cocaine as a part of the stimulant disorders, you specify cocaine or amphetamine type.

The current *DSM-5* made significant changes to the prior SUDs classification system by eliminating the abuse and dependency classifications and instead utilizing the diagnosis of "substance use disorder" on a continuum from mild to severe. Rationales for these changes were well discussed in the literature (e.g., Hasin et al., 2013; O'Brien, 2011) and are beyond the scope of this chapter. Furthermore, as these changes are now at least 3 years old (by the time you are reading this text), reviewing the history of now-irrelevant diagnostic matters is not warranted.

The *DSM-5* diagnostic criteria for a SUD specified a maladaptive pattern of behaviors related to substance use. These behaviors fall into 11 criteria with overall groupings of impaired control, social impairment, risky use, and pharmacological criteria. For some substances symptoms are less prominent, and in a few instances not all symptoms apply.

Impaired Control

Impaired control over substance use is the first criteria grouping and consists of the first four diagnostic items: (1) the individual may take the substance in larger amounts or over a longer period than was originally intended; (2) the individual may express a persistent desire and/or unsuccessful history to cut down, cease, or regulate substance use; (3) the individual may spend a great deal of time obtaining the substance, using the substance, or recovering from its effects; and (4) craving is manifested by an intense desire or urge for the drug that may occur at any time. From the clinician's chair, these four criteria could present in the following manner:

1. Taking larger amounts than intended.
   - When questioned about the current amount of the substance(s) ingested, the individual discusses experiences where he or she "lost control" or "lost track" and may have felt bad or worried about the excessive substance(s) consumed.
   - For those who qualify for more than one SUD (e.g., cocaine use disorder and AUD), is the larger amount being taken consistent across both substances or only for one substance? For instance, does the loss of control in taking larger amounts of cocaine than intended lead to drinking more alcohol than intended? Though the *DSM-5* SUD is the same for each substance class, the clinician still must assess this criteria for each substance. Thus, be careful to verify that the larger amounts than intended criterion is applied to only the proper substance(s).

2. Persistent desire and/or unsuccessful efforts to reduce or cease substance use.
   - The client may discuss a long history of many episodes of brief (less than 1 month) or longer abstinence only to repeatedly relapse. There is no magic number, but look for a history. This may require probing, as the client may not consider their period of nonsubstance use as a period of abstinence. For example, I once had a client who at first did not inform me of abstinence periods of only 1 month, saying, "Those don't count to me." So you may need to ask, ask, and then ask again and in various ways.
   - Look for a "motivation" for recovery reported in these prior abstinence episodes. Why did the client start abstinence? Why did he or she relapse? Note that clients may specifically express the reason for starting but may not be able to verbalize why they relapsed.
   - Similar to the prior criterion, was the desire to cut down or cease substance use applicable to all substances or just some?

3. Great deal of time spent acquiring substance, using substance, and/or recovering from effects.
   - When actively using, how much time is occupied by the substance use? For instance, I once worked with a client who drove many miles round-trip to purchase heroin during the workday.

4. Craving.
   - How has the client experienced the desire to use both now and in the past?
   - If use of multiple substances exists, does craving occur for all or just some of the substances?
   - Do cravings increase or decrease over length of abstinence?
   - Do cravings for one substance influence a craving for another?
   - Do cravings coincide with psychological symptoms (e.g., anxiety, depression)?
   - Do cravings cause guilt or worry in the client?
   - How often in the client's addiction history has a craving led to a lapse or relapse?

Social Impairment

Social impairment due to substance use is the second criteria grouping and consists of diagnostic items 5 to 7: (5) recurrent substance use may result in a failure to fulfill major role obligations at work, school, or home; (6) the individual may continue substance use despite having persistent or recurrent social or interpersonal problems caused or exacerbated by the effects of the substance; and (7) important social, occupational, or recreational activities may be given up or reduced because of substance use.

These three criteria all seem to overlap in regard to the types of client/collateral reports a clinician would experience in an interview. Some examples are as follows:

- A client who reports a pattern of drinking during lunch hour and then failing to return for important afternoon meetings.
- A client who reports frequently "half-assing" work projects because he or she was too hung over to give them a true effort.
- A client who was too under the influence from opioids and failed to pick up his or her child after school.
- You may see a typical pattern of clients coming with a history of repeated work terminations and/or reprimands due to substance use.
- You may see a parent who temporarily or permanently lost custody of his or her children due to substance use.

Risky Use

Continued risky use of the substance is the third criteria grouping and consists of diagnostic items 8 and 9: (8) the recurrent substance use in situations in which it is physically hazardous (such as driving while intoxicated); and (9) the individual continues substance use despite knowledge of having a persistent or recurrent physical or psychological problem that is likely to have been caused or exacerbated by the substance. You may hear reports similar to some of the following:

- A client repeatedly driving home drunk from the bar despite knowing he or she is drunk and could get caught.
- Clients who tell you they keep using cocaine despite the effects use has on their anxiety and self-esteem.

Tolerance and Withdrawal

Tolerance and withdrawal are the final grouping consisting of Diagnostic Criteria 10 and 11: (10) tolerance is signaled by requiring a markedly increased dose of the substance to achieve the desired effect or a markedly reduced effect when the usual dose is consumed. Tolerance may be reported in some of the following ways:

- A client who reports a change in primary substance in order to get a "better" high.
- A client who discusses a frustration in not achieving the same level of intoxication from the amount of substance ingested.
- Clients who report that they changed substance and administration routes to feel a better high (e.g., the Percocet user who moves to injecting heroin for a quicker and stronger high).

Withdrawal, Diagnostic Criteria 11, is a syndrome that occurs when blood or tissue concentrations of a substance decline in an individual who had maintained prolonged heavy use of the substance. After developing withdrawal symptoms, the individual is likely to consume the substance to relieve the symptoms. Withdrawal symptoms vary greatly across the classes of substances, and separate criteria sets for withdrawal are provided for the drug classes. In general, withdrawal syndromes must cause impairment and distress as well as not be better explained by a co-occurring psychological and/or medical disorder (this includes symptoms due to intoxication from the same substance or withdrawal from another substance). Each is briefly reviewed below.

1. Alcohol Withdrawal *DSM-5* (APA, 2013) Criteria Review:
   - Withdrawal symptoms must include two or more of the following occurring within a few days post last drink: Pulse greater than 100 beats/minute, increased hand tremors, insomnia, nausea, temporary hallucinations, psychomotor agitation, tonic-clonic seizures (a seizure affecting the entire brain), anxiety.
   - Withdrawal is only diagnosable if there is moderate or severe alcohol use disorder. (pp. 499–500)

2. Cannabis Withdrawal *DSM-5* Criteria Review:
   - Withdrawal symptoms must include three or more of the following occurring within one week of last use: Irritability/anger, anxiety/general nervousness, sleep difficulties, decreased appetite, restlessness, depression, and a somatic symptom such as abdominal pain or headache.
   - Withdrawal is only diagnosable if there is moderate or severe cannabis use disorder. (pp. 517–518)

3. Opioid Withdrawal *DSM-5* Criteria Review:
   - Withdrawal symptoms must include three or more of the following occurring within a few minutes to a few days post last use: Depressed mood, nausea, body aches, lacrimation (excessive tears) or rhinorrhea (excessive nose running), pupil dilation or sweating, diarrhea, yawning, fever, insomnia.
   - Withdrawal is only diagnosable if there is a moderate or severe opioid use disorder. (pp. 547–548)

4. Sedative, Hypnotic, or Anxiolytic Withdrawal *DSM-5* Criteria Review:
   - Withdrawal symptoms must include two or more of the following occurring within a few hours to a few days post last use: Pulse rate greater than 100 beats/minute, hand tremor, insomnia, nausea, auditory hallucinations, psychomotor, agitation, anxiety, clonic-tonic seizure.
   - Withdrawal is only diagnosable if there is a moderate or severe sedative, hypnotic, or anxiolytic use disorder.
   - Notice the similarity between withdrawal symptoms from alcohol and sedative, hypnotic, or anxiolytic substances. (pp. 557–558)

5. Stimulant Withdrawal *DSM-5* Criteria Review:
   - Withdrawal symptoms must include dysphoric mood and two or more of the following occurring within a few hours to a few days post last use: Fatigue, unpleasant vivid dreams, insomnia or hypersomnia, increased appetite, psychomotor agitation or retardation.
   - Withdrawal is only diagnosable if there is a moderate or severe stimulant use disorder. (p. 569)

Severity Ratings

In the prior substance use diagnostic classification system in *Diagnostic and Statistical Manual of Mental Disorders* (4th ed., text rev.; *DSM-IV-TR*; APA, 2000), substance *abuse* was considered (accurate or not) the less severe of the two diagnoses, with substance *dependence* deemed as a more severe diagnosis. This paradigm resulted in numerous clinical and diagnostic difficulties and inconsistencies (e.g., O'Brien, 2011). In *DSM-5* (APA, 2013), SUDs are now rated on a continuum of severity based on the number of diagnostic criteria (out of 11) endorsed via client self-report (e.g., interview or screening/assessment), clinician observation, collateral report (e.g., family or friends), and/or biological (e.g., urine) testing. The ratings run from mild (two to three criteria endorsed), moderate (four to five criteria endorsed), and severe (six or more criteria endorsed).

Course Specifiers

Though some individuals may come to the diagnostic process as actively using, others may already be in some degree of recovery. Therefore, beyond the type and severity of diagnosis, *DSM-5* also provides the diagnostician an opportunity to specify details regarding any period of abstinence. Early remission occurs if the individual had met the full SUD criteria but now has gone between 3 and 12 months without experiencing any of the diagnostic criteria with the exception of craving. Sustained remission occurs if the individual had met the full SUD criteria but now has gone greater than 12 months without experiencing any of the diagnostic criteria with the exception of craving.

Of note is how the *DSM-5* carved out a craving exception. Craving is a new diagnostic criteria to the *DSM-5* SUDs and demonstrates that the *DSM* now considers active craving symptoms as a commonplace symptom for more than 1 year into full recovery. This decision fits the broader literature that clearly shows how treatment-seeking individuals experience strong craving symptoms and that cravings are the focus of clinical interventions (Heinz, Beck, Grüsser, Grace, & Wrase, 2009; Oslin, Cary, Slaymaker, Colleran, & Blow, 2009). Consequently, craving should not be considered a criterion of relapse but rather a general gauge for how comfortable and stable clients are during their recovery and how they cope with negative affect and experiences without returning to substance use.

Two other course specifiers remain: "In a controlled environment" pertains to those who ceased substance use but did so in a context that (in theory) restricted their access to the substance(s), such as inpatient treatment or prison; and "on maintenance therapy" is reserved for opioid use disorder and stipulates whether no SUD criteria are met due to the client being prescribed and using agonist and/or antagonist medication, such as methadone or oral naltrexone.

Taken together, the specifiers and severity ratings produce a comprehensive and clear diagnosis, for instance, severe opioid use disorder; on maintenance therapy (Suboxone); in a controlled environment; or moderate cannabis use, early remission.

International Statistical Classification of Diseases, Version 10

As of October 1, 2015, there was a mandatory updating of the codes from Version 9 to Version 10 of the World Health Organization's International Statistical Classification of Diseases and Health-Related Problems (World Health Organization, 2011; ICD-10) for the billing of substance use treatment services. As discussed above, the *DSM-5* defines SUD on the basis of severity, from mild to severe. The ICD-10, however, has two primary categories: (1) harmful use requiring physical or mental harm, and (2) dependence, which requires a minimum of three of the following six criteria endorsed:

- Strong desire or compulsion to use the substance (this may entail craving).
- Difficulties in controlling substance use in terms of onset, termination, or level of use.
- Withdrawal or using the same substance to relieve or avoid withdrawal symptoms.
- Tolerance.
- Neglect of alternative pleasures or time spent to obtain, use, and recover from use.
- Continued use despite having a physical, psychological, or cognitive problem(s) related to substance use.

The ICD-10 dependence criteria include some *DSM-5* criteria typically found in more severe SUD diagnoses (Kopak, Proctor, & Hoffman, 2012; Proctor, Kopak, & Hoffman, 2012, 2014). These *DSM-5* criteria are desire/unsuccessful effort to cut down or cease substance use, craving, strong desire or compulsion to use, failure to fulfill responsibilities due to substance use, sacrificing social/occupational/ recreational activities in favor of substance use, and withdrawal. There are, however, questions about how the SUD severity scale in the *DSM-5* matches with the ICD-10 categorical style.

CO-OCCURRING PSYCHIATRIC DISORDERS

According to the *DSM-5* (APA, 2013), psychiatric symptoms may occur alongside substance use in the intoxication or withdrawal diagnosis (e.g., anxiety demonstrated during cocaine intoxication or depressed mood shown during cocaine withdrawal). However, the *DSM-5* also provides for diagnoses of substance-induced psychiatric disorders within other classification areas other than substance related.

For our purposes in this chapter, these include substance-induced anxiety disorders, substance-induced depressive disorders, substance-induced bipolar disorders, and substance-induced psychotic disorders.

The induced disorders come with a specific set of criteria designed to facilitate the differential diagnosis from psychiatric symptoms due to withdrawal, intoxication, or a non-substance-related co-occurring disorder. In brief, the following summarizes the requirements for a substance-induced psychiatric disorder as per the *DSM-5*.

- The psychiatric symptom in question (anxiety for induced-anxiety, for example) needs to be a prominent factor in the overall clinical picture. The diagnosis of induced, and not intoxication or withdrawal, is made when these psychiatric symptoms are more intense than expected in the intoxication or withdrawal period.
- The psychiatric symptoms developed soon after intoxication and/or withdrawal from the substance.
- The substance is capable of inducing the psychiatric symptom(s) in question.
- Psychiatric symptoms that are not better explained by a non-substance-related version of this disorder (e.g., major depressive disorder as opposed to substance-induced depressive disorder). For instance, do the symptoms last one month or longer after acute withdrawal/severe intoxication, or is there evidence of a preexisting psychiatric condition (i.e., evidence of preexisting bipolar disorder would nullify the ability to diagnose a substance-induced bipolar disorder)?
- The psychiatric symptoms appear to not be better explained by delirium.

The 2013 Substance Abuse and Mental Health Services Administration (SAMHSA) TEDS-A data showed that one-third of all SUD treatment admissions also presented with a *DSM*-diagnosed co-occurring psychiatric disorder ($n = 408,737$, 33.1%). Thus, just knowing how to diagnose an SUD is only half the clinical picture (and typically the easier component of the diagnostic process). This next section covers the challenging psychiatric diagnoses inherent within the SUD population.

The prevalence of co-occurring psychiatric symptoms within the SUD population is now the norm and not the exception or specialized clinical case (e.g., CSAT, 2005; Helseth, Samet, Johnsen, Bramness, & Waal, 2013; Thombs & Osborn, 2013). For example, Rosenthal (2013) noted the high rates of psychiatric disorders and symptoms within an SUD treatment population as well as a high rate of substance use and SUD in a psychiatric treatment population. Consequently, if experiencing an SUD case, though you will of course need to diagnose one or more SUDs, you will also very likely need to diagnose one or more co-occurring psychiatric disorders and/or understand the interplay between the exhibited and reported psychiatric symptoms and the substance use.

Grant and colleagues (2015) demonstrated just how prevalent psychiatric disorders/symptoms are in the SUD population when they conducted face-to-face interviews with a representative U.S. noninstitutionalized civilian adult (18 years and older) sample ($N = 36,309$) in the 2012–2013 National Epidemiologic Survey on Alcohol and Related Conditions III (NESARC-III). They found significant associations between 12-month and lifetime AUD and other SUDs, major depressive and bipolar I disorders, and antisocial personality disorder (ASPD) and borderline personality disorder (BPD) across all levels of AUD severity, with odds ratios (ORs) and confidence intervals (CIs) ranging from 1.2 (95% CI, 1.08–1.36) to 6.4 (95% CI, 5.76–7.22). Associations were also found between AUD and panic disorder, specific phobia, and generalized anxiety disorder (ORs ranging from 1.2 (95% CI, 1.01–1.43) to 1.4 (95% CI, 1.13–1.67) across most levels of AUD severity.

In the NESARC-III, Grant et al. (2016) also found significant associations between 12-month and lifetime drug use disorder (DUD) and other SUDs. Significant associations were found between any 12-month DUD and major depressive disorder (OR 1.3; 95% CI, 1.09–1.64), dysthymia (OR 1.5; 95% CI, 1.09–2.02), bipolar I (OR 1.5; 95% CI, 1.06–2.05), posttraumatic stress disorder (PTSD) (OR 1.6; 95% CI, 1.27–2.10), and antisocial (OR 1.4; 95% CI,1.11–1.75), borderline (OR 1.8; 95% CI, 1.41–2.24), and schizotypal (OR 1.5; 95% CI, 1.18–1.87) personality disorders. Lifetime DUD was also associated with generalized anxiety disorder (OR 1.3; 95% CI, 1.06–1.49), panic disorder (OR 1.3; 95% CI, 1.06–1.59), and social phobia (OR 1.3; 95% CI, 1.09–1.64).

Sunderland, Slade, and Krueger (2015) emphasized that although we clearly see a relationship between SUD and psychiatric disorders, what remains unknown is whether this relationship can best be explained by some general factor or whether there is a unique contribution made by specific substances. For instance, a general factor may be genetic vulnerability or psychological hardiness. However, the unique contribution hypothesis very much muddies the waters as evidenced by the myriad findings regarding psychiatric symptoms in the wake of substance use or withdrawal. For example, major depression is theorized to possibly cause increased alcohol use (Kahler, Ramsey, Read, & Brown, 2002). Brick (2008) added that psychotic symptoms during alcohol withdrawal, as due to the GABA/glutamate imbalance, may appear as early as 2 days after the last drink.

Other substances share this literature. Oldham and Ciraulo (2013) discussed paranoia, depression, and suicidal ideation/acts in benzodiazepine and barbiturate users. Numerous studies noted anxiety, depression, and psychosis in methamphetamine users (e.g., Chen et al., 2005), though most symptoms may subside within one week of last use (Newton, Kalechstein, Duran, Vansluis, & Ling, 2004). However, not all methamphetamine users experience psychiatric symptom remission. For instance, Ujike and Sato (2004) noted a prolonged psychosis for 6 months or longer in one-third of methamphetamine users, whereas Glasner-Edwards et al. (2009) found that 50% of methamphetamine users met the *DSM* criteria for a psychiatric disorder 3 years posttreatment.

Cocaine is associated with a cocaine-induced psychosis severe enough to be misdiagnosed as schizophrenia (Kandel, Huang, & Davies, 2001), though upon closer look the symptoms are different due to lesser instances of thought disorder, fewer bizarre thoughts, and fewer negative schizophrenia symptoms (Harris & Batki, 2000; Thirthalli & Benegal, 2006). Cocaine also demonstrates how symptoms due to use greatly resemble psychiatric symptoms. For instance, Gorelick (2013) reviewed the presence of tactile hallucinations of bugs crawling under the skin (formication). Furthermore, panic symptoms common in cocaine use may transform into a panic disorder (Schuckit, 2006).

Similar psychiatric symptom associations are seen with other substances as well. Panic and intense anxiety are reported as adverse reactions in cannabis users, and though it may resolve postabstinence, there is evidence that this cannabis-associated anxiety can develop into panic attacks or panic disorder independent of cannabis use (Zvolensky et al., 2008). In addition, there are high rates of co-occurring psychiatric symptoms such as psychosis in opioid users (Strain, 2002).

Over the years, numerous models have attempted to explain the complicated relationship between co-occurring psychiatric disorders and SUDs. A few are discussed next. The common factor model maintains that the co-occurring SUD and psychiatric disorder originate from a single risk factor (Mueser, Drake, & Wallach, 1998). This risk factor increases the risk for both substance use and psychiatric disorder. Some common risk factors are genetic vulnerability, disordered mesolimbic activity in the brain, or psychosocial factors such as poverty or homelessness (Mueser, Noordsy, Drake, & Fox, 2003).

Other models pose a more complex hypothesis. The random multiformity and extreme multiformity models state that one disorder can take heterogeneous or atypical forms (Klein & Riso, 1993). Thus, symptoms will appear that seem associated with other disorders. This complicates the diagnostic accuracy and also seems to underscore the need for consistent and frequent reevaluation to determine the true origin of the symptom(s). The extreme multiformity model assumes the atypical form will appear only when the severity of the risk factor for either or both of the disorders is elevated. For example, the co-occurrence of cocaine use disorder and psychotic symptoms may not occur unless the frequency of cocaine use reaches a certain (likely unknown) critical threshold and/or there exists an extensive family history of psychosis (such as schizophrenia).

The correlated liabilities model proposes that the onset of co-occurring conditions arise due to shared common sets of risk factors (Neale & Kendler, 1995). For example, co-occurring SUD and depression in adolescence may arise from a variety of forms of neglect and abuse during childhood.

Three types of causation models examine the temporal order of onset of substance use and other psychiatric disorders (Mueser et al., 2003). The secondary substance abuse model proposes that psychopathology precedes and causes SUD, whereas the secondary psychiatric disorder model states that SUD precedes and causes psychiatric disorders. Finally, the reciprocal causation model proposes that one disorder will exacerbate the other. This model is less concerned with the order of onset and more focused on the integration of SUD and psychiatric disorders for the sake of best-fitting treatment options (Mueser et al., 2003).

Another perspective on the substance use/psychiatric disorders paradigm comes from research in the area of behavioral economics and states that SUD clients prefer immediate reinforcement, even if small in magnitude, as opposed to delayed reinforcement of greater magnitude. In addition, they may prefer that punishment be delayed, even if this delay means the punishment magnitude will increase (Bickel & Marsch, 2001; Higgins, Heil, & Lussier, 2004). For example, SUD individuals with psychosis report that despite being aware of the long-term physical and psychological consequences of continued substance use, they still use substances in order to obtain immediate relief from dysphoria and unpleasant side effects of antipsychotic medication via the substance-induced euphoria (Charles & Weaver, 2010). Consequently, those with co-occurring disorders suffer with various psychiatric symptoms and select the immediate (though brief) relief from symptoms via substance use despite the psychological, physical, and interpersonal damage that come later. If this model is correct, it does answer the question many ask of "why would they use if they know the consequences soon to come?" For many, the decision to use or cease substance use may be less a matter of "willpower" or "motivation" and more so a cost-benefit analysis calculated while under psychiatric distress.

The question of whether you are seeing a substance-induced psychiatric symptom or a non-substance-related psychiatric symptom/disorder is critical to clarify. However, this question is also highly complex and at times heterogeneous in presentation. Two recent studies (Foulds, Adamson, Boden, Williman, & Mulder, 2015; Foulds, Sellman, et al., 2015) demonstrated the complexity inherent in the induced versus non-substance-related diagnostic process.

Foulds, Adamson, et al. (2015) noted the presumption that antidepressants would work for non-substance-related but not induced disorders has not been clearly evaluated, at least as it pertains to AUD and depression. They also argued that the induced versus non-substance-related distinction is an "oversimplification" (p. 57) and typically not feasible due to the recall skills required by the client (see the frontal cortex and memory impairments discussed in Chapter 1). Furthermore, they emphasized that the relationship between alcohol use and depression is fluid throughout the patient's lifetime, thus making it challenging to construct a singular diagnostic paradigm between substances and psychiatric disorders/symptoms. As echoed by McKay (2005), if the client uses substances to reduce and/or manage depressive symptoms, then obviously the relationship will adjust as the depressive symptoms and/or substance use changes.

Foulds, Sellman, et al. (2015) studied outpatients with alcohol dependence and major depression (*n* = 138). They found that improvements for drinking and depression occur by week 3 of alcohol treatment. As expected, they found that in the first 3 weeks of treatment, the substance-induced depression group showed greater improvement than the non-substance-related group for depression symptoms (likely due to the passing of the immediate withdrawal period and the associated psychiatric symptoms). Of interest, though, was that for both the induced and non-substance-related groups, poorer depression outcomes were found for those who did not reduce or cease drinking or drank more. Foulds, Sellman, et al. argued that this finding runs counter to the common notion that only the alcohol-induced depressive disorder patients would experience poor depression outcomes if drinking did not cease/reduce. This points to a complicated and nuanced relationship between substances and psychiatric disorders/symptoms and may support (in part) the finding by Nunes, Liu, Samet, Matseoane, and Hasin (2006), who noted a high rate of non-substance-related psychiatric disorders in patients originally diagnosed as having the psychiatric symptoms due to a substance-induced disorder.

Part of this error may be due to the rigid notion of co-occurring disorders only consisting of an integration of one substance disorder and one psychiatric disorder. However, it is common for patients to present with multiple co-occurring psychiatric disorders. For instance, a recent study (Hidalgo-Mazzei, Walsh, Rosenstein, & Zimmerman, 2015) examined 3,651 psychiatric patients and found that 63 of these patients were diagnosed with both bipolar disorder and BPD, and that these patients were significantly more likely to have an SUD compared with bipolar patients without BPD. The study highlighted how both bipolar and BPDs together increased SUD risk as compared to bipolar-only clients and showed how two psychiatric disorders can combine into a perfect storm that increases SUD risk as a mechanism of psychiatric symptom coping.

First (2014) reviewed several critical thinking points in this complicated diagnostic process:

- Is a temporal relationship present between the substance use and the onset/ maintenance of the psychopathology? Unfortunately, this determination is difficult (if not impossible) due to the order of onset of substance use and psychopathology being impossible to accurately determine. In such situations, the clinician must wait out the withdrawal period to determine what happens to the psychiatric symptoms because (in theory) after the period of abstinence following the withdrawal phase the psychiatric symptoms—if induced via withdrawal and substance cessation—should spontaneously resolve. Persistence of the psychiatric symptomatology for a significant period of time beyond periods of intoxication or withdrawal suggests that the psychopathology is primary.

- Regular substance users who report a significant change in the amount used (either a large increase or a decrease sufficient to induce withdrawal symptoms) may develop psychiatric symptoms.
- The substance-taking behavior can be considered a form of self-medication for the psychiatric condition. Substance users often preferentially choose certain classes of substances for their effects. For example, patients with anxiety disorders often prefer central nervous system (CNS) depressants such as alcohol. The principal criterion for a primary psychiatric disorder with secondary substance use is that the primary psychiatric disorder occurs first and/or exists in the patient's lifetime while substance free.
- Even if initially independent, the co-occurring disorders may interact and exacerbate one another.

Below, several common psychiatric conditions are reviewed. Look for the degree of complexity in the integration of SUD and psychiatric symptoms. As you do, it should start to become clear as to why the misdiagnosis of a substance etiology is a very common diagnostic error, especially in clinicians not well versed in substance use diagnostics.

Anxiety/Depression

Myriad findings (e.g., Brooner, King, Kidorf, Schmidt, & Bigelow, 1997; Stewart, Zvolensky, & Eifert, 2002) support the conclusion that anxiety and depressive symptoms occur frequently within the SUD treatment population. For instance, in an SUD population, the lifetime rates of affective and anxiety disorders run between 49% and 79% (Langås, Malt, & Opjordsmoen, 2012). Other studies have documented the temporal sequencing of SUD and anxiety. First, a preexisting anxiety disorder leading to self-medication increases as predicting (OR = 2.50–4.99) the risk of SUD onset (Robinson, Sareen, Cox, & Bolton, 2011). Second, Menary, Kushner, Maurer, and Thuras (2011) documented that approximately 20% of the anxiety disorder population self-medicates with alcohol due to the anxiolytic effect of alcohol. Third, anxiety disorder onset seems to come prior to opioid use disorder onset (Fatséas, Denis, Lavie, & Auriacombe, 2010) or AUD onset (Birrell,

Newton, Teesson, Tonks, & Slade, 2015). Fourth, it is reported that at least 25% of individuals with depressive disorders use substances to relieve symptoms (Bolton, Robinson, & Sareen, 2009).

Mood disorders commonly co-occur with SUDs and trigger a significant risk for suicidal behavior (CSAT, 2009a; Darke & Ross, 2002; Dhossche, Meloukheia, & Chakravorty, 2000). For example, a review of psychological autopsy studies showed that mood disorders (particularly major depression) and SUDs were the most common disorders for those who died by suicide. Furthermore, 38% of these suicidal individuals had one or more SUD plus one or more other psychiatric disorder (Cavanagh, Carson, Sharpe, & Lawrie, 2003). The SUD/mood disorder co-occurring condition also produces a heightened risk for attempted suicide (e.g., McCloud, Barnaby, Omu, Drummond, & Aboud, 2004). Aharonovich, Liu, Nunes, and Hasin (2002) stressed that the suicide risk is present regardless if the depressed mood is due to an independent co-occurring mood disorder or a substance-induced mood disorder. Consequently, it is the symptom and not the origin of the symptom that seems most important.

The severity of these mood symptoms could be quite high. Alcohol use-disordered clients may enter treatment with high levels of depression (e.g., Davidson, 1995; Schuckit, 1994). Those with cocaine use disorder may come to treatment with mood disorder symptom severity greater than that of the general population but still falling short of those with a mood disorder (Siqueland et al., 1999). Rigg and Monnat (2015) examined data from the 2010–2013 National Survey on Drug Use and Health in regard to three classes of substance users: heroin only, prescription opiate use only, and a combined heroin and prescription opiate use. They found that the individuals who misused prescription opiate medication and used heroin were greatly burdened by numerous psychiatric symptoms such as anxiety and depression. Their findings also mirror a common clinical finding in that many clients who started with prescription opiate misuse eventually moved over to heroin due to cost (heroin is much cheaper), rapid onset of effect (injection heroin much quicker onset of effect as opposed to oral opiate pills that must move through the first-pass metabolism before reaching circulation and causing an effect), and a tolerance developed to the oral opiate medication. A client with a co-occurring anxiety disorder with whom I once worked who experienced this very transition from prescription opiate to injection heroin explained the shift in substance in the following way:

> At some point, the oxy wasn't making me feel any less worried or sad or angry or anxious. I was just feeling blah. My friend suggested heroin and holy crap! I felt better. No more negative. No more sad. At least for a while. Could use more of it as it is a lot cheaper. Got a quicker rush from it. So, I never looked back. That's how I wound up here.

Bipolar Disorders

Bipolar disorder and SUDs are a common (e.g., Hawton, Sutton, Haw, Sinclair, & Harriss, 2005) and complex combination. Evidence from treatment populations indicates that one third of bipolar clients met the old *DSM-IV* abuse or dependence criteria (Baethge et al., 2005; Bauer et al., 2005). The co-occurring relationship between these disorders complicates the course and duration of the bipolar depressive and manic episodes (Strakowski & DelBello, 2000). These clients are also dangerous to self as they demonstrate medication nonadherence (Teter et al., 2011) as well as a higher risk for suicide (CSAT, 2009a; Comtois, Russo, Roy-Byrne, & Ries, 2004; Dalton, Cate-Carter, Mundo, Parikh, & Kennedy, 2003; Harris & Barraclough, 1997; Kessler, Borges, & Walters, 1999). Specifically, the mixed episode (most recent depressed and manic) bipolar client with rapid cycling seems to most commonly report a co-occurring SUD (Agrawal, Nurnberger, & Lynskey, 2011).

Psychotic Disorders

Psychotic symptoms are also common in SUDs, whether due to withdrawal, substance-induced, or non-substance-related co-occurring disorder (SAMHSA, 2005; Veatch & Becker, 2005). Hides et al. (2015) recently reported on the high proportion of methamphetamine users having co-occurring psychotic disorders. Hartz et al. (2014) found that severe psychotic disorders increased the risk for heavy alcohol use (OR = 4.0), heavy cannabis use (OR = 3.5), and recreational substance use (OR = 4.6). In regard to cannabis use, Johns (2001) discussed how cannabis use could induce psychosis, whereas Rubio et al. (2012) underscored the commonalities of symptoms between cannabis-induced psychotic disorder and a recent onset non-substance-related psychotic disorder. Though alcohol is found as significantly related with psychotic disorders, Jordaan and Emsley (2014) cautioned how little is actually known regarding alcohol-induced psychotic disorder, specifically in regard to how to distinguish the symptoms from alcohol withdrawal delirium or schizophrenia. Thus, there may be ample cases of misdiagnosis.

One of the most interesting issues regarding psychotic disorders and substance use rests in the debate regarding the antipsychotic quality of opiates. This dialogue dates as far back as the early 1970s when there was some discussion regarding the antipsychotic qualities of heroin (Wellisch, Gay, Wesson, & Smith, 1971). More recently, 23 psychotic heroin-dependent patients, at their first agonist opioid treatment, were compared with 209 nonpsychotic individuals. Findings showed that psychotic heroin-dependent clients presented for agonist opioid treatment demonstrating more severe psychopathology but a shorter, less severe addiction history than the nonpsychotic comparison group. Maremmani et al. (2012) reasoned that since the psychotic clients requested agonist opioid treatment earlier, and with a less severe addiction history, these clients primarily benefited from an opioid medication alleviating their psychiatric symptoms and not necessarily their heroin addiction. However, Maremmani and colleagues noted that psychotic symptoms may also develop after substance use (i.e., heroin) onset, thus confusing the non-substance-related versus substance-induced diagnostic deliberation.

This finding supports earlier research regarding how methadone maintenance helps prevent psychotic relapses in clients with a history of psychotic episodes. The cessation of methadone with these clients led to a reemergence of psychotic symptoms (Levinson, Galynker, & Rosenthal, 1995). Similarly, research involving heroin addicts admitted for inpatient treatment of manic and/or acute psychotic episodes found that regardless of the reasons for hospitalization, those receiving increasing dosages of methadone were found to be less in need of antimanic and antipsychotic drugs at discharge (Pacini & Maremmani, 2005). Interestingly, the proposed antipsychotic effects of methadone may make it challenging to effectively diagnose co-occurring disorders which are non-substance-related, such as schizophrenia. It may also dampen the psychotic features in some other disorders that commonly co-occur with SUD, such as severe major depressive disorder, which can contain a psychotic feature.

Personality Disorders

Rosenthal (2013) noted that ASPD and BPD are the two personality disorders most commonly associated with co-occurring SUD. Research shows that consistently high levels of comorbidity between SUDs and ASPD have been reported within samples of individuals with SUDs in treatment (Cottler, Price, Compton, & Mager, 1995). ASPD clients present as complex cases (Goldstein, Dawson, & Grant, 2010; Westermeyer & Thuras, 2005) and are associated with a more severe course of SUD (Ford et al., 2009; Hesselbrock, 1986). Among clients with co-occurring disorders, ASPD is associated with more severe addiction and worse overall functioning (Crocker et al., 2005). Furthermore, those diagnosed with co-occurring ASPD and another serious mental illness reported higher rates of substance misuse than those with serious mental illness but not co-occurring ASPD (Tengström, Hodgins, Grann, Långström, & Kullgren, 2004).

BPD is also prevalent within the SUD treatment population. One study (Sansone, Whitecar, & Wiederman, 2008) found a prevalence rate of BPD in those seeking buprenorphine treatment for opioid addiction exceeding 40%. Sansone and Wiederman (2009) found that nearly 50% of individuals with BPD reported a history of prescription drug misuse. A large survey found that 50.7% of individuals with a lifetime BPD diagnosis also qualified for a diagnosis of an SUD over the previous 12 months. This same survey found that for individuals with a lifetime diagnosis of an SUD, 9.5% also had a lifetime diagnosis of BPD (Grant et al., 2008).

Co-occurring SUD and BPD present a few challenges. Both BPD and SUD are associated with emotional dysregulation (Beatson & Rao, 2012) and high rates of disorder relapse (Darke, Ross, Williamson, & Teeson, 2005). Thus, differential diagnosis may be difficult if the client is in the midst of a depressive, manic, or mixed episode. BPD is difficult to treat primarily due to the pervasive and inflexible nature of personality disorders. Furthermore, BPD is linked with impulsivity, suicidality, and self-harm risks, and all these risk factors are likely exacerbated by substance use. Thus, it is plausible to conclude that BPD may contribute to the severity of SUD symptoms and that SUD treatment may be more complicated for clients who also have BPD (e.g., SAMHSA, 2014b), especially in regard to treatment alliance building (e.g., Luborsky, Barber, Siqueland, McLellan, & Woody, 1997). For instance, a large-scale study of alcohol-dependent inpatients showed that BPD alone was associated with a lifetime suicide attempt after controlling for other risk factors and personality disorders (Preuss, Koller, Barnow, Eikmeier, & Soyka, 2006). However, the role of other personality disorders in suicide attempts and suicide among individuals with SUDs is not well established (CSAT, 2009a). For example, a study of alcohol-dependent clients failed to find ASPD as significantly associated with suicide attempts, even after controlling for other risk factors (Preuss et al., 2006).

Posttraumatic Stress Disorder

PTSD is common in the SUD population (Coker, Stefanovics, & Rosenheck, 2016; Morgen, Maschi, Viola, & Zgoba, 2013; Saxon & Simpson, 2015), with one quarter to one third of SUD clients in treatment meeting PTSD diagnostic criteria (Dreissen et al., 2008). Those with a PTSD diagnosis have nearly a twofold risk of a lifetime SUD diagnosis (Pietrzak, Goldstein, Southwick, & Grant 2011). Furthermore, many SUD clients have a heightened risk of developing PTSD and/or other co-occurring psychiatric disorders (Green, Calhoun, Dennis, & Beckham, 2010). Like many other substances mirroring psychiatric symptoms, careful diagnostic deliberation is required with PTSD as many of the symptoms of this trauma disorder (such as arousal or reactivity) strongly resemble some symptoms of use and/or withdrawal (Saladin, Brady, Dansky, & Kilpatrick, 1995; Saxon & Simpson, 2015).

The exact nature of any causal relationship between SUD and PTSD is still not clear (Fontana, Rosenheck, & Desai, 2012), though there is clear empirical evidence showing that PTSD is associated with poorer substance use outcomes (Jacobsen, Southwick, & Kosten, 2001). The combination of PTSD and SUD is associated with complex clinical challenges because of the adverse relationship between these two disorders (Back, Waldrop, & Brady, 2009). For example, some research demonstrates that trauma cues can increase craving for addictive substances (Coffey et al., 2002).

In addition, Maschi and colleagues (Maschi, Gibson, Zgoba, & Morgen, 2011; Maschi, Morgen, & Viola, 2014; Maschi, Morgen, Zgoba, Courtney, & Ristow, 2011; Maschi, Viola, Morgen, & Koskinen, 2015) have noted the potential for consistent reexposure and retraumatization as a contributing factor in deteriorating psychiatric well-being. This phenomenon is also noted in the SUD literature. For instance, previous research found that 27% of active injecting substance users not receiving consistent treatment contacts experienced a new traumatic event each month (Peirce, Kolodner, Brooner, & Kidorf, 2012). Peirce and colleagues (2012) also noted how traumatic reexposure was associated with an increased risk of later drug use and a desire for SUD treatment. However, this desire for treatment does not lead to an increase in treatment admissions (Peirce, Brooner, Kolodner, Schacht, & Kidorf, 2013). Furthermore, a recent study underscored how 18% of methadone clients with a co-occurring psychiatric disorder were reexposed to a traumatic event each month during the 12-month study, and this trauma reexposure doubled the risk of SUD treatment interruption within the next 60 days (Peirce, Brooner, King, & Kidorf, in-press). Though in no way explanatory, it does point to how SUD clients may continually turn to substances as a trauma symptom coping mechanism and how the addiction is perpetuated if the individual is not actively engaged in treatment.

PROCESS ADDICTIONS

In discussions regarding co-occurring SUD and other disorders, the traditional bias has been to only consider substance use (e.g., alcohol, cocaine, heroin) and psychiatric disorders (e.g., anxiety, mood, trauma). However, the process addictions are also of critical relevance and play a role in the co-occurring disorder experience. Unfortunately, as of the *DSM-5* release, only one process addiction (pathological gambling) is considered an official *DSM-5* diagnosable disorder. This is despite the clinical, research, and anecdotal evidence that other process addictions do indeed exist. This next section covers pathological gambling as well as three others: sex addiction, food addiction, and nonsuicidal self-injury (NSSI).

Pathological Gambling

Pathological gambling is the only process addiction included in the *DSM-5* (APA, 2013, p. 585). This process addiction causes considerable problems across the areas of finances (debt, bankruptcy), family conflict, career/educational issues, as well as the experiencing of co-occurring psychiatric and/or SUDs (Ledgerwood & Petry, 2015). The criteria, in brief, target "persistent and problematic gambling behavior" that cause impairment over a 12-month period in four or more of the following ways: (1) an increasing need to gamble with greater amounts of money to achieve an exhilaration from the gambling; (2) restlessness and irritability when the individual tries to reduce or stop gambling; (3) repeated and unsuccessful efforts to reduce or cut down gambling; (4) a preoccupation with gambling; (5) gambles when experiencing negative affect and/or mood; (6) tries to "get even" immediately after losing large amounts of money: (7) lying to conceal gambling behaviors; (8) important family, relationship, work, or school obligations jeopardized or lost due to gambling; and (9) requires money from others to support gambling behaviors. Severity ratings are four or five criteria endorsed (mild), six or seven criteria (moderate), and eight or more criteria (severe).

Cowlishaw and Hakes (2015) cautioned that pathological gambling is a common but undetected diagnosis in the SUD population and that the presence of a gambling condition may highlight the presence of underlying psychopathology. Other reviews confirm their claim. Korman, Torneatto, and Skinner (2010) noted that pathological gambling typically occurs along with co-occurring disorders, citing SUDs (50% of cases), depression (72% to 76% of cases), and personality disorders (93% of cases) met the criteria for a *DSM* personality disorder diagnosis. Lorrains, Cowlishaw, and Thomas (2011) added to the evidence via their meta-analysis of 11 studies where they reported pathological gamblers experience high rates of co-occurring SUD (57.5%), mood disorder (37.9%), and anxiety disorder (37.4%).

Sex Addiction

Carnes (1983) introduced sex addiction to the recovery and treatment population. Unfortunately, though widely accepted within the mental health community, Southern, Ellison, and Hagwood (2015) indicted the persistent lack of a diagnostic consensus as the key explanation as to why there is still no inclusion of sex addiction within the *DSM*. For instance, the ICD of the WHO does include two relevant categories for sex addiction: There is "Excessive Sexual Drive," which is divided into satyriasis for males and nymphomania for females, and "Excessive Masturbation." However, Giugliano (2013) underscored the pertinent clarification needed as to what exactly is "excessive" in regard to quantifying sex drive and/or masturbation.

As emphasized by Hall (2014), there is no clear diagnostic paradigm for sex addiction. That sets up the paradox that even though the *DSM* refuses to include sex addiction as an official diagnostic option and the profession cannot agree on a diagnostic definition, there is still much known about sex addiction. For example, Kuzma and Black (2008) documented sexual behaviors by gender and showed that men are more likely to compulsively masturbate, use pornography, pay for sex, and have one-night stands, whereas women are more likely to engage in sex as a business transaction. Furthermore, Schwartz and Southern (1999) cautioned that women who engage in dysfunctional and out-of-control sexual behaviors likely also present with an adult attachment disorder and show difficulties with stress, intimacy expectations, and emotion regulation (Schneider & Schneider 2004). Southern (2002) hypothesized that the sexual behaviors are implemented in an effort to cope with stressors or psychological symptoms.

The closest yet to a clear diagnostic paradigm for sex addiction comes courtesy of Kafka (2010), who presented the hypersexual disorder criteria. In brief, for at least the past 6 months there needs to be recurrent and intense sexual urges and/or behaviors demonstrated in four or more of the following ways: (1) a great deal of time is spent on sexual fantasies or sexual behaviors; (2) the individual repeatedly engages in sexual fantasies and/or behaviors as a response to dysphoric mood; (3) the individual repeatedly engages in sexual fantasies and/or behaviors as a response to stressful life events; (4) there have been repeated unsuccessful efforts to cut down or cease the hypersexual fantasies, urges, and/or behaviors; and (5) the sexual fantasies, urges, and/or behaviors are continued despite the risk of harm to self and/or others. Kafka also includes specifiers regarding whether the sexual activity is focused on masturbation, pornography, sex with consenting adult(s), cybersex, phone sex, or strip clubs.

Food Addiction

The National Center on Addiction and Substance Abuse (2016) recently produced a comprehensive review of food addiction. Specifically, this report noted that similar to sex addiction, food addiction is not a recognized disorder in the *DSM-5*. The National Center on Addiction and Substance Abuse recommended using the Yale Food Addiction Scale (YFAS) (Gearhardt, Corbin, & Brownell, 2009), a valid and reliable measure, for the diagnostic assessment of a potential food addiction. The YFAS criteria are as follows:

1. Substance taken in larger amount and for longer period than intended;

2. Persistent desire or repeated unsuccessful attempts to quit;

3. Much time/activity to obtain, use, recover;

4. Important social, occupational, or recreational activities given up or reduced;

5. Use continues despite knowledge of adverse consequences (e.g., failure to fulfill role obligations, use in physically hazardous situations);

6. Tolerance (marked increase in amount; marked decrease in effect);

7. Characteristic withdrawal symptoms; substance taken to relieve withdrawal; and

8. Use causes clinically significant impairment or distress.

According to the YFAS, endorsement of three or more symptoms demonstrate clinically significant impairment or distress within the past 12 months and meets the criteria for a food addiction diagnosis.

The National Center on Addiction and Substance Abuse (2016) cautioned that individuals with *DSM-5* diagnosable eating disorders (e.g., anorexia nervosa, bulimia nervosa, and binge eating disorder) may demonstrate such addiction-related symptoms as obsessions, compulsions, or impulsivity. The report argued that there is a key difference between eating disorders and food addiction:

> Still, the emphasis in eating disorder research and treatment has concentrated less on food than on the individual's cognitions and feelings with regard to food and weight, whereas in addiction research and treatment, the power of the addictive substance to "hook" the person is paramount. The advent of the food addiction construct bridges these two traditions and, like substance addiction, puts significant emphasis on the target of the addiction: certain types of food (i.e., those that are highly palatable and usually highly processed or refined) and their ability to "hook" those with certain psychosocial vulnerabilities or risk factors. (p. 4)

The report also implied a similarity between food and sex addictions. Specifically, both are biologically common in all individuals and represent natural rewards for which the human system was designed. Thus, it is challenging to reduce the disordered and addictive eating (or sex) behaviors.

Nonsuicidal Self-Injury

I spent 4 months debating whether to include NSSI in the list of process addictions for this text. As discussed below, some may agree with my decision, whereas others will not. As with any text, the content is objective but the perspective through which the content is reviewed comes with an author bias. The review of the NSSI literature and my clinical experiences with individuals who engaged in NSSI and had co-occurring psychiatric and SUDs finally led me to take the stand that NSSI should be considered a process addiction. I will now briefly make the case as to why.

The *DSM-5* (APA, 2013) lists NSSI as a condition in need of further study. Though present in the manual, NSSI does not have an ICD-10/*DSM* diagnostic code. The proposed criteria stipulates that in the past year on at least five occasions the individual has engaged in "intentional, self-inflicted damage" such as cutting, burning, stabbing, punching, or excessive rubbing that is not culturally sanctioned (i.e., as part of a religious or cultural ceremony/ritual) (p. 803). Of importance, this damage is not inflicted as part of a suicidal act. As per the *DSM-5*, NSSI is inflicted for one or more of the following reasons: to seek relief from a negative emotion, to produce a positive emotion, and/or to resolve interpersonal difficulties. In addition, the NSSI occurs in the context of at least one or more of the following: negative affect/mood (e.g., anxiety, depression) in the lead-up to the NSSI act, preoccupation with the NSSI behavior that is difficult to control, and/or frequent rumination regarding NSSI acts (even if not acted upon).

A review of these proposed diagnostic criteria mirrors the experiences of those who struggle with SUDs. Furthermore, as discussed below, co-occurring psychiatric and SUDs are to be considered the norm, so why not co-occurring psychiatric and process addictions (such as the proposed process addiction of NSSI)? In brief, it appears that the individual with NSSI struggles with issues that overlap substantially with those of substance-related disorders—for instance, in the context of psychiatric difficulties via the experiencing of negative affect, mood, or thought; in the use of NSSI to cope with or counter these negative experiences; and in the uncontrollable thoughts (or obsessions) regarding NSSI acts. For example, a commonly cited study (Nixon, Cloutier, & Aggarwal, 2002) showed the similarity between NSSI and addiction. A sample of adolescents who engaged in NSSI were diagnostically evaluated via the *DSM-IV* (APA, 2000) substance abuse and dependence criteria but with the wording edited to accommodate NSSI and not substance use. The results showed that 97.6% of the adolescents met at least three of the seven substance dependence criteria and 81% met at least five of the dependence criteria.

I ask my substance use-disordered clients in recovery about their cravings and/or thoughts regarding substance use in each session. I do the same of my NSSI clients via asking about any NSSI ideation, intent, plans, or acts. I have seen similarities in the following scenarios:

- Both report a constant daily thinking about substance use or NSSI.
- Both report a heightened frequency and/or intensity of these thoughts when experiencing life stressors and/or co-occurring psychiatric disorder symptom flare-ups.
- After excessively using the substance or NSSI for years, they both have reported a tolerance effect. The NSSI clients have discussed not getting the same "relief" or "control" from the acts that they used to achieve. This causes them frustration as their principal coping skill is deteriorating.

These experiences of my NSSI clients sound quite analogous to the affect regulation function of NSSI discussed by some (e.g., Brain, Haines, & Williams, 2002). Buser and Buser (2013) agreed. They provided a comprehensive review of the NSSI literature and concluded that NSSI entails issues of compulsion, loss of control, continued use despite negative consequences, and the development of tolerance, which are all indicative of an addiction.

However, Victor, Glenn, and Klonsky (2012) did not see NSSI as a process addiction. Their reasons for excluding NSSI as a process addiction include the following:

- Substances are craved in a variety of contexts, while NSSI is craved only in context of negative emotion.
- Substance use is maintained via positive reinforcement (e.g., euphoric feelings due to intoxication), whereas NSSI is maintained via negative reinforcement (e.g., reduction of negative affect or mood).

Their argument may be flawed if you consider the co-occurring disorder paradigm as the norm and not the exception in all addictions. For instance, Zetterqvist (2015) reviewed numerous studies and demonstrated the high rates of various co-occurring disorders within the NSSI population such as anxiety, mood, substance use, and eating disorders as well as symptoms of emotional dysregulation and heightened general psychiatric distress. Consequently, it is plausible to suggest that—if you accept the co-occurring paradigm as the norm for all addictions (substance and process)—the positive reinforcement argument falls flat. Whether ingesting cocaine, gambling, being involved in excessive hypersexual behaviors, or engaging in an NSSI act such as cutting, the client is primarily engaged in negative reinforcement. The addiction is not perpetuated to induce a euphoric feeling as much as it is to use that euphoric feeling as a way to (temporarily) reduce the negative affect and/or mood they are experiencing. Addicted individuals do not so much chase the "high" as they instead perpetually return to their coping skill (i.e., the addiction) to escape the hurt.

SPECIAL POPULATIONS

Adolescents

Among adolescents, SUDs and psychiatric disorders exist within a bidirectional relationship, with each increasing the risk for the other (Essau, 2011). For example, a recent study found that 25% of 13- to 17-year-olds who received any type of psychiatric attention at a large medical center presented with at least one co-occurring

SUD (Wu, Gersing, Burchett, Woody, & Blazer, 2011). The 2013 Treatment Episode Data Set (SAMHSA, Center for Behavioral Health Statistics and Quality, 2015) showed that 27.1% of the adolescents admitted for SUD treatment also presented with a co-occurring psychiatric disorder diagnosis. Table 3.1 reports on the most commonly reported substances by adolescents at admission. Many of these substances, as discussed throughout this chapter, have a direct or indirect relationship with psychiatric symptoms. However, many of the normative thoughts, emotions, and behaviors experienced during adolescence may resemble psychiatric symptoms, thus blurring the diagnostic clarity for addressing co-occurring disorders (Brown et. al., 2008).

Virtually any psychiatric disorder may occur with SUDs, such as any of the following:

- Attention-deficit/hyperactivity disorder
- Oppositional defiant disorder
- Conduct disorder
- Depression
- Anxiety disorders
- Posttraumatic stress disorder
- Bipolar disorder
- Psychotic disorder

So similar to adult SUD, there is a large commonality of symptoms shared by the substance use and psychiatric disorders. A few recent studies underscore this complexity. First, Saranga and Coffey (2010) demonstrated the innate complexity in adolescent co-occurring disorders cases via the review of an adolescent demonstrating manic and schizophrenic symptoms along with cannabis and other substance misuse.

Table 3.1 Substances Reported at Admission in Minors Ages 12 to 17 Years (Minimum 5%): SAMHSA Treatment Episode Data Set (2013) Results

Substance	N	%
Alcohol	46,010	45.3%
Marijuana	11,517	11.3%
Other Opiates	5,951	5.9%
Methamphetamine	5,573	5.5%

Source: SAMHSA (2015).

Second, Milin (2013) reviewed the strong association between bipolar disorder and SUD onsets within an adolescent population. What both of these studies also emphasize is that there is still much to know regarding the intersection of substance use and psychiatric disorders in adolescents.

Consequently, in regard to adolescents, it is the collateral report from parents, family, teachers, and school counselors (among others) that first tip off the potential for a substance use issue. Though not exhaustive, there are behavioral and cognitive signs/symptoms to look for, which include the following:

- Change in overall attitude/personality with no other identifiable cause
- Changes in friends, new hang-outs, sudden avoidance of old crowd, doesn't want to talk about new friends, friends are known drug users
- Change in activities or hobbies (e.g., giving up sports)
- Drop in grades at school or performance at work
- Change in habits at home, loss of interest in family and family activities
- Difficulty in paying attention, forgetfulness, blackouts
- General lack of motivation, energy, self-esteem, "I don't care" attitude
- Sudden oversensitivity, temper tantrums, or resentful behavior
- Moodiness, irritability, nervousness, aggressiveness, depression or suicidality
- Paranoia
- Confusion
- Excessive need for privacy
- Secretive or suspicious behavior
- Car accidents
- Taking risks, including sexual risks
- Chronic dishonesty
- Unexplained need for money, stealing money or items
- Change in personal grooming habits
- Possession of drug paraphernalia
- Use of room deodorizers and incense

In addition, there are numerous physical signs associated with substance use, intoxication, or withdrawal in adolescents, and these include the following:

- Change in appetite
- Unexplained weight loss or gain
- Poor physical coordination
- Sleep difficulties
- Red, watery eyes; pupils larger or smaller than usual

- Smell of substance on breath, body, or clothes
- Extreme hyperactivity, excessive talkativeness
- Runny nose, persistent hacking cough
- Nausea, vomiting, or excessive sweating
- Tremors of hands, feet, or head
- Irregular heartbeat, rapid heartbeat, chest pain
- Difficulty breathing
- Difficulty speaking
- Dark-colored urine

The *DSM-IV* (APA, 2000) substance abuse/dependence criteria were designed for adults and did not fit well with adolescent substance use clinical presentation. For example, adolescents may experience substance use issues without signs of withdrawal or physiological dependence (Stewart & Brown, 1995). In addition, Chung and Martin (2001) noted how some degree of tolerance is considered normal in adolescent substance use. Thus, some key *DSM-IV* diagnostic criteria are muddied in an adolescent population. As it stands now, evidence suggests that the *DSM-5* did not improve upon this flaw.

Winters, Martin, and Chung (2011) reported on some areas of the *DSM-5* with questionable validity when applied to adolescent substance users. First, as discussed earlier, tolerance may be normative in adolescent and young adult drinkers (Chung, Martin, Winters, Cornelius, & Langenbucher, 2004) in that it is easier to meet this criterion earlier in the career of the substance user. Thus, a younger user would have had fewer years of substance use history. Second, withdrawal symptoms are rare in adolescents because they only emerge after years of heavy drug use. Third, the hazardous use criterion is questionable. For instance, Winters, Martin, and Chung argued how hazardous use is developmentally bound and more common in adults (likely due to adolescents having less access to dangerous contexts while using, such as driving a car). Fourth, Winters, Martin, and Chung discussed that more research is needed to determine the effectiveness of the craving criterion for adolescents. Fifth, Winters, Martin, and Chung also pointed toward more research being needed for the severity criteria of the 2/11 threshold for SUD in youth, citing how this may wind up diagnosing many mild SUD cases that may not reflect the true definition of an SUD.

In addition, this is another adolescent-specific pragmatic issue for SUDs and the *DSM-5*. The switch to *DSM-5* eliminated the substance abuse diagnostic category. As a reminder, the old *DSM-IV* (APA, 2000) substance abuse criteria involved a pattern of substance use leading to clinically significant impairment or distress, as manifested by one (or more) of the following, occurring within a 12-month period:

1. Recurrent substance use resulting in a failure to fulfill major role obligations at work, school, or home (e.g., repeated absences or poor work performance related to substance use; substance-related absences, suspensions, or expulsions from school; neglect of children or household).

2. Recurrent substance use in situations in which it is physically hazardous (e.g., driving an automobile or operating a machine when impaired by substance use).

3. Recurrent substance-related legal problems (e.g., arrests for substance-related disorderly conduct).

4. Continued substance use despite having persistent or recurrent social or interpersonal problems caused or exacerbated by the effects of the substance (e.g., arguments with spouse about consequences of intoxication, physical fights).

A common treatment occurrence is a client referred/mandated by his or her high school to receive an assessment and possibly receive some brief treatment intervention for substance use. This usually involves a scenario such as a high school student who was caught on school grounds smoking marijuana. Considering that marijuana (in my practicing state of New Jersey) is an illegal substance, coupled with the school's zero tolerance policy, the high school student can get in some trouble at school, which usually involves the need for an assessment.

Many of these high school students may not be addicted to marijuana. You could argue that they are "casual" or "recreational" users. In these instances, they typically wind up endorsing only one of the above substance abuse criteria, usually using when hazardous, poor academic work performance, or continued use despite persistent social/interpersonal problems. However, as per the *DSM-IV* (APA, 2000), one endorsed criterion was the minimum number needed for a diagnosable substance abuse disorder, so they would be diagnosed as cannabis abuse, and that diagnosis was sent over to their (parent's) medical insurance plan. Insurance plans need a diagnosable disorder that is biologically based (thus the reason why the adjustment disorders and v-codes can possibly receive some third-party reimbursement resistance).

However, *DSM-5* (APA, 2013) now requires that at least two criteria be endorsed for a mild SUD diagnosis. In addition, the unspecified other (or unknown) substance-related disorder articulates the following:

This category applies to presentations in which symptoms characteristic of an other (or unknown) substance-related disorder that causes clinically significant distress or impairment in social, occupational, or other important areas of functioning predominate but do not meet the full criteria for any specific other (or unknown) substance-related disorder or any of the disorders in the substance-related disorders diagnostic classes. (p. 585)

Here, this diagnostic choice is not an option as it seems to better reflect an atypical collection of substance use symptoms, with the key term being the plural symptoms. As written, it does not seem to imply that this diagnosis can be used when the person only meets one of the SUD criteria.

In the instances listed above, the high school students would not be diagnosable for an SUD. The students only present with one symptom, and despite a thorough assessment, only seem to experience that one symptom as a casual user. In this case, they are more diagnosable for "poor decision making" for smoking on school grounds. But the schools still want an assessment. And health care coverage for the session is usually only obtainable if there is a diagnosis. So at the end of the session, there is a dilemma in that your client does not have a *DSM-5* diagnosis due to having only one criterion endorsed. Now the parents, who expected to pay nothing more than the co-pay, may have to cover the full session as benefits may be denied. Furthermore, some schools request that the student have a few sessions with a counselor as part of the intervention process. Without a diagnosable (for example in this instance) cannabis use disorder, will this be possible?

In brief, something to consider is that schools were used to the *DSM-IV* substance abuse diagnosis as being an easy catchall where zero tolerance policy, school discipline, and counseling intervention all met. That paradigm does not exist any longer. Consequently, it could be possible that you encounter a student and his or her family who were encouraged (or mandated) to seek an assessment and perhaps some counseling sessions. But this student is not *DSM-5* diagnosable for an SUD. This type of case, based on anecdotal evidence from colleagues nationwide and my own experiences, is becoming common.

Older Adults

Substance use within the older adult population continues to rise (Han, Gfroerer, Colliver, & Penne, 2009), and the challenges of older adult SUDs are documented in a quickly growing body of research (e.g., Blow & Barry, 2014; Morgen et al., 2013; Salmon & Forester, 2012; Satre, 2013). For instance, recent national data demonstrated that of the population 60 years old and older, 5.4% reported illegal drug use in the past year (SAMHSA, 2014a). Liu and Satterfield (2015) underscored that numerous complications exist for older adults with SUD. For instance, older adults may be more sensitive to substances ingested at low levels (CSAT, 1998), have interactions between substances and prescribed medications (Pringle, Ahern, Heller, Gold, & Brown, 2005; CSAT, 1998), demonstrate increased tolerance levels (Schonfeld & MacFarland, 2015), and struggle with increased dementia and other cognitive impairments (Doweiko, 2015).

There are a few key issues relevant to diagnosing older adults. First, older adults may be more likely than younger adults to demonstrate and experience SUDs while not meeting the diagnostic criteria. For example, a study using *DSM-IV* abuse/dependence criteria found that 19% of clients age 55 and older did not meet the dependence criteria (Satre, Mertens, Areán, & Weisner, 2003). It is still unclear as to whether this issue would also occur with the *DSM-5* SUD criteria. Second, Moore, Beck, Barbor, Hays, and Reuben (2002) cautioned that older adults may experience AUD problems without experiencing tolerance or physiological dependence. The amount of alcohol considered problematic differs in older adults when compared to younger drinkers (i.e., 49 years old and younger). The National Institute on Alcohol Abuse and Alcoholism (2005) stipulated no more than three standard alcohol drinks per day. Satre, Gordon, and Weisner (2007) presented maximum alcoholic drinks per day as one (for women) or two (for men). Consequently, there is not a rigid benchmark for problematic drinking. Third, issues of early or late-life onset of the SUD are still unclear, with some evidence indicating late onset SUD is less severe than SUD developed earlier in life (Satre, Chi, Mertens, & Weisner, 2012). Fourth, are symptoms of substance intoxication and/or withdrawal simply dismissed as being what older people do (Morgen, 2015)?

In addition to alcohol and illegal drug use, older adults also struggle with prescription medication. Older adults (age 65 and older) may consume large amounts of over-the-counter (OTC) medications, many of which have strong abuse potentials (Simoni-Wastila & Yang, 2006; Simoni-Wastila, Zuckerman, Singhal, Briesacher, & Hsu, 2006). Medications with strong abuse potential include benzodiazepines (for anxiety, insomnia, or seizures), opioids (for pain), and stimulants (for weight management or attention/concentration). Wu and Blazer (2011) noted that adults ages 50 to 64 years old were more likely to misuse prescription medications than their peers ages 65 years and older. However, these individuals in their 50s and early 60s will eventually grow into adults ages 65 and older. Furthermore, older adults with cognition issues are at risk of taking medications that further impair cognition (Weston, Weinstein, Barton, & Yaffe, 2010).

Interestingly, SAMHSA TEDS (2013) data show that alcohol is by far the most commonly reported substance at admission (regardless of primary, secondary, or

Table 3.2   Substances Reported at Admission in Adults Age 55 Years and Older (Minimum 5%): SAMHSA Treatment Episode Data Set (2013) Results

Substance	N	%
Alcohol	91,182	72.8%
Cocaine/Crack	25,334	20.2%
Heroin	23,344	18.6%
Marijuana	18,009	14.4%
Other Opiates	10,093	8.1%

Source: SAMHSA (2015).

tertiary designation). Table 3.2 shows that other opioid use (i.e., prescription pain medication) was a far less commonly reported substance. This may point to either the client underreporting, the counselor missing the degree of opioid use, and/or the older adult pattern of using opioids in combination with alcohol.

QUESTIONS TO CONSIDER AS YOU MOVE ON TO CHAPTER 4

Question 1: Considering the neurocognitive deficits from Chapter 1 in regard to memory, how would long-term substance use influence an early (a few weeks) recovery client's ability to accurately report temporal or other more sophisticated diagnostic data? How would you work around this issue (or can you)?

Question 2: In Chapter 2, we discussed interviewing and assessment. How do you see the DSM-5 diagnostic criteria interacting with these assessments? As a clinician, if the endorsed DSM-5 diagnostic criteria for SUD tell a different story than a substance use instrument, which of the two would you "trust" more and why? How would this discrepancy influence your further interviewing, assessment, and diagnostic efforts?

Chapter 4

TREATMENT MODALITIES AND CLIENT PLACEMENT

This chapter covers the various settings where substance use disorder (SUD) treatment occurs. Critical to this chapter is the fact that addiction is a chronic disorder. Consequently, there is a sequential component to the treatment process. The client starts at a level appropriate for higher severity, and the level of care adjusts as the client severity decreases or increases. Unfortunately, some persuasive bodies (e.g., insurance companies) dictate length-of-stay limits that are the antithesis of the needs of a client with a chronic disorder. That is why in this chapter you see the constant notes leading you to think about how this process is applied in the real-world, third-party reimbursable context within which we all work. In specific, the chapter covers detoxification services, inpatient and outpatient levels of care, along with the treatment placement procedures to best match client need with level of care. As you can see in Table 4.1, there are numerous subcategories within each level of care. Each is addressed below, starting with detoxification services.

Table 4.1 Type of Care: National Survey of Substance Abuse Treatment Services

Level of Care	National Number of Programs
Outpatient	
Outpatient	11,542
Intensive Outpatient	6,363
Partial Hospitalization or Day Treatment	1,742

Level of Care	National Number of Programs
Detoxification	1,362
Pharmacotherapy (e.g., Vivitrol, Buprenorphine)	1,848
Inpatient/Residential (Non-Hospital)	
Short-Term Residential	1,736
Long-Term Residential	2,858
Detoxification	861
Hospital-Based Inpatient/Residential	
Any Type of Treatment	753
Detoxification	660

Source: SAMHSA (2013).

DETOXIFICATION SERVICES

Doweiko (2015) stressed that detoxification programs are not a form of treatment but rather serve as a prerequisite phase to assist the SUD client to safely withdraw from substance use while having medical and psychological monitoring/control of withdrawal symptoms. The primary clinical question is whether medically supervised detoxification is warranted and whether this process should occur on an inpatient or outpatient basis, as detoxification services are available at varying inpatient and outpatient settings. Brick (2008) underscored how the withdrawal process from some substances (such as benzodiazepines or barbiturates) can be life threatening and must be conducted under close medical supervision. Regardless of detoxification location, it is imperative that detoxification serve as a prelude to treatment. This must be emphasized prior to any detoxification program implementation. This is because time and again research shows that clients who successfully finish a detoxification program but do not follow up with SUD treatment are far more prone to a relapse (Craig, 2004).

CSAT (2006a) reviewed some general questions a clinician must ask when making the determination of inpatient or outpatient detoxification: (1) Is there a history of withdrawal-related seizures or delirium? If yes, then inpatient detoxification is recommended; (2) Is there a co-occurring psychiatric and/or medical disorder (or evidence of such) or a history of suicidal ideation or acts? If the answer is yes to any of these criteria, then inpatient detoxification is again warranted; and (3) Is the client seemingly motivated and willing to adhere to the withdrawal process? If the answer is no (or if there are doubts), then inpatient detoxification is recommended.

Even though these questions are general, the actual detoxification process is quite specific. Different substances require a different approach to detoxification due to the unique symptoms and severity of the withdrawal process caused by different substances. Although as a counselor you will not be primarily responsible for managing the withdrawal process (this is a function of an addiction psychiatrist and other physicians/nurses), you should know about the process for two reasons: first, as a counselor, you may work in a detoxification program in a mental health support role, and second, many of your clients may come to you directly or indirectly from a detoxification program. Consequently, an understanding of the general process will enhance your ability to work with the client. Thus, withdrawal symptom onset, withdrawal symptom experiences, and pharmacotherapy information are reviewed for the substances that currently have an established or developing pharmacotherapy process in the detoxification process.

Alcohol

Onset. The onset of alcohol withdrawal tends to occur 6 to 24 hours post last drink. However, if the individual consumes a benzodiazepine (e.g., Xanax), the withdrawal onset may be delayed. Be warned that heavy drinkers (those with a *Diagnostic and Statistical Manual of Mental Disorders* [5th ed.; *DSM-5*; American Psychiatric Association (APA), 2013] severe alcohol use disorder) may actually experience withdrawal symptoms by only reducing their daily alcohol intake (as opposed to complete cessation of drinking). The withdrawal period typically runs 2 to 3 days without any medical management but could run upward of 10 days.

Withdrawal Symptoms. Alcohol produces numerous withdrawal symptoms (as discussed in the *DSM-5* withdrawal diagnosis criteria) across three general areas. There is autonomic nervous system overactivity as demonstrated by sweating, rapid heart rate, tremors, insomnia, and hypertension. Gastrointestinal issues demonstrate via symptoms that include indigestion, nausea, and vomiting. Cognitive issues are demonstrated via vivid dreams, hallucinations, or delirium. Another cognitive issue in alcohol withdrawal is grand mal (i.e., generalized) seizures, which occur in about 5% of all alcohol withdrawal cases and can occur within 7 to 24 hours after the last drink.

The most severe alcohol withdrawal symptom is the experience of delirium tremens (DTs) which may occur within 2 to 5 days of the last drink (or alcohol reduction in a heavy, chronic drinker) and constitutes a medical emergency. The DTs may last anywhere from 3 days to upward of 14 days. Clients who present with a history of DTs—by default—experienced an intense withdrawal process that may have included cognitive disorientation, gross tremors, extreme agitation that may have required restraints, paranoid ideation, and/or hallucinations.

Medical Treatment. Symptom-triggered benzodiazepine treatment is the current standard of care in alcohol detoxification to manage symptoms and avoid the more severe withdrawal stages. Trials comparing different benzodiazepines demonstrated that all appear equally effective in the reduction of withdrawal symptoms (Mayo-Smith, 1997; Mayo-Smith et al., 2004). Mayo-Smith (1997), among others, recommended a long-lasting benzodiazepine (diazepam) for treating alcohol withdrawal. Recommendations are to implement diazepam treatment as early as possible in the withdrawal process to prevent the client from regressing to a more severe withdrawal experience. However, Breggin (2013) noted that lorazepam is a preferred benzodiazepine because it can be administered intravenously, intramuscularly, or orally with consistent results. Other medical issues relevant to alcohol detoxification, such as nausea or dehydration, are treated with varying medications and/or intravenous rehydration procedures.

Unique to alcohol detoxification and withdrawal is the risk of Wernicke's encephalopathy and Korsakoff's psychosis. In brief, Wernicke's encephalopathy is the experience of neurological symptoms caused by biochemical lesions of the central nervous system after exhaustion of B-vitamin reserves, in particular thiamine (vitamin B1). Thiamine deficiency is common in chronic heavy drinkers. If left untreated it can become Korsakoff's psychosis, which can produce permanent brain damage and result in memory loss. Consequently, one other medical intervention during the alcohol detoxification period is the provision of daily thiamine.

Benzodiazepines

Onset. Withdrawal occurs approximately 2 to 5 days post last use, with the maximum experience of symptoms somewhere between 7 and 10 days after last use.

Withdrawal Symptoms. Withdrawal from this depressant produces "rebound" symptoms on the opposite side of the spectrum. For example, withdrawal consists of numerous typical symptoms including anxiety, insomnia, agitation, irritability, and poor memory or concentration. Though not as common, nightmares, depersonalization, increased sensory perception, ataxia, and panic attacks may also occur. In extreme and uncommon cases, psychotic symptoms and cognitive confusion may also occur.

Medical Treatment. Similar to alcohol, a long-acting benzodiazepine such as diazepam is the preferred medical intervention to facilitate a healthy and safe detoxification process.

Opioids

Onset. Withdrawal from a short-acting substance such as heroin begins 6 to 24 hours after last use, reaches its peak within 24 to 48 hours, and tends to fully resolve in 5 to 10 days. A longer-acting opioid (such as methadone) usually produces withdrawal symptoms 36 to 48 hours after the last dose. The length of the withdrawal is longer and can run anywhere between 3 and 6 weeks (O'Brien, 2006).

Withdrawal Symptoms. The withdrawal experience can produce restlessness, anxiety, piloerection, excessive sweating, rhinorrhea, muscle twitching, gastrointestinal issues, hot and cold flashes, and insomnia. Opiate withdrawal syndrome is quite similar to a severe case of the flu sometimes coupled with psychiatric symptoms such as anxiety. Though unpleasant, opiate withdrawal is not a life-threatening condition (unlike alcohol withdrawal) unless there is a concurrent life-threatening medical condition exacerbated by the physical toll of the opiate withdrawal. Although most patients complain of symptoms of withdrawal, such as cramping or insomnia, these symptoms are tolerable, and initiation of drug therapy can be avoided in many cases.

Medical Treatment. Past pharmacotherapy for opioid withdrawal utilized methadone, a synthetic opiate. Methadone is administered in decreasing doses over a period not exceeding 30 days (for short-term detoxification) or 180 days (for long-term detoxification). A recent review of the research (Amato, Davoli, Minozzi, Ali, & Ferri, 2005) found that slow tapering with temporary substitution of long-acting opioids can reduce withdrawal severity. One issue with methadone treatment was that federal restrictions limited the distribution to a small number of methadone clinics. Thus, there was an inconvenience factor that inhibited the detoxification process. Furthermore, there were limited provisions for home or medical office administration of methadone due to concerns regarding the diversion of the methadone to illicit use (i.e., use of methadone to get high or unlawful sale of methadone).

These concerns were first addressed in 2000 with the passage of the Drug Addiction Treatment Act (DATA), which legalized the office-based management of opioid addiction. This was not legal prior to DATA due to the existing federal laws that had prohibited physicians from prescribing a narcotic for the sole purpose of maintaining the individual in a narcotic-addicted state. Next, in 2002, buprenorphine was approved for opioid withdrawal treatment. The first of two formulations approved, Subutex, contains only buprenorphine and is intended for use at the beginning of treatment. The other, Suboxone, contains both buprenorphine and the opiate antagonist naloxone, and is intended to be used in maintenance treatment of opiate addiction. The use of buprenorphine for medically supervised opioid withdrawal provides a transition from physical dependence to an opioid-free state with minimal withdrawal symptoms (CSAT, 2004a; Orman & Keating, 2009).

CSAT (2004a) reviewed the guidelines for buprenorphine use, which consists of an induction phase and a dose-reduction phase. Recommendations are that patients dependent on short-acting opioids (e.g., oxycodone, heroin) be inducted directly onto buprenorphine/naloxone tablets. The use of buprenorphine (either as buprenorphine alone or the buprenorphine/naloxone combination treatment) to taper off long-acting opioids should be considered only for those patients who have evidence of sustained medical and psychosocial stability. The maintenance treatment with buprenorphine consists of three phases: (1) induction, (2) stabilization, and (3) maintenance. Induction begins the process of switching from the opioid of addiction to buprenorphine. The goal is to find the minimum dose of buprenorphine at which the patient discontinues or greatly diminishes use of other opioids and shows no withdrawal symptoms, minimal to no side effects, and no opioid craving. The stabilization phase begins when no withdrawal symptoms are experienced, there are minimal or no side effects, and no uncontrollable cravings. The longest period that a patient is on buprenorphine is the maintenance phase. This phase may be indefinite.

Stimulants

Onset. Symptoms of withdrawal for amphetamines typically start about 2 to 4 days after last use, peak in severity at around 7 to 10 days, and subside within 2 to 4 weeks. Cocaine withdrawal symptoms start 1 to 2 days after last use, peak in severity at around 4 to 7 days, and subside within 1 to 2 weeks (Breggin, 2013).

Withdrawal Symptoms. Typically, withdrawal symptoms are not a medical emergency but can cause discomfort. The symptoms include fluctuation in mood or energy levels, disrupted sleep including insomnia and/or vivid dreams, general body aches, muscle tension, and the potential for paranoid delusions or hallucinations (Breggin, 2013).

Medical Treatment. Two recent examples demonstrate the attempts to introduce pharmacotherapy into cocaine detoxification and withdrawal treatment. The first, bromocriptine, a dopamine antagonist at low dosages and an agonist at high dosages, has been used to treat cocaine withdrawal symptoms and to reduce cocaine craving. The use of bromocriptine follows the hypothesis that chronic cocaine use depletes dopamine reserves; therefore, the use of a dopamine agonist could activate dopamine receptors. Despite initially promising findings, there is still no evidence that supports the efficacy of bromocriptine to reduce cocaine use or craving (Gorelick & Wilkins, 2006).

A more recent approach is the use of the cocaine vaccine. When cocaine is ingested, it passes into the bloodstream and then into the brain, where it greatly increases dopamine levels and produces its effects. The vaccine's purpose is to help the body's immune system make antibodies against cocaine. Then when cocaine is ingested, the antibodies bind to the cocaine and keep cocaine from crossing into the brain. This basically inhibits the pleasurable effects of the substance. Unfortunately, results have been mixed regarding the ability of the vaccine to blunt cravings and assist with withdrawal symptoms (Kosten et al., 2014; Martell et al., 2009).

INPATIENT TREATMENT

Surprisingly, there is no standard definition of inpatient SUD treatment (Weiss, Potter, Sharpe, & Iannucci, 2008), but basically, inpatient care refers to a variety of treatment forms in varying settings (Weiss & Dreifuss, 2015). Residential treatment programs provide a 24-hour treatment experience and offer a more intensive focus on recovery than outpatient treatment programs (Work Group on Substance Use Disorders, 2007). Some residential programs offer all services in-house, whereas other programs may schedule external appointments with psychiatrists, psychologists, social workers, physicians, and other specialists as needed. The decision to utilize inpatient as opposed to an outpatient treatment is based on the assessed need for a specific level of care.

In general, individuals referred to inpatient SUD treatment are assessed as in need of a more intensive level of care than those referred for outpatient treatment. Inpatient care has the advantage of removing the individual from their living environment so that psychosocial coping skills can be taught (e.g., drug refusal skills) in a substance-free environment. Furthermore, the impact of environmental cues on craving experiences can be explored so that effective coping skills can be cultivated, thus decreasing the potential for relapse. Inpatient care also permits for a 24-hour level of care for individuals struggling with nutritional and/or medical issues. For example, the National Institute on Drug Abuse (2016) cites hypertension, diabetes, hepatitis, sexually transmitted diseases, and coronary disease as some common ailments found within the SUD treatment population. Furthermore, these illnesses are sometimes only first diagnosed in the treatment facility.

Inpatient programs are housed in a medical center, freestanding facility, or in a therapeutic community (TC) setting. Some of these inpatient treatment formats are discussed below. However, many of the services provided exist in all inpatient settings.

Medical Center

Medical center SUD treatment programs offer a range of services that include access to medical treatment and stabilization for ongoing medical problems (related and unrelated to SUD) as well as the standard group, individual, marital/ family therapy programs, and psychoeducational programs, and social service support. Many of these programs used to utilize the Minnesota model, which was developed for alcohol dependency (under the old *DSM* system) but was broadened to all substances. The Minnesota model centers around the treatment team approach in which the addiction counselor, psychologist, physician, nurse, and others made recommendations for clinical areas to focus on, and the document that emerged from this process was the treatment plan. However, there was no definite time frame for treatment length. Health care insurance now demands shorter stays for inpatient clients as evidenced by the common (and arbitrary) 28-day length of stay. Countless times in my career I have seen inpatient clients who were discharged from inpatient care due to the insurance plan refusing to cover the costs for an extended stay beyond 28 days as opposed to a clinical decision made in the best interest of client care. Thus, the original version of the Minnesota model has fallen out of favor, though various components of the model (e.g., interdisciplinary treatment team) remain. In brief, the original Minnesota model may have been popular due to the fact that when developed, there was no other formalized alcohol treatment program available (Willenbring, 2010), and some evidence even suggests that the model is not that effective (Hester & Squires, 2004). It simply was the only game in town, so it naturally became quite popular and synonymous with inpatient SUD treatment at a time prior to the health care insurance model we have today.

Therapeutic Community

De Leon (2000) provided an exhaustive review of the TC history. In brief, the original TC model started in the 1960s as a self-help, milieu-style alternative to the traditional SUD treatment programs at that time (i.e., the Minnesota model). TCs of yesteryear were dramatically different than the models in use today. In the early years of TCs, the focus was on aggressive and harsh "ego-stripping" confrontation-type therapeutic techniques. Two such techniques best reflect this old style of TC work. The first, the 24-hour marathon group, was, as it is stated, an all-day/night intervention and group counseling session with the purpose of moving the TC client toward a recovery-focused/drug-free mentality. The second, the "hot seat" session, was where a member was confronted by all group members regarding personality flaws that inhibit recovery. Counselors in the TC were considered "paraprofessionals" in that most did not possess the graduate degrees we see in programs today. Rather, they were former TC clients themselves who (depending on the era and the state) may not have had any state-sanctioned addiction certification. The most common level of education for the TC counseling staff was a high school diploma or general equivalency diploma (GED).

The TCs today are markedly different in that they now serve as a host for varying programs, including short- and long-term residential and day treatment, as well as serving those with co-occurring SUD and psychiatric disorder (De Leon, 2000). Basically, many of the components of a TC also apply to freestanding clinic programs (Morgen & Kressel, 2002). In addition, as per state mandates, most treatment staff possess graduate degrees and counseling/addiction counseling licenses/ certifications. However, at the core, the TC remains consistent in the view that SUD is actually a disorder of the entire person. De Leon (2000) used the term *habilitation* instead of *rehabilitation*, arguing that the individual never effectively learned basic coping and life management skills, thus turning to substances. The TC habilitates the individual toward a total lifestyle change without the need for substance use (De Leon, 2000) across four areas (Kressel, De Leon, Palij, & Rubin, 2000): (1) developmental, (2) socialization, (3) psychological, and (4) community membership. Positive behavioral, cognitive, and emotional changes across these four areas are hypothesized to facilitate an effective habilitation and provide a strong foundation for substance-free living.

The TC uses a highly structured daily program to achieve this change, as the principal hypothesis is that the community is the agent of change (De Leon, 1997). Within this community-as-change-agent model, there exists a strong emphasis on self-reflection and acceptance of personal responsibility that permeates all facets of community life, such as the daily chores and duties, group or individual counseling, and the mentoring of new TC clients (Kerr, 2015). As with any SUD treatment program, varying versions of group counseling are supplemented with individual counseling and peer interactions in an effort to facilitate lasting change (De Leon, 2015).

For longer-term TC programs, De Leon (2000) advocated for a three-stage model. Stage 1 (orientation) lasts for approximately 60 days and entails an assimilation into the TC milieu treatment model; Stage 2 (primary treatment) occurs in months 2 through 12 and involves the principal components of treatment that facilitate habilitation and total personal change; and Stage 3 (reentry) runs from months 13 through 24 and entails more advanced treatment components, maintenance of changes achieved, the further development of autonomous thought and behavior without substance use, and the acquisition of vocational and/or educational skills (e.g., job training or the provision of in-house educational services for obtaining the GED).

OUTPATIENT TREATMENT

Unlike inpatient treatment, outpatient treatment is more clearly defined. Specifically, outpatient SUD treatment is defined as a nonresidential program focused on SUD treatment and recovery and utilizing a variety of treatment approaches such as individual counseling, group counseling, marital/family counseling, and psychoeducation

(CSAT 2006a; CSAT 2006b). Outpatient SUD treatment is quite common (Work Group on Substance Use Disorders, 2007). For example, the 2013 SAMSHA TEDS admissions data indicated that 60.1% of all SUD treatment admissions were in an outpatient setting, as compared to only 16.9% admitted to an inpatient setting (see Table 4.2). In fact, these 2013 admissions data reflect that more SUD treatment clients were admitted to a detox program than an inpatient treatment program!

In general, outpatient care integrates group and individual counseling with other services such as relapse prevention, anger or stress management, educational programs, job skills training, and marital/family counseling. Most programs adhere to the 12-step philosophy in some manner and may mandate Alcoholics Anonymous/ Narcotics Anonymous meeting attendance as part of a treatment plan. CSAT (2006a, 2006b) stressed that substance use reduction and then abstinence is typically the ultimate treatment goal. The progress toward this goal is monitored via urine toxicology testing.

Outpatient treatment falls into a series of intensity levels. Typically, these move from the most intense (partial hospitalization) to moderate (intensive outpatient) and least intense (outpatient). Each of these outpatient intensity levels will be discussed below.

Partial Hospitalization

These programs may also be called *evening* or *day treatment* (Work Group on Substance Use Disorders, 2007) and are the most intensive of all outpatient formats. Partial hospitalization is a nonresidential treatment program that may or may

Table 4.2   Admissions by Treatment Setting: Treatment Episode Data Set (2013) Results

Setting	*N*	%
Ambulatory, Outpatient	816,122	48.5%
Detoxification, Inpatient/Residential (non-hospital)	313,010	18.6%
Ambulatory, Intensive-Outpatient	195,884	11.6%
Short-Term Inpatient/Residential (≤ 30 days)	155,164	9.2%
Long-Term Inpatient/Residential (> 30 days)	124,340	7.4%
Detoxification, Inpatient/Residential (hospital)	53,033	3.2%
Ambulatory, Detoxification	20,656	1.2%
Inpatient/Residential (no detoxification)	4,977	0.3%
TOTAL	1,683,186	100.0%

Source: SAMHSA (2015).

not be hospital based (e.g., a program may be housed in a medical center or in a freestanding outpatient clinic). The program provides services on a level of intensity relatively equal to an inpatient program but on less than a 24-hour basis. The program is typically more than 20 hours per week and includes treatment services such as medical/nursing, psychiatric evaluation and medication management (including detoxification as appropriate), group and individual/family counseling, psychological testing, vocational counseling, relapse prevention sessions, and other services for typically at least approximately 6 hours per scheduled day. Family involvement from the beginning of treatment is important unless contraindicated. Frequency of interventions and treatment modalities should occur based on individual needs. Partial hospitalization is used as a time-limited response to stabilize acute symptoms. Thus, it serves as both a transitional level of care (i.e., step-down from inpatient) as well as a stand-alone level of care to stabilize a deteriorating condition and avert a more intensive and invasive inpatient placement.

Intensive Outpatient Program (IOP)

Intensive outpatient care involves a structured treatment program that runs 3 to 4 hours per day for between 3 and 5 days per week. The IOP experience runs less than 20 hours per week and involves both group and individual counseling coupled with urine toxicology. Individuals who are at this level of care require less intensive monitoring than at the partial hospitalization or inpatient levels of care. If required, in-house or external referrals may be made for pharmacotherapy, psychiatric evaluation, and marital/family counseling services. IOP is also used as a time-limited response to stabilize acute symptoms. Thus, it may also serve as both as a transitional level of care (i.e., step-down from inpatient or partial hospitalization) as well as a stand-alone level of care to stabilize a deteriorating condition and avert a more intensive and invasive partial hospitalization or inpatient placement.

Outpatient Care

These programs are minimally intensive and restrictive, typically time-limited, and primarily designed for mild to moderate SUDs (CSAT 2006a). Treatment may consist of individual and/or group counseling approximately 2 times per week along with 12-step meeting engagement. This type of program format is most effective for the client who is motivated and ready for treatment, substance cessation, and long-term recovery. This level of care may be referred for either of the following reasons:

- Initial client placement based on required level of care
- Client stepped down in level of care following successfully completing a more intensive level of treatment

The caution for the clinician is to effectively evaluate the client and verify that outpatient care is warranted (that is why assessment is critical in the process and is the first chapter in this text following the biopsychopharmacological primer). Clients typically try to enter treatment at the least intensive level for any number of reasons (denial, perceived "easier" treatment experience, ignorance of problem, or ignorance of treatment process and levels of care). For example, I once conducted an intake for a client seeking admission to outpatient care (one or two sessions per week). Within the first 10 minutes, it was clearly evident that the client was in opiate withdrawal (heroin) and required a different and more intensive level of care. In another example, I performed an intake on a client who was still actively using heroin and alcohol and was experiencing overwhelming cravings, yet this client was seeking outpatient services for only one time per week. Obviously, each of these clients was referred to the appropriate level of care warranted by their symptoms. In each of these cases, part of the referral process was to educate the client on the overall process. In part, I use the analogy of a paper cut and a broken leg. Just as you would never go to the emergency room for a paper cut, you also would not go to your general practitioner for a broken leg. Consequently, when a client comes for an outpatient placement but requires a higher level of care, it is analogous to seeking medical attention for a broken leg at your general practitioner's outpatient medical office.

DUI/DWI Psychoeducation

Technically, driving under the influence (DUI)/driving while intoxicated (DWI) psychoeducation is the least intensive/restrictive of all outpatient care (CSAT 2006a). These programs provide a psychoeducational experience for those convicted of a DUI or DWI violation and consist of group and/or individual counseling coupled with urine toxicology monitoring over a series of weeks. The program is a component of a larger series of tasks and fees the DUI/DWI violator must complete and pay prior to application for the reinstatement of their driving license. The program is typically quite structured, with different content areas for coverage in each session such as how alcohol and substances influence the body and brain, stress management, and substance refusal skills. In addition, clinical assessment is conducted to determine if the DUI/DWI offense reflects a larger pattern of behavior indicative of an SUD. For example, I formerly ran psychoeducation groups for the DUI/DWI population. I found that not many of the clients were ever diagnosed with an SUD but did present with a wide array of substance use that seemed more pervasive and severe than the general population. Recent New Jersey data seem to support my observation noting how statewide, clients in the DUI/DWI psychoeducation program reported higher lifetime prevalence rates for alcohol, marijuana, cocaine, and heroin as compared to the general New Jersey population (Office of Research, Planning, and Evaluation, and Intoxicated Driving Program Unit,

Division of Mental Health and Addiction Services, New Jersey Department of Human Services, 2014). Consequently, part of your role in running these psychoeducation groups is to try to determine if any individual is in need of more intensive SUD treatment services.

ESTABLISHING THE APPROPRIATE LEVEL OF CARE

Historically, there used to be a rule of thumb that intensive care was the most appropriate format for the treatment of any SUD (Kranitz & Cooney, 2013). However, that homogeneous principle has long since given way to a far more theoretical procedure designed to best match the client's heterogeneous needs to an appropriate level of care. Treatment placement is the natural outcome of the interview, assessment, and diagnostic processes. As a clinician, your role in treatment placement may involve making the initial referral to an appropriate level of care or referring a client to a more or less intensive level of care based on treatment progress. The principal guidelines for treatment placement have been developed by the American Society of Addiction Medicine (ASAM, 2013) and involve a detailed process for determining client detoxification and/or treatment needs. The discussion below focuses on the basics of the current *ASAM Criteria* (2013) in regard to treatment placement and treatment planning.

Biopsychosocial Functioning

These six biopsychosocial domains (ASAM, 2013) take into account the multidimensional ways in which addiction interacts with a person's life and produces dysfunction. By considering these areas, the treatment placement procedures are further clarified and hopefully result in the best possible match between the client and an appropriate level of care. For instance, outpatient treatment placement for homeless individuals or treatment placement for individuals without consideration of their HIV medical needs would be both inappropriate placement and not in the best interests of the clients and their recovery. Treatment is not one-size-fits-all, and the tailoring of person and treatment starts with the six domains below.

Acute Intoxication or Withdrawal Potential. Countless times in my career, I have conducted an intake for a client admission to an inpatient or outpatient program but instead wound up referring the individual to a detoxification program as they were struggling with the physical and psychological symptoms of alcohol, opiate, or benzodiazepine withdrawal. Basically, ASAM is directing the clinician to assess if the individual may first require detoxification services (called *withdrawal management* in the *ASAM Criteria*) prior to SUD treatment.

Biomedical Conditions and Complications. SUD clients are documented as having numerous medical ailments (e.g., Morgen, Astone-Twerell, Hernitche, Gunneson, & Santangelo, 2007). Consequently, SUD treatment services must take co-occurring medical conditions into account through the coordination of medical services.

Emotional, Behavioral, or Cognitive Conditions and Complications. As discussed in the prior chapter, co-occurring SUD and psychiatric disorders are the norm and to be expected. Thus, SUD treatment services must also take co-occurring psychiatric disorders (and symptoms) into account through the coordination of mental health services (e.g., counseling and pharmacotherapy).

Readiness to Change. Is the individual motivated and ready for treatment? Based on the present stage of change, what procedures does the clinician need to implement? For instance, if the client is not fully motivated and ready for change, the initiation into the treatment process should occur via motivational enhancement strategies. On the other hand, if the client is ready to work in treatment, their current action stage should be utilized and built upon.

Relapse, Continued Use, or Continued Problem Potential. Is the client at risk of a relapse? If the client is far along in the treatment and recovery process (e.g., client intake for outpatient placement), the client should be assessed for their readiness to engage with relapse prevention services and learn relapse prevention skills. If the client is early in the treatment and recovery process, the emphasis is shifted to the dangers of continual use (e.g., the risk of a client assuming that they can "control" their drinking).

Recovery Environment. Kranitz and Cooney (2013) stressed that any treatment placement decision and subsequent treatment plan must take into account the physical and social environment of the client. Do they have strong social and familial support? If outpatient placement is warranted, do they have a secure home to return to? Does the client have access to transportation and (if needed) childcare? Is the client experiencing any concurrent legal or financial challenges? Failure to incorporate these (and similar) issues into the treatment placement process may lead to an unsuccessful treatment episode and/or relapse.

ASAM Criteria (2013) Level of Withdrawal Management Services for Adults

The *ASAM Criteria* provides five levels of withdrawal management (i.e., detoxification) services in which to place a client. Decisions are primarily made based on the severity of the withdrawal symptoms and the need for medical care. Of note is that the *ASAM Criteria* does not provide withdrawal management placement criteria for adolescents (this is further discussed later in this chapter in the Adolescents section). Each withdrawal management level of care is briefly discussed below.

Ambulatory Withdrawal Management without Extended On-Site Monitoring (Level 1-WM). This represents the least intensive level of withdrawal management care and is appropriate for clients with mild withdrawal symptoms in daily outpatient care. These clients are likely to complete the withdrawal management phase and continue on to SUD treatment.

Ambulatory Withdrawal Management with Extended On-Site Monitoring (Level 2-WM). These clients present with moderate withdrawal symptoms and require all-day supervision. At conclusion of the day, the client returns to a supportive home and is considered likely to complete the withdrawal management process.

Clinically Managed Residential Withdrawal Management (Level 3.2-WM). This level is for a client with moderate withdrawal symptoms but who needs 24-hour support to complete withdrawal management.

Medically Monitored Inpatient Withdrawal Management (Level 3.7-WM). Clients appropriate for this level experience severe withdrawal symptoms and need 24-hour medical/nursing care as warranted. This medical monitoring is considered a requirement in order to have the client successfully complete the withdrawal management program.

Medically Managed Inpatient Withdrawal Management (Level 4-WM). This is the most intensive of the withdrawal management levels. Clients appropriate for this level experience severe withdrawal and require 24-hour medical care in order to manage their unstable medical and withdrawal conditions.

ASAM Criteria (2013) Levels of Care

Based on client needs, treatment placement may occur in any one of 10 levels. All but one of these levels (3.3) are appropriate for adolescent treatment placement. Each of these levels is briefly discussed below.

Early Intervention (Level 0.5). This level of care is most appropriate for an at-risk individual who uses substances but does not meet the *DSM-5* diagnostic criteria for an SUD. This may present as a high school student referred to mandatory counseling due to having been caught smoking marijuana on school property but does not meet the minimum two criteria required for an SUD diagnosis. The principal content at this level of care is psychoeducation on the dangers of continual substance use.

Outpatient Services (Level 1). Placement here consists of treatment and associated care for less than 9 hours per week for adults and less than 6 hours per week for adolescents. This could present as an adult who has already completed more intensive treatment phases and now is receiving individual counseling twice per week for 2 hours total.

Intensive Outpatient (Level 2.1). Placement here consists of treatment and associated care for more than 9 hours per week for adults and more than 6 hours per week for adolescents. This may present as an adolescent attending three groups per week (at 2 hours per group) coupled with one individual counseling session per week.

Partial Hospitalization (Level 2.5). For adults or adolescents, a minimum of 20 treatment hours per week to treat instability. Of importance is that the client does not require 24-hour care. This is typically the first step down from an inpatient program, where the client still requires extensive counseling and supervision along with associated services but is now stable enough to no longer be on an inpatient unit. Clinicians should be cautious at this phase because, due to insurance coverage issues, many clients are referred to partial hospitalization because of exhaustion of inpatient service coverage as opposed to a referral based purely on clinical reasons.

Clinically Managed Low Intensity Residential (Level 3.1). This is the least intensive/restrictive of the inpatient care levels and entails 24-hour care where at least 5 hours per week focus on clinical services. It provides ongoing therapeutic care for clients not yet ready for a partial-hospitalization level of care. For adolescents, this level of care also fits well for adolescent treatment where the teen client still requires extended treatment to sustain and/or further therapeutic gains made at a more intensive level of care. This level is also sometimes warranted as a substitute for or supplement to the deficits in the adolescent's recovery environment, such as a chaotic home situation (e.g., drug-using caretakers or siblings) or a lack of daily structured activities (e.g., not yet clinically cleared to return to school.

Clinically Managed Population Specific High Intensity Residential (Level 3.3). This is 24-hour care to stabilize the client across multiple dimensions (such as addiction and co-occurring psychiatric and/or medical issues). The milieu and group formats are less intensive than a therapeutic community. This level of care is appropriate for clients whose co-occurring psychiatric and/or medical issues produced a degree of cognitive impairment so that the client would best benefit from a slower-paced and repetitive treatment environment. Of note is that this is the only ASAM level of care designated as not applicable for adolescents.

Clinically Managed High Intensity Residential (Level 3.5). This is a 24-hour level of inpatient care for clients who struggle with instability across varying SUD and co-occurring areas. As opposed to Level 3.3, clients placed in Level 3.5 are fully capable of managing the intensity and pace of a milieu or therapeutic community program.

Medically Monitored Intensive Inpatient (Level 3.7). This inpatient level of care consists of 24-hour nursing care with physician availability for clients who struggle with significant medical and physical ailments in need of care. Counseling services are available for 16 hours per day as needed.

Medically Managed Intensive Inpatient (Level 4). This inpatient level of care consists of 24-hour nursing care with physician availability for clients who struggle with more severe medical and physical ailments than those placed at Level 3.7. Counseling services are available as needed.

Opioid Treatment Services (Level OTS). Placement appropriate for an opioid treatment program (e.g., methadone) or office-based opioid treatment program (e.g., Suboxone).

MULTICULTURAL ELEMENTS OF TREATMENT PLACEMENT AND PLANNING

Cultural competence is increasingly a requirement of funding and accreditation bodies. For example, cultural competence is a requirement for accreditation by the Joint Commission on Accreditation of Healthcare Organizations (JCAHO). SUD treatment programs must always consider whether the needs of a specific cultural group can be meet within a nonspecialized treatment program or if a specialized program may best benefit these clients.

I recall from my days of working in a therapeutic community that there were some groups and other counseling-related endeavors unique to cultures and genders. Combined with the general treatment program, these unique culturally relevant groups provided another outlet for individuals to shape their recovery. The question then becomes how to set up a counseling program for a specific cultural group (e.g., Muslim, African American, or Lesbian, Gay, Transgender, Bisexual and Queer).

SAMHSA (2014c) reviewed some different worldview perspectives that would influence the process and outcome of SUD treatment. They include the following:

- *Holistic worldview.* Native American and Asian cultures view the world in a holistic sense, as they see the natural world, the animal world, and the spiritual world as an integrated whole world. Health (or recovery) would entail reconnecting with the larger universe.
- *Spirituality.* Spiritual beliefs and ceremonies often are critical to some cultural groups, such as Hispanics and Native Americans. Native American programming should integrate spiritual customs and rituals to enhance the cultural relevance of the SUD treatment services.
- *Community orientation.* The Anglo American focuses on the individual and the individual's welfare. Many other cultures focus on the collective good of the group. For example, Asian American and Native American clients may care far more about how the substance use disorder harms their family group as opposed to their own self-concerns.
- *Multidimensional learning styles.* Since SUD treatment, and counseling in general, utilizes psychoeducational components, learning style can be one of the keys to treatment success. Anglo American culture emphasizes learning through reading and teaching. Cultures with an oral tradition do not believe that written information is more reliable than oral information. They see learning as conveyed via stories that include emotional and narrative components. In some cases, the speaker's authority may be more important than the message. Cultures that embrace the oral tradition include Hispanics, African Americans, Native Americans, and Pacific Islanders.

SAMHSA (2014c) adopted Sue's (2001) multidimensional model of cultural competence as a guide to target critical components of cultural competence in the provision of behavioral health services across three main dimensions (see Figure 4.1). Dimension 1 is called Racially and Culturally Specific Attributes and includes groups as identified by the U.S. Census Bureau as well as other multiracial and culturally diverse groups (i.e., sexual orientation, gender orientation, socioeconomic status). Since there can be so many cultural groups, for simplicity, all the potential groups are not included in the model. However, the model requires a deep cultural degree of understanding so that the counselor assumes that many cultural and ethnic groupings potentially exist and should be considered in a specific application of the model along Dimension 1 (e.g., considering the unique cultural needs and perspectives of gay Hispanic men in SUD treatment).

Dimension 2 is called Core Elements of Cultural Competence and includes cultural awareness, cultural knowledge, and cultural skill development that enables counselors to become more aware of their cultural attitudes, beliefs, biases, and assumptions as these pertain to help seeking, treatment, and recovery. Dimension 3 is called Foci of Culturally Responsive Services and specifies that cultural considerations be integrated at the clinical, programmatic, and administrative levels of a treatment facility, for example, selection of assessment measures validated for a specific culture or offered in a specific language, and in addition, at a more organizational level, perhaps the consideration of where a new treatment program location should be situated within a community.

The model emphasizes that culture needs to be just as relevant a part of the treatment matching and treatment planning process as the client's expressed clinical needs pertaining to SUDs and other conditions. However, such a cultural understanding can only occur if the staff is adequately trained to truly consider these issues on a macro- and microlevel. Figure 4.1 is one example of how to train staff (and counselor trainees) on how to become more culturally aware. Here, the counselor, client, family, treatment program organization, clinical supervisor, and prison/parole systems are all included in a discussion of how a failure to conceptualize culture could impede the overall treatment and recovery process, and how, if culture is considered, the process could run smoother and be of far more personal benefit to the client.

Of critical importance is that the counselor and facility recognize that the application of cultural issues within treatment is not simply reading and using some of

Figure 4.1 Multidimensional Model for Developing Cultural Competence

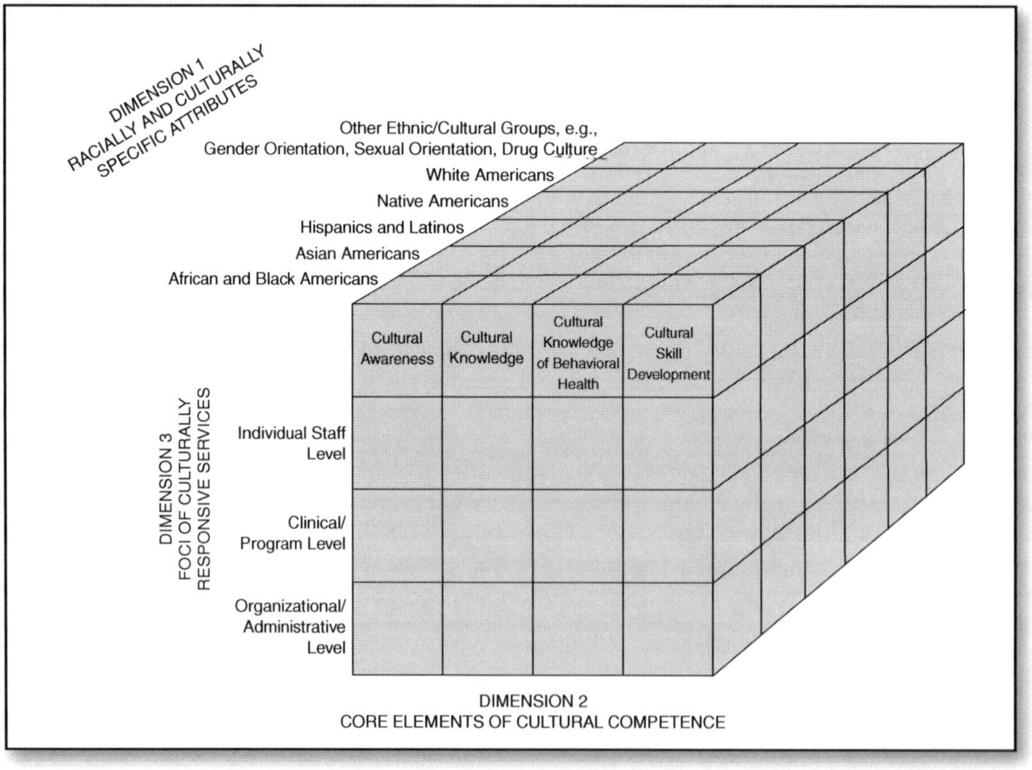

Source: SAMHSA (2014c).

the myriad resources available for culturally relevant treatment. Instead, the most important element is how ingrained cultural issues are into the fabric of the treatment process. For this to occur, the counselor must engage in a meaningful dialogue around culture (however clients define the concept for themselves) and not just treat the material found in various texts and manuals as the all-knowing guide.

For example, *machismo* is used to explain Latino men and their masculinity (Arciniega, Anderson, Tovar-Blank, & Tracey, 2008). Machismo beliefs of Latino men were related to negative mental health, and Latino masculinity was related to restrictive emotionality and depression in males (Fragoso & Kashubeck, 2000). Although men from other cultures show similar behaviors, machismo has become a term to describe only Latino masculinity. However, Arciniega et al. (2008) also emphasized that the masculine Latino role of men includes positive characteristics such as honor, respect, and value for the family. Therefore, Latino masculine identity involves both traditional machismo features and positive features called *caballerismo*. Had I been too reliant on the stereotypical terms and theories, I would expect every Latino client I encountered to be resistant to treatment. Furthermore, they would be resistant due to their machismo attitudes of not showing emotion or weakness. But since I am also aware of the concept of caballerismo, I meet every Latino client with the perspective that they *may* show resistance due to machismo-type characteristics, but they are just as likely to engage with treatment out of honor and respect to their family that needs them to return to health.

CO-OCCURRING LEVELS OF CARE

The *ASAM Criteria* (2013) provided a rigorous and detailed overview of the appropriate placement for a client based on their biopsychosocial functioning and addiction severity. However, the specific degree of co-occurring psychiatric disorder severity also needs to be considered when making a treatment placement. For instance, co-occurring severe major depressive disorder with psychotic features is a more pressing psychiatric need than co-occurring mild generalized anxiety disorder. The co-occurring psychiatric disorder basically results in one of the following scenarios: (1) a co-occurring disorder, (2) a disorder that exacerbates the SUD, and/ or (3) a potential risk factor for relapse and treatment dropout.

The same logic holds for the SUD. Especially since the advent of *DSM-5*, with the disorder severity level taking the place of the old abuse/dependence criteria, symptom severity is critical to understand and utilize in treatment placement. For instance, severe alcohol use disorder is indicative of a higher-risk case as compared with mild cocaine use disorder due to the number of dysfunctional symptoms that need endorsement to qualify for a severe or mild diagnosis. Consequently, the SUD treatment profession developed and utilizes a paradigm for treatment placement that takes into account the severity of both the SUD and psychiatric disorder.

Quadrants of Care

In the 1990s, starting with Ries (1993) and later with the National Association of State Mental Health Program Directors (NASMHPD) and the National Association of State Alcohol and Drug Abuse Directors (NASADAD) (1998), there was the production of a conceptual model that classified clients based on symptom severity and not just diagnosis (see Figure 4.2). Simply put, any client can fall into a category of having high/low addiction symptom severity and high/low mental illness symptom severity. Furthermore, these category placements are not static, and a client can advance or regress through these quadrants as symptoms warrant. One of the goals of this model was to provide a theoretical paradigm that would inform clinicians and other relevant parties across the addiction and mental health professions (NASMHPD & NASADAD, 1998).

Some work has shown that when using high-severity psychiatric diagnoses defined as bipolar, major depression, or schizophrenia, and high-severity addiction as *DSM-IV* (APA, 2000) substance dependence, there was consistency of quadrant placement based on these diagnoses (McGovern, Clark, & Samnaliev, 2007). However, the question remains as to how well such a quadrant system would work when working with symptoms (and not diagnoses), which is typically the experience

Figure 4.2 Quadrants of Care

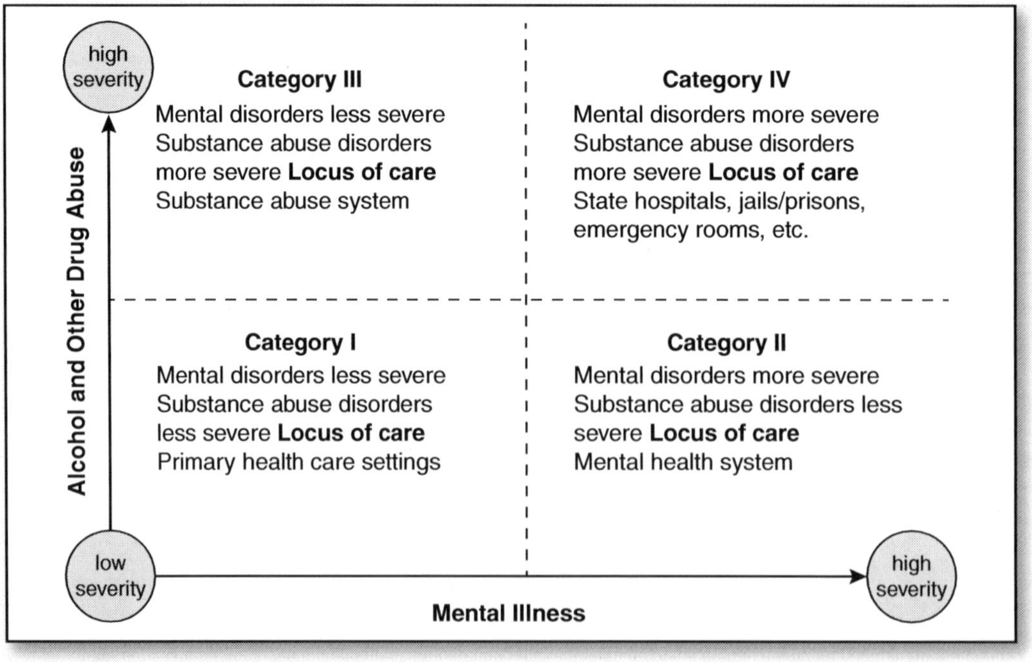

Source: CSAT (2005a, p. 29).

during an inpatient or outpatient SUD treatment intake session. It is one thing to use the quadrant model when provided with a diagnosis. It is entirely different (and far more real-world relevant) to use the quadrant to place a client in treatment using the severity of symptoms demonstrated in the intake session.

Recent work sought to establish if the quadrant model was valid and effective. The validity and stability of the quadrant model was tested using 155 adults presenting at a county hospital with psychiatric, substance use, or medical complaints. The study used data that are routinely gathered in clinical care or available in administrative records (e.g., substance dependence diagnosis, Global Assessment of Functioning scores). Results supported the concurrent validity of the model and showed that quadrant placement was correlated with psychiatric and/or substance use diagnoses, psychiatric symptom severity, drug/alcohol toxicology, and psychiatric and substance use health utilization, supporting the concurrent validity of the model. In addition, both initial and follow-up quadrant placement was significantly correlated, thus demonstrating the stability of the quadrant model (McDonell et al., 2012).

But this model and just about all the supporting research/theory associated with it was developed using the *DSM-IV* (APA, 2000) abuse/dependence diagnostic criteria with dependence defined as the "severe" substance use diagnosis. The development of the mild, moderate, and severe use disorder criteria for the *DSM-5* (APA, 2013) substance use disorder diagnosis likely forces a change to this model. At face value, it appears that the quadrant model needs to expand. For example, there are now three levels of substance use disorder (mild, moderate, severe). There are also multiple levels of the other disorders, such as mild, moderate, and severe major depressive disorder. A 3 × 3 model seems more applicable to the *DSM-5* diagnostic structure. As of the writing of this text, I could find no published/file-drawer update to the model using the new *DSM-5*.

LOGISTICS OF TREATMENT PLANNING

Treatment placement and planning only works if the client can financially afford the services and the services are readily available. Referral to a program for a client lacking insurance coverage and/or recommending treatment that is not readily available to the client (due to distance) are both empty actions. The SUD treatment landscape is actively changing, especially in the wake of the Affordable Care Act (ACA). The next section briefly reviews how this act may contribute to the status of SUD treatment care affordability and availability over the next several years.

The Affordable Care Act

The ACA is one of the largest-ever expansions of mental health and substance use disorder coverage and extends the Mental Health Parity and Addiction Equity

Act of 2008 to provide substance use and mental health care federal parity protections to approximately 62 million Americans by the year 2020 (Beronio, Po, Skopec, & Glied, 2013). It is estimated that approximately 32 million individuals will receive SUD treatment benefits for the first time, while another 30 million will see their behavioral health benefits expanded. The ACA is expected to add 2.7%, or $7.3 billion, to the level of mental health and SUD treatment spending in 2020 as millions who were previously uninsured gain health insurance coverage (SAMHSA, 2014d). The ACA ensures that newly covered individuals receive substance use disorder benefits, thus potentially flooding the behavioral health system with new clients. Beginning in 2014, the ACA established 10 mandatory "essential health benefits" (EHBs) for newly eligible Medicaid enrollees and most individual and small group health plans. Though states have considerable flexibility in determining the details of their EHBs, substance use disorder treatment is one of the 10 EHBs.

Clients and providers will face new systems of care as facilities seek innovative ways to provide high-quality, low-cost care. New opportunities may emerge to access substance use disorder treatment and may be delivered by a changing set of providers, via new payment mechanisms, governed by new coverage guidelines and potentially funded by new payers. SUD treatment providers will face larger client volume and emphasis on coordinated, integrated, and cost-minimizing approaches to treatment (SAMHSA, 2014d). Tai and Volkow (2013) noted how for too long SUD treatment (as part of overall behavioral health care) was carved out of the larger health care system. Tai, Wu, and Clark (2012) added how this isolation impeded earlier detection and treatment referral for numerous individuals struggling with mild and moderate addiction issues. This is critical because it will allow the larger health care field (counseling, medical, etc.) to finally consider substance use disorder as a chronic brain disease that needs consistent care in some degree for years after the cessation of substance use (and the conclusion of successful treatment). For too long, health care has treated and conceptualized addiction as an acute disorder (Miller, 2015), for example, the idea of a 28-day inpatient treatment program. That is why the integration component of the ACA is perhaps one of the biggest assets of the law, as it will require a reconceptualization in regard to treatment services, design, and policy (Capoccia, Grazier, Toal, Ford, & Gustafson, 2012).

DRUG COURTS

Criminal justice system mandated treatment is commonplace within the SUD treatment landscape, with the drug court being one of the most commonly mandated treatment apparatus. A drug court is a special docket within the court system designed to treat addiction via a close integration and collaboration with the SUD treatment field.

The drug court judge leads an interdisciplinary team of professionals, which often includes a court coordinator, the prosecuting and defense attorneys for the case, SUD treatment providers, case managers, and the assigned probation officer (Huddleston & Marlowe, 2011). There are many drug courts throughout the nation (for an accurate identification of drug courts in your area, consult www.nadcp.org/learn/find-drug-court). Table 4.3 Reviews the 10 established components of a drug court.

CSAT (2005b) notes that drug court eligible participants are diagnosable with one or more SUDs and commonly charged with drug-related offenses such as possession of a controlled substance, or other offenses determined to have been related to their addiction such as burglary or forgery. Drug courts refer clients to treatment where they encounter the typical array of clinical services such as SUD and psychiatric disorder treatment, family counseling, vocational training, educational assistance, or help with obtaining medical care. In general, drug court programs tend to run between 12 and 18 months, and to successfully complete the program, a participant must demonstrate continuous abstinence from substances and satisfy treatment and supervision conditions (i.e., adhere to all court rules such as being on time for appointments, arriving for random urine screenings, etc.). In brief, the drug court represents a complicated and integrated treatment placement and planning process as depicted in Figure 4.3.

Though mandatory clients do not voluntarily enter treatment, recent work has demonstrated that mandatory treatment placement can be effective. For example, research has demonstrated that substance abusers who are court ordered to

Table 4.3 10 Components of Drug Courts

1. Drug courts integrate alcohol and other drug treatment services with justice system case processing.
2. Using a non-adversarial approach, prosecution and defense counsel promote public safety while protecting participants' due process rights.
3. Eligible participants are identified early and promptly placed in the drug court program.
4. Drug courts provide access to a continuum of alcohol, drug, and other related treatment and rehabilitation services.
5. Abstinence is monitored by frequent alcohol and other drug testing.
6. A coordinated strategy governs drug court responses to participants' compliance.
7. Ongoing judicial interaction with each drug court participant is essential.
8. Monitoring and evaluation measure the achievement of program goals and gauge effectiveness.
9. Continuing interdisciplinary education promotes effective drug court planning, implementation, and operations.
10. Forging partnerships among drug courts, public agencies, and community-based organizations generates local support and enhances drug court program effectiveness.

Source: National Association of Drug Court Professionals (1997).

Figure 4.3 Substance Abuse Treatment Planning Chart for Treatment-Based Drug Courts

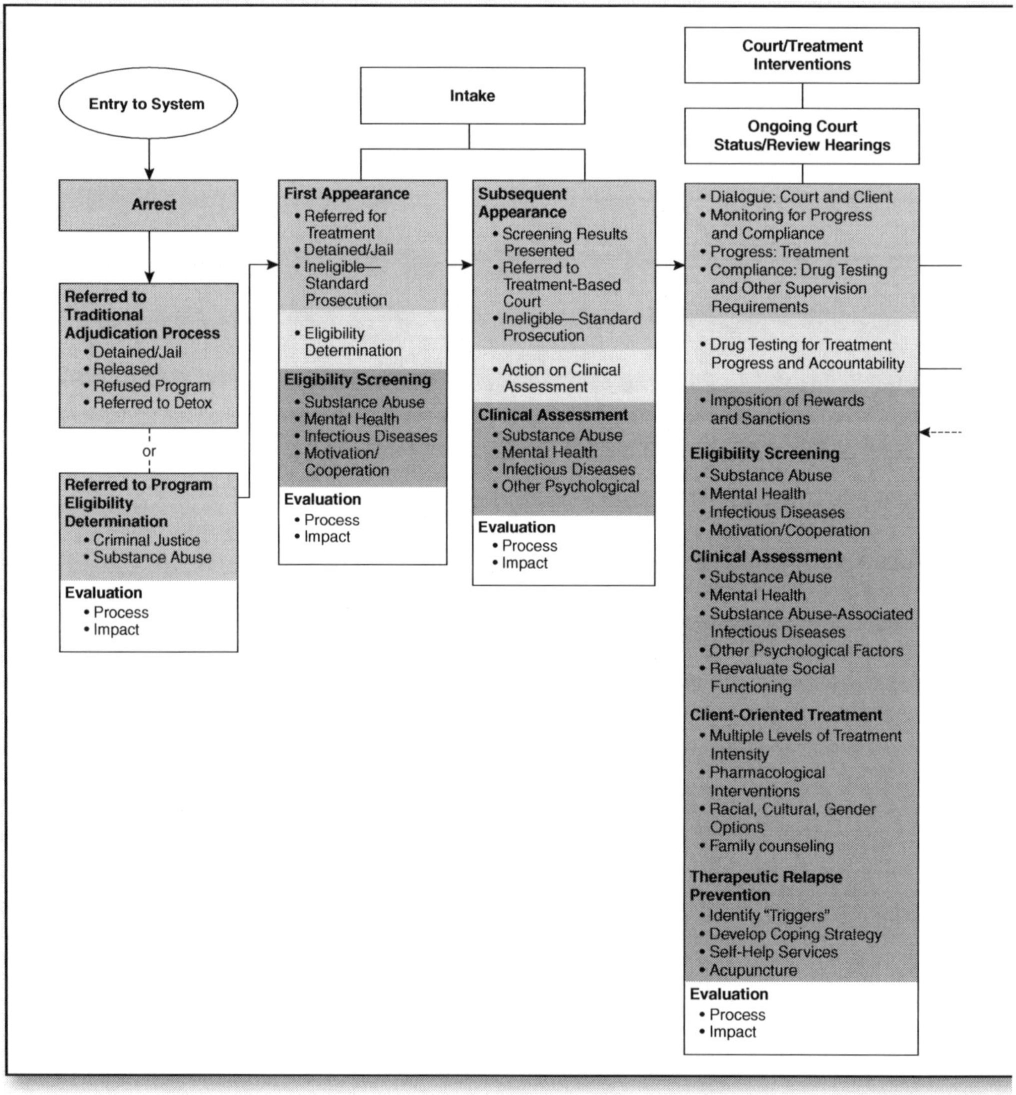

treatment did as well as or better than those who entered voluntarily (e.g., Farabee, Prendergast, & Anglin, 1998; Kelly, Finney, & Moos, 2005; Martin et al., 2003). Similar findings demonstrated the effectiveness of the mandated drug court treatment model. Recent meta-analyses found that adult drug courts significantly reduced crime (Aos, Miller, & Drake, 2006; Downey & Roman, 2010; Latimer, Morton-Bourgon, & Chretien, 2006; Lowenkamp, Holsinger, & Latessa, 2005;

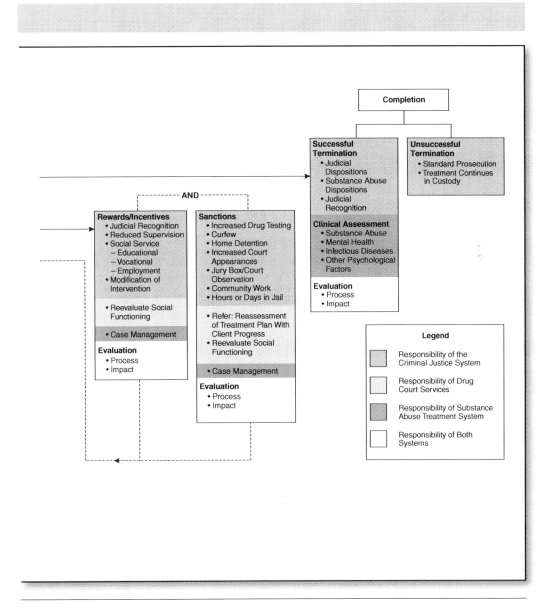

Source: CSAT (2005b).

MacKenzie, 2006; Wilson, Mitchell, & MacKenzie, 2006). Furthermore, drug court recidivism rates have been shown to be anywhere between 8 and 26 percentage points lower than for other justice system responses. These crime reductions have proven to be consistent and long lasting (Finigan, Carey, & Cox, 2007; Gottfredson, Kearley, Najaka, & Rocha, 2005; Gottfredson, Najaka, Kearley, & Rocha, 2006; Turner, Greenwood, Fain, & Deschenes, 1999).

Drug courts are also highly cost effective. For instance, a recent analysis found an average of $2.21 in direct benefits to the criminal justice system for every $1 invested (Bhati, Roman, & Chalfin, 2008)! This return on the investment grows more impressive when drug courts work with the more serious, higher-risk drug offenders, where the average return on investment was determined to be $3.36 for every $1 invested (Bhati et al., 2008).

SPECIAL POPULATIONS

Adolescents

The N-SSATS (SAMHSA, 2013) found that about half (48%) of the 14,311 substance abuse treatment facilities responding to the survey accepted teens. Unfortunately, adolescent SUD treatment programming is not as common as the numbers may imply. If the percentage of programs accepting teens were further split into whether or not the facility offered a specialized group/treatment program for adolescents, the numbers become more concerning. In this case, only 28% of all SUD treatment programs in the N-SSATS offered care purposefully tailored for the adolescent (SAMHSA, 2013). So nationwide, the numbers imply that only approximately one in four programs offer treatment and ancillary services specially developed for the adolescent. This is a problem because adolescent SUD represents a heterogeneous population (Fishman, 2008), and due to the multiple age-specific problems they face, require a more nuanced treatment placement tailored to their developmental needs (Deas, Gray, & Upadhyaya, 2008). In brief, they need coordination of services such as adolescent-specific psychiatric, medical, family, school support, juvenile justice, and others. However, centralized case management with all required services within a single institution is rare. Some adolescent-specific issues regarding SUD treatment placement are discussed below.

According to Fishman (2011), the trend for treatment of severe opioid withdrawal in adolescents is to adopt the standard for pharmacological intervention for adults. However, other detoxification and withdrawal management strategies deviate from those applied for adults. This is primarily due to the fact that there is no consistent and clear evidence for the effectiveness of detoxification in the ambulatory setting with adolescents (e.g., Clemmey, Payne, & Fishman, 2004). Furthermore, Fishman (2011) emphasized how (at least for opioid treatment) the typical sequence of adolescent care involves inpatient detoxification, which is usually followed by inpatient treatment. In general, the use of medication treatment in adolescents with SUDs demands careful assessment and documentation (Upadhyaya & Deas, 2008).

Treatment program placement must also take into account the developmentally normal difficulties with self-regulation skills, as these are a developmental work in progress for all adolescents. Thus, adolescent SUD treatment consistently seeks a balance between limit setting/rules and a degree of tolerance for age-appropriate behavior. Basically, a good treatment placement is where the adolescent misbehavior—to a degree—should be expected, but the facility must also have the capacity to manage the behavior. Along these same lines, there is a need for enhanced training for adolescent counselors to recognize and diagnose co-occurring disorders. In essence, there needs to be nuanced training in differential diagnosis that permits an adolescent treatment staff to distinguish between symptoms as due to substance use, a co-occurring independent disorder, and/or a developmentally appropriate fluctuation in mood or affect. Adolescent diagnosis is fraught with potential misdiagnosis or underdiagnosis.

Treatment placement for adolescents must take into account the safety of the home environment. For instance, any chosen level of care that involves a return to the home must consider the presence of substance use in the home as well as such toxic home environmental factors as maltreatment or neglect, transportation and/or other child care matters (i.e., can the adolescent be transported to and from treatment on a consistent basis), criminal behaviors, or extreme financial hardships. In severe cases, it may be beneficial to (at least) temporarily remove adolescents from toxic home environments and place them in residential treatment. For especially severe cases, it may be necessary to facilitate a more permanent change in home environment such as placement with other family members, longer-term residential placements (e.g., group homes), or surrogate families (e.g., foster care).

Older Adults

America is growing older (Ortman, Velkoff, & Hogan, 2014), and by the year 2030 it is estimated that there will be 72.1 million older adults, as defined as approximately age 65 and older (e.g., Areán, 2015), with anticipated increases in substance use (Duncan, Nicholson, White, Bradley, & Bonaguro, 2010). Despite these rising numbers, there is limited evidence to guide the treatment placement and treatment management of substance use disorders in older adults. Considering that the older adult does experience SUD differently (Liu & Satterfield, 2015; Morgen, 2015; Morgen, Denison-Vesel, Kobylarz, & Voelkner, 2015), this lack of overall treatment guidance is problematic.

Despite this lack of direction, several sources do provide some structure for determining the best treatment placement and plan for an older adult. Regarding detoxification and withdrawal management, Mannelli, Wu, and Brady (2015) offered the guidance that in the absence of older-adult specific guidelines, pharmacological treatment should follow recommendations offered by the treatment of the general adult population but with appropriate dose adjustments for age-related pharmacokinetic and pharmacodynamic changes. In addition, they argue for a lower criteria threshold for inpatient treatment admission.

The limited amount of older adult SUD treatment guidance is also evident in that the CSAT (1998) guidelines for older adult SUD care are nearly 20 years old! Though dated, these guidelines do provide a general framework for considering the needs of an older adult. CSAT stated that treatment must be age-specific with a focus on coping with depression, loneliness, and loss (e.g., death of a spouse, retirement), as these are critical areas of co-occurring psychiatric distress in older adults with SUD (Liu & Satterfield, 2015; Schonfeld & MacFarland, 2015). Clinical staff must understand how psychiatric disorders and subsyndromal symptom expressions present in an older adult. For instance, Morgen (2015) reviewed how many depressed older adults may report no feelings of *sadness*. Their complaints may emphasize symptoms such as low motivation, fatigue, or physical problems. Thus, treatment placement must take into account that the facility staff understands the nuanced clinical presentations and needs of the older adult.

The staff needs to have more than just the clinical mastery of older-adult diagnostic issues. They also must have a commonsense appreciation for the specific treatment placement needs. For example, during my clinical training, I ran a psychoeducation group focused on the recovering individual becoming more autonomous in areas of work and school. In what I can now see (years later) as an example of poor treatment placement, an 81-year-old recovering man was placed in this psychoeducation group. This content had no relevance to his current situation and immediate goals, thus he grew increasingly frustrated. In addition, the group ran for about 2 hours and he just was not able to handle that duration of sitting in a group. The content and pace of the treatment were inappropriate for this older adult. Even though the ASAM placement criteria (based on biopsychosocial dysfunction) matched this treatment setting, the pragmatics of the day-to-day operations failed to match his needs.

QUESTIONS TO CONSIDER AS YOU MOVE ON TO CHAPTER 5

Question 1: How would the ASAM Criteria *(2013) look if it took client neurocognitive deficits into account? How would programs need to adapt to accommodate these needs?*

Question 2: In Chapter 2, we discussed interviewing and assessment. Does client preference in an interview (where warranted) play any role in the treatment placement process, for example, cultural requests by the client regarding treatment type or location?

Question 3: Do you feel that the ASAM Criteria *does a good enough job in regard to the placement of clients with co-occurring SUD and psychiatric needs? Furthermore, do you feel the* ASAM Criteria *addresses treatment placement for process addictions?*

SECTION II REVIEW

CASE OF SAMANTHA: ASSESSMENT, DIAGNOSIS, AND TREATMENT PLACEMENT

Assessment

So you sat down with Samantha. As discussed, you had a typical initial interview of approximately 1 hour. Below, we review what information you collected in this dialogue. Though assessment measures are important and will be discussed in a bit, there is no better clinical assessment tool than a thorough and supportive dialogue between counselor and client.

Substance Use History

You hear in her history review that the opiate use began a little over a year ago. You also asked other questions that gave you additional and critical data. These inquiries and her answers are below.

> *Counselor:* You discussed taking three pills instead of one pill right when you started using. Once you recuperated and returned to work, can you please let me know how many pills you were taking at a time, what their dosage was, and how often per day you were doing this? Was it always just Percocet?

> *Client:* I was usually taking four at a time but sometimes five. I would do this maybe 3 times per day at work then maybe once more when home. I'd try to cut any tired feelings as they wore off with coffee. Seemed to help enough to get through, though I did take advantage of having a private office with no exterior windows to the hall. I'd sometimes lock the door and take a fast nap, but with my iPhone, iPad, and desk computer all set to alarms within 2 minutes of one another so I'd wake up. I mainly used 5 mg pills, but if I could only find 2.5 mg pills I'd use those, just more of them. I was afraid of the higher dose ones. I knew enough to know I was at the high end of the maximum dose per day and I think I passed it on a few occasions by a pill or two. I tried to keep it Percocet only. Sounds weird, but I knew Percocet so I went out of my way to only buy those. I was afraid of trying a different med and having a bad side effect.

> *Counselor:* That's a lot of pills. Did you go right to four or five per day or did that number rise because you noticed you needed more pills for a similar effect?

> *Client:* No. I started with the three, or even two pills a few times per day. Don't remember exact numbers. But I do remember being frustrated that I wasn't feeling the same high anymore after I'd use three pills. I'd wait for it but it never showed up. So yeah, I went to more pills because I couldn't get the same high anymore with fewer pills. It worried me because I knew enough to know that these things are dangerous in higher doses and amounts per each day. I was noticing

it again in the days before I went to rehab. Lucked out that way, I didn't have to experiment with more pills or a higher dose pill.

Counselor: I know they detoxed you during inpatient care. But I also know you said it was 2 or 3 days between when you called out sick from work and then got admitted to the hospital program. You said you refused to use during that time. Can you think back to how you felt in those 2 or 3 days you weren't using? How did you feel? Physically? Psychologically?

Client: Awful. I was sweating, shaking, and just awful. Felt like the flu. Plus, I was jittery and just felt "off" the whole time. It was scary how bad my body and everything got just because I stopped the pills.

Counselor: You obviously used prescription opiates. Did you ever use heroin?

Client: Never. That stuff scared me. Plus, I liked that I knew the pills were made in a pharmaceutical company following FDA rules and stuff. God knows where the heroin comes from or what's in it. You hear stories, I heard some inpatient. Guys dying or getting real hurt from shooting heroin cut with rat poison. So, no. I'm glad I never.

Counselor: You ever use any other substances? Recent to your inpatient placement or in the past?

Client: No, I'm boring that way. I mean, I'd drink a couple glasses of wine out to dinner. Got drunk at college parties way back. But no, nothing else. I maybe had five glasses of wine a month spread over the month. I'd go out to eat with friends a few times. I haven't been drunk or buzzed in I can't remember how long. Years.

Counselor: Did you use any substances, besides the medications they helped you to detox with, while in inpatient or partial hospitalization?

Client: No, just the Suboxone. And that was only for around 6 or 7 days or so when I started.

Counselor: It's been 2 days since you were discharged from the partial program and now here for your intensive outpatient screening. Have you used anything?

Client: No. Urine should be clean.

Counselor: Any cravings now? How do you feel?

Client: I think I still kind of "miss it" but more like I feel like I need it to function. Like people with the morning coffee. I'm not physically sick or really messed in the head from no pills if that's what you're asking me.

Based on her answers to these questions (and other similar inquiries), we can derive the following conclusions regarding Samantha's substance use history:

- She only misused prescription opiate pain medication, primarily Percocet.
- She had been using on a regular basis for a little over 1 year prior to inpatient admission.
- She demonstrated evidence of tolerance with increasing dosages of Percocet.
- She demonstrated evidence of dependence upon cessation of Percocet.
- Suboxone helped her initially withdraw safely off the opiate.
- She has not used a substance (other than Suboxone for detoxification services) since her inpatient admission.
- She is currently not using any substances and not on Suboxone.

Mental Health History

You heard Samantha review her experiences with depression. You also heard her discuss the interrelationship between her depression, opiate use, and sexual behavior. Consequently, it would make clinical sense to assess her depression history in conjunction with her substance (opiate) and process (sexual) addictions. Even though the depression, as per her report, seems to clearly predate the addictive behaviors (thus, for example, ruling out substance-induced mood disorder), you still want to see exactly how each disorder exacerbates one another, so your questioning relevant to depression will also include queries for addictive content as well.

Counselor: This may be asking a lot, so just give the best answer you can, but when did you recall first feeling depressed?

Client: I don't know. I can remember feeling like that in my early teens. That's the first time I heard how being depressed or showing emotion is "weak." So, 12 or 13 or so.

Counselor: OK. Now, let's jump to when you were an adult. So now we're talking anywhere from college up through right now. Have you ever felt down, hopeless, sad for just about every day for a period?

Client: Definitely.

Counselor: Longer than 2 weeks or so?

Client: Yes. Sometimes like 3 or 4 or maybe 5 weeks.

Counselor: You remember feeling like that before you started Percocet? And for that long?

Client: Definitely.

Counselor: You ever lose interest in hobbies, work, people, other enjoyable things when you were feeling down?

Client: Yes. Lots of times. I used to knit but never when I felt depressed.

Counselor: And this loss of interest in, for example, knitting, predates Percocet use? You felt this loss of interest only due to the depression?

Client: Well, I didn't knit when I was using a lot, but that's different. So yeah, I used to feel no interest in stuff due to my depression before the pills started.

Counselor: Let me run a few more things by you. When you were depressed, you ever gain or lose weight?

Client: No, not really.

Counselor: Did you feel fatigued when down?

Client: Yeah, but I just pushed through it. I wouldn't sleep a lot a bunch of times, so I just would sort of veg-out all night till I dozed off.

Counselor: How was work or school when depressed?

Client: Much harder to focus, but again, I just did what I had to do and did my best. Some days I limped through but I did it though.

Counselor: How's your self-esteem? Now, and then.

Client: Always shitty. It's a little better now 'cause I'm proud I stopped the pills and the sex, but I still feel like a loser most days.

Counselor: So, to recap, you have felt all these things, before you started using pills, for at least 2 weeks, right, on occasion?

Client: Yes.

Counselor: This may be a reach, but how many times had you experienced this bundle of symptoms for about 2 weeks?

Client: A bunch. I can't tell you. A bunch. Like maybe 3 or 4 or 5 times a year or maybe more. Sorry. Can't get specific.

Counselor: OK. When was the last time you felt this way for at least 2 weeks?

Client: Probably now. I'm doing better but I still feel like this. Since I started inpatient I think.

This exchange of information clearly shows a history of recurrent major depressive disorder episodes with an initial episode onset long predating the start of the opiate addiction or sex behaviors. Next, we need to delve into the more complicated interrelationship between these three disorders. This is a more difficult task and it is likely that there may not be clear answers that come out of the interview. However, with the substance-induced mood disorder diagnosis now officially off the table as a possibility, the discussion becomes more of how the addictions and depression played off one another. Examples of some relevant inquiries are as follows.

Counselor: You stated that the sex behaviors began as your answer to managing the depression you were not willing to seek help for. How did the sex influence the depression symptoms?

Client: Sex is a rush and fun in general. So there's that. It also gave me something to attack the depression with. I felt like, even if it was only for a bit, I was in control. I could turn the knob on the depression down a little. It did help. All of it, the rush from the sex and the fact I could control things.

Counselor: This might sound odd, but did you notice that sex was not getting you as much of a "rush" anymore? Like the pills, did you need more to get the same effect?

Client: Yeah. It's horrible to say, I probably sound like a total slut. But yeah, I would need to have sex with more guys. Then, to make it more exciting I'd start things like only guys who were strangers. I did craigslist, I did one-night stand hook-ups at bars. I'm not a lesbian but I would pick up and have sex with women. Sometimes I would have sex with multiple partners, like three, four, or five over a weekend. I just kept needing the release and it would take more to get and keep that feeling.

Counselor: Did this happen more often when you were experiencing a depressed episode?

Client: Absolutely. But I stopped when I started the pills.

Counselor: So the sexual behaviors you discussed ended when you started the pills?

Client: Kind of. I felt like a slut toward the end, so I liked the pills got me off the hook and gave me a new outlet. But I still kept up the sexual stuff, just, well, just with myself.

Counselor: So you would chronically masturbate.

Client: Yes. When I felt like I needed to deal with a depressed mood or just a bad day. I started using this as a coping skill also. On bad days, I would masturbate upwards of six times per day. Once early in the morning, then right before work, once at work, then once or twice at home. At some point it wasn't even pleasurable anymore. I just did it for the act, not the effect.

Counselor: So this is where the opiates became more of the primary tool?

Client: Yeah, almost the same as the sex. I used them to deal with my depressive stuff. I felt like I was in control by being able to numb myself. Plus, I didn't feel like a slut and have to worry about STDs, pregnancies, or guys who didn't understand they were just a lay.

Counselor: At the end, right before treatment, like the day you raced to buy more pills during lunch hour, were the pills working as well?

Client: No, the depression was really bad. But at that point it sort of became a double-headed depression. Kind of like yeah, I'm depressed, but now I also have the pill taking to be depressed about. And I was thinking about maybe more sex again, so there was that also. I was just a sad, sad mess. And the damn things weren't even working that well anymore. I was getting more lost in my head about my depressed mood, low self-esteem. Even started having suicidal thoughts, like on my way back, what if I just drove the car off the highway into the trees off to the side? I die and nobody else gets hurt or has car damage.

Counselor: Can you think of how and why that idea came to you?

Client: I talked about that a little in inpatient. I guess because my two ways of dealing with the depression, sex and drugs, no longer worked and I was at my wit's end.

Based on this exchange and her history, it is also clear that Samantha experiences recurrent episodes of major depressive disorder. In addition, she also seems to align with many of the symptoms Kafka's (2010) conceptualization of hypersexual disorder. More on this in the diagnostic section further down.

Social

There would be a few key issues to target here: (1) Does she have an interest in joining a 12-step support system? If yes, she would need to be linked up with an NA group in her area. In addition, if she so desired, she would also need assistance finding a sex addiction support group as well. (2) How did she leave matters with work? Is she welcome to come back? How does she feel about going back? (3) Now that she is no longer using pills or sex, has she reconsidered how many healthy friends she may have? Is she leaning on them for support? Or if she has no friends who are good for her recovery, then she would need help to slowly build a new social support system. (4) The client would need to strongly consider eliminating from her life the regular "sex partners" from her time of dysfunctional sex use.

Family

How are things with her family? Do they know the full story? The counselor role here is to provide the client the space to decide how she wants her family included in her recovery process. Consequently, inquiries need to be made into relationships with parents and other members.

Medical

Considering her history, even if she did just get a full battery of testing during her inpatient stay, I would want her to receive a full assortment of STD testing (including HIV as well as Hepatitis B). I would also want her liver, kidneys, and gastrointestinal system evaluated for any damage due to excessive opiate use.

Mental Status

Following the recommendations from Chapter 2, I assessed the following:

- Appearance
  - o Dressed appropriately. Poor eye contact at times in session.

- Characteristics of Talk
  - o Seemed appropriate.
- Emotional State
  - o Appeared depressed in body posture. Poor eye contact. Became anxious/fidgety when discussing her sexual behaviors.
- Content of Thought
  - o Denied any hallucinations or delusions.
- Orientation
  - o Oriented x3 (person, place, and time). No cognitive confusion evident.
- Memory
  - o Demonstrated good recent and longer-term memory.

Urine Monitoring

Considering her opiate use history, I would recommend urine testing twice per week with optimal spacing between testing so any use could be captured throughout the week. Considering that most substances (with exception of marijuana) are detectable within the urine for only 1 to 3 days post use, a Monday and Thursday schedule would allow me to capture any Tuesday or Wednesday use. Furthermore, without a window to use without detection, this aggressive urine test schedule may serve as another external motivator for sustained substance abstinence.

Assessment of Substance Use, Depression, and Sex Addiction

The list of potential assessment sources is expansive. However, my selection process is narrowed by Samantha's history and current status. First, I obviously want to evaluate her depressed mood right now. That is why I selected the Beck Depression Inventory-II (BDI-II). I can obtain a baseline score and track her depressed mood changes as the treatment progresses. Second, I would also want to give Samantha the Drug Abuse Screen Test (DAST-10). Though she is not actively using, the DAST-10 would provide another piece of data to coincide with the *DSM-5* opiate use disorder criteria. I would want to see if the "severity" level of the DAST-10 was consistent with the *DSM-5*. Third, I would administer the Compulsive Sexual Behavior Inventory to assess the severity of her apparent sexual behavior patterns.

The DAST-10 is a yes/no measure where one point is assigned for each item endorsed that reflects problematic substance use. Though these answers were from her past year and not current, she scored a 9 out of 10. As per the DAST-10, this rates as "severe." The BDI-II contains 21 questions, each answer being scored on a scale value of 0 to 3. Higher total scores indicate more severe depressive symptoms. She scored a 28, which placed her in the BDI-II moderate depression range. Of note, unlike the primarily historical DAST-10 score, the BDI-II score reflects a current level of functioning. The Compulsive Sexual Behavior Inventory is a 28-item measure and includes items such as "How often have you had trouble controlling your sexual urges?" "Were you sexually abused as a child?" and "Have you ever hit, kicked, punched, slapped, thrown, choked, restrained, or beaten any of your sexual partners?" Respondents rate each item on a 5-point Likert-type scale ranging from 1 (*very frequently*) to 5 (*never*). Total scores range from 28 to 140, with higher scores indicating lower sexual addiction. Samantha received a score of 46, which seemed to match the addictive and out-of-control quality of her reported history of and current sexual behavior.

Diagnosis

Based on the *DSM-5* (APA, 2013) Opioid Use Disorder criteria (pp. 541–542), Samantha's diagnosis seems to be *Opioid Use Disorder, Severe, in early remission.* Specifically, through the dialogue shown above plus other discussions with Samantha, it was obvious that she took larger amounts over a longer period, had unsuccessful efforts to cut down, experienced craving and urges, continued use despite noted social problems, avoided important activities due to substance use, continued use despite noting several times in early sessions how the opiate use exacerbated her depression or sexual behaviors, and she experienced symptoms of both tolerance and withdrawal. That is a count of eight criteria endorsed, which qualified her for a severe disorder specifier.

Samantha also, as per the *DSM-5* (APA, 2013) Major Depressive Disorder criteria (pp. 160–162), met the diagnosis of Major Depressive Disorder, Recurrent, Moderate. Since she is currently reporting the symptoms of depressed mood, fatigue, feelings of worthlessness, and diminished interest in prior healthy hobbies, that is her endorsing of four criteria. I am initially going with this diagnosis (and not considering her depressed mood as reflective of a longer-term withdrawal syndrome) for the following reasons: (1) she successfully detoxed prior to meeting me, and (2) she has a long-term history of recurrent depressive episodes prior to any opiate use. I am, of course, considering her major depressive disorder symptoms as perhaps being somewhat amplified by the stress of withdrawal, abstinence, and the rigors of treatment.

Finally, though I could not diagnose her, Samantha is very consistent with many of the criteria for hypersexual disorder. She spent a great deal of time focused on and engaging in sexual behaviors, she engaged in these sexual behaviors as a response to her depressed mood, she engaged in the sexual acts as a response to day-to-day stressful events, she tried to cut down or cease the sexual behaviors, and since she rarely used condoms, the sexual behaviors continued despite the risk of harm to self. The sexual behavior focused on sex with consenting adults and masturbation.

Treatment Placement

Samantha seemed to follow the *ASAM Criteria* (2013) for treatment placement. She began in an OTS program (Suboxone) and then progressed to a Level 3.5 treatment facility (Clinically Managed High Intensity Residential) followed by a Level 2.5 (Partial Hospitalization) facility. Having successfully completed those phases of her treatment, she now arrives at Level 2.1 (Intensive Outpatient). Hopefully, if Samantha maintains her recovery, she will eventually move down to Level 1 (Outpatient) and eventually discharge from formal treatment.

LEGAL, ETHICAL, AND CURRICULAR ISSUES IN SUD SCREENING, ASSESSMENT, AND TREATMENT PLACEMENT

Legal Protections of Data

Addiction-related clinical interview and assessment records are subject to a level of privacy protection not afforded any other health data (Geppert, 2013; Geppert & Roberts, 2008). This is due to the stigma and illegal nature of much substance use (whether an adult addicted to heroin or an adolescent using alcohol). That is why Congress enacted the Confidentiality of Alcohol and Drug Abuse Patient Records, Part 2 of Title 42 of the Code of Federal Regulations (CFR), which is commonly abbreviated as CFR 42 Part 2. This regulation applies to any treatment program providing assessment, diagnosis, treatment, or referral services to SUD treatment.

Most SUD treatment programs receive some type of federal assistance (CSAT, 2006a). However, for-profit programs and private practitioners that do not receive federal assistance of any kind would not be subject to the requirements of CFR 42 Part 2 unless the state licensing or certification agency requires them to comply. The regulations restrict the disclosure and use of alcohol and drug client records which are maintained in connection with the performance of any federally assisted alcohol and drug abuse program. Basically, the protections provided by CFR 42 Part 2 is for any information disclosed by a covered program that identifies an individual directly or indirectly as having a current or past drug or alcohol problem, or as a participant in a covered program. Thus, obviously this applies to the client interview, screening, and assessment data, and with few exceptions, CFR 42 Part 2 requires client consent for disclosures of protected health information even for the purposes of treatment, payment, or health care operations. Consent for disclosure must be in writing.

CFR 42 Part 2 is typically interpreted as a more stringent protector of client confidentiality and privacy than the Health Insurance Portability and Accountability Act (HIPAA), which focuses on all private health information and not just substance-related information. One interesting area of CFR 42 Part 2 and HIPAA conflict is when a client requests access to their clinical records (including interview and assessment data). Under HIPAA, clients have the right to inspect and obtain copies of their information except for counseling notes and any information compiled for a civil, criminal or administrative action/proceeding. However, CFR 42 Part 2 does not prohibit client access to records, including the opportunity to inspect and copy any records maintained about the client. The program is not required to obtain written authorization from the client in order to provide access. Consequently, an ethical dilemma or (at the very least) a challenging clinical situation is what occurs if a client wants to see their assessment data.

On one hand, these data are about the client. The CFR 42 Part 2 protections are afforded to that client so they are buffered from stigma and potential legal action in the hope that they seek and remain in treatment. So the client should be free to see their information as they are not at risk of self-stigmatizing or triggering legal action against themselves. On the other hand, assessment data (particularly the more complicated psychiatric or personality measures) are easily misinterpreted by a layperson and could be quite distressing (e.g., Hays, 2013; Millon

& Davis, 1996). It is therefore incumbent upon the addiction professional to be at the ready to be able to explain these assessment data and findings in a manner that is accurate, understandable, and useable by the layperson client, all while being sensitive to the client reaction. For instance, consider this quote from a former client of mine who, in addition to substance use, also struggled with impulsive sexual behavior indicative of what is commonly called sex addiction:

> I knew I screwed a lot of guys sometimes when I didn't feel like using, but when I saw it in your report, well, all of a sudden I was horrified and embarrassed. I felt like you saw me as a slut. I didn't like that.

American Counseling Association *Code of Ethics*

The American Counseling Association *Code of Ethics* (2014) dedicates a full section to the practice of assessment use and interpretation (Section E, pp. 11–12). This section starts with the following preamble:

> Counselors use assessment as one component of the counseling process, taking into account the clients' personal and cultural context. Counselors promote the well-being of individual clients or groups of clients by developing and using appropriate educational, mental health, psychological, and career assessments. (p. 11)

Some specific components of section E that seem most relevant to the use of assessments in the SUD treatment process are E.2.a (Limits of Competence), E.2.b (Appropriate Use), and E.6.a (Appropriateness of Instruments). These three components all speak to how a counselor must know about the assessment they intend to apply or interpret. For instance, there are many, many measures listed in Table 2.7. It is not feasible or even expected that a counselor is knowledgeable in all of them. Furthermore, some measures may not be accessible for the counselor to use as some instruments mandate a doctoral-level training for purchase and use (Hays, 2013). Thus, instrument choice must be tailored to the client (as discussed earlier) and tailored to the counselor's training, experience, and expertise. For instance, when I have needed a thorough neuropsychological assessment of a client, I have referred to a neuropsychologist who clearly has the expertise to administer, interpret, and report those specific findings.

Interestingly, the National Association of Alcoholism and Drug Abuse Counselors (NAADAC) *Ethical Standards of Alcoholism and Drug Abuse Counselors* (2011) offers no specific guidelines on the rendering and/or use of diagnoses. However, the American Counseling Association *Code of Ethics* (2014) provides guidance on the application and use of *DSM* diagnoses across a few areas. First, the counselor is ethically obligated to be certain that the client understands the implications of a diagnosis (A2.b; p. 4). This also seems to apply to the ethical guideline regarding how the counselor must respect the stigma of a psychiatric diagnosis (E.5.c.; p. 11), especially one as sensitive as substance use disorder. Taken together, these mandate that the counselor helps the client understand how such a diagnosis was derived, normalize the symptoms, and explain the consequences (positive and negative) of such a diagnosis. For example, explaining (in easy to understand terms) how/why the individual in alcohol withdrawal may be experiencing tactile hallucinations of "bugs under the skin" or explaining what the term *psychotic features* means in a nonthreatening way that assists clients to better comprehend their psychiatric state of being. The client may learn how to self-monitor his or her own overall well-being by learning to recognize symptoms as indicative of potential recovery challenges ahead. Think of this as the same as learning that a fever is indicative of being ill. You feel a fever, you seek medical attention.

The American Counseling Association *Code of Ethics* also stipulates that counselors must be cautious to provide the proper diagnosis (E.5.a.; p. 11). Going back for a moment to the work of First (2014) as an example, you can see the complexity of the substance use diagnosis process. Consequently, ample classroom and applied training must take place before a clinician can competently render a diagnosis in the presence of so many overlapping and similar cognitive, emotional, and behavioral symptoms.

NAADAC Ethics Code

The NAADAC Ethics Code (2011) is smaller in scope and detail as compared to the American Counseling Association *Code of Ethics* in regard to assessment use. Specifically, the NAADAC Ethics Code states the following:

> The addiction professional uses assessment instruments as one component of the counseling/treatment and referral process taking into account the client's personal and cultural background. The assessment process promotes the well-being of individual clients or groups. Addiction professionals base their recommendations/reports on approved evaluation instruments and procedures. The designated assessment instruments are ones for which reliability has been verified by research. (p. 2)

There may be some state-specific issues relevant to testing, specifically centered on the primary license of record for many NAADAC members. While many of members of NAADAC operate as licensed professional counselors or licensed social workers, just as many operate as licensed or certified addiction counselors. Consequently, the ethics of assessment would pertain to the scope of practice for an addiction counselor as defined by their state. So if the addiction counselor can only work within the *DSM-5* scope of substance-related disorders and process addictions (i.e., pathological gambling), there would likely be a boundaries of competence issue regarding which assessments the addiction counselor could use due to their graduate training and their state scope of practice guidelines. As I tell all my students in my graduate ethics course, once you decide upon the state where you wish to practice counseling, the first thing you must do is study the counseling regulations for that state.

Council for Accreditation of Counseling and Related Programs (CACREP) Curricular Content

The most recent CACREP Standards (2015) highlight the manner via which master's and doctoral programs should cover assessment within the curriculum (pp. 11–12) and while on practicum or internship (pp. 13–14) via professional training. However, there does seem to be a flaw in how CACREP reviews assessment for the counseling profession, which is indicative of the fragmented nature of the counseling profession as it pertains to the question of whether addictions counseling should be considered a counseling specialization or just the practice of counseling as it relates to one *DSM-5* diagnostic class (Henriksen, Nelson, & Watts, 2010; Morgen, Miller, & Stretch, 2012).

Perusal of the assessment and testing guidelines for counselor training makes specific reference to "trauma" (Section 2, F.1.7.d) or "mental disorders" (Section 2, F.1.7.l) as well as more general statements regarding diagnosis and treatment planning (Section 2, F.1.7.e). But here is where the confusion may occur. For instance, in the human growth and development curricular standards there is specific reference to "theories and etiology of addictions and addictive behaviors" (p. 9). So why is there no specific reference to substance-related or process addictions in the assessment and testing standards, but there is a specific reference to "addictions" in the human growth and development standards? Furthermore, in the addiction counseling specialization criteria there is a clear reference to addiction assessment where CACREP (2015) stipulates "screening, assessment, and testing for addiction, including diagnostic interviews, mental status examination, symptom inventories, and psychoeducational and personality assessments" (p. 19).

As discussed in the Author's Preface, specifically for new graduate students and trainees, the way our profession is explained matters. Our words matter. A professional like me who sees addiction as a clear part of the counselor scope of practice would read things such as "mental health" and "diagnosis" as obviously including substance-related and process addictions. But for a new student or trainee, the confusion is present and clear (e.g., Morgen & Miller, 2013; Morgen, Miller, Chasek, DePue, & Ivers, 2015a, 2015b; Morgen et al., 2012). There is a separate specialization for addiction with a clear addiction assessment training mandate whereas the words *addiction* or *substance-related disorder* are never included in the assessment and testing criteria for counseling. Thus, there lie the seeds of confusion regarding whether addiction work (such as assessment) is something that a licensed professional counselor does. Too often, students and post-master's trainees have told me that they believe they are not permitted to do addiction work because they are working toward their licensed professional counselor's certification, and those who wish to work with addiction pursue the addiction license/certification. In brief, any counseling assessment course (whether for the licensed professional counselor or for the addiction counselor license/certification) must contain a comprehensive section devoted to the assessment and screening for substance-related disorders as reviewed in this chapter.

The CACREP Standards (2015) for addiction counseling make specific reference to the complexity of diagnoses for SUDs and co-occurring psychiatric disorders by mandating that addiction counselors from CACREP programs must understand the "diagnostic process, including differential diagnosis and the use of current diagnostic classification systems, including the *Diagnostic and Statistical Manual of Mental Disorders* (DSM) and the International Classification of Diseases (ICD)" (p. 19). This educational and training requirement runs parallel with the International Certification and Reciprocity Consortium's revised standards for the Advanced Alcohol and Drug Counselor (AADC) credential, one of the largest addiction credentials with over 5,000 AADC professionals worldwide. The AADC credentialing exam recently changed (May 15, 2015) with emphases on diagnosis (and differential diagnosis) of co-occurring SUDs, psychiatric disorders, and physical disorders.

The Addiction Counseling Competencies (CSAT, 2006c) also highlight the requirement for effective diagnostic skills via Competency 30 where counselors "apply accepted criteria for diagnosis of substance use disorders in making treatment recommendations" (p. 43). Furthermore, the Competencies for Substance Abuse Treatment Clinical Supervisors (CSAT, 2007) emphasized how only supervisors trained and skilled in diagnostic assessment should supervise such clinical endeavors. This disclaimer is likely included due to one of two potential scenarios: (1) A grandfathered or long-standing addiction counselor who entered the field when it was considered a paraprofession and *DSM* diagnostic skills were not utilized or emphasized in training or practice (e.g., Morgen et al., 2012), or (2) As a caution to a mental health professional that they cannot supervise an SUD case without diagnostic and differential diagnostic training in SUDs and co-occurring disorders. Too often, this lack of training is unfortunately a reality, especially in counselor/psychologist training programs (e.g., Miller, 2015).

SECTION III

COMMON COUNSELING THEORIES APPLIED TO SUBSTANCE USE DISORDERS AND ADDICTIONS

CHAPTERS 5-8

These chapters cover three common treatment approaches to substance use disorders (SUDs) and addictions—motivational interviewing, cognitive-behavioral therapy, and family systems—as well as an approach not as commonly adopted but still relevant to the practice of counseling for substance use disorders and addictions—existential. Toward the end of each of these chapters, I include some recent meta-analysis study reviews to reinforce the empirically supported nature of these theories toward the treatment of SUDs and addictions. Finally, after Chapter 8, the case of Samantha is revisited from each of these theoretical perspectives to give just a glimpse of how each theory would tackle her case. Last, ethical and other issues are reviewed.

Chapter 5

MOTIVATIONAL INTERVIEWING

GENERAL MOTIVATIONAL INTERVIEWING CONTENT

One of the most common counseling practices applied to SUDs is motivational interviewing (MI). MI is defined as "a collaborative, person-centered form of guiding to elicit and strengthen motivation for change" (Miller & Rollnick, 2009, p. 137). MI is supported by myriad clinical trials that show the effectiveness of the technique (e.g., Miller & Rollnick, 2002; Miller & Rose, 2009; Rosengren, 2009). As designed, MI is a short-term, directive style of counseling that helps clients explore and resolve ambivalence. Typically, via counselor interventions such as empathic listening and reflective statements, the client-perceived need for behavior change occurs (i.e., substance cessation, entering into SUD treatment). Once motivated for the change, MI is integrated or replaced with another counseling orientation (e.g., cognitive-behavioral) during the actual treatment process (Rollnick & Miller, 1995; Satre & Leibowitz, 2015). Entire texts are devoted to MI. The purpose of this chapter is to summarize the critical model components in an attempt to demonstrate how/why MI functions so effectively in the treatment of SUD.

Motivational Interviewing Goals

As defined, MI has three goals:

1. MI strives to increase client intrinsic motivation for behavior change. Intrinsic motivation has a greater impact on behavior change than extrinsic motivation. This is primarily due to the client investment in the proposed behavior change. Extrinsic motivation entails others defining the desired behavior change (e.g., family dictates that the client stops drinking), whereas intrinsic

motivation involves the client defining the desired change (e.g., client decides that he or she needs to stop drinking independent of other opinions).

2. MI helps lower resistance in treatment. Note that this goal is not to eliminate resistance entirely, as that is impossible (Miller, Rollnick, & Moyers, 1998).

3. MI helps resolve ambivalence. Miller and Rollnick (2002) argued that ambivalence, defined as having two opposing thoughts/feelings on an issue, is a key factor as to why some problematic and dysfunctional behaviors remain unchanged. For example, adolescent clients engage in nonsuicidal self-injury because they feel that they need the emotional control and release, but they also feel guilt and concern regarding their continuing process addiction of self-harm and do desire to stop. The client feels pulled in both directions and remains stuck between these two competing forces. MI helps clients to explore and to potentially resolve ambivalence so that behavior change can commence.

MI has a few counseling theory influences. One is person-centered theory, which is evident in the role that empathic listening (a key Rogerian concept) plays in the MI process. The concept of empathy and patience are critical to how MI attempts to effect behavior change in those who may see little to no reason to change.

Another influence, cognitive-behavioral therapy, is evident in how MI works to adjust client thought processes. You will see several MI examples where the intervention is designed to challenge the current perception of the problem and introduce an awareness of a discrepancy between what a client thinks and the reality of the situation.

The stages of change model (Prochaska, DiClemente, & Norcross, 1992) has also influenced MI (Miller & Rollnick, 2002). In the stages of change model, a client cognitively and behaviorally moves through a series of stages toward behavioral change. In the first stage, Precontemplation, clients do not see a need for behavior change and consequently see no reason for treatment. In Stage 2, Contemplation, clients display ambivalence about behavior change. They see both the advantages and disadvantages of behavioral change. Clients are more open to treatment, as compared to those in precontemplation, but still remain unsure about their desire to put forth the effort to engage in treatment and the associated behavioral change (e.g., cessation of substance use). Stage 3 is Preparation, and this is where clients start to cognitively recognize the importance of the behavioral change but remain uninformed (and perhaps overwhelmed) regarding how exactly to start the change process. Stage 4 is the Action stage where clients actively take behavioral change steps (e.g., entering and engaging in treatment, joining an Alcoholics Anonymous [AA]/Narcotics Anonymous [NA] group). After about 6 months of abstinence, clients enter Stage 5, which is Maintenance. Here, clients maintain gains made in treatment, and some may actually move out of the change cycle due to sustained abstinence and stability (Prochaska et al., 1992). However, for many there is Stage 6, which is Relapse. The inclusion of this stage reinforces the common occurrence of relapse and how addiction is a chronic, and not acute, disorder. Clients enter treatment at any stage of the process. For example, a client may enter outpatient counseling with you in the Action stage after having moved through the prior stages in earlier and more intensive levels of treatment. Though MI and the stages of change model have more in common, it is important to note that it is not necessary to know a client's stage of change in order to engage in MI treatment interventions (Miller & Rollnick, 2009).

MOTIVATIONAL INTERVIEWING SPIRIT, PRINCIPLES, AND PROCESSES

MI Spirit

MI is a collaborative process that emphasizes the autonomy of the client while evoking reasons for a behavioral change that are considered in the treatment session. Recently, Miller and Rollnick (2013) added *compassion* as a fourth component of MI spirit. Adding compassion to MI spirit was done to reinforce that all facets of MI are performed in the best interests of the client. It would be easy for a counselor to impose issues in need of discussion or change in session. However, the MI spirit underscores that the client must be involved in the process and eventually endorse any behavioral change matters.

Rollnick (2010) reviewed three common communication styles within professional helping relationships. The *directive style* involves the counselor directing, prescribing, or advising in the session. For instance, a counselor prescribes more relaxation activities for a client experiencing heightened stress. The *guiding style* has the counselor encouraging the client in regard to a behavioral change, for example, a counselor who encourages the client to consider making a behavioral change that may not be popular within the family. The counselor offers support for the client in this process. The *following style* is where the counselor simply exists in the same space as the client, for example, a counselor who just listens to a client discuss his or her traumatic experience of attempting suicide without any direct intervention. Rollnick (2010) argued that counselors use all these communication styles in MI and counseling. The key is to strike the correct balance and use the appropriate style at the right time.

MI Principles

Originally, Miller and Rollnick (1991) discussed five principles of Motivational Interviewing. These were not actually techniques but rather represented a philosophy via which MI was conducted. Principle 1 was to avoid argumentation, as such confrontation only enhances client resistance. Principle 2 was to roll with resistance. Here, resistance is not directly confronted but rather "rolled with," in that the resistance is discussed while valuing the client's perspective on the matter. This approach to resistance led to new perspectives on the issue while also demonstrating counselor empathy. Principle 3 was expressing empathy. The creation of a welcoming and understanding environment with unconditional acceptance assists the client to uncover personal reasons for desiring a behavioral change. Principle 4 was developing discrepancy and was based on Festinger's theory of cognitive dissonance (Miller & Rollnick, 1991) where individuals experience dissonance when behaviors, values, and goals do not line up or move in the same direction. Dissonance is reduced, and motivation is enhanced, when a greater degree of consistency develops between what is desired by the client and the client behaviors that support this goal. Principle 5 was the support of self-efficacy. MI reinforces hope and optimism, and helps the client believe the targeted behavioral change is indeed possible.

However, the principles of MI have evolved since the onset of these principles more than 2 decades ago. Recent discussions of the MI principles utilize the acronym RULE (Rollnick, 2010), which stands for the following:

Resisting the righting reflex. Clinicians cannot make right what is going wrong in the client's life. This can involve providing unsolicited advice, stubbornly fixating on an issue, or even arguing with the client.

Understanding the client's own motivations. For any behavioral change to work, the desire for such change needs to intrinsically come from the client. For a client to develop his or her own motivations for change, the counselor must elicit ideas from the client and reflect this content back to the client for consideration and further development.

Listen with empathy. This remains a defining characteristic of MI as well as any other counseling theory.

Empower the client. Basically, the counselor must support and nurture the client's sense of self-efficacy. If clients believe they can change, then change is possible. Just as critical, if clients see no way in which they can achieve change, MI (or any other intervention) will fail.

MI Processes

Miller and Rollnick (2013) discussed four key therapeutic processes: engaging, focusing, evoking, and planning. *Engaging* refers to establishing a collaborative relationship with the client. *Focusing* is where clinicians help clients find direction in terms of treatment goals and behavior change via involving clients in a dialogue about the process of behavior change. *Evoking* is respecting the client's thoughts and emotions about change. Evoking is a unique element of MI because the client is encouraged to discuss his or her ambivalence and discomfort regarding making any type of change. For example, when I use MI, evoking for me may involve my welcoming prompt where I state to the ambivalent client, "If you think I'm full of crap about this, just tell me. We'll spend the hour discussing how and why I'm way off here." And last, *planning* refers to developing a collaborative plan for realistic and obtainable behavioral change.

THE NUTS AND BOLTS OF MOTIVATIONAL INTERVIEWING

Below, I review several specific strategies and techniques used in MI. These are the "nuts and bolts" of MI. The concepts, strategies, and techniques discussed here would occur as a part of any of the MI processes discussed above.

Reflective Listening

Reflective listening is a core component of the MI technique (Rollnick, 2010) and also a core counseling skill in general. By reflectively listening, the clinician can reduce resistance while communicating empathy. This is accomplished via the counselor offering a summary statement regarding the client's meaning in what was just discussed. There are two types of reflections: simple and complex.

A simple reflection states back to clients what was said by paraphrasing. An example of a simple reflection would be as follows:

Client statement: I do not see any point to my being in treatment. This seems like a waste of time. But I'm forced to come.

Counselor simple reflection: You don't see any benefit to being in treatment.

A complex reflection adds meaning to the client statement by including emotional content. A complex reflection for the above client statement might run as follows:

Counselor complex reflection: You see treatment as a waste of time, and all it seems to accomplish is that you feel annoyed that you have no say in your own life.

The simple reflection does nothing other than restate the client's words. Note how the complex reflection interjects emotional content into the client statement. The type of emotion chosen by the counselor may not be fully accurate, but the mere inclusion of the emotionality will elicit emotional-based dialogue from the client. For instance, clients may disagree with the term *annoyed* but will likely offer their own feelings by correcting you (e.g., they tell you they feel "disrespected" instead of "annoyed"). Regardless of counselor accuracy, this is a winning intervention for the clinician, as the complex and simple reflection processes facilitate a deeper dialogue and demonstrate counselor empathy.

OARS

The acronym OARS stands for open-ended questions, affirmations, reflections, and summary. OARS strategies build rapport, show counselor empathy, and help the client recognize the importance of behavioral change. However, OARS is in no way unique to MI, as these counseling techniques are some of the core foundational components of basic counseling microskills (Ivey, Ivey, & Zalaquett, 2014). They do, though, form a foundation for MI work, and each will briefly be reviewed below.

Open-Ended Questions

Open-ended questions allow for greater exploration as the client is forced to respond with more than just one-word answers. This is critical, as there cannot be a dialogue that discusses thoughts and emotions regarding behavior change, and any ambivalence regarding such change, if the client is only providing one-word answers (Rollnick, 2010). You can also look at open-ended questions as a mechanism to avoid resistance. Too often, a resistant client will demonstrate hesitancy via one-word answers. Open-ended questions force the client to at least provide a more well-articulated rationale for resistance or ambivalence.

Session Summaries

These are designed to help keep the momentum of counseling moving forward (Rollnick, 2010). A general aim is for two summaries per counseling session, one in the middle of the session and the other placed toward the end. Think of these as nothing more than specialized reflections that capture a full session instead of just a small moment of the session.

Counselor: So here's where you are. You're trying to be a good guy and give her space, but you also see how your heroin use damaged your relationship with your girlfriend and your family. While you're trying to get your relationships and life back on track, you are also seeing how stressful it is. That's why you're still occasionally drinking, just to deal with the stress. But now you're also feeling guilty and worried about drinking and may want to stop that as well. So you're anxious, confused, worried, and feeling lost. Does this sound accurate?

As per Rollnick (2010), the above summary statement is appropriate because it references client ambiguity and utilizes "you" language. Such a summary can serve as a meaningful springboard to the remainder of the session or (if summarized at the end) the next session.

Change Talk

Change talk is an important MI concept housed in the premise that the more a client talks about change, the more likely that change will occur (Rollnick, Miller, & Butler 2008). MI clinicians listen for change talk and reinforce it whenever possible. If change talk is not happening, then MI clinicians use open-ended questions to facilitate the development of change talk.

MI theory notes the existence of six types of change talk (Amrhein, Miller, Yahne, Knupsky, & Hochstein, 2004; Amrhein, Miller, Yahne, Palmer, & Fulcher, 2003). The first type focuses on a client's desire to change. The second type of change talk reflects a client's ability to change. The third type involves reasons for desiring change. The fourth type focuses on the need for change. The fifth type examines the client commitment to the behavior change. The sixth type of change talk looks at the specific steps taken thus far toward achieving the change.

These six types of change talk can be broken down into two mnemonics. The first one, DARN, is focused on preparatory change talk—in brief, ways the client is shifting motivation, reducing ambivalence, and preparing for the behavioral change. The mnemonic DARN specifically stands for:

Desire (I want to change)

Ability (I can change)

Reason (It is important to me to change)

Need (It would benefit me to change)

The other mnemonic CAT focuses on the implementation change talk and stands for the following:

Commitment (I will make a change)

Activation (I am ready, prepared, and willing to change)

Taking steps (I am performing tasks to accomplish my intended change)

There are specific MI strategies designed to elicit and sustain change talk. Besides change talk, these strategies can also bolster client confidence in that they are capable of implementing and sustaining behavior change. Each is briefly reviewed as follows:

Ask Evocative Questions. Asking open-ended questions by default produces some type of fuel for change talk.

Explore Decisional Balance. Too often, the pros (benefits) of substance use are ignored. If using the substance produced nothing but despair and pain, the addiction would never have been sustained. By exploring how the substance helped the client (e.g., numbs emotional pain, assists with affect management) as well as the dysfunctional consequences of use, a change talk environment may occur.

Ask for Elaboration. Think of this as a supplemental tactic to coincide with open-ended questions. Probing for more information leads to change talk.

Looking Forward. Ask about what may happen if things remain the same.

Query the Extremes. Ask about what is the best that may happen if the behavior change is made. In addition, inquire about what may be the worst that could happen if the change is not accomplished.

Using Change Rulers. This is an excellent concrete strategy to produce change talk. Ask clients on a scale of 1 (not at all important) to 10 (very important) about how important it is for them to make the intended change, and follow up with inquiries regarding their numeric score. For example, if they stated a 6, ask them why not a 5 or a 7 on the scale? Also, probe regarding what would need to happen in order for them to move from a score of 6 to perhaps a score of 7 or 8 on this scale.

Coming Alongside. In order to facilitate change talk, perhaps the counselor must explicitly side with the ambivalence. For instance, a counselor may say, "Perhaps gambling is so important and critical in your life, you will not stop no matter the personal costs." Especially for a client experienced with SUD treatment and AA/NA culture, receiving this type of MI intervention to elicit change talk is quite powerful and can also strengthen the trust between counselor and client.

Especially with clients who lack confidence to change or who are engaging in unhealthy and self-destructive behaviors, Rosengren (2009) stated that some practitioners may feel pressure to give advice to clients so that the obvious (at least to the counselor) dysfunctional behaviors may cease. In addition, oftentimes clients who are low on confidence (or motivation) solicit ideas to help them reach their recovery goals. For instance, I cannot count the number of times clients have relayed a series of dysfunctional issues in their life and then ended their list with the question, "So what should I do?" Rosengren offered five guidelines for counselors so that they can effectively dispense information and advice, which spell the acronym FOCUS. These guidelines are as follows:

First ask permission. Client resistance will spike, and the client will feel disrespected, if unwanted advice is offered. This will especially be true if the advice runs counter to their current thoughts/feelings regarding change.

Offer suggestions, thoughts, and ideas, but avoid trying to convince. The counselor should serve as a source of informed but objective information.

Concise. Do not offer too much information so as to overwhelm the client.

Use a menu of options. Offer two or three options from which the client can choose so that the client feels a sense of autonomy. For instance, if possible, permit clients to select their psychoeducation group schedule as opposed to a prescribed schedule. When I worked at an inpatient SUD treatment facility, whenever possible, the clients were allowed to select from two concurrent psychoeducation sessions.

Solicit. What does the provided advice and feedback mean to the client? Was it helpful? Was the information received as intended? Did the client's state of ambivalence change in any manner as a result of this advice?

WHEN IS A CLIENT READY FOR CHANGE?

MI states that clients are ready to change when there is an abundance of change talk, the client sees a need for a change, and possesses both the self-efficacy and readiness to implement the change. At this point, counseling moves from exploration into action mode. However, the counselor must be cautious to not move the client toward change that is too broad in scope as that may increase the likelihood of failure. In order to effectively map out change in the MI process, Miller and Rollnick (2002) recommended the use of change plans.

Change Plans

These plans are completed during the entire session or in stages across a series of sessions (e.g., completing one part of the plan per session). Good change plans should contain the following content. First, a good change plan is specific and includes an awareness of any barriers to change as well as some ways to possibly overcome them. Second, the goals are written in measureable and behavioral terms. Third, the change plans include a time frame as to when clients will start and a roster of who provides them with recovery support and how (Miller & Rollnick, 2002). Change plans can be a written or verbal counseling exercise (see Figure 5.1 for an example of a change plan worksheet).

Figure 5.1 Motivational Interviewing Change Plan Worksheet Example

The changes I would like to make are . . .
The reasons I want to make these changes are . . .
The ways others can help me are . . .
I will know my plan is working because . . .
Things that may interfere with my plan are . . .
What I will do if my plan is not working . . .

META-ANALYSES OF MOTIVATIONAL INTERVIEWING: TWO EXAMPLES

Meta-Analysis 1: de Roten, Zimmermann, Ortega, and Despland (2013)

MI is an approach to counseling. Trainings and workshops are common, where clinicians (experienced and novice) are educated and trained on the specific MI techniques and concepts and their applications. However, considering the technical nature inherent in the correct application of MI, reviews of the training effectiveness seem warranted. That is why one of the meta-analyses I chose to provide as an example is the de Roten et al. (2013) meta-analysis of MI training studies that consisted of 15 studies with 715 clinicians (n = 601 MI trained clinicians, n = 114 control clinicians). Specific results from this meta-analysis are reviewed below.

- In the majority of studies (12 out of 15), the training was delivered in a 2-day workshop (12 to 16 hours). Pre- and postcomparisons showed medium to large effect sizes for MI training, which were maintained over a short period of time.
- When compared to a control condition, results with moderate effect sizes suggested higher MI proficiency in the MI-trained professionals as compared with the nontrained professionals. De Roten et al. cautioned that this finding may be due, in part, to potential publication bias.
- MI skills (behaviors, adherence, and empathy) improved more in the MI-trained groups as compared with the nontrained groups, with the exception of the MI spirit application. However, de Roten et al. cautioned that clinicians in the control group received MI books and videotapes and that self-training with MI books and videotapes may be enough to comprehend and learn the concept of MI spirit.
- The results between a control group with no training and a control group with self-training (book and video) confirmed that training is effective as compared to a nontraining condition. But de Roten et al. found that the self-training condition seemed as effective as training in the posttraining assessment. However, they argued that the practitioners who self-trained may have had a longer period of time to study the training materials.
- Training conditions compared to nontraining conditions showed great benefits for nonmental health professionals and more experienced (i.e., more than 5 years of experience with a specific population) professionals. Training benefits for the nonmental health professional may be just that they gain a

basic foundational understanding of MI and counseling skills. For the experienced professional, their training benefits may be that, as experienced professionals, they can conceptualize a more advanced manner in which the MI skills can integrate into the counseling process.

- No meaningful difference was found between training and nontraining conditions in mental health professionals, which de Roten et al. argued is in line with the psychotherapy empirical literature that indicates no benefits of training for therapists.

Meta-Analysis 2: Yakovenko, Quigley, Hemmelgarn, Hodgins, and Ronksley (2015)

Yakovenko et al. (2015) conducted a meta-analysis of randomized controlled trials that examined the effects of motivational interviewing interventions compared to no treatment or interventions without motivational interviewing on gambling frequency and gambling expenditure in adults with pathological gambling disorder. They also assessed the stability of the effects of motivational interviewing over time. The meta-analysis consisted of five studies ($N = 477$ participants), and the results indicated some evidence of a positive effect following treatment. Specific meta-analysis results are discussed below.

- For average dollars lost as an outcome, there was a significant positive effect of motivational interviewing compared to the controls at posttreatment. Yakovenko and colleagues found approximately 10% less dollars being spent per month.
- For average days gambled per month as an outcome, there was a significant mean reduction of 1.30 days gambled per month for the motivational interviewing groups as compared to the controls.
- Yakovenko and colleagues found that the benefits of therapy persisted at 12-month follow-up for gambling frequency but not for gambling expenditures.
- Overall, evidence for the effects of motivational interviewing for disordered gambling over time was mixed. Short-term (6 months) outcome, using the average days gambled per month as an outcome variable, produced significant positive results, with an average reduction of 1.22 days gambled per month. Using log of average dollars spent per month as an outcome variable, Yakovenko and colleagues found a nonsignificant positive trend, with an average reduction of .26 units spent per month.
- In the long-term (12 months) outcome analysis, the same pattern held where days gambled showed a significant positive effect while dollars spent remained not significant.

SPECIAL POPULATIONS

Adolescents

The results for MI use with adolescents are promising as clinicians and researchers have noted for years the difficulty in engaging and retaining adolescents in SUD treatment, particularly due to the fact that many adolescents have explicitly or implicitly been coerced into attending treatment (e.g., parents, school, criminal justice system) and do not believe their substance use is problematic (Kaminer, Spirito, & Lewander, 2011). MI may be of benefit in helping treatment staff to instill some degree of behavior change consideration in the adolescent. Macgowan and Engle (2010) reported that MI has met the American Psychological Association's criteria for promising treatments of adolescent substance use. In general, MI appears to be a good match with an adolescents' developmental need for autonomy while also respecting their increased levels of psychological reactance (Baer & Peterson, 2002). MI also seems to be a good match with an adolescent who may respond in a negative manner to an authoritarian style (Nunes, 2010). However, adolescents who benefit from MI as a mechanism to instill the perceived need for change may also require additional treatment in order to fully address their symptoms (Bekman, Wilkins, & Brown, 2013).

Numerous studies have suggested preliminary support for the effective use of MI with adolescents. For instance, a recent meta-analytic review of MI effectiveness with adolescents showed an overall small but promising effect size and demonstrated a significant overall decrease in alcohol consumption (Jensen et al., 2011). Two other analyses also demonstrated the effectiveness of MI with adolescents. Apodaca and Longabaugh's (2009) meta-analysis found evidence that adolescent client change language (Moyers et al., 2007; Moyers, Martin, Manuel, Hendrickson, & Miller, 2005), the adolescent experience of discrepancy (McNally, Palfai, & Kahler, 2005), and techniques such as decisional balance (LaBrie, Feres, Kenney, & Lac, 2009; Strang & McCambridge, 2004) are positively related to improved treatment outcomes. Furthermore, a meta-analysis of 39 studies found that when compared with treatment as usual, MI interventions were significantly more likely to reduce problematic alcohol use in all but one of the reviewed studies. In addition, when compared with control subjects, adolescents receiving MI were more likely to increase readiness to change and alcohol knowledge (Barnett, Sussman, Smith, Rohrbach, & Spruijt-Metz, 2012).

Older Adults

Few studies or theoretical papers were found that focused on MI applications with older adults in SUD treatment. Cummings, Cooper, and Cassie (2009) reviewed 15 studies that reported on the use of MI with older adults. However, the definition of *older adult* was not consistent in that only four of the reviewed studies had samples where the participant mean age was 60 years or older. Though there are guidelines for screening older adults for some substances (e.g., alcohol), the lack of MI-related guidelines for engaging with older adults is problematic considering the large numbers of older adults struggling with SUD or risky substance use (Satre & Leibowitz, 2015). MI can be adjusted for older adult use in some potential ways, but the counselor must be specifically trained in older adult SUD treatment as there are some critical differences when working with the older adult.

MI can be used to assist the older adult to recognize the existence of a substance use issue in need of change. For a host of reasons, older adults may not notice the extent of their substance use. Furthermore, many other older adults may not have a diagnosable SUD but rather engage in risky or excessive substance use. Consequently, Cooper (2012) advocated for the integration of psychoeducation into the MI process. Though advice giving is typically done sparingly and with client consent, the counselor can facilitate this educational dialogue in the following manner:

- Understand any physical and medical problems, and the associated medication regimen, the client must face.
- Inquire how these illnesses, physical limitations, and medications influence their day.
- See how and why the problematic substance use enters the picture and respect the benefits the client perceives from this use.

For example, I once worked with an older adult woman with serious knee and back ailments. She was at first using a walker but quickly regressed to needing a wheelchair. In addition to her long list of medications for orthopedic and other medical ailments, she was also struggling with major depression and drinking heavily several times per week. She reported drinking to cope with the loneliness, pain, and frustration of her body "failing her." MI spirit emphasizes respect for the client. To discount the role alcohol played in combatting her physical and emotional pain would be nothing short of patronizing and disrespectful. However, she also should not drink that heavily, especially combined with her other medications. MI work here focused on working with her and her physicians to come up with an alcohol use guideline that would not negatively react with her medications and would provide her with the psychological comfort she needed as she worked on her depressive symptoms and continued to cope with her medical and physical issues.

QUESTIONS TO CONSIDER AS YOU MOVE ON TO CHAPTER 6

Question 1: What specific neurocognitive deficits do you see as a possible impediment to implementing effective MI and why?

Question 2: Do you see MI as a unique counseling approach, or do you conceptualize MI as simply counseling microskills that are adapted for the SUD client?

Question 3: Can you think of any co-occurring disorders—based on symptoms—that would pose a challenge to the successful implementation of MI?

Question 4: How would you utilize MI to motivate clients as they progress from a more intensive to less intensive placement of care? Would MI change in any manner based on client progress, time in recovery, or upcoming placement level?

Chapter 6

COGNITIVE-BEHAVIORAL THERAPY

COGNITIVE-BEHAVIORAL THERAPY BASIC ELEMENTS

Cognitive theory states that thought patterns and cognitive themes (schemas) play a large role in both causing and maintaining psychological distress (Beck, 1976). Cognitive-behavioral therapy (CBT) argues that individuals could be helped if the distorted thought patterns and themes were pointed out and corrected within a therapeutic relationship. Individual beliefs develop throughout life (Sharf, 2004), creating schemas (or basic beliefs) about oneself. Schemas are client-perceived core beliefs about self (Archer & McCarthy, 2007). Often in cases of substance use disorders (SUD) and psychiatric disorders, these schemas tend to be negative, thus setting up the individual for a pattern of unhealthy coping mechanisms and symptoms. For instance, Beck, Wright, Newman, and Liese (1993) noted that addressing these schemas and other dysfunctional thought processes is the fundamental component of cognitive-related work with SUDs. Once schemas in SUD individuals become activated, automatic thoughts, cognitive distortions, and other errors tend to fixate on the use of substance as a source of relief (e.g., I can only calm down if I drink). Below, some of these basic elements of CBT work are reviewed.

Automatic Thoughts

An automatic thought is a brief stream of thought about ourselves and others. Automatic thoughts occur with little to no cognitive effort on the part of the individual, apply to specific situations and/or events, and occur quickly during the client's appraisal of self, context, and future. Maladaptive automatic thoughts are distorted reflections of a situation but accepted as true regardless of the degree of distortion. Think of an automatic thought as the real-time client manifestation of dysfunctional beliefs about self, present, and future. These thoughts are typically brought on and exacerbated by psychiatric distress.

Cognitive Distortions

Cognitive distortions occur when information processing is biased against oneself (Sharf, 2004). These distortions are usually associated with negative affect/mood and explain how and why the distorted thinking may lead to problematic behaviors such as substance use. A few common cognitive distortions are briefly reviewed next.

Overgeneralization. This distortion occurs when one interprets the meaning of one event as applying to all events. For example, a client who has relapsed three times prior pronounces he or she will relapse every time sobriety is achieved because this happened three times before.

All-or-Nothing Thinking. This is the tendency to see events through a dichotomous lens. In essence, one achieves perfection or failure—there is no middle ground. For example, I have worked with clients who felt guilty and as if they failed recovery because they experienced a strong urge to drink. This rigid thinking only perpetuates a state of emotional turmoil and worthlessness that is amplified each time the "failure" occurs.

Magnification and Minimization. This distortion involves magnifying imperfections and minimizing positive events (Sharf, 2004). For example, an individual with co-occurring SUD and major depressive disorder may minimize his or her 6 weeks of reduced depressive symptoms and may refuse to focus on that accomplishment, instead underscoring numerous severe depressive episodes. Any attempt to demonstrate his or her strength or progress is met with a "yeah, but . . ." comment from the client. This type of distortion can be frustrating for the counselor as it appears that the client, despite expressing a desire to change, seems intent on holding on to the negative, even at the expense of the positive.

Mind Reading. This is the cognitive distortion where one person swears they know what the other person is thinking about them. However, this definite stance is built on a negative and distorted cognitive foundation and often leads to false conclusions (Leahy, 2003).

COGNITIVE MODEL OF SUBSTANCE USE

According to the cognitive theory of substance abuse, the dysfunctional beliefs about substances and their effects perpetuate the disorder (Beck et al., 1993).

Dysfunctional beliefs are problematic in that they distort reality and produce self-justifications for how/why substances serve as a coping mechanism. These beliefs become self-fulfilling in that the client believes they cannot cope with anything negative without the substance. Furthermore, these beliefs tend to appear most strongly during periods of attempted abstinence. For example, the client may state, "I can't cope with work without drinking," or "My cravings are too strong, I'll return to cocaine at some point."

Beck et al. (1993) argued that dysfunctional beliefs contribute to the formation of urges. The theory stipulates a linear process that starts with a belief, which leads to an expectation, which then produces an urge to use. For instance, I had a client who would tell me that she "could get so much more done at school if I sniffed a few Adderall." The belief (I cannot get school work done) sets up the expectation (using Adderall will help me get this work done), which in turn leads to the urge to illegally purchase and use Adderall to complete her studies. Each time this linear process plays out with a satisfactory result (e.g., good grades on assignments, all school work completed), the model is reinforced. This is because cognitive-behavioral theory holds that the dysfunctional beliefs about the substance use include one of more of the following:

- The substance use will help the client maintain an overall sense of stability.
- The substance will make the client better, smarter, more capable, etc.
- The substance effects will be pleasurable in some manner.
- The substance will relieve negative mood or affect.
- The substance will help manage any cravings.

Beck et al. (1993) also identified two sets of beliefs common in those who use substances. *Permission-giving beliefs* justify the substance use, for example, "One drink won't make me relapse," or "I had a hard day, I need a little fun with online poker." Thus, there is a sense of entitlement despite the known consequences of use. *Anticipatory beliefs* pertain to the anticipated effect of the substance, for example, "If I drink tonight, I'll be more relaxed talking with the trustees at the cocktail party." The anticipation of an easier social engagement due to drinking alcohol leads to the alcohol use.

In brief, the model contains the following points:

- Activating event (including both internal and external signals);
- Activation of core beliefs and schemas;
- Automatic thoughts related to addiction;
- Cravings;
- Permission-giving beliefs; and
- Thinking focused on drug-seeking/using behaviors.

Cognitive therapy can intervene at any one of these points in the process. Because automatic thoughts occur quickly and spontaneously, an individual can become engaged in substance-related behaviors with virtually no warning. Consequently, cognitive therapy aims to help clients become aware of their automatic thoughts and underlying thought patterns that maintain addiction (Beck et al., 1993). This is accomplished through a number of ways, some of which are addressed next (see Beck et al., 1993, for a thorough review).

Current Difficulties

Basically, the theory recommends assessing when the substance and other problems started. Usually some type of temporal sequence is created to see if some life problems may have served as a facilitator of substance use or are a result of substance use.

Core Beliefs

Core beliefs (or schemas) serve as the foundation for the development of cognitive distortions and automatic thoughts. Maladaptive schemas usually comprise the client's entire being, with such statements as "I am worthless" or "I am stupid" (Sharf, 2004). These core beliefs are an essential component of the cognitive-behavioral work with SUDs as they contribute to the addictive behaviors.

Vulnerable Situations

Environmental stimuli often stir up core schemas, leading to automatic thoughts and substance use. For example, a client may attend a wedding where he sees people drinking the whiskey he used to drink. Almost instantaneously, schemas are triggered leading to biased thinking, difficulty with varying emotions, and eventually inappropriate coping (such as using substances). Assessing high-risk situations plays an important role in preventing relapse.

COGNITIVE-BEHAVIORAL SESSION

Session Format

Structured sessions with common elements are the norm in CBT (Liese & Beck, 2000), but there will be variability between clients and sessions. One common therapeutic component is called *setting the agenda* (Beck et al., 1993). This strategy respects client issues while also producing a collaborative therapeutic environment where both counselor and client understand what issues are of relevance today.

Another common therapeutic component is called a *mood check*. This is where negative affect and mood states (such as anxiety, depression, worthlessness, loneliness) that can trigger substance use are assessed. As covered in Chapter 2, a mood check can be conducted using formal cognitive-based measures such as the Beck Depression Inventory, Beck Anxiety Inventory, or Beck Hopelessness Scale. The advantage of these instruments is that they take little time to administer and interpret while providing an objective picture of the client's mood or affect. This data informs the agenda setting and also may indicate a client at heightened risk of relapse.

Bridging from the last session is another cognitive-behavioral therapeutic element. To establish continuity, clinicians can summarize the last session and inquire regarding any unresolved issues that should be placed on the current agenda (Beck et al., 1993). The bridge from the last session is about awareness on the clinician's part in regard to how the prior counseling content fits into the current discussion. This empowers the clinician with the ability to refocus the session where warranted and avoid disruptive tangential dialogue.

Once started, there are numerous techniques applied both within the session and assigned as homework. These techniques are where the distorted thought process is remedied via exploration and discussion of prior thoughts and the subsequent emotions and behaviors. These techniques are addressed below.

EXAMPLES OF SOME CBT TECHNIQUES

Socratic Questioning

The purpose of Socratic questioning is to prompt the examination of the accuracy of maladaptive thoughts producing SUD and psychiatric distress. Although nondirective, Socratic questioning does require an active counselor asking challenging questions in order to identify maladaptive thoughts or errors in logic. Socratic questioning is used throughout the session where warranted with a basic goal of teaching the client how to self-question via the Socratic method. Some examples of Socratic questioning are as follows:

Clarification Questions. Here, clients examine beliefs or assumptions at a deeper level by the counselor requesting more information. Some examples include:

- What do you mean when you say . . . ?
- How do you understand this?
- Why do you say that?
- What exactly does this mean?
- What do we already know about this?

Probing Assumptions. These questions challenge presuppositions and unquestioned beliefs upon which the client bases his or her (flawed) argument. Some examples are as follows:

- How did you come to this conclusion?
- What else could we assume?
- Is this thought based on certain assumptions?
- How did you choose those assumptions?

Probing Reasons and Evidence. These questions help the client examine the actual (typically weak to nonexistent) evidence supporting their beliefs. Some examples are as follows:

- How do you know this?
- Show me . . . ?
- Can you give me an example of that?
- What do you think causes . . . ?
- Are these the only explanations?

Questioning Viewpoints and Perspectives. These questions encourage clients to develop alternative perspectives than the ones adopted. Some examples are as follows:

- What alternative ways of looking at this are there?
- What does it do for you to continue to think this way?
- Who benefits from this?
- What is the difference between . . . and . . . ?

Analyzing Implications and Consequences. These questions help explore any unpleasant outcomes that flow from holding certain maladaptive beliefs. Some examples are as follows:

- Then what would happen?
- What are the consequences of that assumption?
- How could . . . be used to . . . ?
- What are the implications of . . . ?

Questions About Questions. These questions place the focus back on clients when they ask challenging or inappropriate questions of the counselor. Some examples are as follows:

- What is the point of asking that question?
- Why do you think you asked this question?

- What does that mean?
- What would getting an answer either way mean to you?

Daily Thought Record

When clients who abuse substances become aware of their automatic thoughts, they have a better potential to see dysfunctional patterns and the contribution these distortions play in maintaining substance use. According to CBT, if a client is more aware of negative thought patterns, they can start the process of replacing maladaptive for adaptive thoughts. The daily thought record (Burns, 1989) is one of the most common techniques in cognitive therapy to accomplish this shift (see Figure 6.1).

The daily thought (or mood) record has several content areas (Burns, 1989). The thought record helps identify situations, thoughts, and emotions that can lead to substance use. Perhaps more important, the thought record places a natural pause

Figure 6.1 Automatic Thought Record Content Example

Context

✓ What led to this context?
✓ What unpleasant experiences are you having?

Automatic Thoughts

✓ What are the automatic thoughts you are having (be specific)?
✓ Rank them on how much you believe them right now from 0% (not at all) to 100% (absolutely).

Emotions

✓ What emotions are you having right now?
✓ How intense is each emotion from 0% (none at all) to 100% (extremely intense)?

Return to this sheet a few hours later . . .

Looking Back

✓ How much do you think you may have overreacted to the context in some manner from 0% (you did not overreact) to 100% (I absolutely let the context and my automatic thoughts get the better of me)?

Adaptive Response

✓ What may have been some more adaptive styles of thinking in regard to this context?
✓ How may your actions have differed if you engaged in this more adaptive style of thinking?
✓ How may your emotions have differed if you engaged in this more adaptive style of thinking?

between automatic thoughts and potential substance-using behavior. This may interrupt the automatic process from and slowly lead to adjusted thought processes (Beck et al., 1993).

Imagery. Imagery is a type of cognitive rehearsal technique where the client visualizes an upcoming situation and how it would be handled. It provides a virtual experience in which clients can learn to restructure images in a positive direction (Prochaska & Norcross, 2013). The client internally rehearses several of the techniques taught in counseling, leading to a satisfactory resolution to the situation (Beck et al., 1993). I have used imagery to assist clients who needed to attend large banquets where there would be drinking. Using this technique, I was able to walk the clients through a series of scenarios where they faced potential cues for drinking. In these virtual contexts, but in the comfort and safety of the counseling session, we were able to gauge their thoughts, behaviors, and emotions and troubleshoot various ways to effectively manage the relapse risk.

I have found that these CBT techniques facilitate a sense of efficacy in the client. Too often, clients place more power and influence on contexts and cues than may actually exist. Over the years, using CBT as a guide, I have engaged clients in discussions regarding the differences between a stressor and a trigger. For example, being at a wedding and needing to go up to the bar for a soda can be a very stressful context for clients new to their recovery. However, their automatic thoughts reclassify this stressor into a trigger. This is a critical concept.

Triggers are automatic. Once a trigger is implemented, the process goes forward without any ability to stop. For example, a bullet leaves a gun barrel once the trigger is pulled. Consequently, a trigger holds significant weight. However, I have come to find that most clients misclassify stressors as triggers. Going to a bar for a soda is a stressor—a major stressor. There will be countless emotions and thoughts flooding the minds of individuals as they stare at the liquor bottles. But there is no mandate for use. There is no unwavering absolute and rigid outcome dictating that clients must drink alcohol since they stood by the bar. Thus, their automatic thoughts and associated negative schemas ("I cannot be around alcohol without drinking") effectively turns a stressor (for which there is control to manage) into a trigger (for which, by definition, there is no control). After much work with clients using numerous CBT tactics, clients have continually come to the conclusion that people, places, and things (to borrow from Alcoholics Anonymous) defined as triggers were in reality stressors that they were unable and/or unwilling to manage. This is never to say that the management of stressors may not be challenging, scary, confusing, exhausting, and just overwhelming. It is, and more. But it is possible to manage, and CBT helps instill the self-efficacy back into the client by simply stating that this context is stressful but not predetermined for failure. It is in the client's hands to craft the ultimate outcome as opposed to an ultimate outcome forced upon a client with no other options.

RATIONAL EMOTIVE BEHAVIOR THERAPY

Numerous variations of CBT exist for the treatment of substance use and addiction issues. Too many exist in one capacity or the other to review in this chapter, so for sake of brevity, this section reviews one of the most commonly applied—rational emotive behavioral therapy (REBT). REBT, founded by Albert Ellis (1982), was actually one of the first CBTs (Corey, 2009). Ellis theorized that the suffering experienced by an individual (such as substance use and addiction) was a choice. Thus, the responsibility for all self-destructive behaviors (again, including substance use and addiction) rests with the client. REBT argues that no one event, person, or other situation drove the client toward addiction. Instead, REBT theorizes that the addicted client purposefully drove themselves into addiction via their philosophical belief systems. As Ellis theorized, if their belief systems drove them to addiction, they have the power to change these belief systems and overcome addiction.

The REBT model of addiction emphasizes the dynamics of irrational beliefs related to abstinence combined with a low frustration tolerance (LFT) (DiGiuseppe & McInerney, 1990). REBT argues that most SUD clients struggle with LFT (Ellis, McInerney, DiGiuseppe, & Yeager, 1988). Clients can overcome LFT by disputing irrational beliefs producing distress (e.g., anxiety due to LFT) using the ABCs of behavior, where *A* is the activating event. In the wedding example just referenced, this would be the client deciding to be at the bar but not drinking alcohol. *B* is the irrational belief system the client holds in regard to the activating event, in this case, "I cannot be around alcohol without drinking," or "I'm too early in my recovery to manage my urges." Notice the absolute quality of these beliefs. Thus, *C* is the consequence of these irrational and absolute beliefs. This consequence is the experienced LFT symptoms, such as anxiety (Archer & McCarthy, 2007; Ellis, 1982, 1985).

The goal of this model is for the client and counselor to debate the irrational beliefs. Out of this debate may come a new feeling the client experiences in the context of the activating event. For instance, I sometimes have my clients mentally repeat the phrase "It's just a stressor, not a trigger." Out of this disputing framework may come new feelings such as "calmer," or the client may still feel anxiety but just at a lower and much more manageable level because they now feel more in control of the situation (Archer & McCarthy, 2007; Ellis, 1982, 1985).

However, this is much easier said than done. Clients often struggle with this process because they are simply not accustomed to experiencing negative affect and mood. Years of substance use has atrophied their ability to manage the negative. REBT terms this difficulty as *discomfort anxiety* (Ellis, 1980). The definition, though, is imprecise and vague for a reason. Anxiety is not the collection of various *DSM* symptom criteria. Rather, it is described by Ellis and colleagues (1988) as follows:

> Pick your most prevalent addiction or obsession, such as food, liquor, or cigarettes. Now try to imagine all the enjoyment you would get from indulging in that substance. Now tell yourself how unbearable it would be to deprive yourself of it. Really *whine* about it. Now try to label that emotion. What is it called? (p. 27)

REBT argues that one flaw of most addiction counseling is that when a client reports a relapse or use, the counselor first goes to the ABCs before engaging in the disputing task. For instance, if the client uses, the discomfort anxiety as facilitated by the irrational beliefs has since passed. The crisis is over along with all the emotionality regarding the decision to use or not. Though the client is perhaps feeling guilty about the relapse, the actual ABCs of the event (the context, their beliefs about that event, and their eventual use) have passed, so any discussion of those ABCs fails to target the issue. As per REBT, their discomfort anxiety and inability to sit with negative affect (related to substance use or other matters) are the critical issues. If these are not addressed, another ABC moment will soon occur, resulting in another relapse, and the pattern continues. Consequently, much of what I do entails assisting the client to become "OK" with the negative and to recognize that stability is never the absence of negative but rather how they effectively manage the negative and avoid the dysfunction (i.e., substance use, poorly managed psychiatric symptoms). This is why, when I teach students about addiction counseling, I state that after the first or second session you do not really talk about drugs anymore. To use REBT language, you instead spend all your time focused on discomfort anxiety.

The REBT model argues that all irrational belief systems are dictated by absolutes known as the *Three Musts*. These "musts" are inflexible demands that REBT seeks to replace with new, flexible philosophies and beliefs. Though the irrational beliefs vary widely person to person, the Three Musts could be generally summarized as follows:

- I must succeed and have the approval of others or I am no good.
- Other people should do the right thing or they are no good and should be punished.
- I am entitled to a life free from stress, confrontation, or inconvenience.

Following some basic cognitive skills, REBT clinicians utilize several strategies to identify low frustration tolerance and dispute these irrational beliefs and their associated "must" philosophies. Some techniques designed to facilitate disputation of irrational thinking are discussed next.

Role Playing

Although this strategy contains cognitive, emotional, and behavioral elements, the clinician only focuses on the emotional in the role-play as a strategy to explore the cognitions involved in this context (Corey, 2009). For example, I once worked with a client who struggled with a gambling disorder. His wife also struggled with gambling. We role-played him telling his wife how he no longer wanted to gamble and would rather spend time with her in a nongambling context. During the course of a role-play, the client explored the irrational belief that "if I stop gambling then we will no longer have any fun together and she'll leave me." Through numerous interventions, this irrational belief was challenged.

Shame Attacking

Ellis (1999) believed that individuals can refuse to feel shame by convincing themselves that it is not horrible if someone believes they are foolish. Shame-attacking exercises often involve the client doing something out of the ordinary in public (but not illegal or harmful), such as singing out loud in a grocery store line (Corey, 2009). The purpose of these exercises is to help clients realize that others are not as interested in their behavior as they think.

Forceful Dialogues

In this activity, clients are taught to engage in a dialogue where they take the roles of both the rational and irrational voices. This is less of a dialogue and more resembles an argument where new and healthy rational belief systems try to overtake the irrational ones that led to substance use. A brief example of a forceful dialogue involving a woman struggling with sex addiction runs below.

Irrational: It's not really just randomly sleeping around if I screw one of my friends from work. It's not really using anyone, it's just sex.

Rational: No. They're using you just as much as you use them. You've screwed enough guys there that they all know you're good for a quick screw whenever 'cause you're just there for sex.

Irrational: No, they don't really see me like that. I've been in therapy for sex addiction. I've gone to the sex addict support groups. I know what screwing when using sex for an addiction looks like. This ain't it.

Rational: Yes it is. You're stressed and upset and want to have sex with anyone just to no longer be stressed anymore. He was just the first guy who came along today.

Irrational: So what's the big deal? Sex makes people feel good. I feel bad, so why I can't I do something to feel good? It's legal. No one is getting hurt.

Rational: You're getting hurt. When you go to sex to feel better it's never just one guy. Last time it was five guys in only 2 days!

Irrational: No harm done. They had fun.

Rational: But you felt like crap afterward. You always do. That's why you're still in therapy, so harm *is* done to you. Because you know you want more than just this. So stop. Harm is done. There are other ways to deal with your life besides, to borrow your words from a prior session, nailing anything that moves for days on end.

Forceful Coping Statements

These are rational coping statements taught to clients. They learn to not just parrot these phrases to themselves but rather to truly invest in their meaning as a mechanism to overcome addiction and the associated irrational belief systems and discomfort anxiety. I use often use this intervention with clients. For example, I once worked with a client who struggled with figuring out the reasons why others in his life treated him poorly. This constant struggle led to much distress and substance use. The forceful coping statement I taught this client is as follows:

In this world you will only meet three kinds of people: (1) those who like you, (2) those who do not like you, and (3) those who do not give a damn about you either way. Furthermore, the reason(s) why they fall into any given category may be meaningful or superficial. Regardless, that is how the world operates.

This forceful coping helped the client manage the discomfort with any individual whom he perceived (right or wrong) as disliking him. It also opened up the client to be able to focus on some legitimate reasons why others may dislike him (e.g., behaviors he engaged in when using substances) as they were now no longer distracted with other matters for which they had no control.

META-ANALYSES OF CBT EFFECTIVENESS WITH SUDs: TWO EXAMPLES

CBT is one of the most commonly applied treatment approaches in working with SUDs. Since the 1990s, the National Institute on Drug Abuse has advocated for CBT use as an empirically supported treatment (e.g., Carroll, 1998). Below are two recent meta-analyses of the CBT literature pertaining to the treatment of SUD.

Study 1 (Magill & Ray, 2009) examined CBT effectiveness against treatment comparison and control conditions. In Study 2, Windsor, Lermal, and Alessi, 2015, performed a meta-analysis with the focus of comparing Black/Hispanic and non-Hispanic White samples on CBT effectiveness. Each is briefly reviewed next.

Meta-Analysis 1: Magill and Ray (2009)

Magill and Ray conducted a meta-analysis that consisted of 53 randomized trials of CBT for adults diagnosed with SUDs published between 1982 and 2006. Of these studies, 25% were published outside of the United States. The mean sample size was 179 participants (range: 20–1,656). The treatment focused on alcohol ($n = 23$), cocaine/stimulants ($n = 11$), polydrug ($n = 11$), marijuana ($n = 6$), and opiates ($n = 2$). The samples' mean (SD) age was 38 (5.7) years. The majority of studies enrolled only individuals with a diagnosis of alcohol or drug dependence (80.1%), whereas the remaining studies also allowed individuals with a diagnosis of alcohol or drug abuse (this was before the *DSM-5* revision from abuse/dependence to substance use disorder). Approximately 64% of studies allowed non-substance-related co-occurring diagnoses (with exception of suicidal ideation, homicidal ideation, and active psychosis). Over half of the interventions were delivered in an individual format (57.7%), there was a mean of 18 (SD = 11.9; range: 1–48) sessions, and the service delivery was either stand-alone ($n = 31$) or as aftercare following another treatment ($n = 22$).

Overall, Magill and Ray (2009) found that CBT for adult SUDs demonstrated a small, but statistically significant, effect. A strength of their meta-analysis was the use of the *U3* index, which transforms effect size into a percentage of treated individuals who performed better than the median for the comparison group (Rosenthal & Rubin, 1982). Using this statistical technique, Magill and Ray found that 58% of the participants who received CBT fared better than the comparison condition. Some other specific meta-analytic findings are highlighted as follows:

- The CBT effect for marijuana was the only substance-related effect that deviated from the others, with a *U3* value of 69%.
- CBT combined with an additional psychosocial treatment had a larger effect than either CBT combined with pharmacological treatment or CBT alone.
- *U3* value of 79% indicated that individuals treated with CBT showed rates of substance use reduction above the median as compared to those assigned to a wait list or to a similar no-treatment control group.
- CBT treatment effects diminished over time, with lower effects at 6- to 9-month follow-up and even lower effects at 12 months. This indicated to Magill and Ray that CBT is better suited toward longer-term outcomes, and

this may be why it is often used as an aftercare treatment strategy (i.e., the effects of the treatment withstand as the CBT theory is applied in the long-term maintenance/aftercare phase as opposed to a strategy learned at the start of treatment/recovery and then—in theory—called upon for use several months later after initial treatment concluded).

- The meta-analysis results reflected no difference in CBT effectiveness between the group or individual CBT treatment formats.

Meta-Analysis 2: Windsor et al. (2015)

Concerns exist regarding whether CBT is effective for marginalized populations (David, 2009; Eamon, 2008). Griner and Smith (2006) noted, for example, how CBT theory may align more closely with Western culture. Consequently, Windsor et al. conducted a meta-analysis that compared the impact of CBT in reducing substance use between studies with a predominantly non-Hispanic White sample and studies with a predominantly Black and/or Hispanic sample. The final meta-analytic sample comprised 15 research reports, describing 16 studies, and contributing 126 effect sizes resulting in a sample of 3,784 individuals. Windsor et al. failed to find support that CBT, when compared with existing treatments, is less effective in Black/Hispanic study samples as compared to non-Hispanic White samples. Other meta-analysis results are reviewed as follows:

- Overall analysis results (Black/Hispanic and non-Hispanic White together) showed that CBT is an effective intervention for reducing substance use. However, even though the effects were approximately the same amount in both racial samples, Windsor et al. cautioned that the majority of the studies included in the meta-analysis used a comparison treatment group as opposed to a true control group. Since they did not know if the comparison treatments worked equally well for both racial groups, the current findings may not be replicated if conducted using studies with a true control group.
- In a pre-posttest comparison, CBT demonstrated an impact in the reduction of substance use among Black/Hispanic participants. Thus, the individuals in these studies benefited from treatment with CBT. However, the results from the pre-posttest comparison were significantly less effective in reducing substance use in Black/Hispanic samples as compared with non-Hispanic White samples. But Windsor et al. cautioned again how the lack of a true control group in these studies limits the conclusions drawn from this finding.
- Results from the *t* test comparison analysis that assessed differences in retention, engagement, and follow-up completion rates revealed that Black/Hispanic participants had lower percentages on all measures when compared

with the non-Hispanic White samples. However, the retention and engagement analyses failed to reach statistical significance.

- A metaregression analysis was conducted at CBT versus comparison analysis and at pre-posttest comparison analysis to examine the moderating impact of race, gender, employment, treatment format (group, individual, both), substance type, sample size, number of CBT sessions, type of study (efficacy vs. effectiveness), and use of intention-to-treat analysis on overall effect size. Though they did not find a significant moderating relationship in the CBT versus comparison analysis, Windsor et al. did note that studies with higher numbers of White individuals, efficacy studies, and studies with a larger sample size had significantly larger effect sizes.

SPECIAL POPULATIONS

Adolescents

Kaminer and Waldron (2006) noted that establishing support for CBT use in adolescents has been challenging due to the varying CBT strategies across treatments and studies. However, a meta-analysis using the Chambless and Hollon (1998) system for classifying treatments found adolescent group CBT as (to use their terms) a *well-established* treatment and adolescent individual CBT as a *promising* treatment (Waldron & Turner, 2008). The CBT model dictates that to understand the rationale for substance use by an adolescent, treatment must first explore which core beliefs support the addictive behavior.

Working with adolescents follows the structured and collaborative approach typical of CBT. Each session includes setting the agenda for that session, review of any homework from the previous session (e.g., daily thought record), and other matters for discussion within the session. CBT works well with adolescents, as each session involves frequent summary statements, which permits feedback from the adolescent. For example, making a problem list clarifies issues but also shows that treatment is indeed collaborative and that the counselor is trying to understand the adolescent's perspective and priorities. Considering that most adolescents experience adults as directing their lives (e.g., parents, teachers), having an adult listen and truly collaborate is powerful. This concept dates back to the 1970s with Bordin's (1976) conceptualization that the alliance is built on goals, tasks, and bonds. For instance, I worked with an adolescent client who struggled with drinking, nonsuicidal self-injury (NSSI), and severe major depressive disorder. He also smoked cigarettes. The client did not want to give up cigarettes as he felt this was a stress-reduction outlet he needed as he managed to abstain from alcohol and NSSI behaviors while also addressing his depressive symptoms. He expected a lecture from me regarding the need to stop smoking. I explained that my philosophy is you have to pick your battles, and right now he had enough to fight. So if cigarettes were not on his list of behaviors to change, that was fine by me and I would not inform his parents. The collaborative and concrete approach of CBT in this case enabled me to establish a strong alliance as I was an adult who listened to his needs. Granted, adolescents do not get a blank check to request anything, but where you can, CBT's collaborative format is powerful.

CBT's concrete approach is beneficial to adolescents. For example, making diagrams in session may be more helpful than words. Here, positive or negative feedback loops, which may be crucial in maintaining substance use and other functional/dysfunctional problems, can be more easily identified via a diagramming exercise as opposed to dialogue alone. Thus, adolescent self-monitoring is enhanced via the use of charts, thought records, or diaries where adolescents note their cognitions and begin making links to how these thoughts facilitate emotions and behaviors.

Older Adults

CBT was an expert panel-recommended treatment of choice for older adults struggling with SUD (CSAT, 1998). Confusingly, literature searches devoted specifically to older adult SUD CBT treatment produced few findings (whereas older adult treatment of depression using CBT produced far more publications). This is problematic considering how CBT may need some adaptation to effectively work with an older adult struggling with substance issues.

In one finding, Cox and D'Oyley (2011) recommended making logistical adjustments for the older adult. For example, since many CBT therapeutic products are written (e.g., manuals, daily thought records, diagrams of feedback loops), type size should be enlarged. Furthermore, additional sessions should be added to the program in order to permit a slower pacing so there is ample time for the summary and review components critical to CBT.

The counselor also needs to consider the cognitive state of the older adult. Aging brings with it a series of cognitive issues that are only exacerbated and/or complicated via substance use (recall some of the content from Chapter 1). Though mild cognitive impairment is not necessarily an impediment to effective CBT, the limited number of case studies, reviews, and meta-analyses of older adult SUD treatment using CBT calls into question how to take into account cognitive deficits when considering the application of CBT. Unfortunately, it is very plausible that many older adults have experienced a noneffective treatment experience because their cognitive deficits impaired their capability to engage in CBT work. Consequently, as echoed time and again (e.g., Morgen, Denison-Vesel, Kobylarz, & Voelkner, 2015; Qualls, 2015), clinical SUD treatment staff must be trained and experienced in working with the older adult population.

QUESTIONS TO CONSIDER AS YOU MOVE ON TO CHAPTER 7

Question 1: What specific neurocognitive deficits do you see as a possible impediment to implementing effective CBT and why?

Question 2: How does the structure of CBT assist the counselor in the interview process?

Question 3: How does CBT's or REBT's addressing of distorted thinking assist the counselor in the assessment of co-occurring psychiatric disorders?

Question 4: How would you utilize CBT with clients as they progress from a more intensive to lesser intensive placement of care? In theory, would the need/focus area(s) for CBT change in any manner based on client progress, time in recovery, or upcoming placement level?

Question 5: Do you see MI as distinct from CBT or an application of CBT?

Chapter 7

FAMILY COUNSELING INTERVENTIONS

BASIC FAMILY COUNSELING CONCEPTS

Miller, Forcehimes, and Zweben (2011) noted that effective addiction treatment addresses not only clients' substance use problems but also the clients' relationships with significant others (such as their family) in order to facilitate the best possible scenario for recovery. Addiction impacts all members of the family. Similarly, dysfunction within a family tends to remain steadfast and not easily changed. The challenge is to understand the needs of each individual member (including the addicted family member), the various subgroups within the family, and the family as a whole. That is what this chapter covers—the various models that inform the counselor regarding the potential origins and current perpetuation of the addictive and other dysfunctional disorders.

Boundaries

Families live by rules of interaction called *boundaries* (CSAT, 2004b). Boundaries can be rigid or diffuse and ideally are clear. Clear boundaries entail mutual respect for one another, clear communication, and the ability of all family members to individuate. Clear boundaries mean that family members do not attempt to control or manipulate others, and they feel that others do not control them. Furthermore, all family members accept responsibility for their behavior, emotions, and thoughts (Reiter, 2015).

Many families who struggle with addiction typically live by a series of rigid rules. Lawson, Peterson, and Lawson (1983) documented how alcoholic families have diffuse boundaries and specific rules of interaction. Specifically, these families tend to have three rules: (1) don't talk about the alcoholism, (2) don't confront the alcoholic behavior, and (3) protect the alcoholic so that things don't become worse (Lawson et al., 1983, p. 42). These rules silence the problem, but in reality, they just perpetuate the drinking behavior and produce a vicious cycle where the addicted family member embarrasses the family, leading to family isolation, which leads to greater conflict between family members, which in turn leads to more drinking behaviors, and the pattern continues and strengthens the addiction (CSAT, 2004b; Lawson et al., 1983).

Homeostasis

Stanton (1980) conceptualized family homeostasis as a pathological equilibrium in which the nonaddicted family members make some type of dysfunctional emotional investment in the addicted family member's addiction. If substance use ceases, the family is then out of balance and the nonaddicted members may actually (consciously or unconsciously) sabotage the addicted member's recovery so the family can return to homeostasis. For example, I once worked with a family where many members were unsupportive of the addicted family member's recovery in that they would at the last moment cancel their agreement to drive the family member to a treatment session, mandatory urine test, or Alcoholics Anonymous group. Unfortunately, the individual returned to alcohol use. From the standpoint of the family's dysfunctional investment in the addiction, the end result was a return to homeostasis. For families, just as it is for individuals, the overwhelming notion of change can sometimes lead to dysfunctional and destructive outcomes.

It is not necessarily that the family wants the member to remain addicted; it is just that the family typically has other difficulties such as marital problems, family crises, or an aversion to express honest emotions. Consequently, if the family member is addicted and struggling with that dysfunction, the family basically does not have the "time" to invest in their own issues, so the family can focus on the addiction and ignore the other issues plaguing the family (CSAT, 2004b).

Subsystems

Subsystems are smaller systems within the larger family system (Gladding, 2015). Multiple subsystems usually exist, and each one helps carry out the family rules while maintaining boundaries. The most obvious subsystem is the marital subsystem, where both partners assume the role of caretaking for the other as well as the roles of financial management and social activities (to name a few). In healthy families, subsystems help to maintain appropriate family boundaries and rules. In substance-addicted families, these subsystems become dysfunctional. For example, if one spouse has a substance problem, the nonaddicted spouse often takes on most of the household roles such as cooking, cleaning, shopping, and taking care of the children. Though this scenario works for a while, eventually the nonaddicted spouse typically becomes resentful at having to take care of everything (CSAT, 2004b; Gladding, 2015). However, the marital tension as a result of this resentment produces heightened stress, which likely leads the substance-using spouse to continue within the cycle of addiction.

BOWENIAN THEORY

CSAT (2004b) highlighted that Bowenian systems theory is commonly applied with addicted families. Bowenian systems theory views the family members as engaging in complex family patterns where they assume certain roles within the family system (Gladding, 2015). Bowen saw the family as an organic living system (Kerr & Bowen, 1988). Bowenian theory operates from several core principles described in the following paragraphs.

Differentiation

Differentiation is a person's ability to separate the emotional and reactive self from the intellectual self. Well-being depends on one's level of "differentiation of self." Bowen (1978) described a differentiated self as "one who can maintain emotional objectivity while in the midst of an emotional system in turmoil, yet at the same time actively relate to key people in the system" (p. 485).

Bowen (1978) theorized that individuals fall on a spectrum between fusion (i.e., no ability to maintain emotional objectivity) and complete differentiation. People who have a low level of differentiation (e.g., fusion) lack the ability to distinguish their emotional from their intellectual processes and thus live in an emotionally saturated world where they consistently seek acceptance from others. Bowen argued that psychological distress/dysfunction only occurs if the person's need for approval is not met. Conversely, highly differentiated people are less emotionally reactive and experience a healthy balance of individuality and closeness with others (Bowen, 1978).

Triads

Bowen (1978) noted that within a two-person emotional system there will be a constant fluctuation between closeness and distance. This fluctuation produces an unstable dyad, especially when any anxiety becomes overwhelming. To alleviate the anxiety, dyads sometimes "bring in" a third member to create a triad. The triad shifts the anxiety from the original dyad to one member of that dyad and the new member completing the triad. The other member of the original dyad is outside this relationship and gets relief from anxiety (Brown, 1999). Bowen (1978) discussed how the triad is fluid and that when anxiety overwhelms one dyad, the triad shifts so that the other member from the original dyad can now take their break from anxiety. This pattern continues and the triangle gains momentum (Bowen, 1978).

Emotional Cutoff

Emotional cutoff is a psychological coping mechanism designed to withdraw from intense emotional feelings within family relationships (Gladding, 2015). The cutoff can occur both physically and/or emotionally. The cutoff could be a withdrawing emotionally from the family relationship or withdrawing via moving far away and keeping the relationship alive on only a superficial level from a great distance. Of note, because the cut-off family member never resolves their emotional issues, their degree of differentiation remains unchanged and any family processes for that individual will repeat (Bowen, 1978).

Bowenian Therapy: Theory and Techniques

Bowen (1978) discussed the importance of orienting the family by establishing a working relationship designed to decrease anxiety while ensuring all members are heard, all while working from a stance of emotional neutrality. From a Bowenian systems perspective, the clinician needs to conceptualize the degree of anxiety and disruption within the emotional system of the family and how that disruption led to substance use. In Bowen family therapy, the clinician's goal is to encourage family members to talk to the counselor and through the counselor, as opposed to directly with one another, until the family members can engage without excessive emotionality (Bowen, 1978). Differentiation is cultivated at a slow and purposeful pace via counselor encouragement of family members using "I statements." This assists each family member to take ownership of his or her behavior, thoughts, and emotions (Gladding, 2015). The counselor being in the room with the family imposes an added triangulated dimension within the family system. By requiring the family to directly address the counselor (who is emotionally stable and objective), the family repeatedly practices the development of a "healthy" triangle. In theory, the various dyads stabilize and members slowly develop a healthy differentiation (Bowen, 1978).

When conceptualizing addiction within a Bowenian systems theory, the clinician sees the substance-using member as simply seeking emotional and cognitive relief from the family system (CSAT, 2004b). Consequently, family counseling involves an intensive and lengthy discussion regarding how the client experiences the various components of the family system and how the family system and subsystems experience the substance-using member. For example, some areas of discussion may include what family issues the client finds the most stressful or what perceived conflicts the client has with other family member(s). Some specific systems techniques for use with Bowenian theory are addressed below.

Genograms. The genogram permits the counselor and client to outline various relational patterns in the family through the use of lines, symbols, and pictures that represent the various relational and emotional aspects of the family system. The visual diagramming of the family system and the associated emotionality helps the client gain insight into the family patterns and his or her reaction to/role in these patterns. This process encourages differentiation by providing the client with the opportunity to examine the emotionality without actively experiencing the emotional distress (CSAT, 2004b).

Joining. This is the tactic where the counselor establishes a strong and supportive alliance with the family. Joining is critical because it facilitates the establishment of trust and demonstrating empathy to all members of the family system. Basically, as discussed by Stanton and Standish (1997), joining is simply the therapeutic alliance development required for effective work in any type of counseling.

Creating Enactments. Many times in family counseling, individual members talk about another member to the counselor. This can at times be beneficial when an objective and calm analysis of the issue is warranted. However, there are other times when this communication pattern only maintains and perpetuates the family dysfunction. That is why I have spent many family sessions saying the following phrases: "Don't tell me, tell him" or "Why are you talking to me, she's right here. Tell her." This tactic is called *creating an enactment* and it is a powerful tool that forces the start of an uncomfortable dialogue between family members. The enactment can be planned by the counselor as an exercise in the session or just naturally occur in the natural flow of the family session (CSAT, 2004b).

SEQUENTIAL FAMILY ADDICTIONS MODEL

Juhnke and Hagedorn (2006) created a model of family counseling, the sequential family addictions model, based on the hypothesis that family counseling works best as a sequential model that starts with briefer family counseling interventions focused on the here-and-now, and then, as warranted, progresses toward longer-term insight-driven treatment. The sequential family addictions model utilizes such common counseling interventions as motivational interviewing (MI), cognitive-behavioral therapy (CBT), solution-focused counseling, and family systems theory. The model includes seven stages that focus on a specific issue for the family. The model is flexible in that although there are seven stages, the family does not need to complete all stages. For example, the counselor may see enough healthy change by a certain stage and that the family is no longer in crisis and in need of counseling assistance. This model is explained in the excellent text by Juhnke and Hagedorn (2006), so the following is just a brief synopsis of each stage.

Stage One

Here, the counselor begins work with the family using MI techniques because the family needs to be ready and willing to change in order for any treatments to work. Juhnke and Hagedorn (2006) stated that this part of the process takes approximately one or two sessions.

Stage Two

Once the family is appropriately motivated to begin treatment, the model adopts a brief solution-focused orientation. Consistent with solutions-focused techniques, the family counselor works with the system to establish a dialogue regarding how the family system would be different if addiction were no longer present. This stage may run anywhere from three to seven sessions (Juhnke & Hagedorn, 2006).

Stage Three

Here, the focus falls on understanding the role of thoughts and behaviors in maintaining the addictive behavior via an exploration of both the benefits and detriments to the presence of addiction in the family. Family members are taught cognitive restructuring methods to counter the dysfunctional "addictive thinking" family patterns. This stage runs from three to eleven sessions (Juhnke & Hagedorn, 2006).

Stage Four

This stage entails family systems work such as establishing clearer communication patterns and healthier relationships. Structural family therapy is generally concerned with two overarching goals. First, the clinician strives to promote healthy relationships and communication patterns. Second, the basic systems goal is to help the family return to a stable system that does not engage in varying forms of dysfunction that only perpetuates substance use. This stage can run from five to 10 sessions (Juhnke & Hagedorn, 2006).

Stage Five

Here, more insight-oriented interventions occur. The focus of this stage mirrors much of Bowenian theory where family members work on differentiation and eliminating intense and dysfunctional emotionality (i.e., via work with genograms). Also of emphasis here is the multigenerational manner in which addictive behaviors may pass between generations. This stage runs from five to 10 sessions (Juhnke & Hagedorn, 2006).

Stage Six

This stage is an optional one and helps adult clients reconnect with their families of origin and their childhood addiction experiences. The model conceptualizes this stage as a strategy to assist adult clients make peace with their dysfunctional childhood and move forward with their adult life without the impediment of these unresolved emotions and thoughts (Juhnke & Hagedorn, 2006).

Stage Seven

This is a stage designed for families who have unsuccessfully resolved the addiction issues in the other stages. This stage uses psychodynamic object relations principles and is a long-term treatment with no fewer than 15 sessions (Juhnke & Hagedorn, 2006).

THE ADDICTED FAMILY

The addicted family is a rigid and isolated system that CSAT (2004b) argued leads to increased distress and family dysfunction. This discomfort must be managed, so family systems make adjustments and assume specific roles within the family in order that the focus is no longer on the addiction and associated consequences (CSAT, 2004b). Wegscheider (1981) devised the most common role classifications in work done on chemically addicted families and included such well-known roles as the hero, scapegoat, enabler, lost child, and mascot. These roles are useful in that they provide the counselor with a tangible example of how the family system works to maintain homeostasis. The family, ideally, would then more clearly see the degree of their dysfunction in the attempt to not focus on the pressing matter of the addiction. Each role is briefly described below.

The Addicted Family Member

This is the individual who brought addiction into the family system. This person has abdicated any responsibilities in the family (e.g., parental responsibility for a child) and has become emotionally withdrawn (e.g., distant from their spouse). For the addicted family member, their world revolves around the substance use (CSAT, 2004b).

The Enabler

In many cases, the enabler is the nonaddicted spouse and serves the role of protecting the addicted spouse from the consequences of their addiction (Wegscheider, 1981). Their goal is to reduce the tension in the family system that occurs due to the addiction (CSAT, 2004b).

The Family Hero

Typically, this is the oldest child who tries to help the other nonaddicted family members. For example, a family hero (with one or both parent[s] struggling with addiction) may assume parental duties such as caring for siblings, cooking, and cleaning. In addition, this family member tries to divert attention from the addiction via high levels of accomplishment (e.g., scholastic, athletic). Consequently, the attention thrust onto the family is positive and thus further obscures the addictive issues (CSAT, 2004b; Wegscheider, 1981).

The Scapegoat

Typically, this the second-born child who struggles with authority figures (Wegscheider, 1981). This family member acts out to divert attention away from the addiction and other problematic family issues (CSAT, 2004b).

The Lost Child

This child simply fades into the background and tries to cause no problems, no matter how small (Wegscheider, 1981), with a goal to avoid any conflict. Lost children may internalize the family tension created by the addiction, leading to psychological issues of their own in years to come.

The Mascot

The mascot is the family clown who attempts to lighten the mood. This family member is insecure and uses humor to divert the stress away from the addiction and break the tension within the family (Wegscheider, 1981).

Enabling and Codependency

Enabling. Family systems are an entity, and like the individuals within the family, conflict and tension are not welcome experiences. The presence of addiction in the family is overwhelming in that there is virtually no control over the addicted member. Families cannot scream, threaten, or bribe the addiction away. This may be why—in part—some family members behave in a dysfunctional manner that reduces or eliminates the consequences of the addiction. Some examples include not confronting lying, taking the blame for a problem caused by the addicted member, excusing/ covering up the addictive behavior and negative consequences, or simply ignoring the problem. However, the critical component is that enablers are fully aware that they are doing these behaviors, and the nonaddicted member sees these actions as the appropriate behaviors of a "good" family member or spouse (CSAT, 2004b).

Codependency. Doweiko (2015) explained the difference between enabling and codependency: Enabling refers to specific behaviors, and codependency pertains to the relationship pattern with the dependent spouse or other family member. Thus, there can be enabling behaviors without an underlying codependent relationship.

Codependency is an unhealthy relationship pattern resulting from being too closely involved with an addicted individual. Doweiko (2015) described a few key components of codependency: (1) There is excessive overinvolvement with the addicted family member; (2) There are repeated attempts to control the addicted member's behaviors; (3) The codependent individual requires others to validate their self-worth; and (4) The codependent individual makes repeated personal sacrifices in trying to help the addicted member stop the addictive behaviors. In general, codependent individuals lose their sense of self in the (failed) attempt to protect the addicted individual and maintain the secrecy surrounding the addiction (CSAT, 2004b). Furthermore, the clinical paradox is that if the addicted family member achieves sobriety, then the codependent individual may not feel needed any longer, and more important, would have lost a principal source of self-worth (i.e., helping the addicted individual on a daily basis).

META-ANALYSES OF FAMILY SYSTEMS INTERVENTIONS: TWO EXAMPLES

Family therapy applications with substance use disorders (SUDs) are varied and complicated, in part based on the family member(s) with the addictive behavior, the makeup of the family itself, and the countless interpersonal and intrapersonal dynamics inherent in family work. Many (though not all) family therapy techniques and studies are focused on the adolescent as the family member with the addictive behavior and associated dysfunctional issues (e.g., delinquency). Thus, two recent meta-analyses examining family therapy applications for adolescents are reviewed below.

Meta-Analysis 1: Baldwin, Christian, Berkeljon, Shadish, and Bean (2012)

Baldwin et al. (2012) conducted a meta-analysis of 24 studies comparing brief strategic family therapy (BSFT), functional family therapy (FFT), multidimensional family therapy (MDFT), or multisystemic therapy (MST) to treatment-as-usual (TAU), an alternative therapy, or a control group in the treatment of adolescent substance abuse and delinquency. In general, the findings suggested that family therapy has some added benefit beyond what is achieved via TAU or alternative treatments. A review of the meta-analysis findings is as follows:

- Participants with delinquency or substance abuse problems receiving BSFT, FFT, MDFT, or MST fared better than participants receiving either TAU or an alternative therapy. Though statistically significant, the differences were relatively small ($d = 0.21$ for family therapy vs. TAU, and $d = 0.26$ for family therapy vs. alternative therapy).
- The difference between family therapy and control conditions, though somewhat large ($d = 0.70$) was not statistically significant. Baldwin and colleagues reasoned that the lack of significance was due to only four studies using a control condition.

Meta-Analysis 2: Vermeulen-Smit, Verdurmen, and Engels (2015)

Vermeulen-Smit et al. (2015) reviewed 39 papers describing 22 randomized controlled trials (RCTs). The 39 articles represented 18 different programs. Vermeulen-Smit et al. made a few general conclusions based on their review of the research: first, that the elements of family programs aimed at high-risk families may differ from those in general populations because high-risk and substance-using adolescents demonstrate problem behaviors requiring a more sophisticated treatment approach; second, that programs aimed at high-risk adolescents that start when adolescents are 15 to 16 years old may be too late to address marijuana and other substance use; and third, Vermeulen-Smit and colleagues also emphasized that more research is needed to best understand the strategies and practices that best attract and attain high-risk youth and their parents. Some of the specific meta-analysis results are described below.

- Nine RCTs were found examining the effect of family interventions on illicit drug use in general populations. Overall, universal family programs targeting adolescents (ages 10–14) as well as their parents produced a small favorable effect on the initiation of marijuana use. However, there was no clear evidence of the efficacy of family interventions in preventing adolescent initiation of substances other than marijuana.
- Among high-risk groups, there was no clear evidence of the effectiveness of family interventions on illicit drug initiation (six RCTs).
- Among high-risk groups, there was no clear evidence of the effectiveness of family interventions on the frequency of illicit drug use (seven RCTs).
- Among high-risk groups, there was no clear evidence of the effectiveness of family interventions on drug disorders (three RCTs).
- Three small RCTs showed some positive effect of family interventions in reducing the frequency of illicit drug use among substance-using adolescents.

SPECIAL POPULATIONS

Adolescents

Family systems that work for addicted adolescents and their families represent one of the few instances where there does indeed exist a theoretical and empirically supported treatment approach especially crafted for the unique needs of the adolescent. These two treatment approaches are BSFT (Szapocznik, Hervis, & Schwartz, 2003) and MDFT (Liddle, 1995). Each is addressed below.

Brief Strategic Family Therapy. BSFT is endorsed as an effective evidence-based approach by the Substance Abuse and Mental Health Services Administration and National Institute on Drug Abuse (Fischer, Pidcock, & Fletcher-Stephens, 2007). This approach has an overall goal of reducing adolescent behavior problems by strengthening family relationships. Furthermore, BSFT links the family to various resources to promote positive youth engagement (Robbins et al., 2011). BSFT is short term and problem focused across the following primary steps: (1) BSFT works to cultivate a strong therapeutic alliance with each family member, (2) BSFT identifies both the individual and family patterns that negatively impact the adolescent's behavior, (3) BSFT creates a problem-focused and practical change plan that focuses on strengths in the process of correcting the problematic family relationships, and (4) BSFT reinforces family interactions that promote abstinence and clearer interfamily communication (Fischer et al., 2007).

Szapocznik and Coatsworth (1999) listed numerous family problems associated with adolescent problem behaviors that included

- parental drug use or other antisocial behavior,
- parental under- or overinvolvement with the adolescent,
- parental over- or undercontrol of the adolescent,
- poor quality of parent-adolescent communication,
- lack of clear rules and consequences,
- inconsistent application of rules and consequences,
- lack of adult supervision of the adolescent's activities, and
- poor family cohesiveness.

BSFT, whenever possible, strives to keep the family intact when addressing these (and other) problems. While preserving the family system is important, this must only be accomplished if family preservation will enable the elimination or reduction of the adolescent's substance use and associated problem behaviors and if the change can occur within the family interactions that are associated with the adolescent's substance use. At the family systems level, the counselor intervenes to change the way family members interact, thus changing how they communicate and behave with one another. In theory, this would promote more positive family interaction, which in turn paves the way for the adolescent to reduce substance use and other problematic behaviors.

Numerous BSFT resources underscore the applicability of the model with adolescents (Szapocznik et al., 2003; Szapocznik & Kurtines, 1989; Szapocznik et al., 1988). Some of these strengths include the following:

- BSFT creates a treatment intervention that is built into the adolescent's daily family life.
- BSFT is relatively short term and can be implemented in eight to 24 sessions.
- BSFT is "manualized," so counselors can become appropriately trained on a counseling model specifically designed for the adolescent and his or her family.
- BSFT is flexible and applies to a wide range of family problems typically seen in mental health clinics, substance use treatment programs, or other social-service settings such as child protective services.
- BSFT works across all treatment levels of care (inpatient, partial hospitalization, intensive outpatient, outpatient, aftercare).

Multidimensional Family Therapy. Liddle (2013) listed the 10 guiding principles of MDFT. They run as follows:

- Adolescent drug use is a multidimensional problem.
- Family functioning is instrumental in creating new, developmentally adaptive lifestyle alternatives for the adolescent.
- Problem situations provide information and opportunity.

- Change is multifaceted, multidetermined, and stage oriented.
- Motivation is malleable but not assumed.
- Multiple therapeutic alliances are required, and they create a foundation for change.
- Individualized interventions foster developmental competencies.
- Treatment occurs in stages, and continuity is stressed.
- Therapist responsibility is emphasized.
- Therapist attitude is fundamental to success. (pp. 88–89)

MDFT is focused on both the deficits and strengths to obtain a clearer assessment of the family. This includes a multisystem formulation of a theory as to how and why the current situation and behaviors are understandable in the context of the adolescent's developmental history and current degree of risk. Interventions are designed to decrease these risk processes related to dysfunction development or maintenance (e.g., parenting problems, affiliation with drug-using peers, disengagement from school). An example of the flexibility of the MDFT approach is that the counselor intervenes to develop problem solving in the area deemed most accessible and malleable. It may not be the most pressing area, but MDFT takes the approach that change needs to start somewhere, so an accessible area open to change is a good place to commence work.

MDFT is a personal process that works well with the adolescent. In the first session, the counselor will engage the family in a dialogue and note how various individuals contribute to the adolescent's life and current problematic situation (e.g., substance use). MDFT counselors also meet individually with the adolescent, the parent(s), and other family members. These meetings serve the purpose of uncovering the unique perspective of each family member regarding how the events have transpired, what each family member has done to address the problems, what each member believes needs to be changed in regard to the adolescent and the family, as well as the concerns and problems faced by each member that may be unrelated to the adolescent.

MDFT encourages the counselor to facilitate the adolescent's telling of his or her life story during early individual sessions because this increases investment and engagement in the process. In addition, the storytelling provides the counselor with the adolescent's perspective regarding the substance use severity and trajectory, attitudes about substance use, family history, peer relationships, school or legal problems, and any other psychosocial issues. The adolescent, in consultation with the counselor, provides an overview of his or her living context including the neighborhood, hangouts, where friends live, and school or work locations.

The MDFT assessment of the parent(s) includes functioning both as parents and as adults. Strengths and weaknesses are examined in regard to parenting knowledge, parenting style, parenting attitudes and beliefs, and the emotional bond with the adolescent. The counselor promotes parent-adolescent discussions and observes for such issues as supportiveness or emotional disengagement. Parents' mental health status and substance use are assessed due to their potential impediment to improved and effective parenting.

There are four overall areas of attention in MDFT: (1) adolescent, (2) parent, (3) family interaction, and (4) external social systems. The approach works because each area receives a unique focus in order to facilitate change in the entire family system as well as the adolescent behavior. Each area is addressed below.

Adolescent. The counselor establishes a working alliance with the adolescent that in some ways mirrors but is distinct from the parental relationship. The adolescent comes to learn that treatment is a team process via the collaborative establishment of treatment goals that are not only practical but—more important—of value to the adolescent. Adolescents express their perception of their life thus far, and treatment is geared toward addressing some of these issues. The goal is the creation of both pragmatic and obtainable alternatives to substance use and other problematic behaviors (e.g., delinquency).

Parent. The primary objective in the MDFT work with parents involves enhancing the feelings of parental love and emotional connection while appreciating the difficult past and present parental circumstances that their child brings to the family. The goal here is to generate a new sense of hope while changing the parent-adolescent relationship and (where needed) improving the parenting practices. Parents moving through this process come to the decision that they must play a role in their child's change, and in turn, they partner with the counselor to assist the adolescent to change. MDFT conceptualizes the reengagement of parents into their role as parents as the result of "soul searching" about their adolescent, their parenting, and themselves.

Parent-Adolescent Interaction. Fostering changes in the parent-adolescent interaction is primarily accomplished via the family systems technique of enactment. Here, the counselor forces the adolescent and parent(s) to engage with one another, and not through the counselor, in order to facilitate critical and frank discussions. These discussions reveal relationship strengths and problems, which in turn are also discussed. Basically, the enactment helps to train the parent and the adolescent on how to discuss and solve problems in new and healthier ways.

Social Systems External to the Family. Families with an adolescent struggling with substance use likely are involved with multiple community agencies (e.g., school, criminal justice system). The success or failure in working with these agencies can dictate devastating longer-term outcomes. Consequently, a well-working give-and-take collaboration with school, legal, and mental health systems can positively influence the potential for adolescent treatment engagement and lasting change. I have come to learn that an overwhelmed parent deeply appreciates a counselor who understands the nuances of these complex bureaucracies and can assist in the navigation of red tape toward a productive outcome. This act of advocacy helps to lessen the parental stress and bolsters parental efficacy. For example, I have worked with countless parents to organize meetings with school administrators or probation officers. MDFT argues that if the parents (and adolescent) are less stressed regarding these external agencies, their work in the other three areas of focus can occur without impediment.

Older Adults

Unlike adolescents, older adults are not prevalent in the family systems literature pertaining to SUD. However, the older adult could be involved in a family intervention in one of two ways: as a family member engaged in the process focused on another member's addiction or as the addicted family member. In either case, all the general guidelines pertaining to work with older adults (e.g., pacing, consideration of cognitive deficits) need to be considered. In addition, some recent work using narrative therapy techniques for working with older adults with SUDs (Morgan, Brosi, & Brosi, 2011) could also be applied to family systems work in regard to how older adults see addiction (whether a family member's or their own) in the context of their life. Of note is that if an older adult is part of the immediate family (common these days with grandparents living with their children and grandchildren), then the older adult is a part of the immediate system and would be an integral member in any of the systems theories discussed in this chapter and elsewhere.

QUESTIONS TO CONSIDER AS YOU MOVE ON TO CHAPTER 8

Question 1: How do you see a family's misunderstanding of neurocognitive issues in recovery and treatment as a factor within the dysfunctional family system?

Question 2: How would you integrate the family into the assessment and interview process? Do you see any difference for this family intervention for an adult or adolescent addicted family member?

Question 3: How does family systems work with co-occurring psychiatric disorders?

Question 4: Would family systems work be different in various levels of care? How do you see this difference?

Question 5: Can you think of some ways that MI can be integrated into the family systems process?

Question 6: Can you think of some ways that CBT can be integrated into the family systems process?

Chapter 8

EXISTENTIAL COUNSELING

EXISTENTIAL COUNSELING AND SUBSTANCE USE DISORDER

Existential counseling is the only orientation directly influenced by philosophy as opposed to psychology. This makes the theory a unique fit for the addiction population, particularly those with a positive or negative 12-step history (due to the theological and philosophical undercurrents in the 12-step tradition; see Chapter 9). Thus, it is peculiar that although there are some instances of existentialism applied to addiction in the literature (e.g., Ford, 1996; Greaves, 1974, 1980; Lewis, 2014; Morgen, Morgan, Cashwell, & Miller, 2010; Roos, Kirouac, Pearson, Fink, & Witkiewitz, 2015), there are not as many instances as one might expect. For instance, a recent PsychInfo search using the keywords *existentialism* and *addiction counseling* found zero matches.

Applications of existentialism in counseling have been formulated by a number of theorists including Frankl (1964, 1967), May (1958, 1969, 1977, 1983), Laing (1960), Potash (1994), Yalom (1980), and van Deurzen and Adams (2011). Existential counseling is not a specific approach; rather, it presents as a philosophical framework through which one can conduct counseling. The following chapter presents existentialism that includes some components from many of these theorists listed above.

BASIC CONCEPTS

The "I-Am" Experience

The realization of ownership of one's being can strongly affect the client. In essence, they are the ones in charge of their existence. It is not easy to define *being* due to many individuals abdicating their existence-defining power to the external world. For example, people define their being via their job, role, or other external social function. In the substance use disorder (SUD) treatment area, too often clients will define themselves as "addicts." From an existential perspective, I always try to stop this action. What is interesting is the degree of pushback I get from clients. They are so heavily invested in the external definition, in part because it absolves them of needing to create their own definition (and possibly avoid the pain of coming to terms with what the definition produces). My existential rebuttal is that "you are not an addict; rather, you are a person in early recovery from a substance use disorder. But you are also many, many other meanings for many other people."

Existentialism argues that the "I-Am" experience is not the solution to a problem but instead is only the prerequisite condition to achieve an eventual solution. Another key point is that any discussion of *being* also mandates an exploration of *not being,* or nothingness. Nonbeing can be sometimes as clear cut as the inescapable notion of mortality, but it can also manifest as severe and crippling psychopathology (such as addiction and co-occurring psychiatric disorders). The threat of nonbeing is ever present in some degree of intensity. Here lies the paradox. As individuals more clearly define their being and feel a sense of pride in ownership of that being, their fear of nonbeing rises. The following brief counseling dialogue is an example of what I have seen numerous times with clients.

Counselor: You've accomplished a lot. You don't seem too proud or happy.

Client: It's OK.

Counselor: That's a bland response for a situation that would seem to at least warrant some more positive emotion and enthusiasm.

Client: We've discussed this, I don't ever want to be too happy or content, or proud, or at peace with myself.

Counselor: 'Cause if you had a relapse—whether alcohol or depression—you'd lose it.

Client: Yup. So I have a lesser fall if I'm only so-good or just so-happy. Not too much. Won't let myself be that.

Existentially, the client can be theorized as struggling with trying to forge a positive sense of being while also very cognizant of the nonbeing threat.

Normal and Neurotic Anxiety

Existentialism defines anxiety differently. Anxiety arises from our need to assert our being. Rollo May (1977) defined anxiety as "the threat to our existence or to values we identify with our existence" (p. 205). Anxiety shows itself physically in faster beating of the heart or emotionally in a sense of apprehension. The principal counseling function is to assist the client in confronting the normal (i.e., healthy) anxiety within the human condition while moving away from thoughts, behaviors, and emotions associated with the unhealthy neurotic anxiety condition. Each anxiety type is defined below.

Normal Anxiety. This healthy anxiety is comprised of three characteristics. First, the anxiety is proportionate to the situation. Second, normal anxiety is an experience the client can come to terms with and manage. Third, this type of anxiety serves as a stimulus for confronting the dilemma that led to the normal anxiety experience.

Neurotic Anxiety. This unhealthy anxiety is not proportionate to the situation. For example, the client is so fearful of rejection in the career search process that he or she never applies for a job and lives on state assistance. Second, this unhealthy anxiety is internalized and not managed. Third, neurotic anxiety is destructive in that it tends to paralyze the individual rather than facilitate problem solving and growth.

Existential counseling in no way strives to eliminate anxiety. That is impossible. The function of counseling is to help clients live while managing their anxiety (i.e., being) as opposed to shutting down and coping in a dysfunctional manner with anxiety while trying to find some "magic" solution to avoid the conflict (i.e., neurotic anxiety). This is a critical issue for SUD clients in that their addiction, whether substance or process based, shaped a mechanism for coping with anxiety that entailed a rapid and strong (though brief) resolution of anxiety. The heroin or the sex or the gambling or the alcohol became their well-developed coping skill to manage anxiety. From an existential framework, the addiction was just a manifestation of neurotic anxiety.

Guilt

Similar to anxiety, guilt can take either a normal or neurotic form. Neurotic guilt feelings (generally called *guilt*) develop from imagined transgressions. Other forms of guilt, termed *normal guilt,* inform the individual regarding the ethical aspects of behavior.

Boss (1957) reported another type of guilt, which is the guilt toward ourselves for failure to live up to our potentialities, otherwise termed as *forgetting being.* Boss (1957) pointed out that if individuals lock up their potentialities, they are guilty of not defining who they can actually become. This sense of indebtedness can lead to psychological distress.

Forms of World

Existential counseling postulates four modes of the world. The first is *Umwelt,* meaning *world around*, or the *environment*. Van Deurzen and Adams (2011) noted that the issues inherent in this world entail accepting the limits of natural boundaries (e.g., old age), and illness or injury stirs up a reminder of the frailty of the human being.

The second mode is *Mitwelt,* literally the *with-world*, the world of one's fellow human beings or the interpersonal world. This is not necessarily how individuals engage with others but rather how they navigate the world surrounded by others. For example, Potash (1994) defined a conflict in this world as follows:

> If an individual has not developed good self-protective skills, he will not be able to participate in a fully healthy way in his interpersonal world. To be able to have good relationships with others, it is necessary to have a fully developed sense of one's self and one's needs. (pp. 99–100)

The third mode is *Eigenwelt,* the *own-world*, which is the relationship to one's self or the intrapersonal world. May (1983) described the fundamental issue inherent within this mode of the world as follows:

> *Eigenwelt* presupposes self-awareness, self-relatedness, and is uniquely present in human beings. But it is not merely a subjective, inner experience; it is rather the basis on which we see the real world in its true perspective, the basis on which we relate. (p. 128)

The fourth mode of the world is *Uberwelt*, which is the spiritual or ideal version of the world.

Ultimate Concerns

Yalom (1980) identified four ultimate concerns relevant to counseling: death, freedom, isolation, and meaninglessness. Confrontation with each of these constitutes the content of the client's internal conflict from the existential perspective. Each is addressed below.

Death. This is the most obvious ultimate concern and plays a major role in the internal experience. To cope with this fearful concern, we forge defenses against death awareness. These defenses are denial based and if maladaptive can result in pathology. Existentialism sees psychopathology—in part—as basically the failed attempt to defend against the individual terror of death.

Freedom. From the existential frame of reference, freedom is directly linked with the concept of dread. Freedom means that there is no structured design and that clients are solely responsible for their own choices and actions. Sartre (1956) cogently stated that the human being is "condemned to freedom" (p. 631). This existential view of freedom has terrifying implications. If we actually are the only ones responsible for creating our own being, then this also means there is nothing if we fail. We create ourselves or fall into the abyss.

The concept of freedom encompasses many themes with strong implications for addiction counseling (some of which will be reviewed in more detail in Chapter 9), with the most obvious being *responsibility.* Individuals differ in regard to how willing they are to accept responsibility. For example, some individuals displace responsibility for their situation onto other people, whereas others deny responsibility by portraying themselves as "innocent victims" who suffer from external events.

Another aspect of freedom is the concept of *willing.* Willing is the passage from responsibility to action, and as May (1969) stated, it consists first of wishing and then deciding. Psychopathology (such as addiction) has some implications here. For instance, *impulsivity* is the avoidance of wishing by failing to discriminate among wishes and instead acting impulsively and promptly on all wishes. The addicted individual may be struggling with numerous stressors and desires them all eradicated, no matter how impractical. Consequently, the impulsive actions of substance use basically wipes the wishing slate clean without the need to take action—in essence, all the benefits of wish fulfillment without any of the work.

Isolation. A third ultimate concern is isolation. Existential isolation is that no matter how close we are to another individual, there always remains an unbridgeable gap. Mijuskovic (1979) noted how there is a fundamental loneliness in that individuals cannot escape the fact that they can never fully share their consciousness with others. Fear of existential isolation (and the failed defenses against it) greatly influences psychopathology. Here, interpersonal relationships can be seen as dysfunctional and not truthful in that each party *uses* the other to attempt to diminish the distress of isolation.

For example, sex addiction can be conceptualized as a dysfunctional coping skill for isolation. The sexual engagement offers only a temporary remedy for the isolation. The sexual acts only outwardly resemble an authentic relationship, but in reality, the sex-addicted individual only relates to the other in that a need for the feeling of closeness or intimacy is met.

Meaningless. If we are indeed alone in the universe, then what possible meaning can life have? How shall we live? Human beings require a sense of meaning. For those who struggle to understand their meaning, crises arise. For the addicted individual, this is difficult. This is an individual who comes to treatment with no tolerance for experiencing negative affect or cognitions and also requires an immediate resolution of any negative experiences that arise. The dilemma centers on *how does a human being who requires meaning function in a universe that has no apparent meaning?* For some, the dilemma is too intense, and substance use or a process addiction offers a respite from this unavoidable crisis.

THEORY OF COUNSELING

Existential therapy is not a counseling orientation but instead is a model through which client psychopathology is understood. The client handles psychiatric distress via ineffective and maladaptive coping mechanisms that provide a temporary respite from the distress but in the end only cripples the individual's ability to live while also perpetuating the existence of the distressful emotions. In the case of SUD, the client achieves a temporary relief from distress, but as the substance effects subside, they are left with the overwhelming emotions for which they have no answer other than substance use. Thus, the use is repeated and the distressful emotions continue to exist and worsen, which in turn leads to a renewed need for substances. The counselor works with the client to understand this destructive process and address these maladaptive thoughts and behaviors.

Existential counseling emphasizes the depth of the current experience at any given moment, thus, little to no work is focused on the past. The nature of the counselor-client relationship is fundamental considering the emotional and fearful concepts examined in the counseling session (death, freedom, isolation, meaninglessness, isolation, and guilt). Consequently, a good part of counseling is focused on the client's inability to feel and sit with negative affect and cognition. This is a slow process. Within this framework, relapse to substance use is common due to the client struggling with the affect block removal and not feeling confident or competent in his or her ability to sit with the negative. Existential counseling engages in repeated and supportive inquiry where the client is encouraged (and if needed, pressed) to express affect and describe cognitions. Questions posed to the client include "What do you want?" or "What do you feel?" or "What are you thinking right now?" Furthermore, how does the client's experience of not using substances or engaging in the process addiction factor into the individual's feelings and thoughts in this moment? Existential theory argues that the inability to express feelings and thoughts is a pervasive characterological trait that in the end facilitated substance use.

Earlier in the chapter, freedom and decision-making responsibility were discussed. Sometimes, even though clients can wish, they are still unable to act due to indecision. A common reason for such indecision is that clients recognize that if they say one *yes* they also, by default, say *no* to an infinite number of other options. Some of these options may never come again, so the client is paralyzed in fear of saying *no*. Others just become cripplingly overwhelmed at the very idea that they control their own lives.

An existential example of the latter occurs in my review of the 12 steps (Narcotics Anonymous [NA], 1993) with a new client. The 12 steps will be reviewed in the next chapter, but for the sake of this example, Step 1 is, "We admitted that we were powerless over our addiction—that our lives had become unmanageable" (NA, 1993, p. 5). From an existential perspective, this step makes no sense. How it is written, the responsibility for choices and decisions seem carved out from the person. I discuss this matter with the client and offer my rebuttal to Step 1 which is, "My addiction slowly created a scenario where, by my own choices and actions, I lost the ability to effectively manage my life." Life did not magically become unmanageable. Rather, clients' dysfunctional misuse of freedom and choice fueled their inability to effectively manage their lives. Clients typically argue with me regarding this rewrite of Step 1. I hear numerous reasons as to why I am wrong. However, as an existentialist, I process these criticisms as indicative of clients—at some level—recognizing their role in their addiction and refusing to accept ownership due to the pain as well as the recognition of the extensive intrapersonal work they will need to do in order to remedy their plight.

Existential counselors help clients make choices. In doing so, the counselor also teaches the client how and why to *own* one's feelings and decisions. Some clients are panicked by the implications of a decision and the "what ifs" torment them, leading to indecision and stagnation. Thus, the task of the counselor is not to create will but rather to unblock the will. The counselor influences the factors that facilitate willing. Decisions are unavoidable, but some clients decide passively by letting other people and situations dictate their decisions.

In addition, clients have difficulty spending time alone. Consequently, they engage in acts and relationships to reduce their loneliness. However, the client may seek certain kinds of relationships and acts to avoid isolation, for example, the client who fills a void of loneliness with drinking and superficial chitchat with others at the local bar. Though it may feel like an interpersonal connection and it helps reduce or eliminate the discomfort of being alone, nothing healthy is being accomplished in these behaviors. The counselor works with the client to find a healthy and adaptive way to confront isolation. Otherwise, even if the SUD is under control, there is a heightened risk of relapse because the underlying conflict regarding isolation has not been addressed.

Often, SUD clients come to treatment with little to no positive meaning in their lives. Instead, they typically come with countless instances of loss. These clients have lost their relationships, marriage, family, children, career, finances, freedom (if involved with the criminal justice system), and general peace of mind. If there is one existential concept that is a challenge to address within the SUD population, it is meaninglessness and the crafting of some degree of meaning in their life. Some clients used to have meaning and purpose, so for them, the issue of meaninglessness is painful, profound, and pervasive.

Frankl (1964) wrote about the critical importance of meaninglessness in conceptualizing psychopathology and once stated that "happiness cannot be pursued, it can only ensue" (p. 165). In a similar manner, Yalom (1980) wrote that counseling was rarely successful unless the client focused on matters beyond simply obtaining happiness or meaning. Both Frankl and Yalom argued the same principle, that meaning in life is an outcome and not the process. Counseling does not occur to establish meaning and happiness; rather, you counsel to help clients find new ways of being that, one day, may result in them experiencing contentment and meaning in their lives.

Too often, the SUD client is self-centered and selfish. This impacts their ability to craft meaning. For instance, I once worked with a young mother who temporarily lost her children to child protective services because of her substance use. She was obviously distraught and despondent regarding the loss of her children. This caused her to slowly shut down in treatment. In addition, in an almost doubling-down manner, she grew more and more indignant regarding the fact that her children were removed from the home and all the bureaucratic steps she must take to be reunited with them. From an existential perspective, she grew so self-absorbed that she was not able to consider the needs of her young children to be reunited with their mother. To her, the world was unjust, wrong, cruel, and condescending. She was only able to find meaning and purpose when she learned to let go of her needs and consider the needs of her children. She then saw the bureaucracy and treatment as a means to an end to get her children back. Out of this process, she found happiness.

That is why existentialism argues that the primary solution to meaninglessness is the act of engagement. Complete engagement in life's activities (including treatment and recovery) enhances the possibility of finding purpose and happiness. The therapist must deal with engagement in a similar manner as wishing. The desire to engage is actually always present—it is just obscured by obstacles. Thus, counseling activity focuses on the removal of obstacles. A big part of this process is assisting clients as they move away from substance/process addictions as a mechanism of escaping from the world. Here, the counselor helps clients rediscover (or perhaps discover for the first time) how to relate with others and find satisfaction with their lives.

META-ANALYSIS OF EXISTENTIAL COUNSELING: AN EXAMPLE

Vos, Craig, and Cooper (2015)

Only recently has quantitative research been conducted on the outcomes of existential therapies (Vos, Cooper, Correia, & Craig, 2015; Walsh & McElwain, 2002). This may best be explained by the reluctance within the existential community to engage with quantitative research methods and research (Spinelli, 2005). However, Vos, Craig, and Cooper (2015) conducted a meta-analysis focused on 15 randomly controlled trials (RCTs) focused on existential therapy. Though none of the studies reviewed focused on substance use disorders, one general finding of the meta-analysis still seemed relevant for a review. This specific meta-analysis result from Vos, Craig, and Cooper is reviewed below.

- Six studies using positive meaning in life as an outcome had a total of 245 participants. The mean posttreatment effect size was large ($d = 0.65$) and significant. Vos, Craig, and Cooper reasoned that clients seemed to benefit from meaning-based interventions as compared with participating in a social support group, being on a waiting list, or receiving treatment as usual.
- Vos, Craig, and Cooper noted that the participants seemed to find greater meaning or purpose in life, a decreased level of psychopathology, and a somewhat strengthened sense of self-efficacy.

If you examine the one area of the meta-analysis where significance was found (the meaning in life findings reported above), there seems to be a link to the application of existential theory with substance use disorders. Though in no manner conclusive or extensive, these findings do at least suggest the potential of existential work with substance use disorders, and more meta-analyses, controlled trials, and clinical case studies seem warranted.

SPECIAL POPULATIONS

Adolescents

There is not much literature focused on adolescent SUD treatment from an existential perspective. However, Fitzgerald (2005) argued that the developmental process within adolescence is appropriate for various existential discussions. Consistent with existential theory, there are no specific techniques to use for adolescents; rather, it is a state of being in the counseling relationship. For example, Potash (1994) noted the following:

> Pragmatic-existential therapists change their response manner when working with patients in varied age groups. For example, adolescent and young adult patients have a pressing developmental need to become independent adults. Even though these patients are satisfying their desires to participate in psychotherapy, this particular need for assistance is in basic conflict with their healthy need to function independently. As a result, the therapist must minimize instances in which he expresses himself as an authority figure. Such comments undermine the patient's basic needs to be a self-sufficient decision maker. (p. 199)

Potash's stance on the nature of the relationship is critical for the following reason: The adolescent brain is often compared to a car with a fully functioning gas pedal (the reward system) but weak brakes (the prefrontal cortex; Robertson, David, & Rao, 2003). Adolescents are highly motivated to pursue pleasurable rewards and avoid pain. Furthermore, their judgment and decision-making skills are limited. Thus, the existential work must primarily occur within the context of the relationship where adolescents are encouraged, supported, and *trained* to make proactive and healthy decisions. They are not used to being permitted to utilize their freedom and responsibility. If anything, this is usually the first thing taken away.

For example, I have worked with countless adolescents who struggled with co-occurring SUD and major depressive disorder or bipolar disorder. They also had a history of one or more suicide attempts, typically immediately preceding starting treatment with me. Their complaints about their home life at that time centered on the following themes:

- They watch me like a hawk. I can't even go to the bathroom in private.
- It's like I'm 5 years old again. They give me my medicine. I can't take it.
- It's weird. Stuff that used to get me nailed and grounded, or the very least yelled at, is now only met with a calm and mild "Please don't do that." They treat me like I'm made of glass and that I can shatter at any moment.

Two existential points are relevant here. First, with so much autonomy and privacy removed from the adolescent client, it becomes that much more challenging to engage the adolescent in a process focused on embracing freedom and responsibility. Here, the relationship as described by Potash enables counselors and clients to discuss the frustrations with having existential freedom taken away and ways in which their autonomy may come back over time. If adolescents feel free to complain and express outrage or embarrassment over the issue, then they are also slowly taking ownership of the idea of freedom and autonomy. A counselor who merely parrots the parental concern as valid would hamper the adolescent treatment progress, as clients would see the counselor as just one more adult denying their being.

Second, the adolescents I have worked with find being treated like they are made of glass rather uncomfortable. Sure, at first they relish the idea of a primarily (within reason) consequence-free environment. But they slowly and steadily grow uneasy with the parental reaction to behaviors that typically would have resulted in some form of parental punishment or at minimum a stern talking-to. For example, one adolescent girl once told me this in session:

So, my mom and I are yelling at each other. My dad is there as well. During the fight I call my mom a bitch. I immediately stopped arguing, expecting a lot of trouble. It was weirdly quiet for about 10 seconds, then my mom just walked away and my dad said it was OK, you're tired and been through a lot and to just try to not say that again. I just stood there. I remember thinking I should be excited that I got off so easy, but instead I just felt off. Something, and I don't know what, wasn't right and I didn't like it. I felt scared, like maybe they know I'm more fragile than I think I am.

Adolescents, especially ones with co-occurring SUD, severe mental illness, and a suicide history, face these types of scenarios. From an existential perspective, they were granted freedom of choice, and (how they see it) they failed at the task of managing that responsibility. This bothers them. It reinforces their notion that maybe they cannot make choices toward being and instead are always putting themselves at risk of nonbeing. When they see how their actions radically altered their parents' behaviors (which are interpreted as scared), adolescents' fears about being able to engage with freedom, make decisions, and craft a being are amplified. They see the parental behaviors as a measure of just how "bad" they were at developing their being. Self-doubt settles in, and the counselor, again through the mutual relationship, assists the client to understand how these dysfunctional choices do not dictate that all future attempts at being will end in the same manner. This is the primary obstacle the counselor must work toward removing so that treatment can be effective. Imagine trying to engage an adolescent in that dialogue if he or she sees the counselor as just another authority figure. For instance, one adolescent client reported to me that she left a prior therapist because

all she seemed to do was focus on how I screwed up and how my screw-ups deserve my parents being mad and scared with me. I was never allowed to express my side of things. I know I did all of this, but I still had feelings about it.

Older Adults

There is a virtual absence of literature focused on existential counseling with older adults facing SUD. Considering the ultimate concerns regarding death and loss and meaning, one could argue that existentialism would work well with older adults due to the various life contexts they face (retirement, loss of friends/loved ones, physical challenges). However, this would be a superficial reading of the theory. I have found that existential work with older adults with SUD is best applied in helping clients redefine their world perceptions postsubstance use. For example, how has their Mitwelt or Eigenwelt changed due to recovery? Is this change all good, or is there some bad also? Within this discussion, if relevant, of course they will discuss losses of friends or physical challenges due to older age. However, it feels like a form of ageism to assume this is the primary issue that they face. Those crises are present, but they are interwoven into a complicated tapestry being reconfigured in their recovery from substance use.

QUESTIONS TO CONSIDER AS YOU MOVE ON TO CHAPTER 9

Question 1: Do you think that, based on neurocognitive deficits, existential theory is not an appropriate match for a newly recovered client? How and where do you see the reasons why?

Question 2: Can existential theory, in some manner, assist you as a counselor trying to assist a client to express his or her thoughts, feelings, and concerns during the interview process? If yes, can you explain how?

Question 3: Of the theories discussed in this book, which do you think would best fit with your style of counseling as it pertains to co-occurring psychiatric disorders?

SECTION III REVIEW

CASE OF SAMANTHA: MOTIVATIONAL INTERVIEWING (MI), COGNITIVE-BEHAVIORAL THERAPY (CBT), FAMILY SYSTEMS, AND EXISTENTIAL APPROACHES

Chapters 5 through 8 cover various common treatment approaches for working with SUDs. Each one of these treatment theories easily warrants a text to fully do them justice. I refer you to some of these lengthier and more complete sources cited in the various chapters. Below, using the case of Samantha, I try to briefly show you some examples of theory-specific content in the context of a case you are familiar with. The first section below contains some examples of MI applied with Samantha.

The Case of Samantha: MI Examples

Below is a transcript. Follow along and you will see the basic concept of MI spirit throughout the dialogue. In addition, in brackets I point out some more specific MI content. I think the one take-away message from this brief exchange is how MI is, in essence, an application of the basic counseling skills we all learned in graduate school—in brief, how to foster a supportive and trusting relationship where the client feels free to communicate about issues. Considering Samantha's issues of opiate use and sex addiction, and her earlier reported discomfort with expressing emotion and seeking help, these basic counseling skills are critical if Samantha is going to be able to continue her success in intensive outpatient (IOP) treatment.

Counselor: You just came out from detox, inpatient, and partial hospitalization. History of depression and opiate use, namely Percocet. Unmarried, works in the financial field as an MBA. Anything else you would like to add? [MI Notes: Fostering a Collaborative Atmosphere via Respect for Autonomy; Close-Ended Question]

Client: It's just . . . , I've been out for about 2 days now and I'm now supposed to go IOP.

Counselor: OK.

Client: I feel lost.

Counselor: Mm-hmm . . .

Client: I miss my old life, well, not the drugs or the depression or other crazy stuff. Just the stability of knowing a routine, going to work, people not knowing my damn business. I'm so embarrassed, and I really hope nobody at work knows what's going on.

Counselor: By the way you described it, you feel upset about feeling out of touch with a normal routine, and you feel worried people may judge you about your problems.

	Tell me some more about it. [MI Notes: Complex Reflective Statement; Open-Ended Question]
Client:	Well, imagine, after having such a hard life, especially the past few years.
Counselor:	Uh huh . . .
Client:	I always kind of knew in the back of my head the past few years things were screwed up. So many pills a day, the nodding off in the office, all to keep my depression secret so I didn't have to deal with it. And all the guys, and even some girls, for the sex. If I wasn't screwing I was popping pills. But I kept working, getting stuff done, so everything was fine, even though I see now I was not fine.
Counselor:	OK. Keep going . . .
Client:	But I kept telling myself I'm OK. Or, when more honest, I'd say I was going to change, but one day and not today.
Counselor:	Hmmm . . .
Client:	I still can't believe I risked it all to go buy Percocet at lunch. I drove like at least 90 in traffic. I could have lost everything and been found out. Guess that was my rock bottom when I got back to the office with time to spare and just, well, freaked out at what I did and why.
Counselor:	Mm-hmm . . .
Client:	So I went to the hospital, got intake done, then was admitted and went to detox, inpatient, partial, and now here. I'm just a little nervous about this.
Counselor:	OK, you shared some difficult stuff that's also important to who you are now as a person.
Client:	It's embarrassing . . .
Counselor:	But important. You knew you were depressed but for a host of reasons wanted to hide it from others and not manage it in a, let's say, healthy way. That's where the pills and the sex came into play. But after you raced to buy pills and realized how reckless you were in that moment, all done just to cope with things, you finally saw how dysfunctional things had really become. That got you to treatment. [MI Notes: Reflective Statement Summary]

Another exchange shows some other MI topics in use.

Client:	Well, look, honestly I don't even want to think about when I go back to work. I'm terrified. Maybe I can't do the job without the pills? Without the sex?

> Maybe my depression will get worse? Maybe I'll just relapse so all this was a colossal waste.

Counselor: So you are worried all this may just be a waste of time and you're going to relapse soon after returning to work. [MI Notes: Simple Reflective Statement]

Client: I worry about other stuff also.

Counselor: What other stuff do you worry about? [MI Notes: Open-Ended Question]

Below is an MI exchange with Samantha using decisional balance regarding whether to continue in treatment. Consistent with MI, decisional balance would examine both sides of the argument, so this is an MI counseling intervention for Samantha to consider the pros and cons of staying in treatment.

Counselor: Samantha, you talked about not wanting to do any more treatment. You feel like you're not using and that's enough. There are some good reasons why you are currently thinking about stopping treatment. For example, it is far less time consuming and you can get back to work, and as you put it, return to a normal nontreatment or nonhospital life. It can also be less stressful or anxiety provoking, as you won't have to examine your past any longer. And you won't have to ponder the future. So let's take some time and discuss what would be good about stopping treatment now. What else is a benefit to no longer being in treatment after today's session? [MI Notes: Pros of leaving treatment]

Now, a question to address the cons.

Counselor: OK, now Samantha, if you stop treatment today, what is the negative impact potentially for you? Will there be any negative consequences for the people or things that are important to you? What will happen in the long term? How might this impact your life? Your recovery? [MI Notes: Cons of leaving treatment]

Samantha, once she decided to engage in treatment, would create a change plan. An example of a plan she would create in IOP with her counselor follows.

The Changes I Want to Make Are:

- Continue to not use pills
- Continue to not use sex as a drug
- Get a better handle on my depression

The Most Important Reasons Why I Want to Make These Changes Are:

- To take better care of myself
- To give my career a chance to rebound and be successful

The Steps I Plan to Take in Changing Are:

- Keep not using pills one day at a time
- Keep not using sex as a drug one day at a time
- Keep coming to IOP groups and individual sessions
- Keep giving urine tests
- Keep attending NA and Sex Addicts Anonymous (SAA) meetings

The Ways Other People Can Help Are:

- My counselor can help me manage my depression and addictions
- My parents can help me by being supportive listeners
- My counseling groups can help me process through my difficulties with recovery
- My NA sponsor can help me if I feel a craving for Percocet or other drugs

I Will Know My Plan Is Working If:

- I am not using substances
- I am not using sex as a substance
- I am attending IOP regularly as scheduled
- I am providing clean urines
- I attend NA and SAA
- I am making plans to eventually return to work when appropriate

Some Things That Could Interfere With My Plan Are:

- My IOP treatment is extended or I am sent back to inpatient or partial hospitalization due to dirty urines and using again
- I don't plan ahead for cravings and urges
- If I quit treatment
- If I try to return to work too soon

What I Will Do If the Plan Is Not Working:

- Be honest with my counselor and my group and ask for help
- Adjust my plans to manage cravings/urges better
- Adjust my plans to manage my depression symptoms better
- Refuse to feel like a failure and that I am destined to relapse

The Case of Samantha: Cognitive-Behavioral Examples

CBT shares many similarities with MI. However, the difference is primarily that where MI prepares the client to make a decision to engage or disengage with treatment, CBT is the day-to-day therapeutic work done in treatment. Consequently, the scope of examples for CBT are nearly endless. I focus on two CBT areas: testing Samantha's addiction beliefs and assisting Samantha to develop control beliefs.

Addiction Beliefs

Samantha had built numerous maladaptive and distorted beliefs regarding opiate use and sex in the course of her addiction. As she left the more structured and supervised forum of inpatient and partial hospitalization treatment for the less supervised (and less frequent) IOP treatment format, Samantha began to feel old pressures and experience old thoughts regarding how she can only cope with depression, work, and life in general using drugs or sex or both. Like so many clients, as these thoughts and associated emotions grow, clients incorrectly default to a stance of "I cannot control my addiction." The trick is that this belief became ingrained into Samantha over the course of a year (opiates) and much longer (sex). Thus, these beliefs will not dissipate immediately. Beck, Wright, Newman, and Liese (1993) used the term *loosen* to describe the process. Like a tight knot, you slowly loosen the rigid beliefs until the client leaves room for healthier control-based beliefs to develop. A brief example of CBT with Samantha focused on addiction beliefs follows.

Counselor: Let's look some more at your thoughts about the pills, the Percocet.

Client: OK. I'll tell you the truth here. When I'm feeling stressed. After a hard day at treatment. Or, I start getting HR documents pertaining to a return to work date, I miss it. I miss the instant relief from all the stress and stuff.

Counselor: What do you specifically miss about the pills?

Client: Sounds weird, but the peace of mind. With the sex, I always had to convince myself I wasn't a slut or a sex maniac. There was so much baggage attached to it. And most of the time it involved someone else so I wasn't anonymous. But the pills, just a peace of mind that I could privately take some and then just numb out. I knew if the day got too stressful, or I got too depressed, that I had an out. A way to cope that worked. So, peace of mind.

Counselor: So, peace of mind?

Client: Yes. Nothing ever gave me such calming peace of mind that I was able to manage things.

Counselor: Nothing ever? That's a big statement.

Client: Nothing. Big, how? What do you mean?

Counselor: You have said that in your entire adult life you have never, ever, found any action or anything that gave you as much peace of mind as the pills.

Client: That's what I said.

Counselor: How confident are you? What if a lot of money was riding on that bet you just made?

Client: 99% confident.

Counselor: Oh, wait now a moment! You just told me nothing ever. This is an example of nothing ever. How often has the sun risen in the west?

Client: Never, it sets in the west, rises in the east.

Counselor: So what percentage of time does it rise in the west?

Client: 0%.

Counselor: Sure?

Client: Yes.

Counselor: How sure?

Client: Uh, 100%. Why?

Counselor: So you said that you were sure regarding that statement you made of nothing ever gave you as much peace of mind that you could cope with negative stuff as the Percocet. But now it dipped a bit at only 99% sure. So there's room for debate.

Client: OK, maybe there was at some time or two something that helped me cope better, but I don't recall it and it must have been a long while ago.

Counselor: Before the pills you were using sex like a drug. Did you always use sex to cope with stuff?

Client: No. Sometimes, I just couldn't have sex. Like, when I just had a bunch of sex past few days.

Counselor: So did you just suffer and wait it out?

Client: No. I used to swim.

Counselor: What did it do?

Client: Gave me solitude. Exercise. Helped me manage stuff. It didn't really do it as well as sex, but it helped definitely.

Counselor: So why'd you stop?

Client: The accident.

Counselor: So by the time you were healed and could swim again you moved on to the pills?

Client: I guess.

Counselor: And the pills gave you a more instant gratification than swimming, or how it sounds, even sex.

Client: Yeah.

Counselor: So your original belief that nothing [emphasized] ever did the job better than pills wasn't accurate. It sounds more accurate you just gave up on swimming because you found a faster solution for your depression and stress management.

Client: Argh, when you put it like that, I sound even worse. Ok, maybe you were kind of right here.

Control Beliefs

In the exchange above, Samantha was challenged in her thinking that nothing was ever as capable of helping her manage affect and mood as the pills. However, in the course of the CBT dialogue, Samantha flushed out her thinking more and saw how she substituted the pills for swimming when she was physically unable to swim due to her injury. Once her addiction beliefs have been "loosened," it becomes time to slowly instill some control beliefs. An example of CBT attempting to instill control beliefs is below.

Counselor: You discussed swimming. Are you able to swim again physically?

Client: Well, yeah, but I'm totally out of shape. No exercise for over one year.

Counselor: So?

Client: I wouldn't enjoy it. It would suck. I'd be wheezing after two laps.

Counselor: OK, but you probably did that when you first started swimming laps many years back. But let's pretend you could skip over the reacclimation to swimming and you were back in preaccident shape. Would you swim?

Client: You know, especially now with all the emphasis on doing healthy things for me and exercise being reinforced in treatment, I think I would. Plus, it would give me one less thing to worry about. Right now I'm trying to figure out what I can do to exercise. This would solve that problem.

Counselor: You mentioned solitude earlier as an advantage of swimming. What did you mean exactly?

Client: I was free to think. I would sometimes scream through my closed mouth under water. Just one long loud hum for a few seconds. I could get stuff out. I sometimes didn't like what I thought, like if I thought about the sex stuff I was doing, but I was able to think and express.

Counselor: Think that might be helpful to you again? If you had that outlet the worries about returning to the pills or sex might slowly lessen?

Client: Maybe.

Counselor: So maybe you can replace the old addictive beliefs of no control with a healthier statement that I can have control by swimming.

Client: That'd be nice.

The Case of Samantha: Family Counseling Examples

Samantha did not want to include her family in her formal treatment. However, she did want to discuss some of the interpersonal tensions and conflicts within her family, how they impact her present recovery, and how they may have played a role in her addiction. In this instance, the genogram would make the most sense. In her genogram, Samantha would be able to visually demonstrate the conflicts between herself and her mother and father, as well as how she feels cut off from other members of the family. As we move forward in treatment, this information may be valuable. Most critically, Samantha is not forced to engage with her family in treatment if she chooses not to. However, when appropriate, the offer for a family counseling session with all (or some) members will be extended along with how and the reasons why such an intervention may assist in her recovery. The genogram would play a crucial role in mapping out both the argument for the family intervention as well as the initial plan for the family session(s).

The Case of Samantha: Existential Examples

As discussed in this chapter, existentialism is not a counseling orientation but rather a theoretical and philosophical way to conceptualize the counseling process and how clients experience their problems both in the session and the larger world outside treatment. In existential work with Samantha, the crux of the endeavor would be shifting her from an inauthentic to authentic existence, as you could existentially argue that the opiate and sex addictions were a strategy to engage in an inauthentic manner with her life. Clients do small things to demonstrate an inauthentic mind-set. Consequently, an existential counselor picks up on these subtle markers and addresses them in counseling. van Deurzen and Adams (2011) noted a few of these inauthentic indicators as pronoun switching (i.e., the personal "I" pronoun switched out for a less personal term such as *you, they society,* or *people*), excessive referencing to the past (i.e., stubborn and rigid fixation on relaying past events without reflecting on how these past events influence their current existence), and seeing the counselor as the authority (i.e., either deferring to the counselor for making life decisions or being intimidated by the counselor and shutting down in session). Each is briefly demonstrated within the case of Samantha below.

Pronoun switching:

Client: He totally ridiculed my recovery. Said I was one of those 12-step morons who needs a support group for anything.

Counselor: Uh-huh.

Client: That's messed up. Wrong.

Counselor: Wrong how? Why?

Client: People should not put recovery down like that. Society should not allow that!

Counselor: I don't know about people or society, but you seem to find it insulting.

Client: Wouldn't you?

Counselor: Not my recovery. I wasn't the one insulted here.

Client: Fine, forget it.

Counselor: No. I won't forget it because you sure didn't.

Client: What do you want then?

Counselor: How was it to hear what he said? To be insulted like that?

Client: It hurt. Like I was less-than and I was being judged for it.

Counselor: But it's hard for you to admit being hurt, or feeling emotional pain, in front of anyone, especially a therapist.

Client: Yup.

Counselor: Maybe that's why you had the original focus on people and society? And not you, how you felt, you thought.

Client: Maybe.

Notice the resistance to personalize, or own, the hurt feelings. And how that resistance manifests as impersonal phrasing. The counselor working with Samantha would consistently need to be looking out for these instances as they may likely reflect a degree of discomfort and hurt that Samantha struggles with and for effective recovery would need to address.

Excessive referencing to the past:

Client: But you need to know.

Counselor: Why? I have the background. Tell me more about how you now consider your actions when you raced down the highway at 90 mph and back that sent you to treatment? How do you experience that story now?

Client: Back then, I just remember being so stressed.

Counselor: OK, I know that. What I don't know is how do you experience that story now? Like, if you were watching this play out in real time, what would you be thinking and feeling now?

Client: I don't understand.

Counselor: Right now, your thoughts and feelings about having entered treatment. Right now, your thoughts and feelings about the 90 mph incident.

Client: I'm glad about treatment, but I don't like discussing the other thing. Can we just move on?

This is another example of Samantha hiding. Instead of hiding behind impersonal dialogue in session, in this instance she focuses rigidly on relaying her past story and how she felt back then. It takes some work from the counselor to elicit her thoughts and emotions in the present about this topic, and even then, the response is minimal. Effective recovery requires honesty, so Samantha's treatment should, at some point, investigate how and why this event is difficult for her to process in the present.

Below is another example, this time focused on Samantha's overreliance on the counselor for answers, otherwise known as *seeing the counselor as authority*:

Client: So what do I do?

Counselor: I don't know.

Client: Aren't you the expert? Isn't that why I see you? Why you get paid?

Counselor: No, that's not why.

Client: You have the PhD. You have the license. I live by your rules. What good is any of this if you can't help me? Seems like a sham to me.

Counselor: You seem upset.

Client: Yes, I am upset. I pay money to come see you, and I need answers and you give me therapy mumbo-jumbo about not having an answer? I call a plumber and ask why my sink is clogged. Later, I get an answer like hair in the trap. And I get a solution. Sink unclogged. This is a joke.

Counselor: So you want treatment and recovery to be as easy and clear cut as plumbing?

Client: No. Right now I just want you to shut up.

Samantha is lashing out at the counselor because he or she is there. She uses the counselor authority role as an excuse to allow herself to get angry about the ambiguity of treatment and recovery. The best thing a counselor can do here is simply let Samantha be angry. As discussed in the chapter, recognizing one's nonbeing and moving toward a state of being requires courage and time. In that context, this is one small, small step in that lengthy and difficult process.

LEGAL, ETHICAL, AND CURRICULAR MATTERS

One important ethical concept to discuss in regard to the application of counseling for SUDs is that of the recovering counselor. First, we consider the ethical issues relevant to recovering counselors and their specific ethical and personal mandate regarding self-monitoring their own functioning, and where needed, to seek assistance. Second, we address the matter of a counselor being directly questioned about his or her recovery status. Whether in recovery or having never been addicted, this situation poses some meaningful questions one should answer to effectively function in the addiction profession. These are issues that must be embedded into any addiction counseling training/education curriculum.

The Recovering Counselor

Jones, Sells, and Rehfuss (2009) studied counselors recovering from addictions to alcohol and substances. The 1,239 counselor responses documented an overall recovering counselor relapse rate of 37.78%. Thus, recovering addiction counselors are at some degree of risk for relapse (though this is likely influenced by the stability and length of their recovery). It is also difficult to ascertain if this issue is unique to only addiction counselors, as there is not much (if any) literature focused on, for example, counselors with major depressive disorder who experience another episode following work with a depressed client. The Addiction Counseling Competencies (CSAT, 2006c) review the basics of effective counseling from competencies 75 to 88 (pp. 101–112). However, all these basic best practices for counseling require a counselor who is not struggling with personal matters to the point of impairment.

The American Counseling Association (ACA) *Code of Ethics* (2014) makes reference to impaired counselors in C.2.g. Specifically, ACA states:

> Counselors monitor themselves for signs of impairment from their own physical, mental, or emotional problems and refrain from offering or providing professional services when impaired. They seek assistance for problems that reach the level of professional impairment, and, if necessary, they limit, suspend, or terminate their professional responsibilities until it is determined that they may safely resume their work. Counselors assist colleagues or supervisors in recognizing their own professional impairment and provide consultation and assistance when warranted with colleagues or supervisors showing signs of impairment and intervene as appropriate to prevent imminent harm to clients. (p. 9)

In addition, the National Association of Alcoholism and Drug Abuse Counselors Code of Ethics (2011) also seems to address the issue in regard to the ethical concept of professional responsibility:

> The addiction professional espouses objectivity and integrity and maintains the highest standards in the services provided. The addiction professional recognizes that effectiveness in his or her profession is based on the ability to be worthy of trust. The professional has taken time to reflect on the ethical implications of clinical decisions and behavior

using competent authority as a guide. Further, the addiction professional recognizes that those who assume the role of assisting others to live a more responsible life take on the ethical accountability of living responsibly. The addiction professional recognizes that even in a life well-lived, harm might be done to others by words and actions. When he or she becomes aware that any work or action has done harm, he or she admits the error and does what is possible to repair or ameliorate the harm except when to do so would cause greater harm. Professionals recognize the many ways in which they influence clients and others within the community and take this fact into consideration as they make decisions in their personal conduct. (p. 1)

Consequently, recovering counselors must be vigilant regarding their emotional and cognitive stability in their recovery while working with clients. This is why, for example, it is recommended (if not required) that those in recovery have a few years of stable and consistent recovery prior to entering the addiction profession. Unfortunately, this wise advice is sometimes not followed. For example, early in my academic teaching career, I witnessed more than one graduate student who was early in their recovery and had started a counselor education graduate program. They had not yet become capable of processing their own thoughts and emotions from their addiction history, so when these matters (typical of any addiction counseling course) were discussed, they struggled with boundaries and countertransference. Eventually, the students withdrew from the program.

This is why effective addiction counseling supervision is so critical (CSAT, 2007). With the advent of the Approved Clinical Supervisor credential, supervisors now must have adequate graduate-level training in the provision of supervision. A good addiction counselor supervisor is one who is skilled in supervision, understands the addiction profession, and recognizes the potential professional and personal matters unique to the addiction counselor. I have worked with a number of graduate students in recovery who either were doing a practicum/internship in an addictions facility or they desired to obtain such a placement. Our discussions were always focused on their bringing up the question of whether they were "ready" to work in this field. We discussed a few key points:

- How do they know they are ready?
- How would they know they perhaps were experiencing difficulties once on-site?
- How would they address these issues immediately and proactively in a healthy way for both their counseling and their personal recovery?

If they were able to answer these questions in a way satisfactory for them, we discussed that they were probably ready to attempt work in an addiction counseling facility.

Are You in Recovery?

Doyle, Linton, Morgan, and Stefanelli (2008) noted how counselors being asked about their recovery status is a common experience in the practice of working with clients in treatment for SUDs. This is basically a question of self-disclosure (Manual & Forcehimes, 2008; Taleff, 2010), so counselors need to consider how much they wish to self-disclose.

Self-disclosure is effective and appropriate when done for the benefit of clients and their treatment. Thus, the counselor needs to consider the context in which the query was made. For instance, consider the situation of a client who outright states that he or she can tell who is and is not in recovery and declares the counselor as not in recovery, thus disqualifying the counselor's services as valid. I would argue in a case such as this that counselor self-disclosure is not appropriate as it does not contribute to the counseling process. At worst, what would happen is one of the following two scenarios:

- The counselor discloses that he or she is not in recovery and the session becomes one where the counselor may feel on the defensive to prove that their counseling is valid. This is a common scenario for new counselors not in recovery who are posed this question. They feel defensive, and in the end the counseling is not effective.
- The counselor discloses that he or she is, in fact, in recovery. In this case, the counselor is still deferring to the client's inappropriate behavior in session.

In this first scenario, basic counseling skills are called for that attempt to create a dialogue as to why recovery status for his or her counselor is critical. If the question was purely from a defensive or obstructionist point of view, then clients may never hear the answer they want and may leave treatment. Their reason for leaving treatment may seem like it was dissatisfaction with counselor recovery status, but in reality, for various reasons they were just not yet ready for change.

Another scenario reflects a counseling situation where perhaps self-disclosure may, in fact, benefit the relationship. Here, a client is struggling with anxiety regarding an upcoming first-ever Alcoholics Anonymous (AA) meeting. In this case, recovering counselors may choose to self-disclose their recovery status by reflecting on how they felt just as nervous prior to their first AA meeting. The commonality of experience would make for a powerful counseling moment. Of course, a nonrecovering counselor could be just as effective in this moment but from a different perspective. However, what either perspective shares is that the intervention (whether self-disclosure or otherwise) is done for the benefit of the client and the counseling session.

SECTION IV

RECOVERY SUPPORT AND COUNSELOR SUPERVISION

CHAPTERS 9-11

These chapters cover the areas of 12-step philosophy, relapse prevention, and addiction counseling supervision. The latter concept (supervision) is not seen as often in other similar books. Following Chapter 11, I review the case of Samantha from the perspective of what she could/should consider in her 12-step or relapse prevention programs. Both of these are lifetime endeavors that likely extend far beyond the tenure of our counseling together. I end with an ethics review of issues pertinent to supervision.

Chapter 9

12-Step Philosophy

THE 12 STEPS AND TRADITIONS

Any exploration of the 12 steps must address spirituality. At the core of 12-step programs is an understanding of "the spiritual" and a way of living that is rooted in spiritual principles and practices and leads to a "spiritual awakening" (Alcoholics Anonymous World Services [AAWS], 1976, pp. 58–60). This awakening is the 12-step key to survival of alcoholism and addiction (Wilson, 1957/1988). For the 12-step participant, sobriety is the "first gift" of this spiritual awakening (Wilson, 1957/1988, p. 234). Today, many 12-step-inspired programs address a variety of disabling conditions, ranging from alcoholism (Alcoholics Anonymous [AA]) and substance (nonalcohol) addiction (Narcotics Anonymous [NA] or Cocaine Anonymous) to process addictions such as gambling (Gamblers Anonymous) or addictive sexual disorders (Sex and Love Addicts Anonymous). Twelve-step programs also facilitate recovery for people affected by the addictions of others, such as spouses and children of people with alcoholism and addiction (Alanon, Naranon, Alateen). The 12-steps consist of the "steps" as well as the traditions. Each form a philosophy for establishing a healthier and happier way of life for those struggling with addiction either themselves or within their relationship/family. The steps and traditions from AA are below (see Table 9.1 and Table 9.2). For NA, the steps and traditions are the same, with the exception that *alcohol* is replaced with *drug,* and *drinking* with *using.* However, in overall content and scope, they are identical.

Table 9.1 The 12 Steps of Alcoholics Anonymous

1. We admitted we were powerless over alcohol—that our lives had become unmanageable.

2. Came to believe that a Power greater than ourselves could restore us to sanity.

3. Made a decision to turn our will and our lives over to the care of God *as we understood Him.*

4. Made a searching and fearless moral inventory of ourselves.

5. Admitted to God, to ourselves, and to another human being the exact nature of our wrongs.

6. Were entirely ready to have God remove all these defects of character.

7. Humbly asked Him to remove our shortcomings.

8. Made a list of all persons we had harmed, and became willing to make amends to them all.

9. Made direct amends to such people wherever possible, except when to do so would injure them or others.

10. Continued to take personal inventory and when we were wrong promptly admitted it.

11. Sought through prayer and meditation to improve our conscious contact with God, *as we understood Him*, praying only for knowledge of His will for us and the power to carry that out.

12. Having had a spiritual awakening as the result of these Steps, we tried to carry this message to alcoholics, and to practice these principles in all our affairs.

Source: AAWS (1981).

Table 9.2 The 12 Traditions of Alcoholics Anonymous

1. Our common welfare should come first; personal recovery depends upon A.A. unity.

2. For our group purpose, there is but one ultimate authority—a loving God as He may express Himself in our group conscience. Our leaders are but trusted servants; they do not govern.

3. The only requirement for A.A. membership is a desire to stop drinking.

4. Each group should be autonomous except in matters affecting other groups or A.A. as a whole.

5. Each group has but one primary purpose—to carry its message to the alcoholic who still suffers.

6. An A.A. group ought never endorse, finance, or lend the A.A. name to any related facility or outside enterprise, lest problems of money, property, and prestige divert us from our primary purpose.

7. Every A.A. group ought to be fully self-supporting, declining outside contributions.

8. Alcoholics Anonymous should remain forever nonprofessional, but our service centers may employ special workers.

9. A.A., as such, ought never be organized; but we may create service boards or committees directly responsible to those they serve.

10. Alcoholics Anonymous has no opinion on outside issues; hence the A.A. name ought never be drawn into public controversy.

11. Our public relations policy is based on attraction rather than promotion; we need always maintain personal anonymity at the level of press, radio, and films.

12. Anonymity is the spiritual foundation of all our Traditions, ever reminding us to place principles before personalities.

Source: AAWS (1981).

OVERALL PHILOSOPHY OF THE 12 STEPS

"Spiritual Rather Than Religious"

The 12 steps were originally written in 1939 by William Wilson, cofounder of AA, and revised by the earliest recovering members of that organization (Kurtz, 1979, 1992, 1996; Wilson, 1953). They were an attempt to provide insight into the recovery process as they had experienced it, or as they said, an effort to demonstrate "how it works" (AAWS, 1976, pp. 58–71; Forcehimes, 2004).

Wilson (1953) and others were self-conscious about the variety of influences that affected their experiences. They understood that the Oxford Group had provided them with some type of spiritual origins, but they felt the need to break away from the Oxford Group's overt religiosity (Kurtz, 1979). Thus, they proclaimed themselves "spiritual rather than religious," believing that their experiences and the steps they offered provided a wide-open set of beliefs and practices that could complement any religion and accommodate those with no religious faith (AAWS, 1985; Kurtz, 2008). The general philosophy that guided the development of the recovery process was guided by (a) the personal experience of the earliest recovery members, (b) how they understood what had happened to them, and (c) how they communicated this experience to others (Kurtz, 1979, 1982; White & Kurtz, 2008).

Contrary to the misunderstanding of some (e.g., Lé, Ingvarson, & Page, 1995), the founders and earliest members of the 12-step recovery movement underscored "the vital importance of the spiritual" (Kurtz, 1988) while integrating it within a new notion of illness. They simply did not accept a medical view of addiction. Addiction, they said, is a threefold condition of the physical, mental, and spiritual. This redefinition of illness that integrated the spiritual alongside the medical was hypothesized as one of the critical ways that the 12 steps facilitated recovery (Morgan, 1992; Siegler, Osmond, & Newell, 1968).

General 12-Step Structure

Kurtz (2008) concisely reviewed the general structure of the 12 steps. Step 1 captures the experience of "utter defeat," which is the starting point in the 12-step process and typically referenced as "hitting bottom." Steps 2 and 3 start to instill hope and that sobriety comes by turning over one's life to another's care. This is not a passive handing-off our personal responsibility for recovery. Rather, to borrow from existentialism, these steps are in essence individuals admitting they have a problem and becoming less self-absorbed, which the 12-step philosophy argues is far more powerful than simply the cessation of use. Steps 4 and 5 immediately follow this self-admission and focus on self-knowledge and honesty. Steps 6 and 7 assist the recovering person in owning this newly sought personal responsibility via a process of opening one up for the process of personal change. Steps 8 and 9 make the process of personal change quite real (and raw) via the practices of the moral inventory and the philosophic act of confession. Steps 10 through 12 are basically the maintenance steps within a new recovering lifestyle.

The 12-step diagnosis of addiction focuses on "character defects" as the central spiritual problem (AAWS, 1976, 1981). Twelve-step literature discusses concepts such as "selfishness–self-centeredness" and "self-centered fear" as well as "self-will run riot" as the root of the addict's troubles (AAWS, 1976, p. 62; Kurtz, 2008). Thus, the 12 steps focus on spiritual attitudes and practices and not a traditional counseling framework. Kurtz and colleagues go as far as to demonstrate how these 12-step principles (surrender, self-examination, confession, service) are applicable to many Eastern and Western cultures (Kurtz, 2008; Kurtz & Ketcham, 1993).

12 STEPS AND COUNSELING

Despite the uniqueness of the 12 steps, there are still critical associations between the 12 steps and traditional substance use disorder (SUD) counseling. For example, two decades ago Bristow-Braitman (1995) noted the presence of evidence in favor of the integration of evidence-based clinical approaches with the 12 steps. Since that initial observation, other well-established counseling theories have utilized elements of the 12 steps in the conceptualization regarding how and why people change, such as the transtheoretical (DiClemente, 1993; Prochaska & DiClemente, 1986) and motivational enhancement (Miller & Rollnick, 2002) models. For example, Martin and Simh (2009) highlighted the spiritual nature of Miller and Rollnick's (2002) motivational interviewing through counselor-facilitated self-exploration and continual support. However, critical to this chapter is the consideration that motivation is never given by the counselor. Rather, motivation arises if the client desires change. Gorski (1989) described the shift in motivation for a life change as a teachable moment, but this moment is only teachable if it arrives and is accepted by the client.

Thus, 12-step involvement complements other clinical interventions, whether inpatient or outpatient. They are now considered a best practice in the overall process of addiction treatment (Department of Veterans Affairs, Department of Defense, 2015; Gossop, Stewart, & Marsden, 2007; McLellan, 2006; Moos & Moos, 2004, 2006; Tonigan, 2001). For instance, Moos and Moos (2004, 2006) have shown that 12-step participation combined with formal treatment (either concurrently in combination or before/after formal treatment) improves outcomes and may even be equal or superior to current evidence-based treatments alone. Other considerations of the 12 steps see it as one of many facets that help facilitate "recovery capital," which is the amount and quality of internal and external resources expended to achieve and sustain recovery and includes behaviors and attitudes such as having and using (and eventually becoming) a sponsor, regularly attending meetings, and "working" the steps (Laudet, Becker, & White, 2009; Laudet, Morgen, & White, 2006), or conceptualized as a guiding framework for use in integrating spiritual components and discussions into the counseling process (Morgen, Morgan, Cashwell, & Miller, 2010), whereas others see the 12 steps as facilitating the development of important recovery components such as self-efficacy, social support, and positive psychology (Straussner & Byrne, 2009).

12-STEP THEMES

Morgen and Morgan (2011) formulated a thematic organization of the 12 steps centered on the primary conflicts and struggles inherent within that step(s). This thematic guide helps the counselor develop a connective link between the 12-step and SUD treatment client experiences. As conceptualized by Morgen and Morgan, the spiritual, philosophical, and theological 12-step content is quite applicable to the individual and group treatment processes. In fact, being able to bring these matters up in the traditional treatment setting would likely enhance recovery efforts and should be applied to the client's struggles with recovery from other disorders (such as co-occurring psychiatric disorders). The thematic breakdown of the steps as devised by Morgen and Morgan follow below.

Steps 1 Through 3

> We rely on our faith and believe that this decision is one of the best decisions we've ever made.
>
> *—Narcotics Anonymous (1993, pp. 28–29)*

Morgen and Morgan (2011) noted two crucial spiritual, philosophical, and theological components: essential limitation and surrender/confession. Each is addressed individually.

Essential Limitation. Step 1 underscores the consistent, but difficult, truth about the human existence: "To be human, to be essentially limited . . . is to be essentially dependent" (Kurtz, 1982, p. 54). To acknowledge powerlessness (Step 1) is to accept the truth of essential limitation. You cannot do everything and anything. You will make mistakes. Thus, being in the situation of addiction and the associated psychosocial damages and dysfunction is normal. Clients have made mistakes and need to begin understanding how their limitations facilitated their addiction. The notion of limitation is the prerequisite consideration individuals must make before they can move on to the other steps. How and why should you "work" the steps if you do not have a limitation in needed of addressing?

In a paradoxical manner, the notion of acceptance of oneself as limited and flawed brings the calming realization that one is not (nor was one ever) expected to be perfect or consistently in control. To accept oneself as imperfect allows one to also let go of all the cognitive and emotional "tricks" we try to pull on ourselves to maintain an illusion of control. In brief, a major philosophical breakthrough is that the individual recognizes two things: First, it is fine to be human, and second, he or she had been engaged in a futile attempt to not be human (e.g., being perfect, not accepting faults), which was destined to fail every time.

The notion of universal human imperfection helps forge the sense of community within a 12-step meeting. If one is imperfect, then so is everyone else. The self-acceptance of limitation allows the individual to accept the imperfection in the other members. This facilitates a sense of belonging. Accepting the paradox of limitation is not "contrary to the underlying principles of counseling [autonomy, self-efficacy]," as some have maintained (Lé et al., 1995, p. 605). It is just the opposite.

Surrender and Confession. Surrender is a paradox in that to regain power over his or her life, the client must abdicate any control he or she currently possesses (Jensen, 2000; Kurtz, 1982; Swora, 2004). Counseling a client through Steps 1 to 3 entails supporting the client in this difficult task of confronting shame and guilt over past actions (Swora, 2004). The counselor must understand that the addictive behaviors (e.g., drug or alcohol use, gambling, sexual acts) were only a symptom of a larger control issue.

Counseling through Steps 1 to 3 is actually counseling a client toward a state of willingness or readiness to change (AAWS, 1981). However, Gorski (1989) cautioned that before giving up control, the client will first attempt to control the problematic behavior (e.g., drug or alcohol use). Clients may adjust substance dosage or frequency, or change their primary substance used. The counselor should conceptualize these actions as a reluctance to surrender. The counselor should also see this reluctance as normal because surrender is difficult, particularly for an individual who has never before truly surrendered. That is why Morgen and Morgan (2011) saw the early steps as the important preliminary work before one can actually start the process toward a spiritual awakening. Specifically, they argued that these steps entail the combatting of narcissism. In the realm of addiction, narcissism can manifest as a perceived ability to control addiction or that the varied and serious associated life issues can all be handled with no assistance (other than that of substance use). Numerous sources clearly note the obvious, that narcissism is incompatible with spiritual development due to the close-mindedness of the narcissistic individual (AAWS, 1981; Burijon, 2001; Hart & Hugget, 2005). However, the counselor must understand that narcissism is not done out of malice but usually develops as a self-protective shield from the serious issues in need of exploration and change (Morgen & Morgan, 2011). Clients are narcissistic because they are— for lack of a better phrasing—just not ready yet. This is why 12-step programs refuse "none who wish to recover" (AAWS, 1981, p. 189). If they do truly "wish" to recover, by default they are not narcissistic.

Steps 4 Through 9

We are no longer ignorant of our character defects, and this awareness hurts.

—Narcotics Anonymous (1993, p. 60)

Morgen and Morgan (2011) argued that Steps 4 through 9 constitute the bulk of the life-changing work in the process of moving toward a spiritual awakening. They conceptualized this work via the concept of humility.

Humility. Here, the client's perspective and framework for living and being in the world will become clear (Jensen, 2000). Steps 4 to 9 represent a juxtaposition of outward public expressions of regret and remorse alongside an internal debate regarding the new direction of one's life (Maxwell, 1982). Working Steps 4 to 9 means clients have initially overcome the defensiveness and denial resulting from the shame and guilt of past actions. They still feel this pain, but now they are able to manage the discomfort and use it as a guide moving forward. Specifically, they are ready to engage in the development of a moral inventory and making amends.

The moral inventory is a blunt, honest, and comprehensive self-review performed in an effort to construct a new addiction-free way of engaging with the world. Morgen and Morgan (2011) noted that the 12-step philosophy does not mandate with whom the moral inventory must be shared. Thus, a sponsor and a counselor can each play a critical role in the construction and review of the inventory. A counselor working with a client in Steps 4 to 9 helps the client with the process known as "letting go" (Kurtz & Ketcham, 1993). Here, the counselor works within the process in which the client builds the strength and willingness (through 12-step group support, sponsor mentoring, and higher power) to create a moral inventory (a humbling act) that then facilitates enhanced humility, because an effective moral inventory delves deeper into prior wrongful and harmful acts. Ford (1996) cautioned, though, that most SUD treatment programs fail to effectively train clients on the self-reflection and coping skills and strategies required with the high emotionality elicited via a fearless, moral inventory. Consequently, Morgen and Morgan argued that the responsibility for teaching these skills may fall on the counselor.

Knack (2009) pointed out that the 12 steps and counseling share the "talking cure" as a primary mechanism for change. Thus, the counselor role in the process, according to Morgen and Morgan (2011), focuses on engaging the client in spiritual and philosophical discussions on despair, regret, guilt, and self-doubt. Otherwise, clients will not have their negative affect/mood and cognitions under control. Morgen and Morgan also added that this counselor role is heightened if working with an SUD client with a co-occurring psychiatric disorder. This would produce a scenario where the moral inventory would become overwhelming. Furthermore, the act of creating a moral inventory and seeking amends may increase psychological distress so that by focusing on the SUD the client may become more at risk for a relapse of the co-occurring psychiatric disorder (e.g., the client engaging in a fearless moral inventory and revisiting the past ways in which she had been cruel to her spouse may exacerbate her co-occurring major depressive disorder).

Steps 10 Through 12

> The message we carry is that, by practicing the principles contained within the Twelve Steps, we have had a spiritual awakening.
>
> —*Narcotics Anonymous (1993, pp. 118–119)*

Morgen and Morgan (2011) described these steps as indicative of clients having achieved a more stable footing. Having faced their addiction and the damage caused by their dysfunction, they come out the other side healthier, stronger, and more focused individuals. The spiritual awakening is the clarity obtained via facing the addiction, being victorious, and now having a newfound purpose. A client once described it to me like this:

> You ever have the flu for a week? You feel like crap, house goes to crap. Then, you wake up one day and the chills, cough, sweats, aches, and fever are gone. You can smell things again 'cause you're not stuffed up. Your sense of taste is back. You vacuum, do laundry, clean dishes, and get things back to how they should be and it all seems kinda new and wonderful 'cause it wasn't that way for a bit. You have something to do again. You go to work, to school, run errands, whatever.

Morgen and Morgan (2011) described how storytelling and fellowship are the two principle features of these final steps. Each is addressed below.

Storytelling. Morgen and Morgan (2011) described how 12-step recovery is a narrative form of spiritual counseling. In listening to members tell their stories, the new member learns how to tell his or her story, to see things from a unique perspective, to identify character defects, and to "work the steps" toward a solution. In the telling of their story, a new recovery narrative, developed via a serious and deep cognitive, emotional, behavioral, and spiritual exploration, is born and replaces the older addiction self-narrative (Brown, Peterson, & Cunningham, 1988; Morgan, 1992). This process in and of itself is a source of resilience that fuels the recovery potential. But the process must be carefully monitored as it can also serve as an impetus for relapse. For instance, Morgen and Morgan (2011) stated:

> The unfolding story of the costs—and fleeting benefits—of addiction inevitably leads to the experience of regret. Many poor and selfish choices form the heart of the addict's career, and the labeling of one's difficulties as illness or disease does not fully diminish the experience of guilt and shame. Indeed, understanding these choices as part of a spiritual problem invites application of spiritual principles for resolution. As the recovering client remembers poor choices and mixed motives, this regret and shame threaten to reignite stresses that can overwhelm the resolve to stay sober. They can become a catalyst for relapse. (p. 235)

Brach (2004) discussed the "trance of unworthiness" that many live with as a result of their personal narrative. There is a need for healing and freedom from this narrative—freedom to move beyond the negative and start a healing process that enables a new narrative. These last few steps are a sort of debriefing process where all the heavy-lifting work from the prior stages (e.g., essential limitation, surrender and confession, moral inventory, and humility) is appropriately conceptualized by clients in their new self-narrative. This is the new story they take out into the world. This is the new story they will share with other recovering individuals.

Fellowship. The concluding three steps (10–12) also stress the need for fellowship or social support, which is critical to recovery (Laudet et al., 2009; Laudet et al., 2006). The 12th step is never ending. It is a lifelong maintenance and refinement process. What worked once may need adjustment as life changes. Morgen and Morgan (2011) noted that a counselor role of critical importance is to stress a "keep coming back" philosophy and encourage the client to continue attending their home group. Knack (2009) also discussed how client engagement in meetings can enhance their self-esteem. This can happen in a few ways. One is when the client recognizes and explains the value of his or her experiences to a newer 12-step member. Counselors should praise the client's new status as role model. Another way is that clients may also see just how far they have come in their recovery. Seeing a new 12-step member in distress and recalling their own similar plight provides a tangible marker that permits clients to truly see the progress made and that all the work involved was well worth the effort. This also reinforces the need for continual 12-step home group engagement.

Counselors also need to look out for clients who believe they no longer need the support of their 12-step group. For instance, De Leon (2000) discussed the flight-into-health phenomenon where individuals may begin to diminish their need for treatment after the first signs of progress. Gorski and Miller (1986) discussed a similar phenomenon in the recovery phase, noting that the client's new substance-free lifestyle needs continual maintenance. Thus, Morgen and Morgan (2011) noted how one more example of the fellowship is how within the joint role of the 12-step group and counselor there is a continual reinforcement of the 12 steps as a spiritual awakening that influences all other life areas.

12-STEP MEMBERSHIP AND MEETING BASICS

Osten and Switzer (2014) pointed out how 12-step meetings mirror much of the group therapy principles discussed by Yalom (1995). For example, meetings enable individuals to feel less isolated in their recovery, feel a sense of hope in the recovery process, receive information critical to their success, develop a deep bond with others, and learn new socialization and coping skills. Twelve-step meetings are unique, and a new counselor with no addiction counseling experience (academic or applied) would be less likely to have ever seen a meeting (as opposed to the countless hours of watching and facilitating group counseling sessions in graduate training) when compared with a counselor with addiction training and clinical experience. Thus, some of the basics are discussed below.

General Meeting Logistics

Sobriety is not a requirement for 12-step participation. The only requirement is that an individual professes a desire to cease using substances. This means that a member can attend a meeting while under the influence of a substance in order to gain support to stop. Over the years, I have worked with numerous clients who attended an AA or NA meeting while under the influence because—despite being cognitively impaired by the alcohol or heroin—they recognized their degree of dysfunction and sought support. On more than one occasion I have heard of a 12-step member driving an intoxicated member to the local hospital so they could be evaluated and potentially referred to detoxification services. That member, *who was a total stranger,* sat with the intoxicated individual for hours in the emergency room. I typically do not see this degree of dedication and support in any of the treatment groups that I run.

There are two meeting types: open or closed. Open meetings are for anyone who wishes to attend and not just designated for those struggling with addiction or recovery. Typically, these are groups attended by those who are addicted/in recovery alongside family, friends, addiction counseling students, and others who simply want to offer support and/or learn more about addiction and the 12-step process. Closed meetings are only for individuals working on addiction or recovery issues.

Meetings also take a few different formats. A speaker meeting involves a person (called the *lead*) sharing their story of addiction and recovery. A discussion meeting is where members who wish to discuss issues are encouraged to share anything they want in the meeting. The content does not have to be directly or indirectly associated with addiction or recovery. Step meetings involve the group reading parts of the 12-step literature and discussing among one another.

Meetings can run between 1 and 2 hours. A quorum for a 12-step meeting is simply two members in that this is the minimum number of members required in order to have a sharing of personal reflections and thoughts regarding addiction and recovery.

Meetings are well organized. For instance, there is a no cross-talk rule. This prohibits members from talking over one another or having side discussions. Discussions between members are not supposed to be critical. Members do not critique another's sobriety. Instead, members share their experiences (positive and negative) in order to provide inspiration, hope, or example to another member.

A counselor should be well versed regarding the availability of 12-step groups in the area. If needed, there are accurate and up-to-date online sources for locating a meeting via a ZIP code search (see www.aa.org or www.na.org). Furthermore, a counselor should try to attend open groups to foster a better understanding of how these groups work.

Sponsorship

Sponsors have only one role, and it is critical. They (as sponsors) share with the newly recovering individual (the sponsee) how the 12-step experience helped them achieve sobriety and stability. The sponsor-sponsee relationship lasts for as long as it is beneficial.

Newly recovering individuals are encouraged to obtain sponsorship as soon as possible (and as soon as they are ready for this relationship). Individuals can find a sponsor in a few ways. They can approach a member who has said things of importance and relevance to the individual looking for a sponsor, or an individual can approach the 12-step group leader and inquire as to who may make a good sponsor. The sponsor-sponsee relationship starts as a temporary one. Both parties need time to decide if this relationship works for them. There also tends to be a lot of pressure regarding the sponsor-sponsee relationship. Sponsees sometimes hope to find the "best" sponsor on the first attempt. They hope to "nail it" with their first choice and have their lifelong support person in place. Similarly, some sponsors feel a pressure to be the ultimate hall-of-fame sponsor. They either get far too involved in their sponsee's life and/or they feel a tremendous deal of misappropriated responsibility and guilt if the sponsee relapses or leaves the 12-step group. Consequently, the counselor should try to address these misperceptions as early as possible, for instance, checking in with clients who are sponsors to see if they are taking on more personal ownership than warranted, or helping the sponsee work toward a more pragmatic and realistic perspective that, just like recovery, finding the "right" sponsor for them is an imperfect process.

"It's Too Religious for Me" or "It's Not My Religion"

As discussed by Doweiko (2015), the 12 steps have their origins in a Christian religious perspective. The Oxford Group devised their philosophy on a few sources, one of which was the text *The Principles of Jesus* (Speer, 1902). This is why the 12-step programs of AA/NA took on the mantra of spiritual, not religious. They wanted a more open and flexible forum for as diverse a gathering of addicted and recovering men and women as possible. However, there are still a few obstacles for individuals referred to the 12 steps.

First, though God is defined by the individual member, there is still a reference to God. Agnostics and atheists have a problem with the references to God throughout the steps. Second, as noted by Osten and Switzer (2014), the reference to God seems to be from the Judeo-Christian perspective. If one's religion entails the worship of Allah, the omission of the name *Allah* may dissuade the individual from engaging with the 12 steps. Third, though the 12 steps are "spiritual," many meetings do have an underlying bias toward the Christian (as opposed to Jewish) religious perspective. A few papers have addressed the clinical questions and challenges counselors and their clients should consider when referring some Jewish men or women to an AA/NA group (Master, 1989; Steiker & Scarborough, 2011). Over the past few years, though, groups have sprung up dedicated to Jewish men and women struggling with addiction and recovery. Thus, the counselor should seek these meetings out for referral if the Jewish client expresses discomfort due to the Christian perspective of the 12 steps.

SPECIAL POPULATIONS

Adolescents

Alateen is a part of Al-Anon, which is the 12-step support system for families struggling with a loved one's addiction. Alateen is specifically designed for the children of an addicted family member (usually a close relative such as a parent or sibling). Because the adolescent is not struggling with an addiction but rather the ramifications of a loved one's addiction, the purpose of the 12 steps are different. Alateen meetings are almost always closed meetings. Anonymity is tantamount to the success of 12-step support, especially so for adolescents. Furthermore, empirical findings for Alateen or Al-Anon groups are difficult to find, primarily due to the act of research inquiry within the group being seen as contrary to the 12-step traditions (Timko et al., 2013).

Adolescents basically work the 12 steps themselves, despite not struggling with addiction. The 12 steps are a good general guide for anyone struggling with any issue to use in an attempt to enhance personal understanding of thoughts, emotions, and behaviors (Morgen et al., 2010; Morgen & Morgan, 2011). Thus, the adolescent works through the steps in an attempt to make peace with and heal from the emotional wounds caused by the addicted parent/family member. Alateen meetings typically focus on adolescent conflicts and struggles regarding making sense of their parent/family member's addiction and (if possible) facilitating a reconciliation with the family member while establishing a new relationship postaddiction.

Older Adults

Though spirituality is considered a useful tool for working with older adults with SUDs (Diallo, 2013), it was not easy to find many articles that addressed the efficacy of 12-step groups with older adults. However, two studies do demonstrate that the 12-steps seem applicable and effective with older adults. In these two studies, older individuals (ages 55 years or older) with SUDs were matched with younger (ages 21–39 years) and middle-aged (ages 40–59 years) individuals with SUDs on the basis of demographic factors and co-occurring psychiatric disorder status. These three groups all attended a similar number of 12-step meetings during and in 2 years following residential treatment. All had a sponsor. Those who attended more 12-step meetings and those who had a sponsor in the first year experienced better 1-year alcohol and psychiatric outcomes. Furthermore, those who attended more meetings and had a sponsor in the second year reported less alcohol consumption at the 5-year follow-up. Of importance here is that the three age groups did not differ regarding the relationship between 12-step engagement and SUD and psychiatric symptom outcomes (Lemke & Moos, 2003a, 2003b). Consequently, it seems that, at least in these two studies, older adults can obtain just as much benefit from the 12-step experience as younger adults. In brief, there may just need to be some age-appropriate accommodations made to the groups whether in content (e.g., the topics covered in a discussion or speaker group) or general logistics (e.g., meeting locations on a ground floor or a building with an elevator, meetings running closer to 1 rather than 2 hours in length, or the time of day for a meeting).

QUESTIONS TO CONSIDER AS YOU MOVE ON TO CHAPTER 10

Question 1: Can existential theory, in some manner, help you as a counselor trying to assist a client to integrate the 12-step and counseling processes? Do you feel that the other theories of counseling also permit for such a dialogue? Why or why not?

Question 2: Do you think a client can become too engrossed within the concepts of a 12-step program without truly embracing the cognitive, emotional, and behavioral acts implied by these concepts (e.g., one day at a time)? If you encounter such a client, how do you redirect the client to engage with the 12-step program in a more adaptive and active strategy?

Chapter 10

RELAPSE PREVENTION THEORIES

BASICS OF THE RELAPSE PREVENTION IDEA

Substance use disorder (SUD) is a "chronic relapsing condition" (Connors, Maisto, & Donovan, 1996). The act of a relapse is also a chronic process and consists of a few components: slip, lapse, and relapse. Fisher and Harrison (2009) defined a slip as the return to substance use following a period of abstinence. The slip usually is a one-time event that may or may not generate much guilt or distress. The slip can be something as simple as taking one sip of champagne after a wedding toast. Though benign, this act can cause the client much distress. A lapse is also the breaking of abstinence but more so than a slip, while still not returning to pretreatment levels of substance use. For instance, a lapse might refer to having several drinks at a wedding following the champagne toast, but this drinking is immediately followed by a recommitment to abstinence. Of note is that this drinking has not reached pretreatment levels. Relapse, however, is a period of uncontrolled substance use following a period of abstinence when the substance use has returned to pretreatment levels (Fisher & Harrison, 2009).

Marlatt, Parks, and Witkiewitz (2002) noted that relapse prevention is the counseling intervention(s) focused on helping clients reframe a lapse or relapse with the goal of preventing an overreaction to the event (i.e., cognitive distortions regarding the lapse/relapse that lead to negative affect, thus putting the individual at risk of prolonged relapse and other dysfunction). Marlatt and colleagues (2002) recommended replacing the term *relapse*, which has negative connotations, with the term *prolapse*, which they defined as "mistakes that clients learn from that improve their eventual chances of success" (p. 9), the idea being that a lot of the initial angst from the relapse comes from the preestablished negative connotation associated with the term *relapse*. By changing the term, this may give the client more initial room to cognitively process the event without an overwhelming sense of guilt and distress as is usually associated with a relapse.

Recovery refers to the period of purposeful and intentional nonuse of substances. Recovery is a step beyond abstinence, as the cessation of substances is merely the prerequisite for recovery to commence. Recovery is the active cognitive, emotional, and behavioral work done by individuals to improve themselves in all areas of life (not just addiction) and constantly maintain and refine that healthy existence throughout their lifetime. Recovery is so daunting for those new to abstinence because it is a lifelong process (Dimeff & Marlatt, 1998). Some individuals may actually continually relapse because the process is so large in scope and duration.

This chapter starts with a review of some of the major theories that conceptualize the relapse process. Note that each of these models has been described at length in texts and manuals. Here, I try to only summarize the key elements as they pertain to understanding the relapse process.

MARLATT'S MODEL

Marlatt's (1996) model focused on two levels of the individual's circumstances as related to a potential relapse. The first level deals with the immediate high-risk situation and the individual's response. Situations associated with prior substance use (i.e., people, places, and things) can pose a potential risk to continued abstinence. This model suggests that if the person has healthy and effective interpersonal and emotional coping skills, the relapse risk is diminished. More important, the effective coping with the high-risk situation boosts the individual's sense of self-efficacy. Now individuals have seen that they can indeed cope with the situation without substance use and survive. This further boosts their confidence, and this also decreases a potential risk of relapse.

Unfortunately, due to years of substance use as a coping skill (i.e., to numb, forget, or escape negative affect/mood associated with high-risk situations), the individual may not have any effective nonsubstance-related coping mechanisms. I have always discussed with those in treatment the paradox of treatment and recovery. Here they are, facing challenging situations, painful memories of past indiscretions, and the emotional turmoil inherent in rebuilding relationships, and all without their most well-developed (though unhealthy and maladaptive) coping skill. Thus, they are raw, exposed, and vulnerable. In these cases, if individuals do not have an adequate coping response available in a high-risk situation, they experience a rush of self-doubt (i.e., decreased or nonexistent self-efficacy), which results in experiences of helplessness and a perceived diminished sense of self-control, so the expectations about the positive benefits of substance use increases the relapse risk.

According to the model, addiction is the maladaptive coping skill adopted by the individual. Marlatt (1996) and Marlatt et al. (2002) identified several factors across two categories that contribute to a substance use relapse. The first consists of immediate determinants such as high-risk situations, coping skills, outcome expectancies, and the abstinence violation effect (AVE), defined as losing perceived control after the disobeying of self-imposed rules (Curry, Marlatt, & Gordon, 1987). Once the lapse has occurred, experiencing the AVE and the initial positive effects of the substance may increase the potential of a relapse. Conversely, if the individual uses effective coping strategies either when facing a high-risk situation or after an initial lapse, they will likely experience an increase in self-efficacy, which may reduce the risk of relapse. The second factor that contributes to a substance use relapse consists of covert antecedents such as lifestyle imbalances and urges or cravings (Larimer, Palmer, & Marlatt, 1999). Marlatt et al. (2002) broke down determinants into intrapersonal-environmental and interpersonal types. Intrapersonal-environmental determinants can include coping with negative emotional states, coping with negative physiological states, enhancement of positive emotional states, or giving in to cravings or urges. Interpersonal determinants include coping with interpersonal conflict, perceived social pressure, and the enhancement of positive emotional states. As per the model, any one or combination of these factors is capable of triggering a relapse.

The model predicts that if the person uses a substance(s), he or she experiences an abstinence violation effect, which is a predictable series of cognitive and emotional effects that follow the use. For example, individuals may assign responsibility for the slip to internal factors and view this current use as more evidence that they are "addicts" and incapable of recovery. This often is accompanied by a sense of helplessness, depression, resignation, feelings of instability, and guilt. The model stipulates that the extent to which the person experiences these thoughts and feelings after an initial use (i.e., the lapse), the likelihood of continued use (i.e., the relapse) increases.

The second level of Marlatt's model involves the psychosocial context where the individual interacts with others and comes into contact with the high-risk situations. Here, distal factors contribute to the relapse potential. Among these distal factors is the experience of stress. The model conceptualizes a balance between "wants" and "shoulds" and argues that an imbalance between these "wants" and "shoulds" is problematic. Specifically, when an individual's sense of obligation (the "shoulds") is greater than his or her "wants," this increases the degree of stress and in turn increases the vulnerability for a relapse. Due to the heightened stress, the perceived benefits of substance use are amplified. The imbalance also may lead to decisions that though they appear to the individual to have little to no association with a relapse risk, they may in fact eventually leave the individual in a high-risk situation—for example, clients who decide to go socialize at the pub where they used to drink because they feel lonely. Though clients may not see the behavior as problematic and tell themselves (and you) that they "only intend to catch up with friends" and "have a few sodas," this decision puts them in a high-risk setting.

DYNAMIC MODEL OF RELAPSE (WITKIEWITZ & MARLATT, 2004)

This model captures the complexity of behavioral change in the conceptualization of relapse. Witkiewitz and Marlatt (2004) proposed a theoretical model of the alcohol relapse process as a nonlinear dynamical system. The model incorporated distal and proximal risk factors. Distal risks, which are thought to increase the probability of relapse, include background variables (e.g., severity of SUD) and relatively stable pretreatment characteristics (e.g., substance use expectancies). Proximal risks complete the distal predispositions and include transient lapse factors (e.g., stressful situations) and more dynamic individual characteristics (e.g., negative affect, self-efficacy). Myriad combinations of precipitating and predisposing risk factors exist for any specific individual, thus creating a complex system for determining the probability of relapse. Specifically, the model consists of the following six key components:

1. *Distal risks*—Factors that predispose a person toward relapse, such as family addiction history (Witkiewitz & Marlatt, 2007). Distal risks influence coping behaviors and cognitive processes and play a role in the experience of physical withdrawal symptoms.

2. *Cognitive processes*—These processes focus on self-efficacy, outcome expectancies, cravings, and motivation level. These all play a critical role in how individuals cognitively perceive their stability in recovery.

3. *Coping behavior*—Coping behavior is a critical factor in whether one relapses or not. Stronger coping skills enable the individual to ward off any negative affect or cognition that may spur the individual back toward substance use.

4. *Tonic responses*—Tonic activity is a term borrowed from medical science and in this model pertains to an individual's chronic vulnerability (Witkiewitz & Marlatt, 2007). Tonic processes refer to the distal risks, cognitive processes, withdrawal symptoms, coping skills, and affect that may influence a relapse potential.

5. *Phasic responses*—Phasic processes are transient risk factors that are state-based (and not the more consistent trait-based factors) that precede relapse

(Witkiewitz & Marlatt, 2004). Phasic responses can include coping skills, cognitive processes, affect, and substance use. The value of this model is the sophistication and complexity that reflect the nuanced experience of a relapse. That is why cognitive processes, affect, and coping skills are classified as both tonic and phasic processes.

6. *Perceived effects*—Perceived effects refer to processes that occur after a lapse or relapse that can reinforce the continuation of substance use. For example, I worked with a client who struggled with major depressive disorder and alcohol use disorder. This individual saw the relapse of alcohol use at pretreatment levels as a source of relief for depressive symptoms that medication and counseling were failing to achieve.

Evidence exists for the complicated relationship between these six components. Gossop, Stewart, Browne, and Marsden (2002) reasoned how coping skills influence drinking behavior and in turn how drinking influences coping skills. This feedback loops demonstrates the interaction between coping skills, cognitions, craving, affect, and substance use behavior. In addition, others have noted how the relationship between risk factors and substance use behavior is moderated by substance cues (Litt, Cooney, & Morse, 2000).

Witkiewitz and Marlatt (2007) discussed how the dynamic model of addictive behavior relates to catastrophe theory, which is the study of abrupt discontinuous change in a given behavior. They reasoned how relapse seems to reflect the five key components of catastrophe theory: multimodality (more than mode of addictive behavior), sudden jumps (rapidly transitioning between these multiple addictive behavior modes), divergence of linear response (slight changes in relapse risk due to significant changes in addictive behavior), hysteresis (abrupt addictive behavior change corresponds with different values of relapse risk factors), and inaccessibility (the low likelihood of maintaining a lapse state). Witkiewitz and Marlatt also underscored how the catastrophe analysis perspective best captures the relapse process (as compared with other models) because it treats relapse as a continuous process and that the inclusion of distal and proximal risk factors best fits the data for individuals who have experienced at least one lapse. They found that individuals with high distal risks were more vulnerable to the influence of proximal risks, relapsing quickly even after only experiencing small changes in these risks.

Intrapersonal determinants refer to factors influencing relapse at the individual level. Empirical literature shows that these determinants are critical to the understanding of the processes of relapse (Brandon, Vidrine, & Litvin, 2007; Witkiewitz & Marlatt, 2007). Specifically, these determinants are emotional state, distress tolerance, craving, self-efficacy, outcome expectancies, coping and self-regulation, and symptom severity at baseline. Each is addressed below.

Emotional State. Marlatt (1978) suggested that negative affect is a strong predictor of lapse potential after treatment. Negative affect is broadly defined as symptoms of anxiety and/or depression. As discussed throughout this text, substance use is many times motivated by the need to decrease negative affect while also increasing positive affect (e.g., Tennen, Affleck, Armeli, & Carney, 2000). However, anxiety and/ or depression may be defined at too broad a level (Cook, Spring, McChargue, & Doran, 2010). For example, depressed symptoms could run anywhere between depressed mood to diminished self-worth or loss of interest in prior enjoyable tasks. It is feasible that each of these specific symptoms could influence lapse or relapse in a different manner.

Distress Tolerance. The extent to which an individual can tolerate psychological and physical distress dictates how well he or she can maintain the cessation of an addictive behavior despite the distress of withdrawal (Brandon et al., 2007). Low distress tolerance is associated with negative treatment outcomes for SUDs (Daughters et al., 2005; Hsu, Collins, & Marlatt, 2013). In addition, some studies show that pretreatment distress tolerance (i.e., the baseline tolerance ability prior to treatment) predicts treatment outcome (Brandon et al., 2007; Hsu et al., 2013).

Craving. Craving is the urge or desire to engage in the addictive behavior but does not necessarily predict treatment relapse (e.g., Tiffany, Carter, & Singleton, 2000; Witkiewitz & Marlatt, 2004). However, recent research has tried to better clarify the relationship between craving and relapse. For example, Oslin, Cary, Slaymaker, Colleran, and Blow (2009), using a daily diary technique to assess craving during alcohol treatment, found three craving trajectories in the first 25 days: (1) stable, elevated craving; (2) elevated craving followed by decreases in craving; and (3) stable, relatively low craving. Findings showed that those with high, stable craving throughout the 25 days were more likely to relapse within 6 months of treatment, whereas those with stable, low craving were least likely to relapse during that same time period.

Self-Efficacy. Self-efficacy is an individual's level of confidence in performing a behavior in a specific situational context (Bandura, 1977) and is a predictor of treatment outcome (Witkiewitz & Marlatt, 2004). For instance, Gwaltney et al. (2002) explored changes in self-efficacy among smokers who were attempting to quit smoking. Lower self-efficacy at baseline predicted lower self-efficacy across situations, and individuals with low baseline self-efficacy showed increased smoking urges and negative affect that further decreased self-efficacy.

Outcome Expectancies. Outcome expectancy is an individual's anticipation of the effects of a future experience (Brown, Goldman, & Christiansen, 1985). Outcome expectancies do actually predict relapse among a population of SUD treatment dropouts (McKellar, Harris, & Moos, 2006). In this study, those with a positive expectation about substance use and negative expectations about the cessation of substance use at baseline were more likely to experience SUD difficulties 5 years after dropping out of treatment. Outcome expectations are also relevant to the process addictions. For instance, research on pathological gambling seems to indicate that positive outcome expectancies influence the addictive gambling behavior via physiological changes, such as increased heart rate in anticipation of gambling acts (Ladouceur, Sévigny, Blaszczynski, O 'Connor, & Lavoie, 2003; Ledgerwood & Petry, 2006).

Coping and Self-Regulation. Coping is "the thoughts and behaviors used to manage the internal and external demands of situations that are appraised as stressful" (Folkman & Moskowitz, 2004, pp. 746–747). Witkiewitz and Masyn (2008) found that coping skills predicted time to first lapse (i.e., poorer coping skills associated with shorter time to lapse) and the extent of drinking after a lapse (i.e., poorer coping skills associated with heavier drinking after a lapse). Gossop et al. (2002) investigated factors associated with treatment outcome among a sample of heroin-dependent residential treatment clients in the United Kingdom's National Treatment Outcome Research Study. Analyses were conducted for three groups: abstainers, lapsers, and relapsers. Those who were abstainers or lapsers reported that they consistently used cognitive, avoidance, and distraction coping strategies, as compared to the relapsers who did not. Consequently, the cognitive-behavioral processes that occurred during the implementation of coping skills seemed to have enabled these clients to withstand the high-risk situations and associated stressors that could pull toward renewed substance use.

Symptom Severity at Baseline. Baseline SUD symptom severity predicts treatment outcome and relapse potential. For instance, McLellan et al. (1994) examined factors associated with 6-month outcomes among opiate-dependent, cocaine-dependent, and alcohol-dependent clients from inpatient and outpatient programs. Independent of substance type, greater substance use at follow-up was predicted by a higher SUD severity at treatment admission. Furthermore, Witkiewitz and Masyn (2008) found that alcohol dependence symptoms predicted the individual's movement toward heavier drinking.

Interpersonal Determinants. Social support in the dynamic model of relapse (Witkiewitz & Marlatt, 2004) stressed three dimensions of social support: structural, functional, and quality. Structural social supports are the patterns within the social network interrelationships (such as the quantity or duration of social interactions) that enable interactions within the social network (Beattie & Longabaugh, 1997).

This type of social support is typically measured by the availability of supportive resources that help the individual maintain recovery. For example, Havassy, Hall, and Wasserman (1991) examined the relationship between social support and relapse among SUD treatment clients. Stronger structural social support (e.g., the availability of various supportive resources) predicted decreased relapse risk through 3 months of follow-up. In another study discussed elsewhere in this text, Laudet, Morgen, and White (2006) found that a collection of social support resources across numerous categories (e.g., personal, 12 step) helped buffer the effects of stress for those in recovery, thus increasing their overall quality of life. Tracy, Kelly, and Moos (2005) examined how social relationship longevity influences posttreatment. They found that individuals whose partner relationships lasted through the first year posttreatment reported better outcomes than those whose relationships did not persist through the first year.

Functional social support is "the content of each interaction a person has" as well as "perceptions of the availability, content and purpose of these interactions" (Beattie & Longabaugh, 1997, p. 1508). For instance, greater abstinence-specific functional support, as measured by the recovering individual's perceived helpfulness of a partner, predicted a reduced risk of relapse (Havassy et al., 1991). The quality of social support is defined as the subjectively appraised character, strength, and value of the social relationships (Beattie & Longabaugh, 1997). Tracy et al. (2005) found that having a partner who is overly critical, or having a partner perceived as having a substance use problem, harms the success of the treatment and recovery outcomes. Furthermore, Witkiewitz and Marlatt (2004) suggested that support from nonsubstance use-disordered individuals pertains to stronger treatment outcomes, whereas an increased rate of substance use is associated with decreasing support from nonsubstance use-disordered individuals.

GORSKI'S CENAPS MODEL OF RELAPSE PREVENTION THERAPY

Donovan (2003) noted that Marlatt's (1996) model was developed as an academic and research effort, whereas Gorski's model (1989, 1990) came from the perspective of a recovering addiction counselor. Furthermore, Marlatt disseminated his model findings in scholarly journal articles, while Gorski did so via published books and manuals specifically targeted for the practicing addiction counselor. Thus, the Gorski model utilized language and concepts and was obtainable in sources more familiar to a practicing addiction counselor. The CENAPS model of relapse prevention therapy (CMRPT) is a comprehensive method for preventing SUD clients from returning to substance use after initial treatment and also for early intervention should substance use occur.

The CMRPT is a clinical procedure that integrates the disease model of addiction and abstinence-based counseling methods with cognitive, affective, behavioral, and social therapies. The CMRPT is designed to be delivered across all levels of care, though with a primary focus for use in the outpatient treatment systems. The CMRPT has five primary goals: (1) to assess the lifestyle patterns contributing to relapse via comprehensive self-assessment of life, addiction, and relapse history patterns; (2) the construction of a relapse warning signs list; (3) the development of relapse warning sign management strategies; (4) a structured recovery program that helps the individual to identify and manage these critical warning signs; and (5) the development of an early intervention relapse plan, including detailed directions for the individual in an effort to cease substance use, should a relapse occur. The CMRPT uses group and individual counseling sessions and psychoeducational programs that focus primarily on these five primary goals. The treatment engages the client in a structured program of recovery acts.

The CMRPT is an applied cognitive-behavioral therapy program, most similar to rational emotive therapy and Beck's cognitive therapy model. The CMRPT heavily emphasizes affective therapy principles by focusing on the identification, appropriate labeling, and communication and resolution of feelings and emotions. The CMRPT teaches clients that emotions are generated by irrational thinking (cognitive theory) and are stored or repressed (affective theory). Emotional integration work involves both cognitive labeling and expression of feelings designed to bring these emotions to the forefront for treatment. This model is also similar to (influenced by) the cognitive-behavioral relapse prevention model developed by Marlatt and Gordon (1985). The major difference is that the CMRPT integrates abstinence-based treatment and is more compatible with 12-step programs.

The CMRPT is in part formulated from a biopsychosocial model stipulating how SUD is a disease caused by mood-altering substances. SUD is a chronic disease that includes relapse. The CMRPT defines relapse as the process of becoming dysfunctional in recovery, which can lead to renewed substance use. The CMRPT incorporates the roles of brain dysfunction, personality disorganization, social dysfunction, and family-of-origin problems to the problems of recovery and relapse. The long-term use of mood-altering substances causes brain dysfunction that produces emotional, personality, social, occupational, and academic problems. The brain dysfunction occurs during periods of intoxication, short-term withdrawal, and long-term withdrawal. These brain symptoms impair the individual's ability to think clearly and manage emotions, as well as produce difficulties with memory, sleep, and stress management. Gorski (1989, 1990) argued that these symptoms are the most severe during the first 6 to 18 months of sobriety. Total abstinence coupled with major personality and lifestyle changes are essential for effective and lasting recovery. The CMRPT argues that those raised in dysfunctional families may develop self-defeating personality styles (which Alcoholics Anonymous/ Narcotics Anonymous calls character defects) that impede recovery.

Gorski (1989, 1990) argued that the personality disorganization occurs because brain dysfunction interferes with emotions, thoughts, and behaviors. Some personality disorganization is temporary and subsides with abstinence as the brain recovers from the substance use. However, there are other personality traits deeply instilled via the addiction process and can only be remedied via treatment. The social dysfunction (interpersonal, family, career, school, and other areas) is indicative of the disorganization and poor life skills due to the brain and personality dysfunctions.

The relapse syndrome is an integral part of the addiction process. The disease comes in two waves: the first is the substance-based symptoms that manifest during active episodes of substance use, and the second wave is the sobriety-based symptoms that emerge during periods of abstinence. Relapse is the process of becoming dysfunctional due to sobriety-based symptoms that lead to renewed substance use and other problems. The model emphasizes that the relapse process is marked by warning signs that are both predictable and identifiable. Relapse prevention treatment teaches clients to recognize and manage these warning signs so as to interrupt the relapse process and maintain their recovery.

The CMRPT conceptualizes recovery as a developmental process over six stages. The first stage is *transition*, where clients recognize that they have an SUD and need to pursue abstinence as a lifestyle goal. The second stage is *stabilization*, where clients recover from the acute and postacute withdrawal symptoms once they cease substance use. This stage also involves the stabilization of their psychosocial life crises. The third stage is *early recovery*, where clients replace addictive thoughts, feelings, and behaviors with sobriety-centered thoughts, feelings, and behaviors. The fourth stage is *middle recovery*, where clients repair the lifestyle damage caused by the addiction. The fifth stage is *late recovery*, where clients investigate and resolve family-of-origin issues that may impair recovery and act as a relapse trigger. The sixth stage is *maintenance*, where clients continue to maintain an active recovery program.

The CMRPT works best in an outpatient program made up of a minimum of 12 group sessions, 10 individual therapy sessions, and six psychoeducational sessions administered over a period of 6 weeks. After completing the primary outpatient program, the client is transferred to an ongoing group and individual therapy program (four group sessions and two individual sessions per month) to implement the warning sign identification and management. Brief readmission (3 to 10 days) for inpatient stabilization may be required should clients relapse and/or develop severe warning signs that indicate they are at heightened risk for relapse or other serious dysfunction (e.g., suicidal thoughts).

The group counseling sessions follow a highly structured and standard eight-part protocol. The first and last steps of the protocol (preparation and debriefing) are attended by the treatment team only. The other steps occur during the group session. The steps run as follows.

1. *Preparatory session.* The treatment team reviews clients' treatment plans, goals, and current progress. Each client's progress is reviewed, and an attempt is made to predict the assignments and problems that the client will present.

2. *Opening procedure.* The counselor sets the tone for the group, establishes leadership, and helps clients acclimate to the group process.

3. *Reactions to last session.* Each group member reports on thoughts and feelings pertaining to the prior group session and identifies any group members who stood out from that session.

4. *Reports on assignments.* Exercises that clients are working on to identify and manage relapse warning signs, or deal with other matters relevant to relapse prevention, are shared and/or completed during the group session. Immediately following each member's reactions, the counselor asks all group members who received assignments to briefly address the following questions:
   - What was the assignment and why was it assigned?
   - Was the assignment completed, and if not, what happened so that the assignment is incomplete?
   - What was learned by completing (or attempting) the assignment?
   - What feelings and emotions were experienced?
   - Is there anything else related to this assignment that needs to be worked on in group today?

5. *Setting the agenda.* The group counselor identifies members who want to work and announces their names and the order in which they will present. Those who do not present their work during this session are on the agenda for the next group.

6. *Problem-solving group processes.* Clients present their issues to the group, clarify them through questioning and feedback from the group and (if appropriate) from the counselor, and develop their next round of assignments for continued recovery progress.

7. *Closure exercise.* With about 15 minutes remaining in the group session, the counselor asks each member to share the most important thing learned in group today and how this newfound knowledge will immediately contribute to their lifestyle changes and recovery process. At this point, the group is ended for the day.

8. *Debriefing session.* Here, only the treatment team convenes. This session reviews each client's problems and progress, addresses any feedback for the improvement or refinement of counselor group skills, and also provides support and guidance to help prevent counselor burnout. This debriefing process is most helpful if conducted with other counselors running similar recovery groups.

MATRIX MODEL

An example of the application of relapse prevention is found in the work of Rawson and his colleagues (Rawson et al., 2000, 2004, 1995) on the matrix model of treatment for stimulant disorders. The matrix model, described as a "neuro-behavioral" approach, has integrated relapse prevention into a comprehensive outpatient program adapted to the biochemical and biological issues in the recovery from stimulant disorders (such as cocaine use disorder). The program avoids the abstract and theoretical terms that are found in other models of change (e.g., DiClemente & Prochaska, 1998), and instead, the phases of recovery in the matrix model are much more descriptive of client experiences. The five stages of recovery, each tied to the time since the individual last used a stimulant, are (a) withdrawal, (b) honeymoon, (c) the wall, (d) adjustment, and (e) resolution. Furthermore, the model reviews the behavioral, emotional, cognitive, and relationship issues clients can expect in each of the five stages.

As per the model, the wall phase is where clients are thought to be most vulnerable to relapse. Examples of the issues include behavioral (e.g., sluggishness, lack of energy, insomnia), emotional (e.g., depression, anxiety, boredom), cognitive (e.g., euphoric recall of cocaine use, increased frequency of cocaine thoughts and craving, cognitive rehearsals of relapse), and the relationship (e.g., mutual blaming, devaluation of progress, threatened separation).

Clients begin attending the weekly 90-minute relapse prevention group in the second month of this 6-month program, after stabilization. The group is co-led by a professional counselor and a recovering individual. The recovering cofacilitator provides a positive role model for clients and can share relapse prevention techniques from his or her own recovery. The group sessions follow a specific format and address a set of problems previously identified by the group. The group addresses topics such as dealing with cocaine dreams, identifying cognitive/ behavioral warning signs of potential relapse, guilt and shame, and relapse justification.

Another important component in the relapse prevention process is the relapse analysis. This analysis is conducted with the client's therapist in an individual session immediately after a slip or relapse has occurred. The first step here is to let the client talk about the relapse. Next, a structured exercise is used to guide the client and counselor in a review of the cognitive, behavioral, and environmental factors that may have facilitated the relapse. In addition, the cognitive, behavioral, and environmental factors as of right now are also assessed to investigate the degree of support the individual feels postrelapse. Of utmost importance, the client is encouraged to view the relapse as a part of a larger process rather than an isolated and negative event. This is done to diminish the self-deprecating and negative attributions associated with the abstinence violation effect. After analyzing the relapse, changes that may be needed in the treatment plan to restabilize the client's recovery status are implemented.

SPECIAL POPULATIONS

Adolescents

Adolescent SUD interferes with and interrupts normal adolescent development. These developmental deficits negatively influence adolescent recovery efforts (Noyoo, Patel, & Loffell, 2006; van der Westhuizen & De Jager, 2009). That is why aftercare and relapse prevention services are critical to ensure recovery and prevent relapses (Bryan & Stallings, 2002). Relapse is a fairly common occurrence among adolescents (Winters, Botzet, Fahnhorst, & Koskey, 2009. Winters, Botzet, and Fahnhorst (2011) summarized the literature on adolescent relapse and highlighted the adolescent's treatment experience (e.g., counselor rapport, discharge status) and aftercare as influential for the reduction of relapse potential. Basically, the relapse prevention techniques for adolescents are quite similar to adults. For example, the following list of potential relapse risk factors seems applicable to either an adult or adolescent (only the unique presentation of the risk factor varies by age group):

1. Being in social situations or places where drugs are available

2. Being socially isolated

3. Being around drugs or using any mood-altering substance

4. Stress

5. Overconfidence

6. Mental or physical illness or pain

7. Boredom

8. Self-pity

Applications for addressing relapse in adolescents do exist that target the specific developmental characteristics unique to adolescents. One such unique example is described next.

Trudeau, Ainscough, and Charity (2012) studied 16 counselors who were interviewed about peer relationship-related content and features for an adolescent relapse prevention program. Adolescents discussed their approval of a program prototype involving text messaging. The proposed text messaging feature allows adolescents to maintain contact with treatment ideas and objectives. In addition to a connection to a recovery community, the text program can also permit for a series of preset text messages that may include affirmations or reminders about goals and recovery. This type of communication would be most helpful to adolescent clients once they have left treatment and are most vulnerable to some of the risk factors listed above.

However, any effective relapse prevention program for adolescents also includes parents in the process. Goodwin (2000) argued that parents should learn to identify the signs of addiction and understand the recovery process. Consequently, efforts to provide the parents with support for this process are critical. Provision of information pertaining to Al-Anon and Alateen and other support services provide family members with both information on the recovery process as well as support from other families struggling with the same issues with their adolescent child. Finally, Brandt and Delport (2005) discussed how the lack of trust in families leads to the adolescent perception of their parents not trusting them. Aftercare (as a component of relapse prevention) should help adolescents understand the damaging impacts of their addiction on the degree of parental trust. Consequently, relapse prevention for adolescents consists of a heavy family therapy component (see Chapter 7).

Older Adults

CSAT (2005b) developed a cognitive-behavioral and self-management intervention (CB/SM) for older adults comprised of nine modules that are covered in 16 group sessions. In the first module, older adult SUD clients learn about the substance use behavior chain (the antecedents, behaviors during, and consequences of substance abuse). Subsequent modules guide the client through behavioral interventions to teach clients the skills to recognize and interrupt their substance use behavior chain. Sessions in the modules have been developed for older adults with age-appropriate objectives, teaching techniques, and handouts. Furthermore, the pace and content of the sessions are geared to older adults (see Figure 10.1).

Figure 10.1 Module Content and Topics

Modle	Number of Sessions	Topic	Content
1	2	Analysis of Substance Use Behavior	Clients learn how to analyze their behavior by breaking down their individual substance use behavior chains into antecedents, behaviors, and consequences.
2	2	How to Manage Social Pressure	Clients learn the refusal skills they need when social pressure creates high-risk situations for substance abuse relapse. The objective is to teach clients how to control their behaviors and still be able to socialize.
3	½ or 1*	How to Manage Situations at Home and Alone	Clients learn how to cope with feelings of boredom and loneliness and manage leisure time.
4	1½ or 2*	How to Manage Negative Thoughts and Emotions Associated With Substance Abuse	Clients learn how to recognize negative self-talk and repetitive thoughts, interrupt these negative patterns, and find ways other than substance abuse to cope with changes in mood.
5	3	How to Manage Anxiety and Tension	Clients learn how to manage feelings of anxiety, ways to avoid situations that produce these feelings, and skills to reduce these feelings.
6	3	How to Manage Anger and Frustration	Clients learn ways to handle feelings of anger and frustration by using assertive behavior.
7	1	How to Control Substance Abuse Cues	Clients learn how to recognize their personal substance abuse cues, and they practice skills to control these cues.
8	2	How to Cope With Urges	Clients learn that urges last for various periods; have a beginning and an end, even during abstinence; can be waited out; become weaker and end sooner each time they are resisted; and become easier to resist each time they are managed successfully.
9	1	Preventing a Slip From Becoming a Relapse	Clients learn more techniques to help them resist substances. They are taught that one slip does not have to lead to relapse, negative self-talk can be replaced with positive self-talk, and self-management skills and requests for help can be used to avoid a relapse.

* The model permits for the counselor to increase this module session length if needed.

Source: CSAT (2005b).

QUESTIONS TO CONSIDER AS YOU MOVE ON TO CHAPTER 11

Question 1: How can counseling help the client learn and master a sense of self-efficacy so critical to the relapse prevention process? Do you offer specific skills for self-efficacy, or do you bolster a sense of courage so that the client can try for self-efficacy on their own when the moment arrives?

Question 2: How do you, as a counselor, conceptualize the chronic, long-term philosophy of lifelong recovery and relapse prevention skills in a discipline that still seems to see SUDs as an acute disorder (i.e., 28-day programs)?

Question 3: As a counselor, how would you integrate concepts of family, spirituality, and the 12-step concepts of guilt and humility within the relapse prevention process? How and why would these concepts assist you in session as you discuss relapse prevention skills?

Chapter 11

SUBSTANCE USE DISORDERS AND ADDICTION COUNSELING SUPERVISION

OVERVIEW OF SUPERVISION IN THE SUBSTANCE USE DISORDERS AND ADDICTION COUNSELING PROFESSION

There is a growing recognition that clinical supervision is an important part of substance use disorder (SUD) and addiction counseling workforce development (Center for Substance Abuse Treatment [CSAT], 2009b). For example, the publication of the Substance Abuse and Mental Health Services Administration (SAMHSA)/CSAT reports such as *Clinical Supervision and Professional Development of the Substance Abuse Counselor* (CSAT, 2009b) and the *Competencies for Substance Abuse Treatment Clinical Supervisors* (CSAT, 2007) review the importance of supervision as well as the various models and applications possibly applicable to the SUD and addiction workforce. In addition, the 2013 National Survey of Substance Abuse Treatment Services (SAMHSA, 2013) data reflect that 95% of all facilities surveyed mandate a clinical case review with a supervisor. This applied and theoretical interest in supervision is critical because clinical supervision is the primary means through which substance abuse counselors develop the skills, knowledge, and competencies required for effective and ethical practice (Sias & Lambie, 2008). Though ethics will be discussed later in this chapter, the National Association of Alcoholism and Drug Abuse Counselors (2011) ethical code on supervision and consultation encapsulates all that this chapter will review.

Addiction professionals who supervise others accept the obligation to facilitate further professional development of these individuals by providing accurate and current information, timely evaluations and constructive consultation. Counseling supervisors are aware of the power differential in their relationships with supervisees and take precautions to maintain ethical standards. In relationships with students, employees and supervisees he/she strives to develop full creative potential and mature independent functioning. (Code VII, p. 2)

ROLE OF SUPERVISION

CSAT (2007, 2009b) reviewed the critical roles of addiction counselor supervisors. In brief, they serve as a teacher, consultant, coach, and mentor (see Figure 11.1). The teacher role entails the development of counseling knowledge and skills via the identification of learning needs while also determining and underscoring counselor strengths. The consultant role monitors performance while providing another case conceptualization to assist in counselor training. The consultant role also includes professional gatekeeping for the discipline (e.g., addressing counselor impairment such as a recovering counselor not yet stable enough in recovery or a nonrecovering counselor with attitudes about addiction inconsistent with effective counseling). The coach plays a supportive role and offers encouragement and motivation in an attempt to prevent counselor burnout. CSAT (2009b) emphasized that for the entry-level counselor not used to the high rates of client relapse and dropout, the supportive function is critical to the development

Figure 11.1   Roles of the Clinical Supervisor

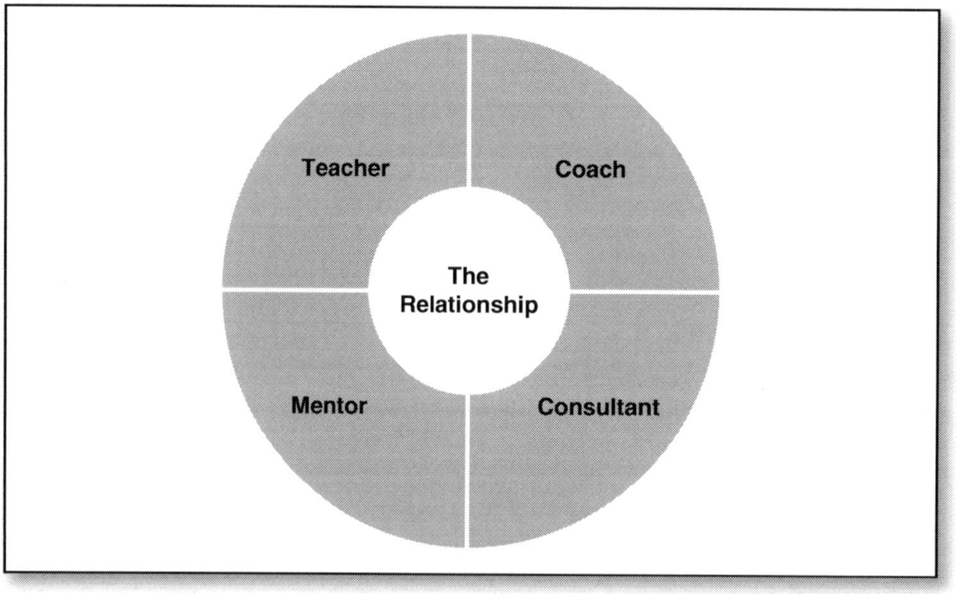

Source: CSAT (2009b).

of a competent and confident counselor. The mentor/role model role is that of the experienced supervisor and mentor that teaches, counsels, and supports the supervisee.

CSAT (2007, 2009b) stated that these four roles all intersect in the provision of supervision for the following reasons.

1. Clinical supervision integrates the program mission, goals, and treatment philosophy with clinical theory and evidence-based practices (EBPs) to ensure quality client care and continued professional development.

2. Clinical supervision enhances staff retention and morale.

3. All clinicians, regardless of level of skill and experience, benefit from clinical supervision. In addition, supervisors benefit from supervision of their supervision.

4. Clinical supervision needs the full support of agency administrators.

5. The supervisor needs to model ethical and legal practice in the supervisory relationship.

6. Clinical supervision is a skill that requires training and experience.

7. Clinical supervision requires balancing administrative and clinical supervision tasks.

8. Culture and other contextual variables influence the supervision process. This includes the culture of the recovery population.

9. Supervisors oversee the successful implementation of EBPs into the treatment program.

10. Supervisors are gatekeepers for the profession. Supervisors maintain professional standards, address impairment, and safeguard the welfare of clients and the supervisees.

11. Clinical supervision involves direct observation methods. Thus, supervisors require training in direct observation, and administrators need to provide resources for implementing direct observation.

Issues in Supervision for Substance Use Disorders and Addiction Counselors

Both CSAT (2009b) and Madson and Green (2012) reviewed key areas of importance for the supervision of SUDs and addiction counseling. First, though the numbers can never be fully known, research consistently shows a substantial percentage of the SUDs and addiction counseling workforce as being in recovery (Curtis & Eby, 2010). Some suggested that their addiction and recovery experiences allow them to quickly and accurately understand their clients, but there is no evidence linking recovery status (recovering or nonrecovering) to addiction counselor effectiveness (White, 2000). However, Madson and Green argued that personal addiction and recovery experience can also be a detriment to effective counseling. Specifically, they argued that recovering clinicians might make assumptions that they understand the client and that these clients have similar addiction and recovery experiences. Consequently, these counselors could experience issues of countertransference and not accurately engage with the client. Furthermore, counselors in recovery may require support to maintain their recovery. This is because counselors in recovery could relapse. Thus, relapse is an issue that a supervisor would need to monitor (Culbreth & Borders, 1999). But it is critical to emphasize that an "impaired" counselor is not a concept limited only to addictions. Counselors are human beings who come to the profession with various personal issues of their own. Counselors can "relapse" with other issues, such as another episode of major depressive disorder. Just like with the supervisor working with the recovering counselor perhaps struggling with a potential relapse, the supervisor of the counselor slipping into another depressive episode needs to be supportive, honest, and vigilant in order to best serve the interests of the counselor and his or her client(s).

In addition, an ethical dilemma unique to the addiction profession is one of a nonrecovering counselor (or counselor in training) being questioned about his or her recovery status (Doyle, Linton, Morgan, & Stefanelli, 2008). The supervisor needs to walk the supervisee through this process. Regardless of the supervisee recovery status, the supervisory task here is to mentor, counsel, and educate the supervisee regarding the act of recovery status self-disclosure. Specifically, the supervisee, both in the counseling session and in supervision, needs to investigate the underlying purpose of the inquiry regarding his or her recovery status.

In a second key area of importance for the supervision of SUDs and addiction counseling, CSAT (2009b) argued that although there is a growing body of the SUDs and addiction counseling workforce with a master's degree, many other addiction counselors (due to certification status or having been grandfathered) lack graduate degrees. Thus, unlike supervision in the mental health professions where all supervisees have a graduate degree or are in a graduate program, SUDs and addiction counselor supervisors can encounter a workforce with an educational range between high school diploma/general equivalency diploma all the way to master's and doctoral degrees. This does set up a scenario where long-term clinical supervisors without formal academic training (i.e., those who had been grandfathered into the profession) are supervising master's level counselors or those in a master's program. Each has a valid and unique perspective on the counseling and addiction process. However, if all perspectives are not respected, this could create a challenge for the supervisor, counselor, and agency.

Madson and Green (2012) also emphasized the issue of counselor experience and training as critical to supervision. For instance, they argued that graduate school-trained clinicians are trained in EBPs. However, many certified practitioners with no graduate degree experience may have been trained from another perspective. Thus, Madson and Green recommended the following.

First, they argued that the supervision of novice clinicians (e.g., those new to addiction treatment) requires a careful process. Especially with a new clinician, attitudes regarding addiction (i.e., moral model, overly simplified perspective on substance cessation without consideration of the neuropsychological and psychopharmacological processes inherent in addiction) need careful monitoring. Specifically, what are the supervisees' attitudes regarding addiction? Clarifying supervisee attitudes and biases toward addiction is critical for the supervisory process with supervisees lacking addiction experience, either professional via a counselor or personal via their own recovery (Jordan, Miller, & Napolitano, 2008). Or what is their degree of education and training, and how well do they apply these academic skills to the practical realm of service delivery? Or how are they adapting their current counseling tools for the new problems and issues unique to SUDs and addictions?

MODELS OF COUNSELING SUPERVISION

Clinical supervision is a complex and theoretically driven dyad comprised of the supervisor and supervisee with the goal of the supervisee gaining technical skills and personal insights for the effective, ethical, competent, and confident practice of counseling (Bernard & Goodyear, 2013; Falender & Shafranske, 2008).

This chapter gives the reader a sample foundation for understanding the different supervision models, but in no way does this chapter review all models of supervision, nor does it comprehensively review the full model. The various schools of supervision, with some specific model examples, run below. I tried to choose models that seemed most applicable to the addiction counseling and supervision process.

Psychotherapy Models

Psychotherapy models of supervision often feel like a natural extension of the counseling orientation applied to the treatment process. Thus, there is a commonality of terminology and theory between the counseling and supervision sessions. This may make for a cohesive and focused learning experience for the supervisee. A few brief examples of psychotherapy supervision models are below.

Feminist Model of Supervision. Feminist theory affirms that the individual's experiences reflect the broader society's institutionalized attitudes and values (Haynes, Corey, & Moulton, 2003). Feminist counselors contextualize the client's experiences within the broader societal content. The counselor needs to acknowledge the power differentials in the client-counselor relationship. In a similar manner, the power differential and other feminist ideas are emphasized in the supervisory relationship in an attempt to empower the supervisee, who may then be able to empower the client (Porter & Vasquez, 1997).

Cognitive-Behavioral Supervision. In this model, the supervisor teaches the techniques of cognitive-behavioral therapy. Similar to the treatment process, the supervisor uses observable and reported cognitions, feelings, and behaviors (specific to the supervisee reaction to the counseling process) in an attempt to train the supervisee in effective counseling. Cognitive-behavioral techniques used in supervision include setting an agenda for supervision sessions, problem-solving skills training, and formative feedback for the supervisee to process (Cummings, Ballantyne, & Scallion, 2015).

Person-Centered Supervision. This style of supervision assumes that the supervisee can effectively develop as a counselor. The supervisor is not an expert in this model but rather a "collaborator" with the supervisee and in that role facilitates the process of the supervisee becoming more open to the experience of practicing and learning counseling through the quality and intensity of the supervisory relationship (Lambers, 2000).

Developmental Models

Developmental models of supervision define progressive stages of supervisee development, with each stage consisting of specific technical and reflective skills. The key to effectively implementing these models is to accurately identify the supervisee's current degree of counseling competency and create a supervisory plan to support further development at this stage while also providing the foundation for progression to the next developmental stage (Stoltenberg & Delworth, 1987). In this process, the dynamic between supervisor and supervisee helps instill more advanced critical thinking skills within the supervisee. A few developmental models are briefly described next.

Integrated Development Model (IDM). This is one of the most well-known developmental models (Stoltenberg, 1981; Stoltenberg & Delworth, 1987; Stoltenberg, McNeill, & Delworth, 1998). The IDM describes three levels of counselor development.

Level 1: Supervisees are generally entry-level students who are both highly motivated and also highly anxious and fearful of supervisory evaluation.

Level 2: Supervisees are at mid-level and experience fluctuating confidence.

Level 3: Supervisees are secure in skill set, stable in motivation, and have developed the ability to use the therapeutic self in the implementation of counseling intervention (i.e., feel comfortable using their personal reactions as a clinical guide in session).

The IDM stresses the need for the supervisor to engage in supervisory practices that correspond to the level of the supervisee—for example, a supervisor who demands that a Level-1 supervisee demonstrate a grasp of the scholarly literature and degree of counseling competence more aligned with a Level-3 supervisee. This obviously is a failed supervisory perspective, but more critical, this approach will amplify the supervisee anxiety and further strengthen his or her discomfort and lack of confidence. For instance, perhaps the supervisee will think "I should be more skilled than I am, so I clearly am not cut out for this profession."

Ronnestad and Skovholt's Model. The most recent revision (Ronnestad & Skovholt, 2003) of their model is made up of six developmental phases. The first three phases (called *The Lay Helper, The Beginning Student Phase,* and *The Advanced Student Phase*) can be conceptualized as somewhat corresponding with the three levels of the IDM. The second three phases (*The Novice Professional Phase, The Experienced Professional Phase,* and *The Senior Professional Phase*) explain the ever-developing course of technical and interpersonal/intrapersonal skills over a counselor's career. Specifically, Ronnestad and Skovholt's (2003) model proposed 14 themes:

1. Professional development involves an ever-developing integration of the professional self and the personal self.

2. The focus of functioning shifts from internal to external to internal.

3. Continuous reflection is a prerequisite for optimal learning and professional development.

4. An intense commitment to learn is mandatory.

5. Beginning counselors rely on external expertise, whereas more experienced counselors rely on internal expertise (e.g., confident and competent use of clinical intuition).

6. Professional development is a slow and nonlinear process.

7. Professional development is a lifelong process.

8. Over time, anxiety is reduced in most counselors as they progress in development.

9. Clients serve as the primary teachers of counseling.

10. Counselor personal life influences professional functioning across the professional life span.

11. Interpersonal sources influence professional development.

12. New counselors see professional elders (e.g., those with countless years of experience, counseling and supervision licensure/certification credentials, or graduate training) with strong emotional reactions (i.e., both impressed/want to learn from but also perhaps intimidated).

13. Extensive experience with suffering allows a counselor to better recognize, accept, and appreciate the myriad expressions of the human existence.

14. Client, not counselor (or supervisor), is seen as the hero.

Integrative Models

Integrative models of supervision rely on multiple theories (Bernard & Goodyear, 2013). These models of supervision are widely practiced. One of the most common models, the discrimination model (Bernard, 1979; Bernard & Goodyear, 2009), is briefly reviewed below.

Discrimination Model. This model is made up of three separate areas of supervisory focus (i.e., intervention, conceptualization, and personalization) and three possible supervisor roles for addressing these areas (i.e., teacher, counselor, and consultant). For example, the supervisor may serve as a teacher while reviewing a specific intervention. Because supervision is fluid and constantly responds to the supervisee's current needs, the roles and foci consistently shift within and between supervision sessions.

SUPERVISION MODELS SPECIFIC FOR ADDICTION COUNSELING

The Blended Model (Powell & Brodsky, 2004)

Though other supervisory applications for the SUDs and addiction counseling workforce have been discussed as relevant to such counseling areas as spirituality (Ogden & Sias, 2011) or recovery status (Culbreth & Borders, 1999), Powell and Brodsky's model is still one of the only supervisory paradigms designed specifically for SUDs and addiction counseling supervision. The model elements are reviewed below.

1. *Self.* Each supervisor has an idiosyncratic style of supervision, largely based upon personality profile and counseling orientation.

2. *Philosophy of counseling.* Supervisors articulate what they do in counseling and what models and techniques are applied.

3. *Descriptive dimension.* The blended model uses a version of Bascue and Yalof's (1991) Descriptive Dimensions. Table 11.1 reviews these dimensions and their relevance to supervision.

Table 11.1   The Blended Model and Descriptive Dimensions of Supervision as Reviewed by Bascue and Yalof (1991)

Influential	Is the supervisor trying to influence the supervisee affect or cognition or skills regarding a case (i.e., where is the supervisory emphasis?)
Symbolic	Is the supervisor focused on the supervisee manifest actions or the underlying intrapersonal/intrapsychic influences?
Structural	Is the supervisor proactive (i.e., agenda setting) or reactive (i.e., seeing where things go in session)?
Replicative	Does the supervisor believe in parallel process in that supervisee personal experiences play out in the counseling process?
Counselor in Treatment	Does the supervisor believe that the supervisee should be in counseling in order to effectively train as a counselor? This seems most relevant to the recovering counselor. However, most recovering counselors I have worked with actively engage in their recovery while in counselor training via engagement with the 12-step community.
Information Gathering	How is data obtained for supervision? Direct observation (one-way mirror, video review) or indirect observation (transcript review, clinical record review)?
Jurisdictional/Relationship	Who has jurisdiction for the client? Supervisor or supervisee? Legally, the supervisor obviously has the official responsibility (for example, see *Almonte v. New York Medical College* 1994; *Gilmore v. Board of Psychological Examiners,* 1986; *Peck v. Counseling Service of Addison County, Inc.,* 1985; *Steckler v. Ohio State Board of Psychology,* 1992), but in the context of supervision, does the supervisor dictate counseling goals or interventions, or does the supervisor engage in a collaborative dialogue on these matters?
Strategy	Is supervision focused on insight-oriented approaches or a skill-based model?

4. *Stages of counselor development.* This model adapts a developmental approach to clinical supervision.

5. *Contextual factors.* The blended model uses the work of Holloway (1995) and other contextual models of clinical supervision, addressing factors affecting supervision such as age, race, gender, ethnicity, recovery–nonrecovery status, professional disciplines, or academic background (among others).

6. *Affective–behavioral axis.* The model views supervision along a continuum of affective and behavioral changes for the counselor.

7. *Spiritual dimensions.* Supervision should focus on the spiritual facet of counseling.

The Three-Dimensional Existential Model

This is a type of psychotherapy model of supervision that I have been developing over the past few years as a natural extension of my own existential orientation that I integrate into much of my counseling. In addition to the landmark and original work by Binswanger (1963), Boss (1957, 1963), May (1969, 1983), Spinelli (2005), and Yalom (1980), my thoughts on existential-themed supervision were influenced by du Plock (2007, 2009), Farber (2010), Pagdin (2013), and Spinelli (2015). I intend here to provide a brief overview of the model. I hope it propels some internal dialogue for you in regard to the practice of supervision (whether existential based or otherwise).

According to van Deurzen and Adams (2011), existential counseling is an act of storytelling. Consequently, existential supervision is also an act of storytelling. So in the supervisory relationship, there are a few narratives being relayed in various relationships:

- The story told by client to counselor;
- The story of the client as told by counselor to client (as a conceptual organization of the client experience);
- The story of the counselor and his or her experience as told by supervisee to supervisor; and
- The story of the counselor and his or her experience as told by the supervisor to the supervisee (as a conceptual organization of the supervisee—and client—experience).

Within the context of counseling for SUDs and addictions, there are countless factors unique to this discipline that may play a role in how these stories are told and heard. These (and myriad others) can interact in numerous ways. A few examples are as follows:

- Recovery status of counselor
- Client reactions to the recovery status of the counselor
- Recovery status of the supervisor
- Supervisor reactions to the recovery status of the supervisee
- Supervisee reactions to the recovery status of the supervisor
- Supervisor reactions to client engagement with recovery
- Client reactions to counselor degree, certification, or credentials
- Supervisor reactions to supervisee degree, certification, or credentials
- Supervisee reactions to supervisor degree, certification, or credentials
- Client belief system about the 12-step process
- Counselor reaction to the client's belief system about the 12-step process
- Supervisor reaction to the supervisee belief system about the 12-step process
- Supervisor reaction to the client's belief system about the 12-step process

Consequently, I think of the stories as being said and heard through the perspective of three means of the world: Umwelt, Mitwelt, and Eigenwelt. To understand supervision, there is a need to see this process in a broad manner. For example, in the supervision relationship, in regard to any issue of discussion, you see the influence of the client, counselor (supervisee), and supervisor Umwelt, Mitwelt, and Eigenwelt. Everybody sees and experiences the world in a different way. Perception is reality.

Consider some brief examples of how these perceptions may differ or overlap. Van Deurzen and Adams (2011) noted that Umwelt deals with the issues inherent in accepting the limits of natural boundaries and illness as demonstrating the frailty of the human being. In this case, thoughts, histories, and (perhaps) concerns regarding relapse may be very different emotional and philosophical experiences for the client, counselor/supervisee, and supervisor. Regardless of the reason(s) why their experiences vary, the point is that they vary; thus, this variability plays a role in the process and needs to be addressed. Potash (1994) conceptualized the Mitwelt as the interpersonal skills at the disposal of the individual for navigating the world. Again, the client, counselor/supervisee, and supervisor all come to their respective dyad with different strengths and limits in this area. Considering the highly interpersonal nature of counseling and supervision, this also seems to be an area in need of discussion. Finally, May (1983) explained the Eigenwelt as the way we internally cope with and relate with the world. Think of IDM Level-1 counselors. They would likely have a much more fragile and underdeveloped internal coping mechanism for handling the stressors of counseling and supervision. The client obviously lacks in the intrapersonal area. The supervisor, though likely strong now, has a history of at one point being much weaker in this area. How do they recall and process their own development?

Therefore, it is imperative that the supervisor and supervisee process (whether in dialogue or via self-reflection) how each of these world perspectives, and the owner of those perspectives, can influence the counseling dyad and the supervision dyad. Though only a brief review of some of my supervision ideas, it does demonstrate the process and the potential benefit of existential theory for supervision model development and the applicability to addiction counseling.

ETHICAL CONCERNS RELEVANT TO ADDICTION COUNSELING SUPERVISION

Supervision, like counseling, is a skill set that requires training and experiential practice. That is why the findings by West and Hamm (2012) are so concerning. Specifically, 57 clinical supervisors in licensed SUD treatment centers were surveyed regarding their supervision credentials. They found that only 28% of the supervisors reported graduate course work in supervision. Other reported supervisory areas were state-sponsored training (21%), workshops (25%), and on-the-job training (19%). So at best, a little less than one in three supervisors had any formal supervision training. Consequently, West and Hamm raised concerns regarding the quality of the clinical supervision provided within the addiction counseling profession.

Thus, well-trained supervisors are key to the effectiveness of addiction counseling. The Approved Clinical Supervisor (ACS) credential allows qualified supervisors to demonstrate their training and experience with the theory and practice of supervision. Based on the work of West and Hamm (2012), this degree of supervisory expertise seems to be required.

The ACS requires that supervisors be a National Certified Counselor, a licensed/certified mental health counselor, or a licensed/certified clinical supervisor with at least 100 hours of documented supervision of their counseling supervision by an eligible/qualified supervisor. They need one graduate course in clinical supervision or a total of 45 hours of workshop training in clinical supervision. The clinical supervision training, whether via graduate course or workshop, must be specific to the provision of supervision and include the following content areas:

1. Roles and functions of clinical supervisors

2. Models of clinical supervision

3. Mental health-related professional development

4. Methods and techniques in clinical supervision

5. Supervisory relationship issues

6. Cultural issues in clinical supervision

7. Group supervision

8. Legal and ethical issues in clinical supervision

9. Evaluation of supervisee competence and the supervision process

I would like to add the obvious—that being a counselor supervisor who earns the ACS credential and works with addiction counseling *must* have adequate and appropriate training and experience in practicing addiction counseling. I would also argue that supervisors need extensive supervision of their addiction counseling supervision with an addiction clinician (qualified to offer supervision) before they can truly practice independent (i.e., nonsupervised) supervision of addiction counseling. For example, Figure 11.2 examines the multitude of decisions that must be made by a supervisor when investigating a potential ethical or legal violation by a supervisee. Consequently, the supervisor *must* be well experienced in the practice and supervision of addiction counseling in order to carry out an effective administrative and clinical supervisory inquiry.

The American Counseling Association *Code of Ethics* (ACA, 2014) contains several concepts relevant to supervision. Below, some of these are reviewed with a small case example afterward that demonstrate what a clinical scenario may look like that requires conceptualization via this ethical consideration.

Ethical Code: F.1.a. Client Welfare.

A primary obligation of counseling supervisors is to monitor the services provided by supervisees. Counseling supervisors monitor client welfare and supervisee performance and professional development. To fulfill these obligations, supervisors meet regularly with supervisees to review the supervisees' work and help them become prepared to serve a range of diverse clients. Supervisees have a responsibility to understand and follow the ACA Code of Ethics. (p. 12)

F.1.a Case Example. The counselor supervisor notices the supervisee struggling with relapse prevention and recovery maintenance strategies for clients. However, the supervisor also wants the supervisee to develop his or her own

Figure 11.2   Supervisor Steps to Determine a Potential Ethical or Legal Violation by Supervisee

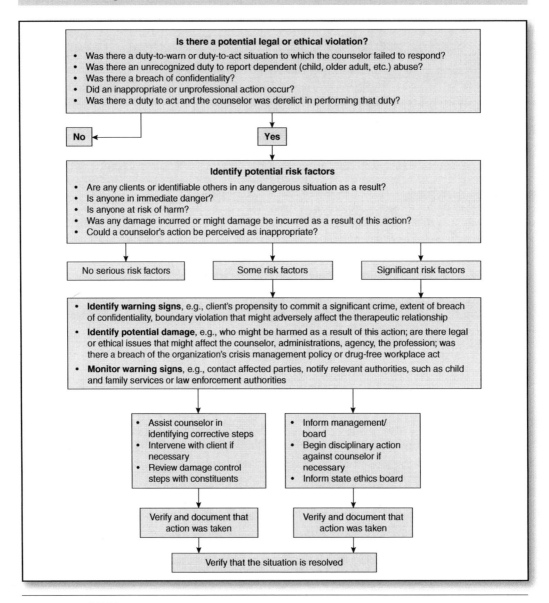

Source: CSAT (2009b).

counseling style and beliefs. Consequently, the supervisor assigns the supervisee to read relapse prevention texts and clinical workbooks from varying perspectives (e.g., Marlatt, Gorski). But this supervision ethic truly comes into being when the supervisor enacts the teacher role and assists the supervisee to learn the theory and to learn the pragmatic application of these techniques in session.

Ethical Code: F.2.a. Supervisor Preparation.

Prior to offering supervision services, counselors are trained in supervision methods and techniques. Counselors who offer supervision services regularly pursue continuing education activities, including both counseling and supervision topics and skills. (p. 13)

F.2.a Case Example. A graduate counseling program with an addictions track decides to offer a post-master's supervision course sequence where the students receive a course in supervision theory and practice and a practicum where new supervisors can be supervised in their supervision of addiction counseling. Thus, this program can produce counselors well trained in the addictions who also could qualify for the ACS credential and provide quality and ethical supervision.

Ethical Code F.2.b. Multicultural Issues/Diversity in Supervision.

Counseling supervisors are aware of and address the role of multiculturalism/diversity in the supervisory relationship. (p. 13)

F.2.b Case Example. The supervisor makes it a point to inquire regarding how the supervisee (in his or her specific cultural viewpoint) conceptualizes addiction. For example, some cultures are more inclusive and wish to involve the family within the treatment process. This cultural belief would inform the supervisee's clinical decisions. Thus, the supervisee's cultural perspective would need to be understood by the supervisor so that he or she could best consult with the supervisee about the most appropriate clinical decision.

Ethical Code F.3.a. Extending Conventional Supervisory Relationships.

Counseling supervisors clearly define and maintain ethical professional, personal, and social relationships with their supervisees. Supervisors consider the risks and benefits of extending current supervisory relationships in any form beyond conventional parameters. In extending these boundaries, supervisors take appropriate professional precautions to ensure that judgment is not impaired and that no harm occurs. (p. 13)

F.3.a Case Example. Consider the following scenario for a supervisor in recovery. This individual went to an Alcoholics Anonymous (AA) home group but also attended another group relatively frequently. At one meeting at this other group site, the supervisor happened to notice a new member who was one of his counseling supervisees. This code required the supervisor to discuss the joint membership in the same AA group. In the end, especially since it was not his home group, the supervisor chose to stop attending the other AA meeting because he felt there was the potential of some type of (unknown) harm or impairment that could come to the counselor or the supervisory relationship.

Ethical Code F.6.b. Gatekeeping and Remediation.

> Through initial and ongoing evaluation, supervisors are aware of supervisee limitations that might impede performance. Supervisors assist supervisees in securing remedial assistance when needed. They recommend dismissal from training programs, applied counseling settings, and state or voluntary professional credentialing processes when those supervisees are unable to demonstrate that they can provide competent professional services to a range of diverse clients. Supervisors seek consultation and document their decisions to dismiss or refer supervisees for assistance. They ensure that supervisees are aware of options available to them to address such decisions. (p. 13)

F.6.b Case Example. Supervisory examples here are many. In one example, the counselor-trainee in early recovery who experiences client data as personal stressors that either can lead the supervisee toward a relapse or ineffective counseling via countertransference reactions. Gatekeeping would not automatically discharge the trainee. Rather, the gatekeeping function would only occur if the supervisee consistently rebuked or failed at the remediation plans developed by the supervisor in consultation with the supervisee. In another example, addiction and the possible associated client psychosocial and medical experiences (i.e., family estrangement or conflict, legal issues, financial issues, child protective services, homelessness, hepatitis, HIV/AIDS) could seem like areas of potential clinical interest for a student in the classroom setting. However, I have encountered many supervisees over the years (as have my colleagues) who were overwhelmed with the issues or pacing (e.g., 28-day program) of an addiction counseling placement. Regardless of recovery status, they found the placement uncomfortable. Via supervisory discussions, whether based on simply being overwhelmed or perhaps biases and opinions they harbored, we discussed how this discomfort impeded the counseling process. The supervisee was just not a good fit for the addiction counseling profession. But many of them went on to find they were good fits for other counseling populations and disorders.

Ethical Code F.6.c. Counseling for Supervisees.

> If supervisees request counseling, the supervisor assists the supervisee in iden-
> tifying appropriate services. Supervisors do not provide counseling services to
> supervisees. Supervisors address interpersonal competencies in terms of the
> impact of these issues on clients, the supervisory relationship, and professional
> functioning. (p. 14)

F.6.c Case Example. Supervision has a counseling component built into the process. But the counseling is embedded into the supervision in order to facilitate the
supervisee's deeper introspection regarding various intrapersonal or interpersonal
factors influencing the counseling (or supervisory) relationship. An ethical
dilemma would be if a recovering supervisor began offering recovery support to
an in-recovery supervisee struggling with remaining in recovery due to various
stressors encountered in the act of providing treatment services. This is a difficult,
complicated scenario. The in-recovery community is both close knit and supportive. In addition, depending on the exact nature of the scenario, the line may not be
clear between whether this is just recovery support between two recovering
individuals or counseling between a supervisor (who, in their supervisory role, is
the more credentialed and experienced of the two in the dyad) and supervisee. It is
imperative that supervisors be mindful of their deliberate interventions with
supervisees so not to cross the line into counseling. A supervisor can have countertransference reactions to a supervisee, so supervisors must also reflect on their
motivations for offering assistance. Finally, the supervisee must also be a
responsible member of the relationship. Thus, supervisees should monitor what
they are asking of their supervisors. Are they going to supervisors in their role as
supervisor, or are they trying to transform the supervisory relationship into a
counseling relationship? Both parties are obligated to be intrapersonally and
interpersonally aware.

SECTION IV REVIEW

CASE OF SAMANTHA: RELAPSE AND 12-STEP IDEAS

Chapters 9 and 10 cover some unique areas to the SUD treatment process. In Chapter 9, 12-step groups are reviewed. However, the counselor plays no role in that process other than facilitating engagement with a group if clients wish to include the 12-step program in their recovery. Furthermore, Chapter 10 covers relapse prevention issues relevant to recovery. In many ways, the relapse prevention issues discussed here (and elsewhere) are not a static intervention but rather the continuous process of self-reflection and growth that both occurs in treatment and is developed by being in treatment. That's why in this final visitation of the Samantha case, our discussions are more theoretical and less applied. First, I consider some potential areas of growth and change that Samantha may pursue while engaged in the Narcotics Anonymous (NA) 12-step process. Second, I review some treatment interventions that may permit for successful recovery and navigation of any potential relapse risk scenarios. Finally, there is no ethics or counseling curricular discussion here because there are no ethical or curricular issues unique to the 12-steps or relapse prevention.

The Case of Samantha: 12-Step Considerations

Rather than addressing some issues step-by-step, I organize the content via the themes as described by Morgen and Morgan (2011). Though not an exhaustive list, these may be some things the client would consider. In addition, though not directly covered in NA, Samantha would also likely engage with Sex Addicts Anonymous and work through the process of understanding how her sex addiction impaired her life and how to move past that dysfunction. For now, we focus on NA.

- Steps 1 Through 3

Basically, the concepts of essential limitation should help Samantha. Considering that her parents (primarily her father) taught her how showing emotion and needing help are weaknesses, Samantha would greatly benefit from a community of individuals with similar substance experiences who model how to express and own emotion and how to ask for help. And this community would embrace, not shun, her discussions of limitations, flaws, and her need for support and help.

- Steps 4 Through 9

Humility is a key theme across these steps and critical for Samantha's recovery. Samantha considered herself as "functional" in her addiction, always noting how she never missed a meeting, messed up a work assignment, or likewise. This dates back to her time in college where she told you how she never let her excessive sexual behaviors get in the way of her academics. Samantha would need to revisit many issues in her addiction and reconsider her prior interpretation of events. In essence, was she as "functional" as she believed?

In an example of how the steps build on one another, the increased comfort with expressing flaws and requesting help will enable Samantha to truly perform a fearless moral inventory. Though it will be difficult for her to accomplish, when she finishes it, her ability to express emotion, process her strengths and weaknesses, and seek out support (whether through NA or counseling) will have grown. That is basically the purpose of the 12 steps—to rebuild (or perhaps build for the first time) the intrapersonal and interpersonal skills required for a successful recovery and a healthy, stable life.

- Steps 10 Through 12

Brach's (2004) "trance of unworthiness" would be critical to Samantha in these last steps. Through her 12-step work and the work she does in treatment, Samantha will craft herself a new narrative. She will take her story to others. I have had many clients who were speakers in a meeting toward the end of their step work. They likened it to a personal and emotional type of graduation and farewell ceremony—graduation in the sense that they could share how they made it through the hard work and are now on stable ground in their recovery, and that their story can inspire others to do the same. It is also a type of farewell ceremony where some of my clients reported feeling the old self-narrative and their past fade away and finally be replaced by a healthier life. This would be powerful for Samantha. This would help Samantha. Being a speaker at a meeting would allow her to share her narrative and further clarify how she finds meaning in her recovery.

The Case of Samantha: Relapse Prevention Considerations

Relapse prevention is the process of self-reflection and avoiding as many high-risk situations as possible. However, relapse prevention is also the process of building one's sense of self-efficacy that an individual can indeed manage the stressors of life (and recovery) without the need for substances. Self-efficacy grows exponentially in that people acquire it after they successfully manage an issue that they initially felt they could not tackle. The analogy is of children learning to ride a bicycle. The more times children can keep the bicycle going without falling down, or the more times that they fell down and were able to get right back up on their own and keep riding, the stronger their sense of self-efficacy becomes.

There are myriad relapse prevention strategies (some of which are discussed in Chapter 10). However, there is one critical concept that helps instill self-efficacy that cannot be found in any technique or model of relapse prevention. That is the concept of courage.

Think about Samantha and when she would face a high-risk situation. At some point, she will need to have faith in herself to apply her skills and face the situation without substance use or sex. To borrow from existentialism, there is a fundamental sense of existential isolation in this moment. The counselor, the treatment group, the 12-step group, and the 12-step sponsor can all help her learn new coping skills and assist her to process and reconceptualize her identity as a woman who is in recovery from addiction. But even with all these tools at her immediate disposal, she still needs to use them. Whether it is something big and complicated (like a cognitive restructuring exercise) or small and simple (like calling her sponsor), Samantha is alone in that moment. One second after she engages with a tool or support system, she has a sense of support and community around her. But in that moment where she needs to decide between a healthy or substance-related reaction to the situation, she is alone.

Now, regardless of treatment orientation, think of all the counseling interventions within SUD treatment (only a very small number are discussed in this book). Also, think of all the philosophical concepts that Samantha needs to navigate in her intrapersonal process through the 12 steps. All these concepts, tools, interventions, and otherwise were performed so that Samantha could feel a sense of self-efficacy that she could manage the problem without substances and also so that she would have the courage to ride through the anxiety and other negative experiences she may encounter as she successfully handles the situation in a nonsubstance-related way.

Relapse prevention is a process, not an outcome or a static counseling intervention. All the skills and tools learned and utilized build upon one another following each application. Self-efficacy grows, techniques are adapted, and Samantha hopefully grows more confident and competent in her ability to own and improve her recovery skills throughout her life.

CLOSING THOUGHTS

This book covers the basics (broadly defined) of what constitutes the information required for competent substance use disorders (SUDs) and addictions counseling. Going back to the Preface for a moment, all this content is obviously applied quite differently depending upon which of the credentials a counselor holds (whether licensure, certification, or Council for Accreditation of Counseling and Related Programs). That is why I am so concerned about the fragmentation of the profession. Recall my client who asked me what the difference would be between receiving addictions treatment from a psychologist, psychiatrist, addictions counselor, professional counselor, or social worker? Well, some of these differences could be considerable, and I try to briefly (on your way out the door from reading this book) leave you with some thoughts about the fragmented profession through the context of some of the content this book reviews.

First, consider the widely accepted and documented fact that co-occurring psychiatric disorders (whether *Diagnostic and Statistical Manual of Mental Disorders*, 5th ed. [*DSM-5*], diagnosable or subsyndromal) are present in just about all moderate/severe SUD cases. In general, licensed professional counselors (LPCs), licensed psychologists, or licensed social workers have a clearer scope of practice and training associated with the diagnosis and treatment of co-occurring psychiatric disorders. But what of the licensed addictions counselor? These professionals do TREMENDOUS work. I have worked with them and overseen their work over the years. I proudly call some of them colleagues. However, I feel the fragmented system did them (and their clients) a disservice.

I have heard the following scenario played out in many states over the years. An addictions counselor (licensed or certified as per their state) was working with a client who presented for alcohol use disorder. However, it soon became evident that the client presented problems that also included (for example) generalized anxiety disorder independent of the alcohol use disorder. Based on the scope of the license/certification, the addictions counselor may need to refer the client to a licensed professional counselor for the anxiety issues but would still see the client for the alcohol issues. The reasoning was that the addictions license/certification does not cover diagnosis and treatment of nonsubstance use disorders. So a client may need to see one clinician for anxiety and another clinician for the alcohol use disorder. This, to me, seems counterproductive to the client's need for care and the unification of the counseling profession, but I hear about similar scope of practice type scenarios nationwide. That is why—though it is slowly starting to happen state by state—I firmly advocate for all licensed addictions counselors to be provided with a series of standardized and sound "mental health diagnosis" training and have their scope of practice expanded to fully and truly cover co-occurring disorders. LPCs and licensed addictions counselors are not competing professions (though some see differently). They are, and should be seen as, colleagues and equals. Some states are better at it than others, but all states should provide the counselors the skills, training, and regulatory ability to work with their clients in a nonfragmented manner.

Second, consider the role that all the certifications and other credentials play in identifying an "addictions counselor." In various treatment centers, clients would encounter staff of numerous titles, degrees, and credentials. For example, my colleagues in different states have experienced this issue, as have my students and I. A client is used to a certain set of credentials (they learn the acronyms quickly) and decide what they see is being an "addictions counselor." When they next encounter (in a new treatment episode or after a transfer to a new level of care) another professional with different credentials, they challenge that counselor's ability to offer services as a counseling professional who works with the SUDs and the addictions.

This has ramifications in the area of (for instance) supervision and counseling. Dating back to the 1970s and 1980s (and up through the 1990s with the work by Culbreth & Borders, 1999), Strong, Welsh, Corcoran, and Hoyt (1992) studied the role of client-perceived counselor similarity, competence, and trustworthiness. Individuals informed different things about a counselor seen in a video (years of training, background, for example) greatly influenced perceptions about this counselor. Despite all watching the same video, different information produced different perceptions. Recovering clients may (from self and others) have a set belief about who is a counselor best qualified to treat them. That belief system directly influences how they would work with the counselor treatment matters or how the supervisee and supervisor may view each other's qualifications for working in the field and what is needed to be considered competent and effective. If you ever review the addiction counseling competencies from the Substance Abuse and Mental Health Services Administration, they are many in number, but they are somewhat vague in description. So it falls to the counselor, supervisor, and perhaps client to make that final specific application.

If all the other disorders which we treat had a similar national landscape, we would all just keep pushing along. But this profession (SUDs and addictions counseling) is unique in that there are so many voices out there stating what "should be" (and some of them even conflict with one another) in regard to the treatment of a *DSM-5* disorder class. In addition, we are unique in that this is the only *DSM-5* disorder class paired with a specific licensure/certification process. That's why, in these last words I have to type, I want to leave you with what I think every good SUDs and addictions professional (i.e., a licensed professional counselor, licensed/certified addictions counselor, psychologist, social worker) should know:

- The full breadth of the *DSM* substance-related and addictive disorders.
- An understanding of a diagnostic scheme for addictions that have not yet made it into the *DSM* mainstream (sex, food, perhaps nonsuicidal self-injury).
- A clear understanding of the basics behind the co-occurring psychiatric disorders condition.
- An ability to balance an appreciation and respect for the neuropsychological and psychopharmacological influences in the addiction and withdrawal processes alongside an ability to instill self-ownership in clients of their actions now in trying to cease substance use and sustain recovery.
- An ability to meet clients on whatever level they need, whether concrete (e.g., cognitive-behavioral therapy) or more esoteric (e.g., existential).
- The flexibility to work with numerous other agencies in the treatment of a client while recognizing that (sometimes) not all parties fully share the same overall goals.
- The capability to question and discuss spirituality matters in a nonrigid manner (i.e., more than just a simple inquiry of *are you spiritual, yes or no?*).
- A true philosophical understanding of the meaning and application of the 12 steps and how to complement and supplement that process for the client's recovery.
- Regardless of your counseling orientation, the ability to challenge a client and the ability to be challenged by a client.
- Knowledge of counseling theories; interviewing skills (not just motivational interviewing); diagnostic and assessment appreciation for SUDs and co-occurring psychiatric disorders; and how the brain, thoughts, emotions, and behaviors are altered by the active use, withdrawal, and recovery periods.

There's a lot of stuff to know and apply. Clients need our help. Students need our training so they can join the ranks of those who can help. Most (if not all) of what I list above falls within any certification, licensure, or accreditation list of required content. We all believe the content I covered in this book is relevant and critical to the treatment of SUDs. My hope is that the profession can figure out a more unified manner via which to make it known what we know, who knows it, and how we can help.

Thanks for reading. If you want to continue the conversation, please feel free to send me an e-mail.

—Keith

morgenk@centenaryuniversity.edu

REFERENCES

Agrawal, A., & Lynskey, M. T. (2008). Are there genetic influences on addiction: Evidence from family, adoption, and twin studies. *Addiction, 103*(7), 1069–1081. doi:10.1111/j.1360-0443.2008.02213.x

Agrawal, A., Nurnberger, J. I., & Lynskey, M. T. (2011). The bipolar genome study: Cannabis involvement in individuals with bipolar disorder. *Psychiatry Researcher, 185,* 459–461.

Aharonovich, E., Liu, X., Nunes, E., & Hasin, D. S. (2002). Suicide attempts in substance abusers: Effects of major depression in relation to substance use disorders. *American Journal of Psychiatry, 159*(9), 1600–1602. doi:10.1176/appi.ajp.159.9.1600

Al-Anon Family Group Headquarters. (2013). *Al-Anon, Alateen service manual 2014–2017.* Virginia Beach, VA: Author.

Alcoholics Anonymous World Services. (1976). *Alcoholics Anonymous* (3rd ed.). New York, NY: Author.

Alcoholics Anonymous World Services. (1981). *Twelve steps and twelve traditions.* New York, NY: Author.

Alcoholics Anonymous World Services. (1985). *Alcoholics Anonymous comes of age: A brief history of A.A.* New York, NY: Author.

Amato, L., Davoli, M., Minozzi, S., Ali, R., & Ferri, M. (2005). Methadone at tapered doses for the management of opioid withdrawal. *Cochrane Database of Systematic Reviews, 20*(3), CD003409.

American Academy of Pediatrics Committee on Substance Abuse. (2011). Substance use screening, brief intervention, and referral to treatment for pediatricians. *Pediatrics, 135*(4), 1330–1340.

American Counseling Association. (2014). *ACA code of ethics.* Alexandria, VA: Author.

American Psychiatric Association. (2000). *Diagnostic and statistical manual of mental disorders: DSM-IV-TR* (4th ed.). Washington, DC: Author.

American Psychiatric Association. (2013). *Diagnostic and statistical manual of mental disorders* (5th ed.). Washington, DC: Author.

American Society of Addiction Medicine. (2013). *The ASAM criteria: Treatment criteria for addictive, substance-related, and co-occurring disorders.* Carson City, NV: The Change Companies.

Amrhein, P. C., Miller, W. R., Yahne, C., Knupsky, A., & Hochstein, D. (2004). Strength of client commitment language improves with therapist training in motivational interviewing. *Alcoholism: Clinical and experimental research, 28*(5) (Suppl.), 403.

Amrhein, P. C., Miller, W. R., Yahne, C. E., Palmer, M., & Fulcher, L. (2003). Client commitment language during motivational interviewing predicts drug use outcomes. *Journal of Consulting and Clinical Psychology, 71*(5), 862–878. doi:10.1037/0022-006X.71.5.862

Anderson, D. A., & Parker, J. D. (1997). The use of a mental status examination in a chemical dependence treatment program. *Journal of Substance Abuse Treatment, 14*(4), 377–382.

Aos, S., Miller, M., & Drake, E. (2006). *Evidence-based public policy options to reduce future prison construction, criminal justice costs, and crime rates.* Olympia, WA: Washington State Institute for Public Policy.

Apodaca T. R., & Longabaugh, R. (2009). Mechanisms of change in motivational interviewing: A review and preliminary evaluation of the evidence. *Addiction, 104*(5), 705–715.

Archer, J., & McCarthy, C. J. (2007). *Theories of counseling and psychotherapy: Contemporary applications.* Columbus, OH: Pearson.

Arciniega, G. M., Anderson, T. C., Tovar-Blank, Z. G., & Tracey, T. G. (2008). Toward a fuller conception of Machismo: Development of a traditional Machismo and Caballerismo Scale. *Journal of Counseling Psychology, 55*(1), 19–33. doi:10.1037/0022-0167.55.1.19

Areán, P. (2015). Introduction. In P. A. Areán (Ed.), *Treatment of late-life depression, anxiety, trauma, and substance abuse* (pp. 3–10). Washington, DC: American Psychological Association. http://dx.doi .org/10.1037/14524-001

Asada, T., Takaya, S., Takayama, Y., Yamauchi, H., Hashikawa, K., & Fukuyama, H. (2010). Reversible alcohol-related dementia: A five-year follow-up study using FDG-PET and neuropsychological tests. *Internal Medicine, 49,* 283–287. doi.org/10.2169/internalmedicine.49.2662

Atkins, C.A. (2014). *Co-occurring disorders: Integrated assessment and treatment of substance use and mental disorders.* New York, NY: PESI.

Back, S. E., Waldrop, A. E., & Brady, K. T. (2009). Treatment challenges associated with comorbid substance use and posttraumatic stress disorder: Clinicians' perspectives. *The American Journal on Addictions/ American Academy of Psychiatrists in Alcoholism and Addictions, 18*(1), 15–20. http://doi.org/10.1080/ 10550490802545141

Baer, J. S., & Peterson, P. L. (2002). Motivational interviewing with adolescents and young adults. In W. R. Miller & S. Rollnick (Eds.), *Motivational interviewing: Preparing people for change* (pp. 320–332). New York, NY: Guilford Press.

Baethge, C., Baldessarini, R. J., Khalsa, H. K., Hennen, J., Salvatore, P., & Tohen, M. (2005). Substance abuse in first-episode Bipolar I Disorder: Indications for early intervention. *American Journal of Psychiatry, 162*(5), 1008–1010. doi:10.1176/appi.ajp.162.5.1008

Baldwin, S. A., Christian, S., Berkeljon, A., Shadish, W. R., & Bean, R. (2012). The effects of family therapies for adolescent delinquency and substance abuse: A meta-analysis. *Journal of Marital and Family Therapy, 38*(1), 281–304. doi:10.1111/j.1752-0606.2011.00248.x

Bandura, A. (1977). Self-efficacy: Toward a unifying theory of behavioral change. *Psychological Review, 84,* 191–215

Barnett, E., Sussman, S., Smith, C., Rohrbach, L. A., & Spruijt-Metz, D. (2012). Motivational interviewing for adolescent substance use: A review of the literature. *Addictive Behaviors, 37*(12), 1325–1334. http:// doi.org/10.1016/j.addbeh.2012.07.001

Bascue, L. O., & Yalof, J. A. (1991). Descriptive dimensions of psychotherapy supervision. *Clinical Supervisor, 9*(2), 19–30. doi:10.1300/J001v09n02_03

Bates, M. E., Bowden, S. C., & Barry, D. (2002). Neurocognitive impairment associated with alcohol use disorders: Implications for treatment. *Experimental and Clinical Psychopharmacology, 10*(3), 193–212. doi:10.1037/1064-1297.10.3.193

Bates, M. E., Buckman, J. F., & Nguyen, T. T. (2013). A role for cognitive rehabilitation in increasing the effectiveness of treatment for alcohol use disorders. *Neuropsychology Review, 23*(1), 27–47. http://doi .org/10.1007/s11065-013-9228-3

Bauer, M. S., Altshuler, L., Evans, D. R., Beresford, T., Williford, W. O., & Hauger, R. (2005). Prevalence and distinct correlates of anxiety, substance, and combined comorbidity in a multi-site public sector sample with bipolar disorder. *Journal of Affective Disorders, 85*(3), 301–315. doi:10.1016/j.jad.2004.11.009

Beatson, J. A., & Rao, S. (2012). Depression and borderline personality disorder. *MJA Open, 1*(Suppl. 4), 24–27. doi:10.5694/mjao12.10474

Beattie, M. C., & Longabaugh, R. (1997). Interpersonal factors and post-treatment drinking and subjective wellbeing. *Addiction, 92*(11), 1507–1521. doi:10.1111/j.1360-0443.1997.tb02871.x

Beck, A. T. (1976). *Cognitive therapy and the emotional disorders.* New York, NY: Meridian.

Beck, A. T., Wright, F. D., Newman, C. F., & Liese, B. S. (1993). *Cognitive therapy of substance abuse.* New York, NY: Guilford Press.

Beckett, C., & Taylor, H. (2010). *Human growth and development* (2nd ed.). Thousand Oaks, CA: Sage.

Bekman, N. M., Wilkins, K. C., & Brown, S. A. (2013). Treatment for adolescent alcohol and drug problems. In B. S. McCrady & E. E. Epstein (Eds.), *Addictions: A comprehensive guidebook* (2nd ed., pp. 708–741). New York, NY: Oxford University Press.

Bernard, J. M. (1979). Supervisor training: A discrimination model. *Counselor Education and Supervision, 19*, 60–68.

Bernard, J. M., & Goodyear, R. K. (2009). *Fundamentals of clinical supervision* (4th ed.). Needham Heights, MA: Allyn & Bacon.

Bernard, J. M., & Goodyear, R. K. (2013). *Fundamentals of clinical supervision* (5th ed.). New York, NY: Pearson.

Beronio, K., Po, R., Skopec, L., & Glied, S. (2013). Affordable Care Act will expand mental health and substance use disorder benefits and parity protections for 62 million Americans. *ASPE Research Brief*, 1–4.

Bhati, A. S., Roman, J. K., & Chalfin, A. (2008). *To treat or not to treat: Evidence on the prospects of expanding treatment to drug-involved offenders.* Washington, DC: The Urban Institute.

Bickel, W. K., & Marsch, L. A. (2001). Toward a behavioral economic understanding of drug dependence: Delay discounting processes. *Addiction, 96*(1), 73–86. doi:10.1046/j.1360-0443.2001.961736.x

Binswanger, L. (1963). *Being-in-the-world* (translated and with a critical introduction by J. Needleman). New York, NY: Basic Books.

Birrell, L., Newton, N. C., Teesson, M., Tonks, Z., & Slade, T. (2015). Anxiety disorders and first alcohol use in the general population. Findings from a nationally representative sample. *Journal of Anxiety Disorders, 31*, 108–113. doi:10.1016/j.janxdis.2015.02.008

Blow, F. C., & Barry, K. L. (2014). Substance misuse and abuse in older adults: What do we need to know to help? *Generations, 38*, 53–67.

Blow, F. C., Brower, K. J., Schulenberg, J. E., Demo-Dananberg, L. M., Young, J. P., & Beresford, T. P. (1992). The Michigan Alcoholism Screening Test—Geriatric Version (MAST-G): A new elderly-specific screening instrument. *Alcoholism: Clinical and Experimental Research, 16*, 372.

Bobby, C. L. (2013). The evolution of specialties in the CACREP standards: CACREP's role in unifying the profession. *Journal of Counseling & Development, 91*(1), 35–43. doi:10.1002/j.1556-6676.2013.00068.x

Bohbot, V. D., Del Balso, D., Conrad, K., Konishi, K., & Leyton, M. (2013). Caudate nucleus-dependent navigational strategies are associated with increased use of addictive drugs. *Hippocampus, 23*(11), 973–984. doi:10.1002/hipo.22187

Bolton, J. M., Robinson, J., & Sareen, J. (2009). Self-medication of mood disorders with alcohol and drugs in the National Epidemiologic Survey on Alcohol and Related Conditions. *Journal of Affective Disorders, 115*(3), 367–375. doi:10.1016/j.jad.2008.10.003

Bordin, E. S. (1976). The generalizability of the psychoanalytic concept of the working alliance. *Psychotherapy: Theory, Research, and Practice, 16*, 252–260.

Boss, M. (1957). *The analysis of dreams.* London, England: Rider.

Boss, M. (1963). *Psychoanalysis and daseinsanalysis.* New York, NY: Basic Books.

Boucher, M., & Sandhu, P. (2013). The neurobiology of adolescent addiction. In R. Rosner (Ed.), *Clinical handbook of adolescent addiction* (pp. 78–87). New York, NY: Wiley.

Bowen, M. (1978). *Family therapy in clinical practice.* New York, NY: Jason Aronson.

Brach, T. (2004). *Radical acceptance: Embracing your life with the heart of a Buddha.* New York, NY: Bantam.

Brain, K. L., Haines, J., & Williams, C. L. (2002). The psychophysiology of repetitive self-mutilation. *Archives of Suicide Research, 6*, 199–210. doi:10.1080/13811110214140

Brand, M., Kalbe, E., Labudda, K., Fujiwara, E., Kessler, J., & Markowitsch, H. J. (2005). Decision-making impairments in patients with pathological gambling. *Psychiatry Research, 133*(1), 91–99.

Brandon, T. H., Vidrine, J. I., & Litvin, E. B. (2007). Relapse and relapse prevention. *Annual Review of Clinical Psychology, 3*, 257–284. doi:10.1146/annurev.clinpsy.3.022806.091455

Brandt, C. J., & Delport, C. S. L. (2005). Theories of adolescent substance use and abuse. *Professional Journal for Social Work, 41*(2), 163–175.

Breggin, P. R. (2013). *Psychiatric drug withdrawal: A guide for prescribers, therapists, patients, and their families*. New York, NY: Springer.

Brick, J. (2008). Characteristics of alcohol: Definitions, measurement, chemistry, and use. In J. Brick (Ed.), *Handbook of the medical consequences of alcohol and drug abuse* (2nd ed., pp. 1–12. New York, NY: Routledge.

Brickman, P., Rabinowitz, V. C., Coates, D., Cohn, E., Kidder, L. (1982). Models of helping and coping. *American Psychologist, 37*, 364–384.

Bristow-Braitman, A. (1995). Addiction recovery: 12-step programs and cognitive-behavioral psychology. *Journal of Counseling & Development, 73*, 414–418.

Brooks, F., & McHenry, B. (2015). *A contemporary approach to substance use disorders and addiction counseling* (2nd ed.). Washington, DC: American Counseling Association.

Brooner, R. K., King, V. L., Kidorf, M., Schmidt, C. W., & Bigelow, G.E. (1997). Psychiatric and substance use comorbidity among treatment-seeking opioid users. *Archives of General Psychiatry, 54*, 71–80.

Brown, A. E., Tonigan, J. S., Pavlik, V. N., Kosten, T. R., & Volk, R. J. (2013). Spirituality and confidence to resist substance use among celebrate recovery participants. *Journal of Religion & Health, 52*(1), 107–113. doi:10.1007/s10943-011-9456-x

Brown, H. P., Peterson, J. H., & Cunningham, O. (1988). An individualized behavioral approach to spiritual development for the recovering alcoholic/addict. *Alcoholism Treatment Quarterly, 5*, 177–192.

Brown, J. (1999). Bowen family systems theory and practice. *Australian and New Zealand Journal of Family Therapy, 20*(2), 99–103.

Brown, S. A., Goldman, M. S., & Christiansen, B. A. (1985). Do alcohol expectancies mediate drinking patterns of adults? *Journal of Consulting and Clinical Psychology, 53*, 512–519.

Brown, S. A., McGue, M., Maggs, J., Schulenberg, J., Hingson, R., Swartzwelder, S., . . . Murphy, S. (2008). A developmental perspective on alcohol and youths 16 to 20 years of age. *Pediatrics, 121*(Suppl. 4), S290–S310.

Bryan, A., & Stallings, M. C. (2002). A case control study of adolescent risky sexual behavior and its relationship to personality dimensions, conduct disorder, and substance use. *Journal of Youth and Adolescents, 31*(5), 337–396.

Burijon, B. N. (2001). Narcissism and grace: Inherent incompatibility. *Pastoral Psychology, 49*, 181–186.

Burns, D. B. (1989). *The feeling good handbook*. New York, NY: Penguin Books.

Buser, T. J., & Buser, J. K. (2013). Conceptualizing nonsuicidal self-injury as a process addiction: Review of research and implications for counselor training and practice. *Journal of Addictions & Offender Counseling, 34*, 16–29. doi:10.1002/j.2161-1874.2013.00011.x

Bush, K., Kivlahan, D. R., McDonell, M. B., Fihn, S. D., & Bradley, K. A. (1998). The AUDIT alcohol consumption questions (AUDIT-C): An effective brief screening test for problem drinking. Ambulatory Care Quality Improvement Project (ACQUIP). *Archives of Internal Medicine, 158*, 1789–1795.

Bush, G., Luu, P., & Posner, M. I. (2000). Cognitive and emotional influences in anterior cingulate cortex. *Trends in Cognitive Sciences, 4*(6), 215–222. doi:http://dx.doi.org/10.1016/S1364-6613(00)01483-2

Calley, N., & Hawley, L. (2008). The professional identity of counselor educators. *Clinical Supervisor, 27*(1), 3–16. doi:10.1080/07325220802221454

Capoccia, V. A., Grazier, K. L., Toal, C., Ford, J. H., II, & Gustafson, D. H. (2012). Massachusetts's experience suggests coverage alone is insufficient to increase addiction disorders treatment. *Health Affairs, 31*(5), 1000–1008.

Carnes, P. (1983). *Out of the shadows: Understanding sexual addiction*. Minneapolis, MN: CompCare.

Carroll, K. M. (1998). *Therapy manuals for drug addiction. A cognitive-behavioral approach: Treating cocaine addiction*. Rockville, MD: National Institute on Drug Abuse.

Cashwell, C., Kleist, D., & Schofield, T. (2009, August). A call for professional unity. *Counseling Today, 52*(2), 60–61.

Cashwell, C. S., & Watts, R. E. (2010). The new ASERVIC Competencies for addressing spiritual and religious issues in counseling. *Counseling & Values, 55*(1), 2–5.

Cattie, J. E., & Grant, I. (2014). Cannabis. In D. N. Allen & S. P. Woods (Eds.), *Neuropsychological aspects of substance use disorders* (pp. 134–156). New York, NY: Oxford University Press.

Cavanagh, J. O., Carson, A. J., Sharpe, M., & Lawrie, S. M. (2003). Psychological autopsy studies of suicide: A systematic review. *Psychological Medicine, 33*(3), 395–405. doi:10.1017/S0033291702006943

Center for Substance Abuse Treatment. (1998). *Substance abuse among older adults* (Treatment Improvement Protocol [TIP] Series, No. 26. HHS Publication No. [SMA] 12-3918). Rockville, MD: Substance Abuse and Mental Health Services Administration.

Center for Substance Abuse Treatment. (2004a). *Clinical guidelines for the use of Buprenorphine in the treatment of opioid addiction* (Treatment Improvement Protocol [TIP] Series 40. DHHS Publication No. [SMA] 04–3939). Rockville, MD: Substance Abuse and Mental Health Services Administration.

Center for Substance Abuse Treatment. (2004b). *Substance abuse treatment and family therapy* (Treatment Improvement Protocol [TIP] Series, No. 39. HHS Publication No. [SMA] 15-4219). Rockville, MD: Substance Abuse and Mental Health Services Administration.

Center for Substance Abuse Treatment. (2005a). *Substance abuse treatment for adults in the criminal justice system* (Treatment Improvement Protocol [TIP] Series 44. HHS Publication No. [SMA] 13-4056). Rockville, MD: Substance Abuse and Mental Health Services Administration.

Center for Substance Abuse Treatment. (2005b). *Substance abuse relapse prevention for older adults: A group treatment approach* (DHHS Publication No. [SMA] 05-4053). Rockville, MD: Substance Abuse and Mental Health Services Administration.

Center for Substance Abuse Treatment. (2006a). *Substance abuse: Administrative issues in outpatient treatment* (Treatment Improvement Protocol [TIP] Series 46. DHHS Publication No. [SMA] 06-4151). Rockville, MD: Substance Abuse and Mental Health Services Administration.

Center for Substance Abuse Treatment. (2006b). *Substance abuse: Clinical issues in intensive outpatient treatment* (Treatment Improvement Protocol [TIP] Series 47. DHHS Publication No. [SMA] 06-4182). Rockville, MD: Substance Abuse and Mental Health Services Administration.

Center for Substance Abuse Treatment. (2006c). *Addiction counseling competencies: The knowledge, skills, and attitudes of professional practice* (Technical Assistance Publication [TAP] Series 21. HHS Publication No. [SMA] 08-4171). Rockville, MD: Substance Abuse and Mental Health Services Administration.

Center for Substance Abuse Treatment. (2007). *Competencies for substance abuse treatment clinical supervisors* (Technical Assistance Publication [TAP] Series 21-A. HHS Publication No. [SMA] 12-4243). Rockville, MD: Substance Abuse and Mental Health Services Administration.

Center for Substance Abuse Treatment. (2009a). *Addressing suicidal thoughts and behaviors in substance abuse treatment* (Treatment Improvement Protocol [TIP] Series, No. 50. HHS Publication No. [SMA] 15-4381). Rockville, MD: Substance Abuse and Mental Health Services Administration.

Center for Substance Abuse Treatment. (2009b). *Clinical supervision and professional development of the substance abuse counselor* (Treatment Improvement Protocol [TIP] Series 52. DHHS Publication No. [SMA] 09-4435). Rockville, MD: Substance Abuse and Mental Health Services Administration.

Chambless, D. L., & Hollon, S. (1998). Defining empirically supported therapies. *Journal of Consulting and Clinical Psychology, 66,* 7–18.

Charles, V., & Weaver, T. (2010). A qualitative study of illicit and non-prescribed drug use amongst people with psychotic disorders. *Journal of Mental Health, 19*(1), 99–106. doi:10.3109/09638230802523039

Chen, C. K., Lin, S. K., Sham, P. C., Ball, D., Loh, el-W., & Murray, R. M. (2005). Morbid risk for psychiatric disorder among the relatives of methamphetamine users with and without psychosis. *American Journal of Medical Genetics Part B, 136B*(1), 87–91.

Chronister, J., Chou, C., & Chan, F. (2016). The roles and functions of professional counselors. In I. Marini & M. A. Stebnicki (Eds.), *The professional counselor's desk reference* (2nd ed., pp. 9–15). New York, NY: Springer.

Chung, T., & Martin, C. S. (2001). Classification and course of alcohol problems among adolescents in addiction treatment programs. *Alcoholism: Clinical and Experimental Research, 25*(12), 1734–1742. doi:10.1097/00000374-200112000-00008

Chung, T., Martin, C. S., Winters, K. C., Cornelius, J. R., & Langenbucher, J. W. (2004). Limitations in the assessment of *DSM-IV* cannabis tolerance as an indicator of dependence in adolescents. *Experimental and Clinical Psychopharmacology, 12*(2), 136–146. doi:10.1037/1064-1297.12.2.136

Clemmey, P., Payne, L., & Fishman, M. (2004). Clinical characteristics and treatment outcomes of adolescent heroin users. *Journal of Psychoactive Drugs, 36*(1), 85–94. doi:10.1080/02791072.2004.10399726

Cloos, J. M. (2010a). Benzodiazepines and addiction: Myths and realities (Part 1). *Psychiatric Times, XXVII*(7), 26–29.

Cloos, J. M. (2010b). Benzodiazepines and addiction: Long-term use and withdrawal (Part 2). *Psychiatric Times, XXVII*(8), 34–36.

Coffey, S. F., Saladin, M. E., Drobes, D. J., Brady, K. T., Dansky, B. S., & Kilpatrick, D. G. (2002). Trauma and substance cue reactivity in individuals with comorbid posttraumatic stress disorder and cocaine or alcohol dependence. *Drug and Alcohol Dependence, 65,* 115–127.

Coker, K. L., Stefanovics, E., & Rosenheck, R. (2016). Correlates of improvement in substance abuse among dually diagnosed veterans with post-traumatic stress disorder in specialized intensive VA treatment. *Psychological Trauma: Theory, Research, Practice, and Policy, 8*(1), 41–48. doi:10.1037/tra0000061

Comtois, K. A., Russo, J. E., Roy-Byrne, P., & Ries, R. K. (2004). Clinicians' assessments of bipolar disorder and substance abuse as predictors of suicidal behavior in acutely hospitalized psychiatric patients. *Biological Psychiatry, 56,* 757–763.

Connors, G. J., Maisto, S. A., & Donovan, D. M. (1996). Conceptualizations of relapse: A summary of psychological and psychobiological models. *Addiction, 91,* S5–S13.

Cook, C. C. H. (2004). Addiction and spirituality. *Addiction, 99,* 539–551.

Cook, J., Spring, B., McChargue, D., & Doran, N. (2010). Effects of anhedonia on days to relapse among smokers with a history of depression: A brief report. *Nicotine & Tobacco Research, 12,* 978–982. doi:10.1093/ntr/ntq118

Cooper, L. (2012). Combined motivational interviewing and cognitive-behavioral therapy with older adult drug and alcohol abusers. *Health & Social Work, 37*(3), 173–179. doi:10.1093/hsw/hls023

Corey, G. (2009). *Theory and practice of counseling and psychotherapy* (8th ed.). Belmont, CA: Brooks/Cole.

Cottler L. B., Price, R. K., Compton, W. M., & Mager, D. (1995). Subtypes of adult antisocial behavior among drug abusers. *Journal of Mental and Nervous Diseases, 3,* 54–161.

Council for Accreditation of Counseling and Related Educational Programs. (2015). *2016 CACREP Standards.* Available from http://www.cacrep.org/wp-content/uploads/2012/10/2016-CACREP-Standards.pdf

Cowlishaw, S., & Hakes, J. K. (2015). Pathological and problem gambling in substance use treatment: Results from the National Epidemiologic Survey on Alcohol and Related Conditions (NESARC). *American Journal on Addictions, 24*(5), 467–474. doi:10.1111/ajad.12242

Cox, D., & D'Oyley, H. (2011). Cognitive-behavioral therapy with older adults. *BCMJ, 53*(7), 348–352.

Craig, R. J. (2004). *Counseling the alcohol and drug dependent client.* New York, NY: Norton.

Critchley, H. D., Wiens, S., Rotshtein, P., Öhman, A., & Dolan, R. J. (2004). Neural systems supporting interoceptive awareness. *Nature Neuroscience, 7*(2), 189–195.

Crocker, A. G., Mueser, K. T., Clark, R. E., McHugo, G. J., Ackerson, T., & Alterman, A. I. (2005). Antisocial personality, psychopathy and violence in persons with dual disorders: A longitudinal analysis. *Criminal Justice and Behavior, 32,* 452–476.

Culbreth, J. R., & Borders, L. D. (1999). Perceptions of the supervisory relationship: Recovering and nonrecovering substance abuse counselors. *Journal of Counseling & Development, 77*(3), 330–338. doi:10.1002/j.1556-6676.1999.tb02456.x

Culliford, L. (2002). Spirituality and clinical care: Spiritual values and skills are increasingly recognised as necessary aspects of clinical care. *British Medical Journal, 325,* 1434–1435.

Cummings, J. A., Ballantyne, E. C., & Scallion, L. M. (2015). Essential processes for cognitive behavioral clinical supervision: Agenda setting, problem-solving, and formative feedback. *Psychotherapy, 52*(2), 158–163. doi:10.1037/a0038712

Cummings, S. M., Cooper, R. L., & Cassie, K. M. (2009). Motivational interviewing to affect behavioral change in older adults with chronic and acute illnesses. *Research on Social Work Practice, 19,* 195–204.

Curry, S., Marlatt, G. A., & Gordon, J. R. (1987). Abstinence Violation Effect: Validation of an attributional construct with smoking cessation. *Journal of Consulting and Clinical Psychology, 55*(2), 145–149.

Curtis, S. L., & Eby, L. T. (2010). Recovery at work: The relationship between social anxiety and commitment among substance abuse counselors. *Journal of Substance Abuse Treatment, 39*(3), 248–254.

Dagher, A., Owen, A. M., Boecker, H., & Brooks, D. J. (1999). Mapping the network for planning: A correlational PET activation study with the Tower of London task. *Brain: A Journal of Neurology, 122*(10), 1973–1987. doi:10.1093/brain/122.10.1973

Dalton, E. J., Cate-Carter, T. D., Mundo, E., Parikh, S. V., & Kennedy, J. L. (2003). Suicide risk in bipolar patients: The role of co-morbid substance use disorders. *Bipolar Disorders, 5,* 58–61.

Darke, S., & Ross, J. (2002). Suicide among heroin users: Rates, risk factors and methods. *Addiction, 97*(11), 1383–1394. doi:10.1046/j.1360-0443.2002.00214.x

Darke, S., Williamson, A., Ross, J., & Teeson, M. (2005). Attempted suicide among heroin users: 12-month outcomes from the Australian Treatment Outcome Study (ATOS). *Drug & Alcohol Dependence, 78*(2), 177–186.

Daughters, S. B., Lejuez, C. W., Bornovalova, M. A., Kahler, C., Strong, D., & Brown, R. (2005). Distress tolerance as a predictor of early treatment dropout in a residential substance abuse treatment facility. *Journal of Abnormal Psychology, 114,* 729–734.

David, E. (2009). Internalized oppression, psychopathology, and cognitive behavioral therapy among historically oppressed groups. *Journal of Psychological Practice, 15,* 71–103.

Davidson, K. M. (1995). Diagnosis of depression in alcohol dependence: Changes in prevalence with drinking status. *British Journal of Psychiatry, 166*(2), 199–204. doi:10.1192/bjp.166.2.199

Deas, D., Gray, K., & Upadhyaya, H. (2008). Evidence-based treatments for adolescent substance use disorders. In R. G. Steele, T. D. Elkin, & M. C. Roberts (Eds.), *Handbook of evidence-based therapies for children and adolescents: Bridging science and practice* (pp. 429–444). New York, NY: Springer. doi:10.1007/978-0-387-73691-4_24

De Leon, G. (1997). *Community as method: Therapeutic communities for special populations and special settings.* Westport, CT: Praeger/Greenwood.

De Leon, G. (2000). *The therapeutic community: Theory, model, and method.* New York, NY: Springer.

De Leon, G. (2015). Therapeutic communities. In M. Galanter, H. D. Kleber, & K. T. Brady (Eds.), *The American Psychiatric Publishing textbook of substance abuse treatment* (5th ed., pp. 511–530). Arlington, VA: American Psychiatric Publishing.

Denering, L. L., & Spear, S. E. (2012). Routine use of screening and brief intervention for college students in a university counseling center. *Journal of Psychoactive Drugs, 44*(4), 318–324.

Department of Veterans Affairs, Department of Defense. (2015). *VA/DoD clinical practice guideline for the management of substance use disorders.* Washington, DC: Author.

de Roten, Y., Zimmermann, G., Ortega, D., & Despland, J. (2013). Meta-analysis of the effects of MI training on clinicians' behavior. *Journal of Substance Abuse Treatment, 45*(2), 155–162. doi:10.1016/j.jsat.2013.02.006

DeVane, C. L. (2004). Principles of pharmacokinetics and pharmacodynamics. In A. F. Schatzberg & C. B. Nemeroff (Eds.), *Textbook of psychopharmacology* (3rd ed.). Washington, DC: American Psychiatric Publishing.

Dhossche, D. M., Meloukheia, A. M., & Chakravorty, S. (2000). The association of suicide attempts and comorbid depression and substance abuse in psychiatric consultation patients. *General Hospital Psychiatry, 22*(4), 281–288. doi:10.1016/S0163-8343(00)00085-2

Diallo, A. (2013). Clients' willingness to incorporate religion or spirituality in counseling: A brief report. *Rehabilitation Counseling Bulletin, 56*(2), 120–122. doi:10.1177/0034355212439425

DiClemente, C. C. (1993). Alcoholics Anonymous and the structure of change. In B. S. McCrady & W. R. Miller (Eds.), *Research on Alcoholics Anonymous: Opportunities and alternatives* (pp. 79–97). New Brunswick, NJ: Rutgers Center of Alcohol Studies.

DiClemente, C., & Prochaska, J. (1998). Toward a comprehensive, transtheoretical model of change: Stages of change and addictive behaviors. In W. Miller & N. Heather (Eds.), *Treating addictive behaviours* (2nd ed., pp. 3–24). New York, NY: Plenum Press.

DiGiuseppe, R., & McInerney, J. (1990). Patterns of addiction: A rational-emotive perspective. *Journal of Cognitive Psychotherapy: An International Quarterly, 4,* 121–134.

Dimeff, L. A., & Marlatt, G. A. (1998). Preventing relapse and maintaining change in addictive behaviors. *Clinical Psychological Science Practice, 5,* 513–525.

Donovan, D. M. (2003). Relapse prevention in substance abuse treatment. In J. L. Sorensen, R. A. Rawson, J. Guydish, & J. E. Zweben (Eds.), *Drug abuse treatment through collaboration: Practice and research partnerships that work* (pp. 121–137). Washington, DC: American Psychological Association. doi:10.1037/10491-008

Donovan, D. M. (2013). Evidence-based assessment: Strategies and measures in addictive behaviors. In B. S. McCrady & E. E. Epstein (Eds.), *Addictions: A comprehensive guidebook* (2nd ed., pp. 311–351). New York, NY: Oxford University Press.

Doweiko, H. E. (2015). *Concepts of chemical dependency* (9th ed.). Stamford, CT: Cengage.

Downey, P. M., & Roman, J. K. (2010). *A Bayesian meta-analysis of drug court cost-effectiveness.* Washington, DC: The Urban Institute.

Doyle, K., Linton, J. M., Morgan, O. J., & Stefanelli, M. (2008). You're not one of us: The age-old question of counselor recovery status. In L. E. Tyson, J. R. Culbreth, & J. A. Harrington (Eds.), *Critical incidents in clinical supervision: Addictions, community, and school counseling* (pp. 3–10). Alexandria, VA: American Counseling Association.

Drake, R. E., Mueser, K. T., Brunette, M. F., & McHugo, G. J. (2004). A review of treatments for people with severe mental illnesses and co-occurring substance use disorders. *Psychiatric Rehabilitation Journal, 27*(4), 360–374. doi:10.2975/27.2004.360.374

Dreissen, M., Schulte, S., Luedecke, C., Schaefer, I., Sutmann, F., Ohlmeier, M., . . . TRAUMAB-Study Group. (2008). Trauma and PTSD in patients with alcohol, drug, or dual dependence: A multi-center study. *Alcoholism: Clinical and Experimental Research, 32*(3), 481–488.

Duncan, D. F., Nicholson, T., White, J. B., Bradley, D. B., & Bonaguro, J. (2010). The baby boomer effect: Changing patterns of substance abuse among adults ages 55 and older. *Journal of Aging & Social Policy, 22,* 237–248. http://dx.doi.org/10.1080/08959420.2010.485511

Dunne, E. M., Burrell, L. E., Diggins, A. D., Whitehead, N. E., & Latimer, W. W. (2015). Increased risk for substance use and health-related problems among homeless veterans. *American Journal on Addictions, 24*(7), 676–680.

du Plock, S. (2007). "A Relational Approach to Supervision": Some reflections on supervision from an existential-phenomenological perspective. *Existential Analysis, 18*(1), 31–38.

du Plock, S. (2009). An existential-phenomenological inquiry into the meaning of clinical supervision: What do we mean when we talk about existential-phenomenological supervision? *Existential Analysis, 20*(2), 299–318.

DuPont, R. L., & Selavka, C. M. (2015). Testing to identify recent drug use. In M. Galanter, H. D. Kleber, & K. T. Brady (Eds.), *The American Psychiatric Publishing textbook of substance abuse treatment* (5th ed., pp. 741–755). Arlington, VA: American Psychiatric Publishing.

Eamon, M. K. (2008). *Empowering vulnerable populations: Cognitive behavioral interventions.* Chicago, IL: Lyceum Books.

el-Guebaly, N., & Violato, C. (2011). The international certification of addiction medicine: Validating clinical knowledge across borders. *Substance Abuse, 32*(2), 77–83. doi:10.1080/08897077.2011.555697

Ellis, A. (1980). Discomfort anxiety: A new cognitive-behavioral construct (Part II). *Rational Living, 15*(1), 25–30.

Ellis, A. (1982). The treatment of alcohol and drug abuse: A rational-emotive approach. *Rational Living, 17*(2), 15–24.

Ellis, A. (1985). *Overcoming resistance: Rational-emotive therapy with difficult clients.* New York, NY: Springer.

Ellis, A. (1999). *Rational emotive behavior therapy diminishes much of the human ego.* New York, NY: Albert Ellis Institute.

Ellis, A., McInerney, J., DiGiuseppe, R., & Yeager, R. J. (1988). *Rational-emotive therapy with alcoholics and substance abusers.* Boston, MA: Allyn & Bacon.

Essau, C. A. (2011). Comorbidity of substance use disorders among community-based and high-risk adolescents. *Psychiatry Research, 185*(1–2), 176–184. doi:10.1016/j.psychres.2010.04.033

Falender, C. A., & Shafranske, E. P. (2008). *Casebook for clinical supervision: A competency-based approach.* Washington, DC: American Psychological Association.

Fama, R., & Sullivan, E. V. (2014). Alcohol. In D. N. Allen & S. P. Woods (Eds.), *Neuropsychological aspects of substance use disorders* (pp. 103–133). New York, NY: Oxford University Press.

Farabee, D., Prendergast, M., & Anglin, M. D. (1998). The effectiveness of coerced treatment for drug-abusing offenders. *Federal Probation, 62,* 3–10.

Farber, E. W. (2010). Humanistic-existential psychotherapy competencies and the supervisory process. *Psychotherapy Theory, Research, Practice, and Training, 47*(1), 28–34.

Fatséas, M., Denis, C., Lavie, E., & Auriacombe, M. (2010). Relationship between anxiety disorders and opiate dependence-A systematic review of the literature: Implications for diagnosis and treatment. *Journal of Substance Abuse Treatment, 38*(3), 220–230. doi:10.1016/j.jsat.2009.12.003

Fein, G., Torres, J., Price, L. J., & Sclafani, V. (2006). Cognitive performance in long-term abstinent alcoholic individuals. *Alcoholism: Clinical & Experimental Research, 30*(9), 1538–1544.

Fernandez-Serrano, M. J., Lozano, O., Perez-Garcia, M., Verdejo-Garcia, A. (2010). Impact of severity of drug use on discrete emotions recognition in polysubstance abusers. *Drug & Alcohol Dependence, 109*(1–3), 57–64. doi:10.1016/j.drugalcdep.2009.12.007

Finigan, M., Carey, S. M., & Cox, A. (2007). *The impact of a mature drug court over 10 years of operation: Recidivism and costs.* Portland, OR: NPC Research. Available at http://www.npcresearch.com

First, M. B. (2014). *DSM-5 handbook of differential diagnosis.* Washington, DC: American Psychiatric Publishing.

Fischer, J. L., Pidcock, B. W., & Fletcher-Stephens, B. J. (2007). Family response to adolescence, youth, and alcohol. *Alcoholism Treatment Quarterly, 25,* 27–41.

Fisher, G. L., & Harrison, T. C. (2009). *Substance abuse: Information for school counselors, social workers, therapists, and counselors* (4th ed.). New York, NY: Pearson.

Fishman, M. (2008). Treatment planning, matching, and placement for adolescents with substance use disorders. In Y. Kaminer & O. G. Bukstein (Eds.), *Adolescent substance abuse: Psychiatric comorbidity and high-risk behaviors* (pp. 87–110). New York, NY: Routledge/Taylor & Francis Group.

Fishman, M. (2011). Placement criteria and treatment planning for adolescents with substance use disorders. In Y. Kaminer & K. C. Winters (Eds.), *Clinical manual of adolescent substance abuse treatment* (pp. 113–141). Arlington, VA: American Psychiatric Publishing.

Fitzgerald, B. (2005). An existential view of adolescent development. *Adolescence, 40*(160), 793–799.

Flynn, P., Joe, G., Broome, K., Simpson, D., & Brown, B. (2003). Looking back on cocaine dependence: Reasons for recovery. *American Journal on Addictions, 12,* 398–411.

Folkman, S., & Moskowitz, J. T. (2004). Coping: Pitfalls and promise. *Annual Review of Psychology, 55,* 745–774. doi:10.1146/annurev.psych.55.090902.141456

Folstein, M. F., Folstein, S. E., & McHugh, P. R. (1975). "Mini-mental state." A practical method for grading the cognitive state of patients for the clinician. *Journal of Psychiatric Research, 12*(3), 189–198.

Fontana, A., Rosenheck, R., & Desai, R. (2012). Comparison of treatment outcomes for veterans with posttraumatic stress disorder with and without comorbid substance use/dependence. *Journal of Psychiatric Research, 46*(8), 1008–1014. doi:10.1016/j.jpsychires.2012.05.004

Forbush, K. T., Shaw, M., Graeber, M. A., Hovick, L., Meyer, V. J., Moser, D. J., . . . Black, D. W. (2008). Neuropsychological characteristics and personality traits in pathological gambling. *CNS Spectrums, 13*(4), 306–315.

Forcehimes, A. A. (2004). De Profundis: Spiritual transformations in Alcoholics Anonymous. *Journal of Clinical Psychology: In Session, 60,* 503–517.

Ford, G. G. (1996). An existential model for promoting life change: Confronting the disease concept. *Journal of Substance Abuse Treatment, 13*(2), 151–158.

Ford, J. D., Gelernter, J., DeVoe, J. S., Zhang, W., Weiss, R. D., Brady, K., . . . Kranzler, H. R. (2009). Association of psychiatric and substance use disorder comorbidity with cocaine dependence severity and treatment utilization in cocaine-dependent individuals. *Drug and Alcohol Dependence, 99,* 193–203.

Foulds, J. A., Adamson, S. J., Boden, J. M., Williman, J. A., & Mulder, R. T. (2015). Depression in patients with alcohol use disorders: Systematic review and meta-analysis of outcomes for independent and substance-induced disorders. *Journal of Affective Disorders, 18,* 547–559. doi:10.1016/j.jad.2015.06.024

Foulds, J. A., Sellman, J. D., Adamson, S. J., Boden, J. M., Mulder, R. T., & Joyce, P. R. (2015). Depression outcome in alcohol dependent patients: An evaluation of the role of independent and substance-induced depression and other predictors. *Journal of Affective Disorders, 174,* 503–510. doi:10.1016/j.jad.2014.11.052

Fragoso, J. M., & Kashubeck, S. (2000). Machismo, gender role conflict, and mental health in Mexican American men. *Psychology of Men & Masculinity, 1*(2), 87–97. doi:10.1037/1524-9220.1.2.87

Frankl, V. E. (1964). *Man's search for meaning.* London, England: Hodder & Stoughton.

Frankl, V. (1967). *Psychotherapy and existentialism.* New York, NY: Simon & Schuster.

Franklin, T. R., Acton, P. D., Maldjian, J. A., Gray, J. D., Croft, J. R., Dackis, C. A., . . . Childress, A. R. (2002). Decreased gray matter concentration in the insular, orbitofrontal, cingulate, and temporal cortices of cocaine patients. *Biological Psychiatry, 51*(2), 134–142. doi:10.1016/S0006-3223(01)01269-0

Frone, M. R. (2009). Does a permissive workplace substance use climate affect employees who do not use alcohol and drugs at work? A U.S. national study. *Psychology of Addictive Behaviors, 23*(2), 386–390. http://doi.org/10.1037/a0015965

Gale, A., & Austin, B. (2003). Professionalism's challenges to professional counselors' collective identity. *Journal of Counseling & Development, 81*(1), 3–10.

Gardner, E. L., & Ashby, C. J. (2000). Heterogeneity of the mesotelencephalic dopamine fibers: Physiology and pharmacology. *Neuroscience and Biobehavioral Reviews, 24*(1), 115–118. doi:10.1016/S0149-7634(99)00048-2

Gearhardt, A. N., Corbin, W. R., & Brownell, K. D. (2009). Preliminary validation of the Yale Food Addiction Scale. *Appetite, 52*(2), 430–436.

Geppert, C. A. (2013). Legal and ethical issues. In B. S. McCrady & E. E. Epstein (Eds.), *Addictions: A comprehensive guidebook* (2nd ed., pp. 625–640). New York, NY: Oxford University Press.

Geppert, C. M. A., & Roberts, L. W. (2008). Ethical foundations for substance abuse treatment. In C. M. A. Geppert & L. W. Roberts (Eds.), *The book of ethics: Expert guidance for professionals who treat addiction* (pp. 1–28). Center City, MN: Hazelden.

Ghitza, U. E., Gore-Langton, R. E., Lindblad, R., Shide, D., Subramaniam, G., & Tai, B. (2013). Common data elements for substance use disorders in electronic health records: The NIDA Clinical Trials Network experience. *Addiction, 108*(1), 3–8. doi:10.1111/j.1360-0443.2012.03876.x

Ghitza, U. E., Gore-Langton, R. E., Lindblad, R., & Tai, B. (2015). NIDA Clinical Trials Network Common Data Elements Initiative: Advancing big-data addictive-disorders research. *Frontiers in Psychiatry, 6,* 33. http://doi.org/10.3389/fpsyt.2015.00033

Gilbody, S., Richards, D., Brealey, S., & Hweitt, C. (2007). Screening for depression in medical settings with the Patient Health Questionnaire (PHQ): A diagnostic meta-analysis. *Journal of General Internal Medicine, 22*(11), 1596–1602.

Giugliano, J. R. (2013). Sex addiction as a mental health diagnosis: Coming together or coming apart? *Sexologies, 22,* e77–e80.

Gladding, S. T. (2015). *Family therapy: History, theory, and practice* (6th ed.). New York, NY: Pearson.

Glasner-Edwards, S., Marinelli-Casey, P., Hillhouse, M., Ang, A., Mooney, L. J., & Rawson R. (2009). Depression among methamphetamine users: Association with outcomes from the Methamphetamine Treatment Project at 3-year follow-up. *Journal of Nervous and Mental Disorders, 197,* 225–231.

Goldman, M. S. (1995). Recovery of cognitive functioning in alcoholics—The relationship to treatment. *Alcohol Health & Research World, 19*(2), 148–154.

Goldstein, R. B., Dawson, D. A., & Grant, B. F. (2010). Antisocial behavioral syndromes in adulthood and alcohol use disorder treatment over three-year follow-up: Results from wave 2 of the national epidemiologic survey on alcohol and related conditions. *Journal of the American Psychiatric Nurses Association, 16*(4), 212–226. doi:10.1177/1078390310375846

Goldstein, R. Z., & Volkow, N. D. (2002). Drug addiction and its underlying neurobiological basis: Neuroimaging evidence for the involvement of the frontal cortex. *American Journal of Psychiatry, 159*(10), 1642–1652.

Goodwin, D. W. (2000). *Alcoholism: The facts* (3rd ed.). Oxford, England: Oxford University Press.

Gorelick, D. A. (2013). Pharmacokinetic strategies for treatment of drug overdose and addiction. *Future Medicinal Chemistry, 4*(2), 227–243.

Gorelick, D. A., & Wilkins, J. N. (2006). Bromocriptine treatment for cocaine addiction: Association with plasma prolactin levels. *Drug & Alcohol Dependence, 81*(2), 189–195.

Gorski, T. T. (1989). Passages through recovery: An action plan for preventing relapse. Center City, MN: Hazelden.

Gorski, T. T. (1990). The CENAPS Model of Relapse Prevention: Basic principles and procedures. *Journal of Psychoactive Drugs, 22*(2), 125–133. doi:10.1080/02791072.1990.10472538

Gorski, T. T., & Miller, M. (1986). *Staying sober: A guide for relapse prevention.* Independence, MO: Herald House/Independence Press.

Gossop, M., Harris, J., Best, D., Man, L., Manning, V., Marshall, J., & Strang, J. (2003). Is attendance at Alcoholics Anonymous meetings after inpatient treatment related to improved outcomes? A 6-month follow-up study. *Alcohol and Alcoholism, 38,* 421–426.

Gossop, M., Stewart, D., Browne, N., & Marsden, J. (2002). Factors associated with abstinence, lapse or relapse to heroin use after residential treatment: Protective effect of coping responses. *Addiction, 97*(10), 1259–1267. doi:10.1046/j.1360-0443.2002.00227.x

Gossop, M., Stewart, D., & Marsden, J. (2007). Attendance at Narcotics Anonymous and Alcoholics Anonymous meetings, frequency of attendance and substance use outcomes after residential treatment for drug dependence: A 5-year follow-up study. *Addiction, 103,* 119–125.

Gottfredson, D. C., Kearley, B. W., Najaka, S. S., & Rocha, C. M. (2005). The Baltimore City Drug Treatment Court: 3-year outcome study. *Evaluation Review, 29,* 42–64.

Gottfredson, D. C., Najaka, S. S., Kearley, B. W., & Rocha, C. M. (2006). Long-term effects of participation in the Baltimore City drug treatment court: Results from an experimental study. *Journal of Experimental Criminology, 2,* 67–98.

Grant, B. F., Chou, S. P., Goldstein, R. B., Huang, B., Stinson, F. S., Saha, T. D., . . . Ruan, W. J. (2008). Prevalence, correlates, disability, and comorbidity of *DSM-IV* Borderline Personality Disorder: Results from the Wave 2 National Epidemiologic Survey on Alcohol and Related Conditions. *Journal of Clinical Psychiatry, 69*(4), 533–545.

Grant, B. F., Goldstein, R. B., Saha, T. D., Chou, S. P., Jung, J., Zhang, H., . . . Hasin, D. S. (2015). Epidemiology of *DSM-5* alcohol use disorder: Results from the National Epidemiologic Survey on Alcohol and Related Conditions III. *JAMA Psychiatry, 72*(8), 757–766. doi:10.1001/jamapsychiatry.2015.0584

Grant, B. F., Saha, T. D., Ruan, J., Goldstein, R. B., Chou, P., Jung, J., . . . Hasin, D. S. (2016). Epidemiology of *DSM-5* drug use disorder: Results from the National Epidemiologic Survey on Alcohol and Related Conditions III. *JAMA Psychiatry, 73*(1), 39–47. doi:10.1001/jamapsychiatry.2015.2132

Grant, I., Gonzalez, R., Carey, C. L., Natarajan, L., & Wolfson, T. (2003). Non-acute (residual) neurocognitive effects of cannabis use: A meta-analytic study. *Journal of the International Neuropsychological Society, 9*(5), 679–689. doi:http://dx.doi.org/10.1017/S1355617703950016

Greaves, G. B. (1974). Toward an existential theory of drug dependence. *Journal of Nervous and Mental Disease, 159,* 263–274.

Greaves, G. B. (1980). An existential theory of drug dependence. In D. Lettieri, M. Sayers, & H. Pearson (Eds.), *Theories on drug abuse: Selected contemporary perspectives* (pp. 24–28) [National Institute on Drug Abuse Research Monograph No. 30]. Washington, DC: U.S. Government Printing Office.

Green, K. T., Calhoun, P. S., Dennis, M. F., & Beckham, J. C. (2010). Exploration of the resilience construct in posttraumatic stress disorder sensitivity and functional correlates in military combat veterans who have served since September 11, 2001. *Journal of Clinical Psychiatry, 71*(7), 823–830. doi:10.4088/JCP.09m05780blu

Greenfield, B. L., & Tonigan, J. S. (2013). The general Alcoholics Anonymous tools of recovery: The adoption of 12-Step practices and beliefs. *Psychology of Addictive Behaviors, 27*(3), 553–561. http://doi.org/10.1037/a0029268

Griner, D., & Smith, T. B. (2006). Culturally adapted mental health intervention: A meta-analytic review. *Psychotherapy: Theory, Research, Practice, Training, 43,* 531–548. doi:10.1037/0033-3204.43.4.531

Gwaltney, C. J., Shiffman, S., Paty, J. A., Liu, K. S., Kassel, J. D., Gnys, M., & Hickcox, M. (2002). Using self-efficacy judgments to predict characteristics of lapses to smoking. *Journal of Consulting and Clinical Psychology, 70*(5), 1140–1149. doi:10.1037/0022-006X.70.5.1140

Hall, P. (2014). Sex addiction—An extraordinarily contentious problem. *Sexual and Relationship Therapy, 29*(1), 68–75. http://dx.doi.org/10.1080/14681994.2013.861898

Han, B., Gfroerer, J. C., Colliver, J. D., & Penne, M. A. (2009). Substance use disorder among older adults in the United States in 2020. *Addiction, 104*(1), 88–96. doi:10.1111/j.1360-0443.2008.02411.x

Harris, E. C., & Barraclough, B. (1997). Suicide as an outcome for mental disorders. A meta-analysis. *British Journal of Psychiatry, 170,* 205–228.

Harris, D., & Batki, S. L. (2000). Stimulant psychosis: Symptom profile and acute clinical course. *American Journal on Addictions, 9*(1), 28–37.

Hart, K. E., & Huggett, C. (2005). Narcissism: A barrier to personal acceptance of the spiritual aspect of Alcoholics Anonymous. *Alcoholism Treatment Quarterly, 23,* 85–100. doi:10.1300/J020v23n04_06

Hartz, S. M., Pato, C. N., Medeiros, H., Cavazos-Rehg, P., Sobell, J. L., Genomic Psychiatry Cohort Consortium (GPCC), . . . Pato, M. T. (2014). Comorbidity of severe psychotic disorders with measures of substance use. *JAMA Psychiatry, 71*(3), 248–254. http://doi.org/10.1001/jamapsychiatry.2013.3726

Hasin, D. S., O'Brien, C. P., Auriacombe, M., Borges, G., Bucholz, K., Budney, A., . . . Grant, B. F. (2013). DSM-5 criteria for substance use disorders: Recommendations and rationale. *American Journal of Psychiatry, 170*(8), 834–851. http://doi.org/10.1176/appi.ajp.2013.12060782

Havassy, B. E., Hall, S. M., & Wasserman, D. A. (1991). Social support and relapse: Commonalities among alcoholics, opiate users, and cigarette smokers. *Addictive Behaviors, 16,* 235–246.

Havassy, B., Wasserman, D., & Hall, S. (1993). Relapse to cocaine use: Conceptual issues. In F. M. Tims & C. G. Leukefeld (Eds.), *Cocaine treatment: Research & clinical perspectives* [Research Monograph #135]. Rockville, MD: National Institute on Drug Abuse. Retrieved from https://archives.drugabuse.gov/pdf/monographs/135.pdf

Hawton, K., Sutton, L., Haw, C., Sinclair, J., & Harriss, L. (2005). Suicide and attempted suicide in bipolar disorder: A systematic review of risk factors. *Journal of Clinical Psychiatry, 66*(6), 693–704. doi:10.4088/JCP.v66n0604

Haynes, R., Corey, G., & Moulton, P. (2003). *Clinical supervision in the helping professions: A practical guide.* Pacific Grove, CA: Brooks/Cole.

Hays, D. (2013). *Assessment in counseling* (5th ed.). Alexandria, VA: American Counseling Association.

Heinz, A., Beck, A., Grüsser, S. M., Grace, A. A., & Wrase, J. (2009). Identifying the neural circuitry of alcohol craving and relapse vulnerability. *Addiction Biology, 14*(1), 108–118. http://doi.org/10.1111/j.1369-1600.2008.00136.x

Helseth, V., Samet, S., Johnsen, J., Bramness, J. G., & Waal, H. (2013). Independent or substance-induced disorders? An investigation of comorbidity in an acute psychiatric unit. *Journal of Dual Diagnosis, 9*(1), 78–86.

Henriksen, R. C., Nelson, J., & Watts, R. E. (2010). Specialty training in counselor education programs: An exploratory study. *Journal of Professional Counseling: Practice, Theory, and Research, 38*(1), 39–51.

Hesselbrock, M. N. (1986). Childhood behavior problems and adult antisocial personality disorder in alcoholism. In R. E. Meyer (Ed.), *Psychopathology and addictive disorders* (pp. 78–94). New York, NY: Guilford Press.

Hester, R., Dixon, V., & Garavan, H. (2006). A consistent attentional bias for drug-related material in active cocaine users across word and picture versions of the emotional Stroop task. *Drug & Alcohol Dependence, 81*(3), 251–257. doi:10.1016/j.drugalcdep.2005.07.002

Hester, R. K., & Squires, D. D. (2004). Outcome research: Alcohol research. In M. Galanter & H. D. Kleber (Eds.), *Textbook of substance abuse treatment* (3rd ed., pp 129–136). Washington, DC: American Psychiatric Press.

Hidalgo-Mazzei, D., Walsh, E., Rosenstein, L., & Zimmerman, M. (2015). Comorbid bipolar disorder and borderline personality disorder and substance use disorder. *Journal of Nervous and Mental Disease, 203*(1), 54–57. doi:10.1097/NMD.0000000000000235

Hides, L., Dawe, S., McKetin, R., Kavanagh, D. J., Young, R. M., Teesson, M., & Saunders, J. B. (2015). Primary and substance-induced psychotic disorders in methamphetamine users. *Psychiatry Research, 226*(1), 91–96. doi:10.1016/j.psychres.2014.11.077

Higgins, S. T., Heil, S. H., & Lussier, J. P. (2004). Clinical implications of reinforcement as a determinant of substance use disorders. *Annual Review of Psychology, 55,* 431–461. doi:10.1146/annurev.psych.55 .090902.142033

Hollar, D., & Moore, D. (2004). Relationship of substance use by students with disabilities to long-term educational, employment, and social outcomes. *Substance Use & Misuse, 39*(6), 931–962.

Holloway, E. (1995). *Clinical supervision: A systems approach.* Thousand Oaks, CA: Sage.

Holtz, J. L. (2010). *Applied clinical neuropsychology: An introduction.* New York, NY: Springer.

Hsu, S. H., Collins, S. E., & Marlatt, G. A. (2013). Examining psychometric properties of distress tolerance and its moderation of mindfulness-based relapse prevention effects on alcohol and other drug use outcomes. *Addictive Behaviors, 38*(3), 1852–1858. doi:10.1016/j.addbeh.2012.11.002

Huddleston, W., & Marlowe, D. B. (2011). *Painting the current picture: A national report on drug courts and other problem-solving court programs in the United States.* Alexandria, VA: National Drug Court Institute.

Hulka, L. M., Wagner, M., Preller, K. H., Jenni, D., Quednow, B. B. (2013). Blue-yellow vision color impairment and cognitive deficits in occasional and dependent stimulant users. *International Journal of Neuropsychopharmacology, 16*(3), 535–547. doi:10.1017/S1461145712000624

Humphreys, K., & Moos, R. (2001). Can encouraging substance abuse patients to participate in self-help groups reduce demand for health care: A quasi-experimental study. *Alcoholism: Clinical and Experimental Research, 25,* 711–716.

Humphreys, K., & Noke, J. M. (1997). The influence of post-treatment mutual help group participation on the friendship networks of substance abuse patients. *American Journal of Community Psychology, 25,* 1–16.

Humphreys, K., Wing, S., McCarty, B., Chappel, J., Gallant, L., Haberle, B., . . . Weiss, R. (2004). Self-help organizations for alcohol and drug problems: Toward evidence-based practice and policy. *Journal of Substance Abuse Treatment, 26,* 151–158.

Iarussi, M. M., Perjessy, C. C., & Reed, S. W. (2013). Addiction-specific CACREP standards in clinical mental health counseling programs: How are they met? *Journal of Addictions & Offender Counseling, 34*(2), 99–113.

Institute of Medicine. (1990). *Broadening the base of treatment for alcohol problems.* Washington, DC: National Academies Press.

Iudicello, J. E., Bolden, K., Griglak, S. R., & Woods, S. P. (2014). Methamphetamine. In D. N. Allen & S. P. Woods (Eds.), *Neuropsychological aspects of substance use disorders* (pp. 183–203). New York, NY: Oxford University Press.

Iudicello, J. E., Weber, E., Dawson, M., Grant, I., Weinborn, M., Woods, S. P., & HNRC Group (2011). Misremembering future intentions in methamphetamine dependent individuals. *Clinical Neuropsychologist, 25,* 269–286.

Ivey, A. E., Ivey, M. B., Zalaquett, C. P., & Quirk, K. (2012). *Essentials of interviewing: Counseling in a multicultural world.* Belmont, CA: Brooks/Cole.

Ivey, A. E., Ivey, M. B., & Zalaquett, C. P. (2014). *Intentional interviewing and counseling: Facilitating client development in a multicultural society.* Belmont, CA: Brooks/Cole.

Jacobsen, L. K., Southwick, S. M., & Kosten, T. R. (2001). Substance use disorders in patients with post-traumatic stress disorder: A review of the literature. *American Journal of Psychiatry, 158*(8), 1184–1190. doi:10.1176/appi.ajp.158.8.1184

Jensen, G. H. (2000). *Storytelling in Alcoholics Anonymous: A rhetorical analysis.* Carbondale, IL: Southern Illinois University Press.

Jensen, C. D., Cushing, C. C., Aylward, B. S., Craig, J. T., Sorell, D. M., & Steele, R. G. (2011). Effectiveness of motivational interviewing interventions for adolescent substance use behavior change: A meta-analytic review. *Journal of Consulting and Clinical Psychology, 79*(4), 433–440. doi:10.1037/a0023992

Johns, A. (2001). Psychiatric effects of cannabis. *British Journal of Psychiatry, 178,* 116–122. doi:10.1192/bjp.178.2.116

Johnson, B. (2001). *A better kind of high: How religious commitment reduces drug use among poor urban teens* [Report #2001-2]. Philadelphia, PA: University of Pennsylvania, Center for Research and Urban Civil Society.

Jones, T., Sells, J. N., & Rehfuss, M. (2009). How wounded the healers? The prevalence of relapse among addiction counselors in recovery from alcohol and other drugs. *Alcoholism Treatment Quarterly, 27*(4), 389–408. doi:10.1080/07347320903209863

Jordaan, G. P., & Emsley, R. (2014). Alcohol-induced psychotic disorder: A review. *Metabolic Brain Disease, 29*(2), 231–243. doi:10.1007/s11011-013-9457-4

Jordan, J. P., Miller, G., & Napolitano, L. (2008). Dealing with supervisee countertransference toward addicted clients. In L. E. Tyson, J. R. Culbreth, & J. A. Harrington (Eds.), *Critical incidents in clinical supervision: Addictions, community, and school counseling* (pp. 19–24). Alexandria, VA: American Counseling Association.

Juhnke, G. A., & Hagedorn, W. B. (2006). *Counseling addicted families. An integrated assessment and treatment model.* New York, NY: Routledge.

Kafka, M. P. (2010). Hypersexual disorder: A proposed diagnosis for *DSM-5. Archives of Sexual Behavior, 39,* 377–400.

Kahler, C. W., Ramsey, S. E., Read, J. P., & Brown, R. A. (2002). Substance-induced and independent major depressive disorder in treatment-seeking alcoholics: Associations with dysfunctional attitudes and coping. *Journal of Studies on Alcohol, 63*(3), 363–371.

Kaminer, Y., Spirito, A., & Lewander, W. (2011). Brief motivational interventions, cognitive-behavioral therapy, and contingency management for youth substance use disorders. In Y. Kaminer & K. Winters (Eds.), *Clinical manual of adolescent substance abuse treatment* (pp. 213–238). Arlington, VA: American Psychiatric Association.

Kaminer, Y., & Waldron, H. B. (2006). Evidence-based cognitive behavioral therapies for adolescent substance use disorders: Applications and challenges. In C. Rowe & H. Liddle (Eds.), *Adolescent substance abuse: Research and clinical advances* (pp. 396–419). New York, NY: Cambridge University Press.

Kandel, D. B., Huang, F. Y., & Davies, M. (2001). Comorbidity between patterns of substance use dependence and psychiatric symptoms. *Drug & Alcohol Dependence, 64,* 233–241.

Kaskutas, L. A., Borkman, T. J., Laudet, A., Ritter, L. A., Witbrodt, J., Subbaraman, M. S., . . . Bond, J. (2014). Elements that define recovery: The experiential perspective. *Journal of Studies on Alcohol and Drugs, 75*(6), 999–1010.

Kaufman, J. N., Ross, T. J., Stein, E. A., Garavan, H. (2003). Cingulate hypoactivity in cocaine users during a GO-NOGO task as revealed by event-related functional magnetic resonance imaging. *Journal of Neuroscience, 23*(21), 7839–7843.

Kelly, J. F., Finney, J. W., & Moos, R. (2005). Substance use disorder patients who are mandated to treatment: Characteristics, treatment process, and 1- and 5-year outcomes. *Journal of Substance Abuse Treatment, 28*(3), 213–223. doi:10.1016/j.jsat.2004.10.014

Kerr, D. H. (2015). *The voices of integrity: Compelling portrayals of addiction and recovery.* Bloomington, IN: Xlibris.

Kerr, M. E., & Bowen, M. (1988). *Family evaluation. An approach based on Bowen theory.* New York, NY: Norton.

Kessler, R. C., Borges, G., & Walters, E. E. (1999). Prevalence of and risk factors for lifetime suicide attempts in the National Comorbidity Survey. *Archives of General Psychiatry, 56*(7), 617–626. doi:10.1001/archpsyc.56.7.617

Kim, S. J., Lyoo, I. K., Hwang, J., Sung, Y. H., Lee, H. Y., Lee, D. S., . . . Renshaw, P. F. (2005). Frontal glucose hypometabolism in abstinent methamphetamine users. *Neuropsychopharmacology, 30,* 1383–1391.

Klein, D. N., & Riso, L. P. (1993). Psychiatric disorders: Problems of boundaries and comorbidity. In C. G. Costello (Ed.), *Basic issues in psychopathology* (pp. 19–66). New York, NY: Guilford Press.

Knack, W. A. (2009). Psychotherapy and Alcoholics Anonymous: An integrated approach. *Journal of Psychotherapy Integration, 19,* 86–109.

Knight, D. K., Becan, J. E., Landrum, B., Joe, G. W., & Flynn, P. M. (2014). Screening and assessment tools for measuring adolescent client needs and functioning in substance abuse treatment. *Substance Use & Misuse, 49*(7), 902–918. http://doi.org/10.3109/10826084.2014.891617

Koob, G. F. (2013). Addiction is a reward deficit and stress surfeit disorder. *Frontiers in Psychiatry, 4,* 72. http://doi.org/10.3389/fpsyt.2013.00072

Koob, G. F., Arends, M. A., & Le Moal, M. (2015). *Drugs, addiction, and the brain.* New York, NY: Elsevier.

Kopak, A. M., Proctor, S. L., & Hoffmann, N. G. (2012). An assessment of the compatibility of *DSM–IV* and proposed *DSM-5* criteria in the diagnosis of cannabis use disorders. *Substance Use & Misuse, 47,* 1328–1338. doi:10.3109/10826084.2012.714039

Kopelman, M. D., Thomson, A. D., Guerrini, I., & Marshall, E. J. (2009). The Korsakoff syndrome: Clinical aspects, psychology and treatment. *Alcohol and Alcoholism, 44*(2), 148–154. doi:10.1093/alcalc/agn118

Korman, L. M., Toneatto, T., & Skinner, W. (2010). Pathological gambling. In J. E. Fisher & W. T. O'Donohue (Eds.), *Practitioner's guide to evidence-based psychotherapy* (pp. 291–300). New York, NY: Springer.

Kosten, T. R., Domingo, C. B., Shorter, D., Orson, F., Green, C., Somoza, E., . . . Kampman, K. (2014). Vaccine for cocaine dependence: A randomized double-blind placebo-controlled efficacy trial. *Drug and Alcohol Dependence, 140,* 42–47. http://doi.org/10.1016/j.drugalcdep.2014.04.003

Kranitz, L. S., & Cooney, N. L. (2013). Treatment decision making and goal setting. In B. S. McCrady & E. E. Epstein (Eds.), *Addictions: A comprehensive guidebook* (2nd ed., pp. 352–373). New York, NY: Oxford University Press.

Kressel, D., De Leon, G., Palij, M., & Rubin, G. (2000). Measuring client clinical progress in therapeutic community treatment: The therapeutic community Client Assessment Inventory, Client Assessment Summary, and Staff Assessment Summary. *Journal of Substance Abuse Treatment, 19*(3), 267–272. doi:10.1016/S0740-5472(00)00108-2

Kroenke, K., Spitzer, R. L., & Williams, J. B. (2003). The Patient Health Questionnaire-2: Validity of a two-item depression screener. *Medical Care, 41,* 1284–1292.

Kuhn, S., & Gallinat, J. (2011). Common biology of craving across legal and illegal drugs—A quantitative meta-analysis of cue-reactivity brain response. *European Journal of Neuroscience, 33*(7), 1318–1326. doi:10.1111/j.1460-9568.2010.07590.x

Kurtz, E. (1979). *Not-god: A history of Alcoholics Anonymous.* Center City: MN: Hazelden.

Kurtz, E. (1982). Why A.A. works: The intellectual significance of Alcoholics Anonymous. *Journal of Studies on Alcohol, 43,* 38–80.

Kurtz, E. (1988). "Spiritual rather than religious": The contribution of Alcoholics Anonymous. In E. Kurtz (Ed.), *The collected Ernie Kurtz* (pp. 51–62). New York, NY: Author's Choice Press.

Kurtz, E. (1992). Research on Alcoholics Anonymous: The historical context. In E. Kurtz (Ed.), *The collected Ernie Kurtz* (pp. 1–22). New York, NY: Author's Choice Press.

Kurtz, E. (1996). Spirituality and recovery: The historical journey. In E. Kurtz (Ed.), *The collected Ernie Kurtz* (pp. 109–144). New York, NY: Author's Choice Press.

Kurtz, E. (2008). Whatever happened to twelve-step programs? In E. Kurtz (Ed.), *The collected Ernie Kurtz* (pp. 145–176). New York, NY: Author's Choice Press.

Kurtz, E., & Ketcham, K. (1993). The spirituality of imperfection: Storytelling and the search for meaning. New York, NY: Bantam.

Kuzma, J. M., & Black, D. W. (2008). Epidemiology, prevalence, and natural history of compulsive sexual behavior. *Psychiatric Clinics of North America, 31,* 603–611.

LaBrie, J. W., Feres, N., Kenney, S., & Lac, A. (2009). Family history of alcohol abuse moderates effectiveness of a group motivational enhancement intervention in college women. *Addictive Behaviors, 34*(5), 415–420.

Ladouceur, R., Sévigny, S., Blaszczynski, A., O'Connor, K., & Lavoie, M. E. (2003). Video lottery: Winning expectancies and arousal. *Addiction, 98*(6), 733–738. doi:10.1046/j.1360-0443.2003.00412.x

Laing, R. D. (1960). *The divided self.* London, England: Penguin.

Lambers, E. (2000). Supervision in person-centered therapy: Facilitating congruence. In E. Mearns & B. Thorne (Eds.), *Person-centered therapy today: New frontiers in theory and practice* (pp. 196–211). London, England: Sage.

Lander, L., Howsare, J., & Byrne, M. (2013). The impact of substance use disorders on families and children: From theory to practice. *Social Work in Public Health, 28*(3–4), 194–205. http://doi.org/10.1080/19371 918.2013.759005

Langås, A., Malt, U. F., & Opjordsmoen, S. (2012). In-depth study of personality disorders in first-admission patients with substance use disorders. *BMC Psychiatry, 12*(180). http://www.biomedcentral .com/1471-244X/12/180

Lank, P. M., & Crandall, M. L. (2014). Outcomes for older trauma patients in the emergency department screening positive for alcohol, cocaine, or marijuana use. *American Journal of Alcohol & Drug Abuse, 40*(2), 118–124. doi:10.3109/00952990.2014.880450

Larimer, M. E., Palmer, R. S., & Marlatt, G. A. (1999). Relapse prevention: An overview of Marlatt's cognitive-behavioral model. *Alcohol Research and Health, 23,* 151–160.

Latimer, J., Morton-Bourgon, K., & Chretien, J. (2006). *A meta-analytic examination of drug treatment courts: Do they reduce recidivism?* Ottawa: Department of Justice Canada.

Laudet, A. B., Becker, J. B., & White, W. L. (2009). Don't wanna go through that madness no more: Quality of life satisfaction as predictor of sustained remission from illicit drug misuse. *Substance Use & Misuse, 44,* 227–252.

Laudet, A., Magura, S., Vogel, H., & Knight, E. (2000). Support, mutual aid and recovery from dual diagnosis. *Community Mental Health Journal, 36,* 457–476.

Laudet, A., Morgen, K., & White, W. (2006). The role of social supports, spirituality and affiliation in 12-step groups in life satisfaction among individuals in recovery from alcohol and drug use. *Alcoholism Treatment Quarterly, 24,* 33–73.

Lawson, G., Peterson, J. S., & Lawson, A. (1983). *Alcoholism and the family: A guide to treatment and prevention.* Rockville, MD: Aspen Systems.

Lé, C., Ingvarson, E. P., & Page, R. C. (1995). Alcoholics Anonymous and the counseling profession: Philosophies in conflict. *Journal of Counseling & Development, 73,* 603–609.

Leahy, R. L. (2003). *Cognitive therapy techniques: A practitioner's guide.* New York, NY: Guilford.

Ledgerwood, D. M., & Petry, N. M. (2006). Psychological experience of gambling and subtypes of pathological gamblers. *Psychiatry Research, 144*(1), 17–27.

Ledgerwood, D. M., & Petry, N. M. (2015). Pathological gambling and gambling disorder. In J. D. Wright (Ed.), *International encyclopedia of the social & behavioral sciences* (2nd ed., Vol. 17, pp. 592–597). New York, NY: Elsevier.

Lee, T. K., Craig, S. E., Fetherson, B. L., & Simpson, C. D. (2013). Addiction competencies in the 2009 CACREP clinical mental health counseling program standards. *Journal of Addictions & Offender Counseling, 34*(1), 2–15. doi:10.1002/j.2161-1874.2013.00010.x

Lemke, S., & Moos, R. (2003a). Treatment and outcomes of older patients with alcohol use disorders in community residential programs. *Journal of Studies on Alcohol, 64,* 219–226.

Lemke, S., & Moos, R. (2003b). Treatment outcomes at 1-year and 5-years for older patients with alcohol use disorders. *Journal of Substance Abuse Treatment, 24,* 43–50.

Levinson, I., Galynker, I. I., & Rosenthal, R. N. (1995). Methadone withdrawal psychosis. *Journal of Clinical Psychiatry, 56*(2), 73–76.

Lewis, T. F. (2014). *Substance abuse and addiction treatment: Practical applications of counseling theory.* New York, NY: Pearson.

Lewis, J. A., Dana, R. Q., & Blevins, G. A. (2015). *Substance abuse counseling* (5th ed.). Stamford, CT: Cengage.

Li, C. R., Huang, C., Yan, P., Bhagwagar, Z., Milivojevic, V., & Sinha, R. (2008). Neural correlates of impulse control during stop signal inhibition in cocaine-dependent men. *Neuropsychopharmacology: Official Publication of the American College of Neuropsychopharmacology, 33*(8), 1798–1806. http://doi.org/10.1038/sj.npp.1301568

Li, Q., Wang, Y., Zhang, Y., Li, W., Yang, W., Zhu, J., . . . Tian, J. (2012). Craving correlates with mesolimbic responses to heroin-related cues in short-term abstinence from heroin. An event fMRI study. *Brain Research, 1469,* 63–72.

Liddle, H. A. (1995). Conceptual and clinical dimensions of a multidimensional, multisystems engagement strategy in family-based adolescent treatment. *Psychotherapy: Theory, Research, Practice, Training, 32*(1), 39–58. doi:10.1037/0033-3204.32.1.39

Liddle, H. A. (2013). Multidimensional family therapy for adolescent substance abuse: A developmental approach. In P. M. Miller, S. A. Ball, M. E. Bates, A. W. Blume, K. M. Kampman, D. J. Kavanagh, . . . P. De Witte (Eds.), *Comprehensive addictive behaviors and disorders, Vol. 3: Interventions for addiction* (pp. 87–96). San Diego, CA: Elsevier. doi:10.1016/B978-0-12-398338-1.00010-5

Liese, B. S., & Beck, A. T. (2000). Back to basics: Fundamental cognitive therapy skills for keeping drug-dependent individuals in treatment. In J. J. Boren, L. S. Onken, & J. D. Blaine (Eds.), *Beyond the therapeutic alliance: Keeping drug-dependent individuals in treatment* (pp. 207–232) [National Institute on Drug Abuse Research Monograph]. Washington, DC: Government Printing Office.

Lima, J. E., Reid, M. S., Smith, J. L., Zhang, Y., Jiang, H., Rotrosen, J., & Nunes, E. (2009). Medical and mental health status among drug dependent patients participating in a smoking cessation treatment study. *Journal of Drug Issues, 39*(2), 293–312.

Lin, N. (1986). Conceptualizing social support. In N. Lin, A. Dean, & W. Ensel (Eds.), *Social support, life events and depression* (pp. 17–30). New York, NY: Academic Press.

Litt, M. D., Cooney, N. L., & Morse, P. (2000). Reactivity to alcohol-related stimuli in the laboratory and in the field: Predictors of craving in treated alcoholics. *Addiction, 95*(6), 889–900. doi:10.1046/j.1360-0443.2000.9568896.x

Liu, J., Qin, W., Yuan, K., Li, J., Wang, W., Li, Q., . . . Tian, J. (2011). Interaction between dysfunctional connectivity at rest and heroin cues-induced brain responses in male abstinent heroin-dependent individuals. *PLoS ONE, 6*(10), e23098. http://doi.org/10.1371/journal.pone.0023098

Liu, N. H., & Satterfield, J. M. (2015). Screening, brief intervention, and referral to treatment (SBIRT) for substance abuse in older populations. In P. A. Areán (Ed.), *Treatment of late-life depression, anxiety, trauma, and substance abuse* (pp. 181–210). Washington, DC: American Psychological Association. doi:10.1037/14524-009

London, E. D., Simon, S. L., Berman, S. M., Mandelkem, M. A., Lichtman, A. M., Braman, J., . . . Ling, W. (2004). Mood disturbances and regional cerebral metabolic abnormalities in recently abstinent methamphetamine users. *Archives of General Psychiatry, 61,* 73–84.

Lorrains, F. K., Cowlishaw, S., & Thomas, S. A. (2011). Prevalence of comorbid disorders in problem and pathological gambling: Systemic review and meta-analysis of population surveys. *Addiction, 106,* 490–498.

Lowenkamp, C. T., Holsinger, A. M., & Latessa, E. J. (2005, Fall). Are drug courts effective? A meta-analytic review. *Journal of Community Corrections,* 5–28.

Luborsky, L., Barber, J. P., Siqueland, L., McLellan, A. T., & Woody, G. (1997). Establishing a therapeutic alliance with substance abusers. In L. S. Onken, J. D. Blaine, & J. J. Boren (Eds.), *Beyond the therapeutic alliance: Keeping the drug-dependent individual in treatment* (pp. 233–243) [National Institute on Drug Abuse Research Monograph No. 165]. Rockville, MD: National Institutes of Health.

Macgowan, M. J., & Engle B. (2010). Evidence for optimism: Behavior therapies and motivational interviewing in adolescent substance abuse treatment. *Child and Adolescent Psychiatric Clinics of North America, 19*(3), 527.

MacKenzie, D. L. (2006). *What works in corrections: Reducing the criminal activities of offenders and delinquents.* New York, NY: Cambridge University Press.

Madson, M. B., & Green, B. A. (2012). Clinical supervision and addiction treatment. In H. Shaffer, D. A. LaPlante, & S. E. Nelson (Eds.), *APA addiction syndrome handbook, Vol. 2: Recovery, prevention, and other issues* (pp. 35–53). Washington, DC: American Psychological Association. doi:10.1037/13750-002

Magill, M., & Ray, L. A. (2009). Cognitive-behavioral treatment with adult alcohol and illicit drug users: A meta-analysis of randomized controlled trials. *Journal of Studies on Alcohol and Drugs, 70*(4), 516–527.

Mannelli, P., Wu, L., & Brady, K. T. (2015). Pharmacological and integrated treatments in older adults with substance use disorders. In I. Crome, L. Wu, R. Rao, & P. Crome (Eds.), *Substance use and older people* (pp. 273–294). New York, NY: Wiley-Blackwell.

Manual, J. K., & Forcehimes, A. A. (2008). The therapeutic relationship in substance abuse treatment. In C. M. A. Geppert & L. W. Roberts (Eds.), *The book of ethics: Expert guidance for professionals who treat addiction* (pp. 29–40). Center City, MN: Hazelden.

Maremmani, A. G. I., Bacciardi, S., Rovai, L., Rugani, F., Dell'Osso, L., & Maremmani, I. (2012). Natural history of addiction in psychotic heroin-addicted patients at their first agonist opioid treatment. *Addictive Disorders and Their Treatment, 12*(1), 31–39.

Marlatt, G. A. (1978). Craving for alcohol, loss of control, and relapse: A cognitive-behavioral analysis. In P. E. Nathan, G. A. Marlatt, & T. Loberg (Eds.), *New directions in behavioral research and treatment* (pp. 271–314). New York, NY: Plenum Press.

Marlatt, G. A. (1996). Taxonomy of high-risk situations for alcohol relapse: Evolution and development of a cognitive-behavioral model. *Addiction, 91,* S37–S49.

Marlatt, G. A. (n.d.). *Addiction and the mind* (Unpublished presentation). Seattle: Addictive Behaviors Research Center, University of Washington.

Marlatt, G. A., & Gordon, J. R. (1985). *Relapse prevention: Maintenance strategies in the treatment of addictive behaviors.* New York, NY: Guilford Press.

Marlatt, G. A., Parks, G. A., & Witkiewitz, K. (2002). *Clinical guidelines for implementing relapse prevention therapy: A guideline developed for the Behavioral Health Recovery Management Project.* Seattle: Addictive Behaviors Research Center, University of Washington. Retrieved from http://www.bhrm.org/guidelines/RPT%20guideline.pdf

Martell, B. A., Orson, F. M., Poling, J., Mitchell, E., Rossen, R. D., Gardner, T., & Kosten, T. R. (2009). Cocaine vaccine for the treatment of cocaine dependence in methadone maintained patients: A randomized double-blind placebo-controlled efficacy trial. *Archives of General Psychiatry, 66*(10), 1116–1123. http://doi.org/10.1001/archgenpsychiatry.2009.128

Martin, B., Clapp, L., Bialkowski, D., Bridgeford, D., Amponsah, A., Lyons, L., & Beresford, T. P. (2003). Compliance to supervised disulfiram therapy: A comparison of voluntary and court-ordered patients. *American Journal on Addictions, 12*(2), 137–143. doi:10.1080/10550490390201399

Martin, J. E., & Simh, E. P. (2009). Motivational interviewing: Applications to Christian therapy and church ministry. *Journal of Psychology and Christianity, 28,* 71–77.

Martindale, S. L., Sejud, L. R., Giardina, A., McGowan, S., & Dolan, S. L. (2013). Changes in coping strategies over time in a residential substance use disorder treatment population: A preliminary assessment. *Alcoholism Treatment Quarterly, 31*(4), 484–494. doi:10.1080/07347324.2013.831683

Maschi, T., Gibson, S., Zgoba, K., & Morgen, K. (2011). Trauma and life event stressors among young and older adult prisoners. *Journal of Correctional Healthcare, 17,* 160–172.

Maschi, T., Morgen, K., & Viola, D. (2014). Unraveling trauma and stress, coping resources, and mental well-being among older adults in prison: Empirical evidence linking theory and practice. *The Gerontologist, 54,* 857–867.

Maschi, T., Morgen, K., Zgoba, K., Courtney, D., & Ristow, J. (2011). Age, cumulative trauma and stressful life events, and post traumatic stress symptoms among older adults in prison: Do subjective impressions matter? *The Gerontologist, 51*(5), 675–686. doi:10.1093/geront/gnr074

Maschi, T., Viola, D., Morgen, K., & Koskinen, L. (2015). Trauma, stress, grief, loss, and separation among older adults in prison: The protective role of coping resources on physical and mental well-being. *Journal of Crime and Justice, 38,* 113–136. doi:10.1080/0735648X.2013.808853

Master, L. (1989). Jewish experiences of Alcoholics Anonymous. *Smith College Studies in Social Work, 59*(2), 183–199.

Master's in Psychology and Counseling Accreditation Council. (2016). *Accreditation manual*. Retrieved from http://www.mpcacaccreditation.org/about/accreditation-manual/

Maxwell, M. A. (1982). *The Alcoholics Anonymous experience: A close up view for professionals*. New York, NY: McGraw-Hill.

May, R. (1958). *Existence: A new dimension in psychiatry and psychology*. New York, NY: Simon & Schuster.

May, R. (1969). *Love and will*. New York, NY: Norton.

May, R. (1977). *The meaning of anxiety* (Rev. ed.). New York, NY: Norton.

May, R. (1983). *The discovery of being: Writings in existential psychology*. New York, NY: Norton.

Mayo-Smith, M. F. (1997). Pharmacological management of alcohol withdrawal. A meta-analysis and evidence-based practice guideline. American Society of Addiction Medicine Working Group on Pharmacological Management of Alcohol Withdrawal. *JAMA, 278*(2), 144–151.

Mayo-Smith, M. F., Beecher, L. H., Fischer, T. L., Gorelick, D. A., Guillaume, J. L., Hill, A., . . . Working Group on the Management of Alcohol Withdrawal Delirium, Practice Guidelines Committee, American Society of Addiction Medicine. (2004). Management of alcohol withdrawal delirium. An evidence-based practice guideline. *Archives of Internal Medicine, 164*(13), 1405–1412.

McCloud, A., Barnaby, B., Omu, N., Drummond, C., & Aboud, A. (2004). Relationship between alcohol use disorders and suicidality in a psychiatric population: In-patient prevalence study. *British Journal of Psychiatry, 184*(5), 439–445. doi:10.1192/bjp.184.5.439

McDonell, M. G., Kerbrat, A. H., Comtois, K. A., Russo, J., Lowe, J. M., & Ries, R. K. (2012). Validation of the co-occurring disorder quadrant model. *Journal of Psychoactive Drugs, 44*(3), 266–273. doi:10.1080/02791072.2012.705065

McGovern, M. P., Clark, R. E., & Samnaliev, M. (2007). Co-occurring psychiatric and substance use disorders: A multistate feasibility study of the quadrant model. *Psychiatric Services, 58*(7), 949–954. doi:10.1176/appi.ps.58.7.949

McKay, J. R. (2005). Co-occurring substance dependence and depression: Practical implications and next questions. *Addiction, 100*(12), 1755–1757. doi:10.1111/j.1360-0443.2005.01320.x

McKellar, J. D., Harris, A. H., & Moos, R. H. (2006). Predictors of outcome for patients with substance-use disorders five years after treatment dropout. *Journal of Studies on Alcohol, 67*(5), 685–693. doi:10.15288/jsa.2006.67.685

McKetin, R., & Mattick, R. P. (1998). Attention and memory in illicit amphetamine users: Comparison with non-drug-using controls. *Drug & Alcohol Dependence, 50,* 181–184.

McLellan, A. T. (2006). What we need is a system: Creating a responsive and effective substance abuse treatment system. In W. R. Miller & K. M. Carroll (Eds.), *Rethinking substance abuse: What the science shows, and what we should do about it* (pp. 275–292). New York, NY: Guilford Press.

McLellan, A. T., Alterman, A. I., Metzger, D. S., Grissom, G. R., Woody, G. E., Luborsky, L., & O'Brien, C. P. (1994). Similarity of outcome predictors across opiate, cocaine, and alcohol treatments: Role of treatment services. *Journal of Consulting and Clinical Psychology, 62*(6), 1141–1158. doi:10.1037/0022-006X.62.6.1141

McNally, A. M., Palfai, T. P., & Kahler, C. W. (2005). Motivational interventions for heavy drinking college students: Examining the role of discrepancy-related psychological processes. *Psychology of Addictive Behaviors, 19*(1), 79–87.

Meadows, R., & Verghese, A. (1996). Medical complications of glue sniffing. *Southern Medical Journal, 89*(5), 455–462.

Mellin, E. A., Hunt, B., & Nichols, L. M. (2011). Counselor professional identity: Findings and implications for counseling and interprofessional collaboration. *Journal of Counseling & Development, 89*(2), 140–147.

Menary, K. R., Kushner, M. G., Maurer, E., & Thuras, P. (2011). The prevalence and clinical implications of self-medication among individuals with anxiety disorders. *Journal of Anxiety Disorders, 25*(3), 335–339. doi:10.1016/j.janxdis.2010.10.006

Mijuskovic, B. (1979). Loneliness and narcissism. *Psychoanalytic Review, 66*(4), 479–492.

Milin, R. (2013). Bipolar disorder and the onset of substance use disorders in adolescents: The emerging story. *Journal of the American Academy of Child & Adolescent Psychiatry, 52*(10), 1004–1005. doi:10.1016/j.jaac.2013.08.005

Miller, G. (2015). *Learning the language of addiction counseling* (4th ed.). Hoboken, NJ: Wiley.

Miller, G., Scarborough, J., Clark, C., Leonard, J. C., & Keziah, T. B. (2010). The need for national credentialing standards for addiction counselors. *Journal of Addictions & Offender Counseling, 30*(2), 50–57. doi:10.1002/j.2161-1874.2010.tb00056.x

Miller, W. R., & Rollnick, S. (1991). *Motivational interviewing: Preparing people to change addictive behavior.* New York, NY: Guilford Press.

Miller, W. R., & Rollnick, S. (2002). *Motivational interviewing: Preparing people for change* (2nd ed.). New York, NY: Guilford Press.

Miller, W. R., & Rollnick, S. (2009). Ten things motivational interviewing is not. *Behavioural and Cognitive Psychotherapy, 37,* 129–140.

Miller, W. R., & Rollnick, S. (2013). *Motivational interviewing: Helping people change* (3rd ed.). New York, NY: Guilford Press.

Miller, W. R., Rollnick, S., & Moyers, T. B. (1998). *Motivational interviewing: Professional training videotape series.* Albuquerque: University of New Mexico.

Miller, W. R., & Rose, G. S. (2009). Toward a theory of motivational interviewing. *American Psychologist, 64*(6), 527–537.

Miller, W., & Thoresen, C. (2003). Spirituality, religion and health: An emerging research field. *American Psychologist, 58,* 24–35.

Miller, W. R., Forcehimes, A. A., & Zweben, A. (2011). *Treating addiction: A guide for professionals.* New York, NY: Guilford Press.

Millon, T., & Davis, R. (1996). Putting humpty dumpty together again: Using the MCMI in psychological assessment. In L. E. Beutler & M. R. Berren (Eds.), *Integrative assessment of adult personality* (pp. 240–279). New York, NY: Guilford Press.

Mioshi, E., Dawson, K., Mitchell, J., Arnold, R., & Hodges, J. R. (2006). The Addenbrooke's Cognitive Examination Revised (ACE-R): A brief cognitive test battery for dementia screening. *International Journal of Geriatric Psychiatry, 21*(11), 1078–1085.

Monnot, M., Lovallo, W. R., Nixon, S. J., & Ross, E. (2002). Neurological basis of deficits in affective prosody comprehension among alcoholics and fetal alcohol-exposed adults. *Journal of Neuropsychiatry & Clinical Neuroscience, 14*(3), 321–328.

Moore, A. A., Beck, J. C., Barbor, T. F., Hays, R. D., & Reuben, D. B. (2002). Beyond alcoholism: Identifying older, at-risk drinkers in primary care. *Journal of Studies on Alcohol, 63*(3), 316–324.

Moos, R., Finney, J., Ouimette, P., & Suchinsky, R. (1999). A comparative evaluation of substance abuse treatment: I. Treatment orientation, amount of care, and 1-year outcomes. *Alcoholism Clinical and Experimental Research, 23,* 529–536.

Moos, R. H., & Moos, B. S. (2004). Long-term influence of duration and frequency of participation in Alcoholics Anonymous on individuals with alcohol use disorders. *Journal of Consulting and Clinical Psychology, 72,* 81–90.

Moos, R. H., & Moos, B. S. (2006). Participation in treatment and Alcoholics Anonymous: A 16-year follow-up of initially untreated individuals. *Journal of Clinical Psychology, 62,* 735–750.

Morgan, M. L., Brosi, W. A., & Brosi, M. W. (2011). Restorying older adults' narratives about self and substance abuse. *American Journal of Family Therapy, 39*(5), 444–455. doi:10.1080/01926187.2011.560784

Morgan, O. J. (1992). In a sober voice: A psychological study of long-term alcoholic recovery with attention to spiritual dimensions. *Dissertation Abstracts International: Section B. Sciences and Engineering, 52*(11), 6069. (UMI No. 92-10480)

Morgen, K. (2011, March). *Will the real addictions specialist please stand?* Paper presented as part of the panel Analysis of Professional and Addiction Counseling Licensure Requirements, Scope of Practice, and Training: National Findings at the American Counseling Association Annual Conference & Exposition, New Orleans, LA.

Morgen, K. (2015, March). *Older adult substance use disorder: National trends at facility and client levels.* Paper presented at the Eastern Psychological Association Conference, Philadelphia, PA.

Morgen, K., Astone-Twerell, J., Hernitche, T., Gunneson, L., & Santangelo, K. (2007). Health-related quality of life among substance abusers in residential drug abuse treatment. *Applied Research in Quality of Life, 2,* 239–246.

Morgen, K., Denison-Vesel, K., Kobylarz, A., & Voelkner, A. (2015). Prevalence of substance use disorder treatment facilities specializing in older adult and trauma care: N-SSATS data 2009 to 2011. *Traumatology, 21*(3), 153–160.

Morgen, K., & Kressel, D. (2002, June). *Evaluating the progress of residential and outpatient TC treatment.* Poster session presented at the 64th Annual Scientific Meeting of the College on Problems of Drug Dependence, Quebec City, Quebec, Canada.

Morgen, K., Maschi, T., Viola, D., & Zgoba, K. (2013). Substance use disorder and the older offender. *VISTAS Online,* Article 97. Retrieved from http://www.counseling.org/knowledge-center/vistas/vistas-2013

Morgen, K., & Miller, G. (2013, March). *Thoughts on addiction counseling licensure.* Paper presented at the American Counseling Association Conference and Exposition, Cincinnati, OH.

Morgen, K., Miller, G., Chasek, C., DePue, K., & Ivers, N. (2015a, March). *LPC and addictions counseling licensure and policy integration.* IAAOC division keynote address at the American Counseling Association Annual Conference and Exposition, Orlando, FL.

Morgen, K., Miller, G., Chasek, C., DePue, K., & Ivers, N. (2015b, March). *Integration of LPC and addictions licensure: IAAOC task force findings.* Poster session presented at the American Counseling Association Annual Conference and Exposition, Orlando, FL.

Morgen, K., Miller, J., & Stretch, L. S. (2012). Addiction counseling licensure issues for licensed professional counselors. *The Professional Counselor: Research and Practice, 2*(1), 58–65. Retrieved from http://tpcjournal.nbcc.org/wp-content/uploads/Addiction-counseling-licensure-issues_Morgen-Miller-Stretch-Article.pdf

Morgen, K., & Morgan, O. J. (2011). 12-step spirituality. In C. S. Cashwell & J. S. Young (Eds.), *Integrating spirituality and religion in counseling: A guide to competent practice* (2nd ed., pp. 225–241). Alexandria, VA: American Counseling Association.

Morgen, K., Morgan, O. J., Cashwell, C., & Miller, G. (2010). *Strategies for the competent integration of spirituality into addictions counseling training and supervision.* Retrieved from http://counseling outfitters.com/vistas/vistas10/Article_84.pdf

Morgen, K., & Voelkner, A. (2014, July). *Clinical and data management issues for the older offender on parole.* Paper presented at the conference on 21st Century Forensic Practice: Moving Beyond Cultural Competence, New York, NY.

Morjaria, A., & Orford, J. (2002). The role of religion and spirituality in recovery from drink problems: A qualitative study of Alcoholics Anonymous members and South Asian men. *Addiction Research & Theory, 10,* 225–256.

Moyers, T. B., Martin, T., Christopher, P. J., Houck, J. M., Tonigan, J., & Amrhein, P. C. (2007). Client language as a mediator of motivational interviewing efficacy: Where is the evidence? *Alcoholism: Clinical and Experimental Research, 31*(10 Suppl.), 40s–47s.

Moyers, T. B., Martin, T., Manuel, J. K., Hendrickson, S. M. L., & Miller, W. R. (2005). Assessing competence in the use of motivational interviewing. *Journal of Substance Abuse Treatment, 28*(1), 19–26.

Mueser, K. T., Drake, R. E., & Wallach, M. A. (1998). Dual diagnosis: A review of etiological theories. *Addictive Behaviors, 23*(6), 717–734. doi:10.1016/S0306-4603(98)00073-2

Mueser, K. T., Noordsy, D. L., Drake, R. E., & Fox, L. (2003). *Integrated treatment for dual disorders: A guide to effective practice.* New York, NY: Guilford Press.

Myers, J. (1995). Specialties in counseling: Rich heritage or force for fragmentation? *Journal of Counseling & Development, 74*(2), 115–116.

Myers, J., Sweeney, T., & White, V. (2002). Advocacy for counseling and counselors: A professional imperative. *Journal of Counseling & Development, 80*(4), 394.

Narcotics Anonymous. (1993). *It works: How and why; The twelve steps and twelve traditions of Narcotics Anonymous.* Van Nuys, CA: World Service Office.

Nassar-McMillan, S. C., & Niles, S. G. (2011). *Developing your identity as a professional counselor.* Belmont, CA: Brooks/Cole.

National Association of Alcoholism and Drug Abuse Counselors. (2011). *Ethical standards of alcoholism and drug abuse counselors.* Alexandria, VA: Author.

National Association of Drug Court Professionals. (1997). *Defining drug courts: The key components.* Washington, DC: Office of Justice Programs, U.S. Department of Justice.

National Association of State Alcohol and Drug Abuse Directors. (2013). *State regulations on substance use disorder programs and counselors: An overview.* Retrieved from http://nasadad.org/

National Association of State Mental Health Program Directors, & National Association of State Alcohol and Drug Abuse Directors. (1998). *National dialogue on co-occurring mental health and substance abuse disorders.* Washington, DC: Authors.

National Center on Addiction and Substance Abuse. (2016). *Understanding and addressing food addiction: A science-based approach to policy, practice, and research.* New York, NY: Author.

National Center on Addiction and Substance Abuse at Columbia University. (2001). *So help me God: Substance abuse, religion and spirituality.* New York, NY: Author.

National Institute on Alcohol Abuse and Alcoholism. (2005). *Helping patients who drink too much: A clinician's guide.* Rockville, MD: Author.

National Institute on Drug Abuse. (2012). *Medical consequences of drug abuse* Retrieved January 28, 2016, from http://www.drugabuse.gov/related-topics/medical-consequences-drug-abuse

National Institute on Drug Abuse. (2016, January). *Commonly abused drugs charts.* Retrieved January 31, 2016, from http://www.drugabuse.gov/drugs-abuse/commonly-abused-drugs-charts

Neale, M. C., & Kendler, K. S. (1995). Models of comorbidity for multifactorial disorders. *American Journal of Human Genetics, 57*(4), 935–953.

Nestler, E. J. (2005). The neurobiology of cocaine addiction. *Science & Practice Perspectives, 3*(1), 4–10.

Newton, T. F., Kalechstein, A. D., Duran, S., Vansluis, N., & Ling, W. (2004). Methamphetamine abstinence syndrome: Preliminary findings. *American Journal on Addictions, 13*(3), 248–255.

Nixon, M. K., Cloutier, P. F., & Aggarwal, S. (2002). Affect regulation and addictive aspects of repetitive self-injury in hospitalized adolescents. *Journal of the American Academy of Child and Adolescent Psychiatry, 41,* 1333–1341. doi:10.1097/01.CHI.0000024844.60748.C

Noël, X., Van der Linden, M., Brevers, D., Campanella, S., Hanak, C., Kornreich, C., & Verbanck, P. (2012). The contribution of executive functions deficits to impaired episodic memory in individuals with alcoholism. *Psychiatry Research, 198*(1), 116–122. doi:10.1016/j.psychres.2011.10.007

Noone, M., Dua, J., & Markham, R. (1999). Stress, cognitive factors, and coping resources as predictors of relapse in alcoholics. *Addictive Behaviors, 24,* 687–693.

Noyoo, N., Patel, L., & Loffell, J. (2006). The human development situation of Johannesburg's youth. *Professional Journal for Social Work, 42*(1), 93–100.

Nunes, E. V. (2010). Drug use disorders among young adults: Evaluation and treatment. In J. E. Grant & M. N. Potenza (Eds.), *Young adult mental health* (pp. 311–334). New York, NY: Oxford University Press.

Nunes, E. V., Liu, X., Samet, S., Matseoane, K., & Hasin, D. (2006). Independent versus substance-induced major depressive disorder in substance-dependent patients: Observational study of course during follow-up. *Journal of Clinical Psychiatry, 67*(10), 1561–1567. doi:10.4088/JCP.v67n1010

O'Brien, C. P. (2006). Drug addiction and drug abuse. In L. Brunton, J. Lazo, & K. Parker (Eds.), *Goodman & Gilman's the pharmacological basis of therapeutics* (11th ed., pp. 607–627). New York, NY: McGraw-Hill.

O'Brien, C. (2011). Addiction and dependence in DSM-V. *Addiction (Abingdon, England), 106*(5). doi:10.1111/j.1360-0443.2010.03144.x

Office of Research, Planning, and Evaluation, and Intoxicated Driving Program Unit, Division of Mental Health and Addiction Services, New Jersey Department of Human Services. (2014). *Intoxicated driving program 2013 statistical summary report.* Trenton, NJ: Author.

Ogden, K. W., & Sias, S. M. (2011). An integrative spiritual development model of supervision for substance abuse counselors-in-training. *Journal of Addictions & Offender Counseling, 32*(1–2), 84–96. doi:10.1002/j.2161-1874.2011.tb00209.x

Oldham, M. A., & Ciraulo, D. A. (2013). Sedative-hypnotic and anxiolytic drugs. In B. S. McCrady & E. E. Epstein, (Eds.), *Addictions: A comprehensive guidebook* (2nd ed., pp. 155–173). New York, NY: Oxford University Press.

Orman, J. S., & Keating, G. M. (2009). Buprenorphine/naloxone: A review of its use in the treatment of opioid dependence. *Drugs, 69*(5), 577–607. doi:10.2165/00003495-200969050-00006

Ortman, J., Velkoff, V., & Hogan, H. (2014). *An aging nation: The older population in the United States.* Baltimore, MD: U.S. Department of Commerce.

Oslin, D. W., Cary, M., Slaymaker, V., Colleran, C., & Blow, F. C. (2009). Daily ratings measures of alcohol craving during an inpatient stay define subtypes of alcohol addiction that predict subsequent risk for resumption of drinking. *Drug and Alcohol Dependence, 103*(3), 131–136. doi:10.1016/j.drugalcdep.2009.03.009

Osten, K. A., & Switzer, R. J. (2014). *Integrating 12-steps and psychotherapy: Helping clients find sobriety and recovery.* Thousand Oaks, CA: Sage.

Pacini, M., & Maremmani, A. G. I. (2005). Methadone reduces the need for antipsychotic and antimanic agents in heroin addicts hospitalized for manic and/or acute psychotic episodes. *Heroin Addiction & Related Clinical Problems, 7*(4), 43–48.

Pagdin, S. (2013). An existential phenomenological model of supervision. *Existential Analysis, 24*(1), 142–152.

Pau, C. W. H., Lee, T. M. C., & Chan, S. F. (2002). The impact of heroin on frontal executive functions. *Archives of Clinical Neuropsychology, 17*(7), 663–670. doi:10.1016/S0887-6177(01)00169-X

Paulus, M. P., Tapert, S. F., & Schuckit, M. A. (2005). Neural activation patterns of methamphetamine-dependent subjects during decision making predict relapse. *JAMA Psychiatry, 62*(7), 761–768.

Peirce, J. M., Brooner, R. K., King, V. L., & Kidorf, M. S. (in press). Effect of traumatic event exposure and PTSD on substance use disorder treatment response. *Drug and Alcohol Dependence.*

Peirce, J. M., Brooner, R. K., Kolodner, K., Schacht, R. L., Kidorf, M. S. (2013). Prospective effects of traumatic event re-exposure and post-traumatic stress disorder in syringe exchange participants. *Addiction, 108,* 146–153.

Peirce, J. M., Kolodner, K., Brooner, R. K., Kidorf, M. S. (2012). Traumatic event re-exposure in injecting drug users. *Journal of Urban Health, 89,* 117–128.

Pellouox, Y., & Baunez, C. (2013). Deep brain stimulation for addiction: Why the subthalamic nucleus should be favored. *Current Opinion in Neurobiology, 23*(4), 713–720.

Piehler, T. F., Véronneau, M.-H., & Dishion, T. J. (2012). Substance use progression from adolescence to early adulthood: Effortful control in the context of friendship influence and early-onset use. *Journal of Abnormal Child Psychology, 40*(7), 1045–1058. http://doi.org/10.1007/s10802-012-9626-7

Pietrzak, R. H., Goldstein, R. B., Southwick, S. M., & Grant, B. F. (2011). Prevalence and Axis I comorbidity of full and partial posttraumatic stress disorder in the United States: Results from Wave 2 of the National Epidemiologic Survey on Alcohol and Related Conditions. *Journal of Anxiety Disorders, 25*(3), 456–465. http://doi.org/10.1016/j.janxdis.2010.11.010

Pinel, J. P. J. (2013). *Biopsychology* (9th ed.). Upper Saddle River, NJ: Pearson.

Pitel, A.-L., Beaunieux, H., Eustache, F., Chanraud, S., Pfefferbaum, A., & Sullivan, E.V. (2010). *Episodic memory heterogeneity in alcoholism: Evidence from neuropsychological and neuroimaging structural and functional studies* (abs). Paper presented at the International Society for Brain Research in Alcoholism (ISBRA), Paris, France.

Porter, N., & Vasquez, M. (1997). Covision: Feminist supervision, process, and collaboration. In J. Worell & N. G. Johnson (Eds.), *Shaping the future of feminist psychology: Education, research, and practice* (pp. 155–171). Washington, DC: American Psychological Association. doi:10.1037/10245-007

Potash, H. M. (1994). *Pragmatic-existential psychotherapy with personality disorders.* Madison, NJ: Gordon Handwerk.

Powell, D. J., & Brodsky, A. (2004). *Clinical supervision in alcohol and drug abuse counseling: Principles, models, methods* (Rev. ed.). San Francisco, CA: Jossey-Bass.

Preuss, U. W., Koller, G., Barnow, S., Eikmeier, M., & Soyka, M. (2006). Suicidal behavior in alcohol-dependent subjects: The role of personality disorders. *Alcoholism: Clinical and Experimental Research, 30*(5), 866–877. doi:10.1111/j.1530-0277.2006.00073.x

Pringle, K. E., Ahern, F. M., Heller, D. A., Gold, C. H., & Brown, T. V. (2005). Potential for alcohol and prescription drug interactions in older people. *Journal of the American Geriatrics Society, 53*(11), 1930–1936.

Prochaska, J. O., & DiClemente, C. C. (1986). Toward a comprehensive model of change. In W. R. Miller & N. Heather (Eds.), *Treating addictive behaviors: Processes of change* (pp. 3–27). New York, NY: Plenum.

Prochaska, J. O., DiClemente, C. C., & Norcross, J. C. (1992). In search of how people change: Applications to addictive behaviors. *American Psychologist, 47,* 1102–1114.

Prochaska, J. O., & Norcross, J. C. (2013). *Systems of psychotherapy: A transtheoretical analysis* (8th ed.). Belmont, CA: Thomson Brooks/Cole.

Proctor, S. L., Kopak, A. M., & Hoffmann, N. G. (2012). Compatibility of current *DSM–IV* and proposed *DSM-5* diagnostic criteria for cocaine use disorders. *Addictive Behaviors, 37,* 722–728. doi:10.1016/j.addbeh.2012.02.010

Proctor, S. L., Kopak, A. M., & Hoffmann, N. G. (2014). Cocaine use disorder prevalence: From current *DSM-IV* to proposed *DSM 5* diagnostic criteria with both a two and three severity level classification. *Psychology of Addictive Behaviors, 28*(2), 563–567.

Prosek, E. A., & Hurt, K. M. (2014). Measuring professional identity development among counselor trainees. *Counselor Education and Supervision, 53*(4), 284–293. doi:10.1002/j.1556-6978.2014.00063.x

Qualls, S. H. (2015). Building competencies in professional geropsychology: Guidelines, training model, and strategies for professional development. In P. A. Areán (Ed.), *Treatment of late-life depression, anxiety, trauma, and substance abuse* (pp. 11–48). Washington, DC: American Psychological Association. doi:10.1037/14524-002

Rass, O., Schacht, R. L., Marvel, C. L., & Mintzer, M. Z. (2014). Opioids. In D. N. Allen & S. P. Woods (Eds.), *Neuropsychological aspects of substance use disorders* (pp. 231–253). New York, NY: Oxford University Press.

Rawson, R., Huber, A., Brethen, P., Obert, J., Gulati, V., Shoptaw, S., & Ling, W. (2000). Methamphetamine and cocaine users: Differences in characteristics and treatment retention. *Journal of Psychoactive Drugs, 32*(2), 233–238.

Rawson, R. A., Marinelli-Casey, P., Anglin, M. D., Dickow, A., Frazier, Y., Gallagher, C., . . . Zweben, J. (2004). A multi-site comparison of psychosocial approaches for the treatment of methamphetamine dependence. *Addiction, 99*(6), 708–717.

Rawson, R. A., Shoptaw, S. J., Obert, J. L., McCann, M. J., Hasson, A. L., Marinelli-Casey, P. J., . . . Ling, W. (1995). An intensive outpatient approach for cocaine abuse treatment: The Matrix model. *Journal of Substance Abuse Treatment, 12*(2), 117–127.

Reiter, M. D. (2015). *Substance abuse and the family.* New York, NY: Routledge.

Remley, T., & Herlihy, B. (2009). *Ethical, legal, and professional issues in counseling* (3rd ed.). Upper Saddle River, NJ: Merrill.

Ries, R. K. (1993). The dually diagnosed patient with psychotic symptoms. *Journal of Addictive Diseases 12*(3), 103–122.

Rigg, K. K., & Monnat, S. M. (2015). Comparing characteristics of prescription painkiller misusers and heroin users in the United States. *Addictive Behaviors, 51,* 106–112. doi:10.1016/j.addbeh.2015.07.013

Rippeth, J. D., Heaton, R. K., Carey, C. L., Marcotte, T. D., Moore, D. J., Gonzalez, R., . . . HNRC Group. (2004). Methamphetamine dependence increases risk of neuropsychological impairment in HIV infected persons. *Journal of the International Neuropsychological Society, 10*(1), 1–14.

Robbins, M. S., Feaster, D. J., Horigian, V. E., Rohrbaugh, M., Shoham, V., Bachrach, K., . . . Szapocznik, J. (2011). Brief strategic family therapy versus treatment as usual: Results of a multisite randomized trial for substance using adolescents. *Journal of Consulting and Clinical Psychology, 79*(6), 713–727. doi:10.1037/a0025477

Robertson, E. B., David, S. L., & Rao, S. A. (2003). *Preventing drug abuse among children and adolescents: A Research-based guide for parents, educators, and community leaders* (2nd ed.). Bethesda, MD: National Institute on Drug Abuse.

Robinson, J., Sareen, J., Cox, B. J., & Bolton, J. M. (2011). Role of self-medication in the development of comorbid anxiety and substance use disorders: A longitudinal investigation. *Archives of General Psychiatry, 68*(8), 800–807. doi:10.1001/archgenpsychiatry.2011.75

Robinson, S. M., Sobell, L. C., Sobell, M. B., & Leo, G. I. (2014). Reliability of the timeline followback for cocaine, cannabis, and cigarette use. *Psychology of Addictive Behaviors, 28*(1), 154–162. doi:10.1037/a0030992

Robinson, T. E., & Berridge, K. C. (2001). Incentive-sensitization and addiction. *Addiction, 96*(1), 103–114. doi:10.1046/j.1360-0443.2001.9611038.x

Rollnick, S. (2010). *Motivational interviewing for mental health disorders.* Eau Claire, WI: PESI.

Rollnick, S., & Miller, W. R. (1995). What is motivational interviewing? *Behavioural and Cognitive Psychotherapy, 23*(4), 325–334. doi:10.1017/S135246580001643X

Rollnick, S., Miller, W. R., & Butler, C. C. (2008). *Motivational interviewing in health care: Helping patients change behavior.* New York, NY: Guilford Press.

Ronnestad, M. H., & Skovholt, T. M. (2003). The journey of the counselor and therapist: Research findings and perspectives on professional development. *Journal of Career Development, 30,* 5–44.

Roos, C. R., Kirouac, M., Pearson, M. R., Fink, B. C., & Witkiewitz, K. (2015). Examining temptation to drink from an existential perspective: Associations among temptation, purpose in life, and drinking outcomes. *Psychology of Addictive Behaviors, 29*(3), 716–724. doi:10.1037/adb0000063

Rosenberg, N. L., Grigsby, J., Dreisbach, J., Busenbark, D., & Grigsby, P. (2002). Neuropsychological impairment and MRI abnormalities associated with chronic solvent abuse. *Clinical Toxicology, 40*(1), 21–34.

Rosengren, D. B. (2009). Building motivational interviewing skills: A practitioner's workbook. New York, NY: Guilford Press.

Rosenthal, R. N. (2013). Treatment of persons with substance use disorder and co-occurring other mental health disorders. In B. S. McCrady & E. E. Epstein (Eds.), *Addictions: A comprehensive guidebook* (2nd ed., pp. 659–707). New York, NY: Oxford University Press.

Rosenthal, R., & Rubin, D. B. (1982). A simple, general purpose display of magnitude of experimental effect. *Journal of Educational Psychology, 74,* 166–169.

Rubio, G., Marín-Lozano, J., Ferre, F., Martínez-Gras, I., Rodriguez-Jimenez, R., Sanz, J., . . . Palomo, T. (2012). Psychopathologic differences between cannabis-induced psychoses and recent-onset primary psychoses with abuse of cannabis. *Comprehensive Psychiatry, 53,* 1063–1070. doi:10.1016/j.comppsych.2012.04.013

Rumpf, H., Bischof, G., Hapke, U., Meyer, C., & John, U. (2002). The role of family and partnership in recovery from alcohol dependence: Comparison of individuals remitting with and without formal help. *European Addiction Research 8,* 122–127.

Saladin, M. E., Brady, K. T., Dansky, B. S., & Kilpatrick, D. G. (1995). Understanding comorbidity between PTSD and substance use disorder: Two preliminary investigations. *Addictive Behaviors, 20*(5), 643–655. doi:10.1016/0306-4603(95)00024-7

Salmon, J. M., & Forester, B. (2012). Substance abuse and co-occurring psychiatric disorders in older adults: A clinical case and review of relevant literature. *Journal of Dual Diagnosis, 8,* 74–84. http://dx.doi.org/10.1080/15504263.2012.648439

Sansone, R. A., Whitecar, P., & Wiederman, M. W. (2008). The prevalence of borderline personality among buprenorphine patients. *International Journal of Psychiatry in Medicine, 38*(2), 217–226. doi:10.2190/PM.38.2.h

Sansone, R. A., & Wiederman, M. W. (2009). The abuse of prescription medications: borderline personality patients in psychiatric versus non-psychiatric settings. *International Journal of Psychiatry in Medicine, 39*(2), 147–154. doi:10.2190/PM.39.2.c

Saranga, V., & Coffey, B. J. (2010). Bipolar disorder or substance-induced mood disorder in an adolescent? *Journal of Child and Adolescent Psychopharmacology, 20*(4), 343–346. doi:10.1089/cap.2010.2043

Satre, D. D. (2013). Treatment of older adults. In B. S. McCrady & E. E. Epstein (Eds.), *Addictions: A comprehensive guidebook* (2nd ed., pp. 742–757). New York, NY: Oxford University Press.

Satre, D. D., Chi, F. W., Mertens, J. R., & Weisner, C. M. (2012). Effects of age and life transitions on alcohol and drug treatment outcome over nine years. *Journal of Studies on Alcohol and Drugs, 73*(3), 459–468.

Satre, D. D., Gordon, N. P., & Weisner, C. (2007). Alcohol consumption, medical conditions, and health behavior in older adults. *American Journal of Health Behavior, 31*(3), 238–248. http://doi.org/10.5555/ajhb.2007.31.3.238

Satre, D. D., & Leibowitz, A. (2015). Brief alcohol and drug interventions and motivational interviewing for older adults. In P. A. Areán (Ed.), *Treatment of late-life depression, anxiety, trauma, and substance abuse* (pp. 163–180). Washington, DC: American Psychological Association. doi:10.1037/14524-008

Satre, D. D., Mertens, J., Areán, P. A., & Weisner, C. (2003). Contrasting outcomes of older versus middle-aged and younger adult chemical dependency patients in a managed care program. *Journal of Studies on Alcohol, 64*(4), 520–530.

Sartre, J. P. (1956). *Being and nothingness* (H. E. Barnes, Trans.). New York, NY: The Philosophical Library.

Saxon, A. J., & Simpson, T. L. (2015). Co-occurring substance use disorders and PTSD. In N. C. Bernardy & M. J. Friedman (Eds.), *A practical guide to PTSD treatment: Pharmacological and psychotherapeutic approaches* (pp. 135–150). Washington, DC: American Psychological Association. doi:10.1037/14522-010

Schneider, J., & Schneider, B. H. (2004). *Sex, lies, and forgiveness: Couples speak out on healing from sex addiction* (3rd ed.). Tucson, AZ: Recovery Resources Press.

Schonfeld, L., & MacFarland, N. S. (2015). Relapse prevention treatment for substance abuse disorders in older adults. In P. A. Areán (Ed.), *Treatment of late-life depression, anxiety, trauma, and substance abuse* (pp. 211–234). Washington, DC: American Psychological Association. doi:10.1037/14524-010

Schreiner, A. M., & Dunn, M. E. (2012). Residual effects of cannabis use on neurocognitive performance after prolonged abstinence: A meta-analysis. *Experimental and Clinical Psychopharmacology, 20*(5), 420–429. doi:10.1037/a0029117

Schuckit, M. A. (1994). Alcohol and depression: A clinical perspective. *Acta Psychiatrica Scandinavica, 89*(377, Suppl.), 28–32. doi:10.1111/j.1600-0447.1994.tb05798.x

Schuckit, M. A. (2006). *Drug and alcohol abuse: A clinical guide to diagnosis and treatment* (6th ed.). New York, NY: Springer.

Schwartz, M. F., & Southern, S. (1999). Manifestations of damaged development of the human affectional systems and developmentally based psychotherapies. *Sexual Addiction & Compulsivity, 6,* 163–175.

Scott, J. C., Woods, S. P., Matt, G. E., Meyer, R. A., Heaton, R. K., Atkinson, J. H., & Grant, I. (2007). Neurocognitive effects of methamphetamine: A critical review and meta-analysis. *Neuropsychology Review, 17*(3), 275–297.

Sharf, R. S. (2004). *Theories of psychotherapy and counseling: Concepts and cases* (3rd ed.). Pacific Grove, CA: Brooks/Cole.

Sias, S. M., & Lambie, G. W. (2008). An integrative social-cognitive development model of supervision for substance abuse counselors-in-training. *Journal of Teaching in the Addictions, 7,* 57–74.

Siegler, M., Osmond, H., & Newell, S. (1968). Models of alcoholism. *Quarterly Journal of Studies on Alcohol, 29,* 571–591.

Simoni-Wastila, L., & Yang, H. K. (2006). Psychoactive drug abuse in older adults. *American Journal of Geriatric Pharmacotherapy, 4,* 380–394. http://dx.doi.org/10.1016/j.amjopharm.2006.10.002

Simoni-Wastila, L., Zuckerman, I. H., Singhal, P. K., Briesacher, B., & Hsu, V. D. (2006). National estimates of exposure to prescription drugs with addiction potential in community-dwelling elders. *Substance Abuse, 26,* 33–42. http://dx.doi.org/10.1300/J465v26n01_04

Siqueland, L., Horn, A., Moras, K., Woody, G., Weiss, R., Blaine, J., . . . Thase, M. (1999). Cocaine-induced mood disorder: Prevalence rates and psychiatric symptoms in an outpatient cocaine-dependent sample. *American Journal on Addictions, 8*(2), 165–169. doi:10.1080/105504999305974

Skinner, H. A. (1982). The Drug Abuse Screening Test. *Addictive Behaviors, 7*(4), 363–371.

Smith, P. C., Schmidt, S. M., Allensworth-Davies, D., & Saitz, R. (2010). A single-question screening test for drug use in primary care. *Archives of Internal Medicine 170,* 1155–1160.

Southern, S. (2002). The tie that binds: Sadomasochism in female addicted trauma survivors. *Sexual Addiction & Compulsivity, 9,* 209–229.

Southern, S., Ellison, D., & Hagwood, M. (2015). Sexual addiction. In R. L. Smith (Ed.), *Treatment strategies for substance and process addictions* (pp. 177–206). Alexandria, VA: American Counseling Association.

Soyka, M., Limmer, C., Lehnert, R., Koller, G., Martin, G., Kufner, H., . . . Haberthur, A. (2011). A comparison of cognitive function in patients under maintenance treatment with heroin, methadone, or buprenorphine, and healthy controls: An open pilot study. *American Journal of Drug & Alcohol Abuse, 37*(6), 497–508. doi:10.3109/00952990.2011.600381

Speer, R. E. (1902). *The principles of Jesus.* New York, NY: Fleming H. Revell Company.

Spinelli, E. (2005). *The interpreted world. An introduction to phenomenological psychology* (2nd ed.). London, England: Sage.

Spinelli, E. (2015). On existential supervision. *Existential Analysis, 26*(1), 168–178.

Spitzer R., Kroenke, K., & Williams, J. (1999). Validation and utility of a self-report Version of PRIME-MD: The PHQ Primary Care Study. *JAMA, 282,* 1737–1744.

Stahl, S. M. (2013). *Stahl's essential psychopharmacology: Neuroscientific basis and practical applications* (4th ed.). Cambridge, England: Cambridge University Press.

Stanton, M. D. (1980). A family theory of drug abuse. In D. Lettieri, M. Sayers, & H. Pearson (Eds.), *Theories on drug abuse: Selected contemporary perspectives* (pp. 147–156) [National Institute on Drug Abuse Research Monograph No. 30]. Washington, DC: U.S. Government Printing Office.

Stanton, M. D., & Standish, W. R. (1997). Outcome, attrition, and family–couples treatment for drug abuse: A meta-analysis and review of the controlled, comparative studies. *Psychological Bulletin, 122,* 170–190.

Steenbergh, T. A., Runyan, J. D., Daugherty, D. A., & Winger, J. G. (2012). Neuroscience exposure and perceptions of client responsibility among addiction counselors. *Journal of Substance Abuse Treatment, 42*(4), 421–428. doi:10.1016/j.jsat.2011.09.015

Steiker, L. H., & Scarborough, B. (2011). Judaism, alcoholism, and recovery: The experience of being Jewish and alcoholic. *Journal of Social Work Practice in the Addictions, 11,* 90–95.

Stevens, P., & Smith, R. L. (2013). *Substance abuse counseling: Theory and practice* (5th ed.). New York, NY: Pearson.

Stewart, D. G., & Brown, S. A. (1995). Withdrawal and dependency symptoms among adolescent alcohol and drug abusers. *Addiction, 90*(5), 627–635. doi:10.1111/j.1360-0443.1995.tb02201.x

Stewart, S. H., Zvolensky, M. J., & Eifert, G. H. (2002). The relations of anxiety sensitivity, experiential avoidance, and alexithymic coping to young adults' motivations for drinking. *Behavior Modification, 26*(2), 274–296.

Stoltenberg, C. D. (1981). Approaching supervision from a developmental perspective: The counselor complexity model. *Journal of Counseling Psychology, 28,* 59–65.

Stoltenberg, C. D., & Delworth, U. (1987). *Supervising counselors and therapists.* San Francisco, CA: Jossey-Bass.

Stoltenberg, C. D., McNeill, B., & Delworth, U. (1998). *IDM supervision: An integrated developmental model for supervising counselors and therapists.* San Francisco, CA: Jossey-Bass.

Stoner, S. A., Mikko, A. T., & Carpenter, K. M. (2014). Web-based training for primary care providers on screening, brief intervention, and referral to treatment (SBIRT) for alcohol, tobacco, and other drugs. *Journal of Substance Abuse Treatment, 47*(5), 362–370. doi:10.1016/j.jsat.2014.06.009

Strain, E. C. (2002). Assessment and treatment of comorbid psychiatric disorders in opioid-dependent patients. *Clinical Journal of Pain, 18*(Suppl. 4), S14–27.

Strakowski, S. M., & DelBello, M. P. (2000). The co-occurrence of bipolar and substance use disorders. *Clinical Psychology Review, 20*(2), 191–206. doi:10.1016/S0272-7358(99)00025-2

Strang, J., & McCambridge, J. (2004). Can the practitioner correctly predict outcome in motivational interviewing? *Journal of Substance Abuse Treatment, 27*(1), 83–88.

Straussner, S. L., & Byrne, H. (2009). Alcoholics Anonymous: Key research findings from 2002–2007. *Alcoholism Treatment Quarterly, 27,* 349–367.

Strong, S. R., Welsh, J. A., Corcoran, J. L., & Hoyt, W. T. (1992). Social psychology and counseling psychology: The history, products, and promise of an interface. *Journal of Counseling Psychology, 39*(2), 139–157. doi:10.1037/0022-0167.39.2.139

Substance Abuse and Mental Health Services Administration. (2001). *Alcohol use among older adults. Pocket screening instruments for healthcare and social service providers.* Rockville, MD: Author.

Substance Abuse and Mental Health Services Administration. (2005). *Substance abuse treatment for persons with co-occurring disorders* (Treatment Improvement Protocol [TIP] Series, No. 42, HHS Publication No. [SMA] 1339920. Rockville, MD: Author.

Substance Abuse and Mental Health Services Administration. (2011a). *Scopes of practice and career ladder for substance use disorder counseling.* Rockville, MD: Author.

Substance Abuse and Mental Health Services Administration. (2011b). *The treatment of depression in older adults: Depression and older adults: Key issues* [HHS Publication No. SMA-11-4631]. Rockville, MD: Center for Mental Health Services, Substance Abuse and Mental Health Services Administration, U.S. Department of Health and Human Services.

Substance Abuse and Mental Health Services Administration. (2012). *Clinical drug testing in primary care* (Technical Assistance Publication [TAP] 32, HHS Publication No. [SMA] 12-4668). Rockville, MD: Author.

Substance Abuse and Mental Health Services Administration. (2013). *National Survey of Substance Abuse Treatment Services (N-SSATS): 2012. Data on Substance Abuse Treatment Facilities* (BHSIS Series S-66, HHS Publication No. [SMA] 14-4809). Rockville, MD: Author.

Substance Abuse and Mental Health Services Administration. (2014a). *Results from the 2013 National Survey on Drug Use and Health: Summary of National Findings* (NSDUH Series H-48, HHS Publication No. [SMA] 14-4863). Rockville, MD: Author.

Substance Abuse and Mental Health Services Administration. (2014b). An introduction to co-occurring borderline personality disorder and substance use disorders. *In Brief, 8*(3), 1–8.

Substance Abuse and Mental Health Services Administration. (2014c). *Improving cultural competence* (Treatment Improvement Protocol [TIP] Series No. 59, HHS Publication No. [SMA] 14-4849). Rockville, MD: Author.

Substance Abuse and Mental Health Services Administration. (2014d). *Projections of national expenditures for treatment of mental and substance use disorders, 2010–2020* (HHS Publication No. [SMA] 14-4883). Rockville, MD: Author.

Substance Abuse and Mental Health Services Administration, Center for Behavioral Health Statistics and Quality. (2015). *Treatment Episode Data Set (TEDS): 2003–2013. National Admissions to Substance Abuse Treatment Services* (BHSIS Series S-75, HHS Publication No. [SMA] 15-4934). Rockville, MD: Author.

Sudai, E., Croitoru, O., Shaldubina, A., Abraham, L., Gispan, I., Flaummenhaft, Y., . . . Yadid, G. (2011). High cocaine dosage decreases neurogenesis in the hippocampus and impairs working memory. *Addiction Biology, 16*(2), 251–260. doi:10.1111/j.1369-1600.2010.00241.x

Sue, D. W. (2001). Multidimensional facets of cultural competence. *Counseling Psychologist, 29*(6), 790–821. doi:10.1177/0011000001296002

Sullivan, E. V., & Pfefferbaum, A. (2005). Neurocircuitry in alcoholism: A substrate of disruption and repair. *Psychopharmacology (Berlin), 180,* 583–594.

Sunderland, M., Slade, T., & Krueger, R. F. (2015). Examining the shared and unique relationships among substance use and mental disorders. *Psychological Medicine, 45,* 1103–1113.

Swora, M. G. (2004). The rhetoric of transformation in the healing of alcoholism: The twelve steps of Alcoholics Anonymous. *Mental Health, Religion, & Culture, 7,* 187–209. doi:10.1080/1367467031000 1602445

Szapocznik, J., & Coatsworth, J. D. (1999). An ecodevelopmental framework for organizing the influences on drug abuse: A developmental model of risk and protection. In M. D. Glantz & C. R. Hartel (Eds.), *Drug abuse: Origins & interventions* (pp. 331–366). Washington, DC: American Psychological Association. doi:10.1037/10341-014

Szapocznik, J., Hervis, O., & Schwartz, S. (2003). *Brief strategic family therapy for adolescent drug abuse* (NIH Publication No. 03-4751). Bethesda, MD: National Institute on Drug Abuse.

Szapocznik, J., & Kurtines, W. M. (1989). *Breakthroughs in family therapy with drug abusing and behavior problem youth.* New York, NY: Springer.

Szapocznik, J., Perez-Vidal, A., Brickman, A. L., Foote, F. H., Santisteban, D., Hervis, O., & Kurtines, W. M. (1988). Engaging adolescent drug abusers and their families in treatment: A strategic structural systems approach. *Journal of Consulting and Clinical Psychology, 56,* 552–557. doi:10.1037/0022-006X.56.4.552

Tagaki, M. J., Lubman, D. I., Cotton, S. M., & Yucel, M. (2014). Inhalants. In D. N. Allen & S. P. Woods (Eds.), *Neuropsychological aspects of substance use disorders* (pp. 254–279). New York, NY: Oxford University Press.

Tai, B., Lindblad, R., Gore-Langton, R., Ghitza, U., & Subramaniam, G. (2012, June). *A clinical decision support model for screening and management of substance use disorders in electronic health records in general medical settings* [Abstract #663]. The College on Problems of Drug Dependence, 74th Annual Meeting, Palm Springs, CA.

Tai, B., & Volkow, N. D. (2013). Treatment for substance use disorder: Opportunities and challenges under the Affordable Care Act. *Social Work in Public Health, 28,* 165–174.

Tai, B., Wu, L., & Clark, H. (2012). Electronic health records: Essential tools in integrating substance abuse treatment with primary care [Commentary]. *Substance Abuse and Rehabilitation, 3,* 8.

Taleff, M. J. (2010). *Advanced ethics for addiction professionals.* New York, NY: Springer.

Taylor, K. S., Seminowicz, D. A., & Davis, K. D. (2009). Two systems of resting state connectivity between the insula and cingulate cortex. *Human Brain Mapping, 30*(9), 2731–2745.

Tengström, A., Hodgins, S., Grann, M., Långström, N., & Kullgren, G. (2004). Schizophrenia and criminal offending: The role of psychopathy and substance use disorders. *Criminal Justice and Behavior, 31*(4), 367–391. doi:10.1177/0093854804265173

Tennen, H., Affleck, G., Armeli, S., & Carney, M. A. (2000). A daily process approach to coping: Linking theory, research, and practice. *American Psychologist, 55,* 626–636.

Teter, C. J., Falone, A. E., Bakaian, A. M., Tu, C., Öngür, D., & Weiss, R. D. (2011). Medication adherence and attitudes in patients with bipolar disorder and current versus past substance use disorder. *Psychiatry Research, 190*(2–3), 253–258. http://doi.org/10.1016/j.psychres.2011.05.042

Thirtalli, J., & Benegal, V. (2006). Psychosis among substance users. *Current Opinion in Psychiatry, 19,* 239–245.

Thombs, D. L., & Osborn, C. J. (2013). *Introduction to addictive behaviors* (4th ed.). New York, NY: Guilford Press.

Tiffany, S., Carter, B., & Singleton, E. (2000). Challenges in the manipulation, assessment and interpretation of craving relevant variables. *Addiction, 95*(Suppl. 2), 177–187.

Timko, C., Cronkite, R., Kaskutas, L. A., Laudet, A., Roth, J., & Moos, R. H. (2013). Al-Anon family groups: Newcomers and members. *Journal of Studies on Alcohol and Drugs, 74*(6), 965–976.

Tonigan, J. S. (2001). Benefits of Alcoholics Anonymous attendance: Replication of findings between clinical research sites in Project MATCH. *Alcoholism Treatment Quarterly, 19,* 67–77. doi:10.1300/J020v19n01_05

Townshend, J. M., & Duka, T. (2003). Mixed emotions: Alcoholics' impairments in the recognition of specific emotional facial expressions. *Neuropsychologia, 41*(7), 773–782.

Tracy, S. W., Kelly, J. F., & Moos, R. H. (2005). The influence of partner status, relationship quality and relationship stability on outcomes following intensive substance-use disorder treatment. *Journal of Studies on Alcohol, 66*(4), 497–505. doi:10.15288/jsa.2005.66.497

Trudeau, K. J., Ainscough, J., & Charity, S. (2012). Technology in treatment: Are adolescents and counselors interested in online relapse prevention? *Child & Youth Care Forum, 41,* 57–71.

Turner, S., Greenwood, P., Fain, T., & Deschenes, E. (1999). Perceptions of drug court: How offenders view ease of program completion, strengths and weaknesses, and the impact on their lives. *National Drug Court Institute Review, 2,* 61–85.

Ujike, H., & Sato, M. (2004). Clinical features of sensitization to methamphetamine observed in patients with methamphetamine dependence and psychosis. *Annals of the New York Academy of Sciences, 13*(2), 181–190.

Upadhyaya, H., & Deas, D. (2008). Pharmacological interventions for adolescent substance use disorders. In Y. Kaminer & O. G. Bukstein (Eds.), *Adolescent substance abuse: Psychiatric comorbidity and high-risk behaviors* (pp. 145–161). New York, NY: Routledge/Taylor & Francis.

van der Westhuizen, M. A., & De Jager, M. S. (2009). Relapsing after treatment: Exploring the experiences of chemically addicted adolescents. *Maatskaplike Werk, 45*(1), 76–90.

van Deurzen, E., & Adams, M. (2011). *Skills in existential counselling & psychotherapy.* Thousand Oaks, CA: Sage.

van Holst, R. J., van den Brink, W., Veltman, D. J., & Goudriaan, A. E. (2010). Brain imaging studies in pathological gambling. *Current Psychiatry Reports, 12*(5), 418–425. http://doi.org/10.1007/s11920-010-0141-7

van Wormer, K., & Davis, D. R. (2012). *Addiction treatment: A strengths perspective.* Belmont, CA: Brooks/Cole.

Veatch, L. M., & Becker H. C. (2005). Lorazepam and MK-801 effects on behavioral and electrographic indices of alcohol withdrawal sensitization. *Brain Research, 1065,* 92–106.

Verdejo-Garcia, A. (2014). Cocaine. In D. N. Allen & S. P. Woods (Eds.), *Neuropsychological aspects of substance use disorders* (pp. 157–182). New York, NY: Oxford University Press.

Vereby, K. G., & Meenan, G. (2011). Diagnostic laboratory: Screening for drug abuse. In P. Ruiz & E. Strain (Eds.), *Lowinson and Ruiz's substance abuse: A comprehensive textbook* (5th ed., pp. 123–137). Philadelphia, PA: Lippincott, Williams, & Wilkins.

Vermeulen-Smit, E., Verdurmen, J. E., & Engels, R. E. (2015). The effectiveness of family interventions in preventing adolescent illicit drug use: A systematic review and meta-analysis of randomized controlled trials. *Clinical Child and Family Psychology Review, 18*(3), 218–239. doi:10.1007/s10567-015-0185-7

Victor, S. E., Glenn, C. R., & Klonsky, E. D. (2012). Is non-suicidal self-injury an "addiction"? A comparison of craving in substance use and non-suicidal self-injury. *Psychiatry Research, 197*(1–2), 73–77. http://doi.org/10.1016/j.psychres.2011.12.011

Voon, V., Mole, T. B., Banca, P., Porter, L., Morris, L., Mitchell, S., . . . Irvine, M. (2014). Neural correlates of sexual cue reactivity in individuals with and without compulsive sexual behaviors. *PLoS ONE, 9*(7), 1–10. doi:10.1371/journal.pone.0102419

Vos, J., Cooper, M., Correia, E., & Craig, M. (2015). Existential therapies: A review of their scientific foundations and efficacy. *Existential Analysis, 26*(1), 49–69.

Vos, J., Craig, M., & Cooper, M. (2015). Existential therapies: A meta-analysis of their effects on psychological outcomes. *Journal of Consulting and Clinical Psychology, 83*(1), 115–128. doi:10.1037/a0037167

Waldron, H. B., & Turner, C. W. (2008). Evidence-based psychosocial treatments for adolescent substance abuse. *Journal of Clinical Child & Adolescent Psychology, 37*(1), 238–261. doi:10.1080/15374410701820133

Walsh, R. A., & McElwain, B. (2002). Existential psychotherapies. In D. J. Cain & J. Seeman (Eds.), *Humanistic psychotherapies: Handbook of research and practice* (pp. 253–278). Washington, DC: American Psychological Association. doi:10.1037/10439-008

Wegscheider, S. (1981). *Another chance: Hope and health for the alcoholic family.* Palo Alto, CA: Science and Behavior Books.

Weiss, R. D., & Dreifuss, J. A. (2015). Inpatient treatment. In M. Galanter, H. D. Kleber, & K. T. Brady (Eds.), *The American Psychiatric Publishing textbook of substance abuse treatment* (5th ed., pp. 499–510). Arlington, VA: American Psychiatric Publishing.

Weiss, R. D., Potter, J. S., Sharpe, J., & Iannucci, R. A. (2008). Inpatient treatment. In M. Galanter & H. D. Kleber (Eds.), *Textbook of substance abuse treatment* (pp. 445–458). Washington, DC: American Psychiatric Association.

Wellisch, D. K., Gay, G. R., Wesson, D. R., & Smith, D. E. (1971). The psychotic heroin addict. *Journal of Psychedelic Drugs, 4*(1), 46–49. doi:10.1080/02791072.1971.10471785

West, P. L., & Hamm, T. (2012). A study of clinical supervision techniques and training in substance abuse treatment. *Journal of Addictions & Offender Counseling, 33*(2), 66–81. doi:10.1002/j.2161-1874 .2012.00005.x

Westermeyer, J., & Thuras, P. (2005). Association of antisocial personality disorder and substance disorder morbidity in a clinical sample. *American Journal of Drug and Alcohol Abuse, 31*(1), 93–110. doi:10.1081/ ADA-200047895

Weston, A. L., Weinstein, A. M., Barton, C., & Yaffe, K. (2010). Potentially inappropriate medication use in older adults with mild cognitive impairment. *Journals of Gerontology Series A: Biological Sciences and Medical Sciences, 65A*(3), 318–321. http://doi.org/10.1093/gerona/glp158

White, W. L. (2000). The history of recovered people as wounded healers: II. The era of professionalization and specialization. *Alcoholism Treatment Quarterly, 18,* 1–25. doi:10.1300/J020v18n02_01

White, W. L., & Kurtz, E. (2008). Twelve defining moments in the history of Alcoholics Anonymous. In M. Galanter & L. A. Kaskutas (Eds.), *Recent developments in alcoholism: Vol. 18. Research on Alcoholics Anonymous and spirituality in addiction recovery* (pp. 37–57). New York, NY: Springer.

Willenbring, M. L. (2010). The past and future of research on treatment of alcohol dependence. *Alcohol Research & Health, 33*(1–2), 55–63.

Wills, T., Yaeger, A., & Sandy, J. (2003). Buffering effect of religiosity for adolescent substance use. *Psychology of Addictive Behaviors, 17,* 24–31.

Wilson, W. G. (1953, July). *Where did the twelve steps come from? A fragment of history by Bill W.* Retrieved from http://www.barefootsworld.net/aa12stepsorigin.html

Wilson, W. G. (1988). The greatest gift of all. In AA Grapevine (Ed.), *The language of the heart: Bill W's Grapevine articles* (pp. 233–236). New York, NY: AA Grapevine. (Original work published December 1957)

Wilson, D. B., Mitchell, O., & MacKenzie, D. L. (2006). A systematic review of drug court effects on recidivism. *Journal of Experimental Criminology, 2,* 459–487.

Windsor, L. C., Jermal, A., & Alessi, E. J. (2015). Cognitive behavioral therapy: A meta-analysis of race and substance use outcomes. *Cultural Diversity and Ethnic Minority Psychology, 21*(2), 300–313.

Winters, K. C., Botzet, A. M., & Fahnhorst, T. (2011). Advances in adolescent substance abuse treatment. *Current Psychiatry Reports, 13*(5), 416–421. http://doi.org/10.1007/s11920-011-0214-2

Winters, K. C., Botzet, A. M., Fahnhorst, T., & Koskey, R. (2009). Adolescent substance abuse treatment: A review of evidence-based research In C. Leukefeld, T. Gullotta, & M. Tindall Staton (Eds.), *Handbook on the prevention and treatment of substance abuse in adolescence* (pp. 73–96). New York, NY: Springer.

Winters, K. C., Martin, C. S., & Chung, T. (2011). Substance use disorders in *DSM-V* when applied to adolescents. *Addiction, 106*(5), 882–884. doi:10.1111/j.1360-0443.2010.03334.x

Witkiewitz, K., & Marlatt, G. A. (2004). Relapse prevention for alcohol and drug problems: That was Zen, this is Tao. *American Psychologist, 59,* 224–235.

Witkiewitz, K., & Marlatt, G. A. (2007). High-risk situations: Relapse as a dynamic process. In K. Witkiewitz & G. A. Marlatt (Eds.), *Therapist's guide to evidence-based relapse prevention.* New York, NY: Elsevier.

Witkiewitz, K., & Masyn, K. E. (2008). Drinking trajectories following an initial lapse. *Psychology of Addictive Behaviors, 22*(2), 157–167. doi:10.1037/0893-164X.22.2.157

Work Group on Substance Use Disorders. (2007). Treatment of patients with substance use disorders. *American Journal of Psychiatry, 164*(Suppl. 4), 5–123.

World Health Organization. (2011). *International statistical classification of diseases and related health problems* (10th rev.). Geneva, Switzerland: Author.

Wu, L. T., & Blazer, D. G. (2011). Illicit and nonmedical drug use among older adults: A review. *Journal of Aging and Health, 23,* 481–504. http://dx.doi.org/10.1177/0898264310386224

Wu, L.-T., Gersing, K., Burchett, B., Woody, G. E., & Blazer, D. G. (2011). Substance use disorders and comorbid Axis I and II psychiatric disorders among young psychiatric patients: findings from a large electronic health records database. *Journal of Psychiatric Research, 45*(11), 1453–1462. http://doi .org/10.1016/j.jpsychires.2011.06.012

Yakovenko, I., Quigley, L., Hemmelgarn, B. R., Hodgins, D. C., & Ronksley, P. (2015). The efficacy of motivational interviewing for disordered gambling: Systematic review and meta-analysis. *Addictive Behaviors, 4372*–4382. doi:10.1016/j.addbeh.2014.12.011

Yalom, I. (1980). *Existential psychotherapy.* New York, NY: Basic Books.

Yalom, I. (1995). *The theory and practice of group psychotherapy* (4th ed.). New York, NY: Basic Books.

Zetterqvist, M. (2015). The *DSM-5* diagnosis of nonsuicidal self-injury disorder: A review of the empirical literature. *Child & Adolescent Psychiatry & Mental Health, 9*(31). doi:10.1186/s13034-015-0062-7

Zvolensky, M. J., Lewinsohn, P., Bernstein, A., Schmidt, N. B., Buckner, J. D., Seeley, J., & Bonn-Miller, M. O. (2008). Prospective associations between cannabis use, abuse, and dependence and panic attacks and disorder. *Journal of Psychiatric Research, 42*(12), 1017–1023. http://doi.org/10.1016/j.jpsychires.2007.10.012

Index

Made in the USA
Las Vegas, NV
22 May 2023

72402959R00190